...bout 2 years since *Naruto* ...g in *Weekly Shonen* ...d I haven't been back to ...rents' house once! While I've been away from home, they've totally remodeled the place, and apparently there's not even a trace left of my shabby, memory-filled room. When I heard that, I got a little sad... Time just keeps flowing by...

岸本斉史

—*Masashi Kishimoto, 2001*

Author/artist Masashi Kishimoto was born in 1974 in rural Okayama Prefecture, Japan. After spending time in art college, he won the Hop Step Award for new manga artists with his manga **Karakuri** (Mechanism). Kishimoto decided to base his next story on traditional Japanese culture. His first version of **Naruto**, drawn in 1997, was a one-shot story about fox spirits; his final version, which debuted in **Weekly Shonen Jump** in 1999, quickly became the most popular ninja manga in Japan.

NARUTO VOL. 8
SHONEN JUMP Manga Edition

This graphic novel contains material that was originally published
in English in **SHONEN JUMP** #31–35.

STORY AND ART BY MASASHI KISHIMOTO

English Adaptation/Jo Duffy
Translation/Mari Morimoto
Touch-up Art & Lettering/Heidi Szykowny
Additional Touch-up/Josh Simpson
Design/Sean Lee
Series Editor/Joel Enos
Editor/Frances E. Wall

Published by VIZ Media, LLC
P.O. Box 77010
San Francisco, CA 94107

10 9 8 7
First printing, November 2005
Seventh printing, April 2011

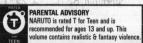

PARENTAL ADVISORY
NARUTO is rated T for Teen and is
recommended for ages 13 and up. This
volume contains realistic & fantasy violence.

ratings.viz.com

www.viz.com

SHONEN JUMP MANGA EDITION

NARUTO

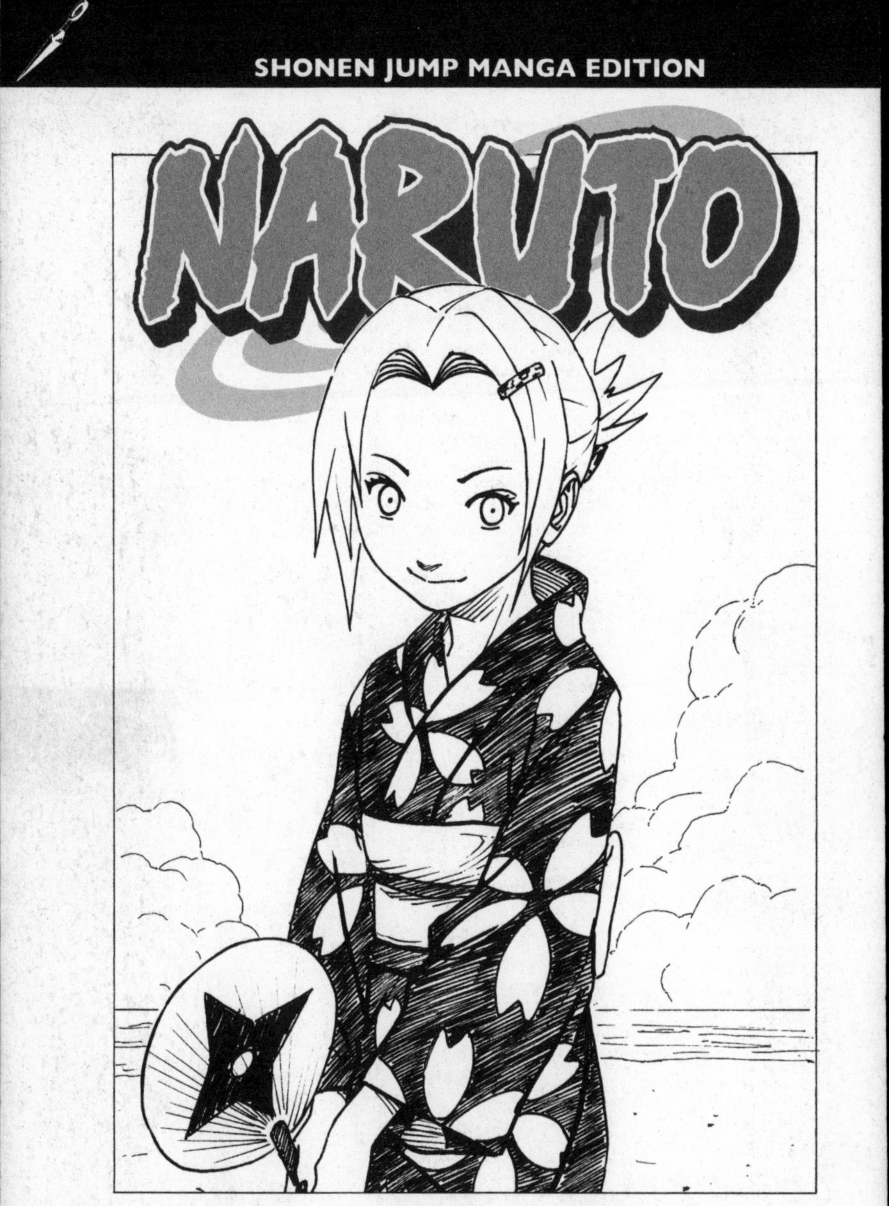

VOL. 8

LIFE-AND-DEATH BATTLES

STORY AND ART BY

MASASHI KISHIMOTO

SAKURA サクラ

Smart and studious, Sakura is the brightest of Naruto's classmates, but she's constantly distracted by her crush on Sasuke. Her goal: to win Sasuke's heart!

NARUTO ナルト

When Naruto was born, a destructive fox spirit was imprisoned inside his body. Spurned by the older villagers, he's grown into an attention-seeking trouble-maker. His goal: to become the village's next *Hokage*.

SASUKE サスケ

The top student in Naruto's class, Sasuke comes from the prestigious Uchiha clan. His goal: to get revenge on a mysterious person who wronged him in the past.

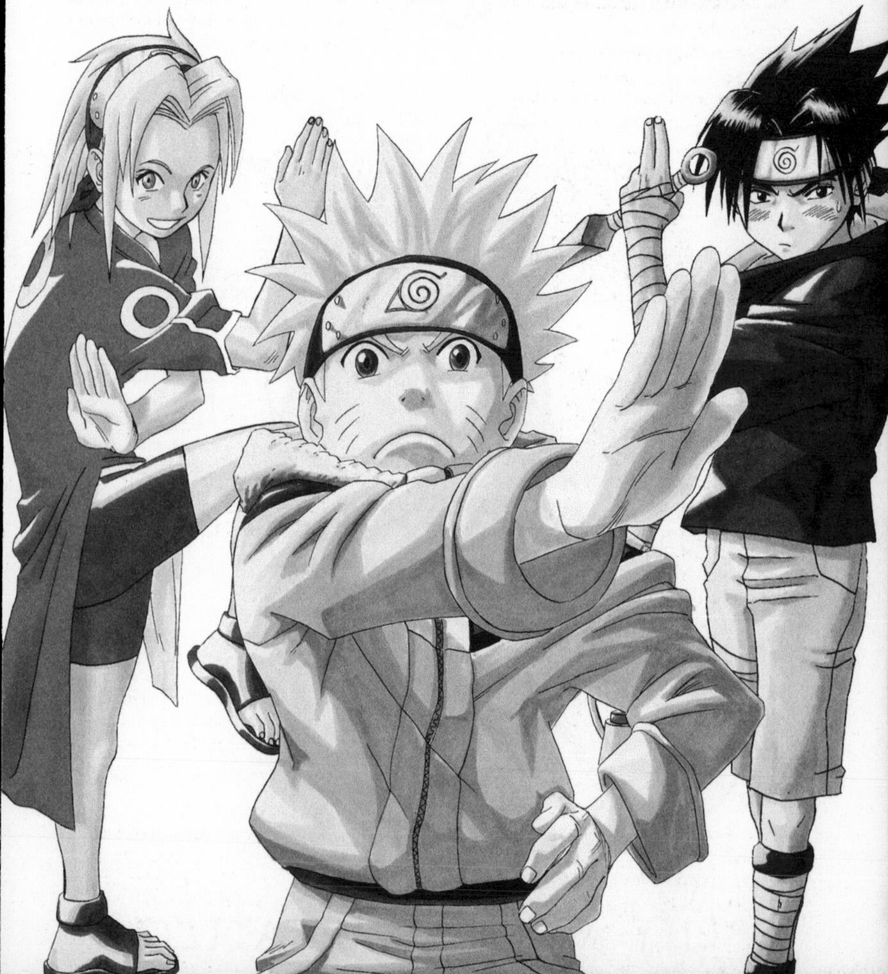

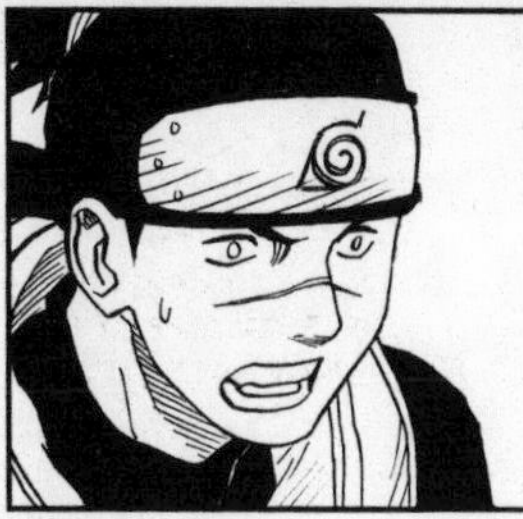

Iruka イルカ

Naruto, Sasuke and Sakura's teacher from their Ninja Academy days. Iruka has a soft spot in his heart for Naruto because he also grew up as an orphan.

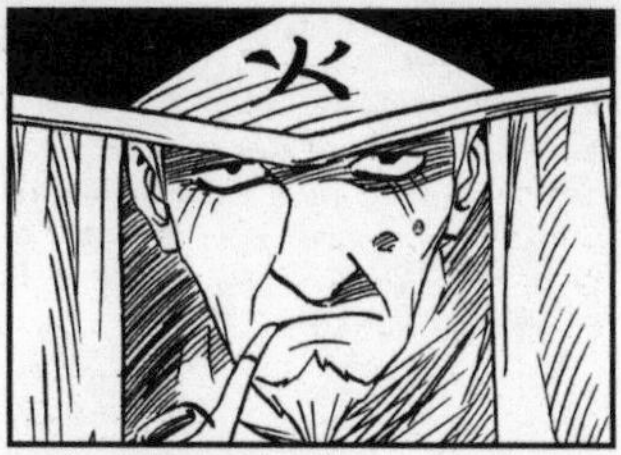
火

The Third Hokage 三代目火影

The head ninja and leader of the village of Konohagakure.

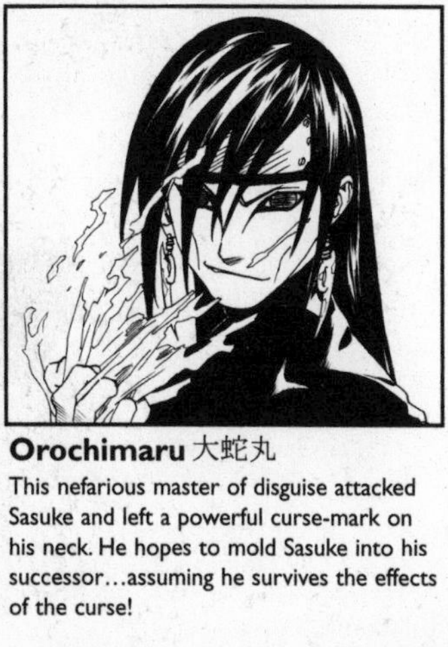

Orochimaru 大蛇丸

This nefarious master of disguise attacked Sasuke and left a powerful curse-mark on his neck. He hopes to mold Sasuke into his successor…assuming he survives the effects of the curse!

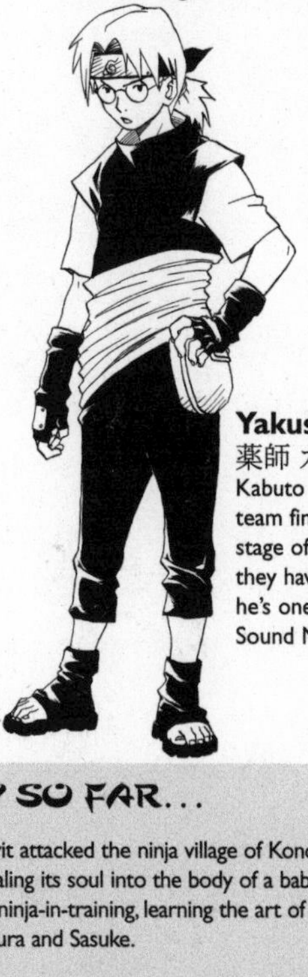

Yakushi Kabuto
薬師 カブト

Kabuto helped Naruto's team finish the second stage of the exam, but they have no idea that he's one of Orochimaru's Sound Ninja spies!

THE STORY SO FAR…

Twelve years ago, a destructive nine-tailed fox spirit attacked the ninja village of Konohagakure. The *Hokage*, or village champion, defeated the fox by sealing its soul into the body of a baby boy. Now that boy, Uzumaki Naruto, has grown up to become a ninja-in-training, learning the art of *ninjutsu* with his classmates Sakura and Sasuke.

After a long and harrowing journey through the Forest of Death, Naruto, Sasuke and Sakura finally secure the scrolls they need to pass the second stage of the Chûnin (Journeyman Ninja) Selection Exam. With Heaven and Earth scrolls in hand, they head to the tower in the center of the Forest of Death that marks the exam's finish line. Inside the tower, Naruto, Sasuke and Sakura are greeted by a cryptic message from The Third Hokage. They understand enough of the message to realize they should open both of their scrolls at the same time, so they prepare to unfurl them, unsure of what they'll find inside…

NARUTO

VOL. 8
LIFE-AND-DEATH BATTLES

CONTENTS

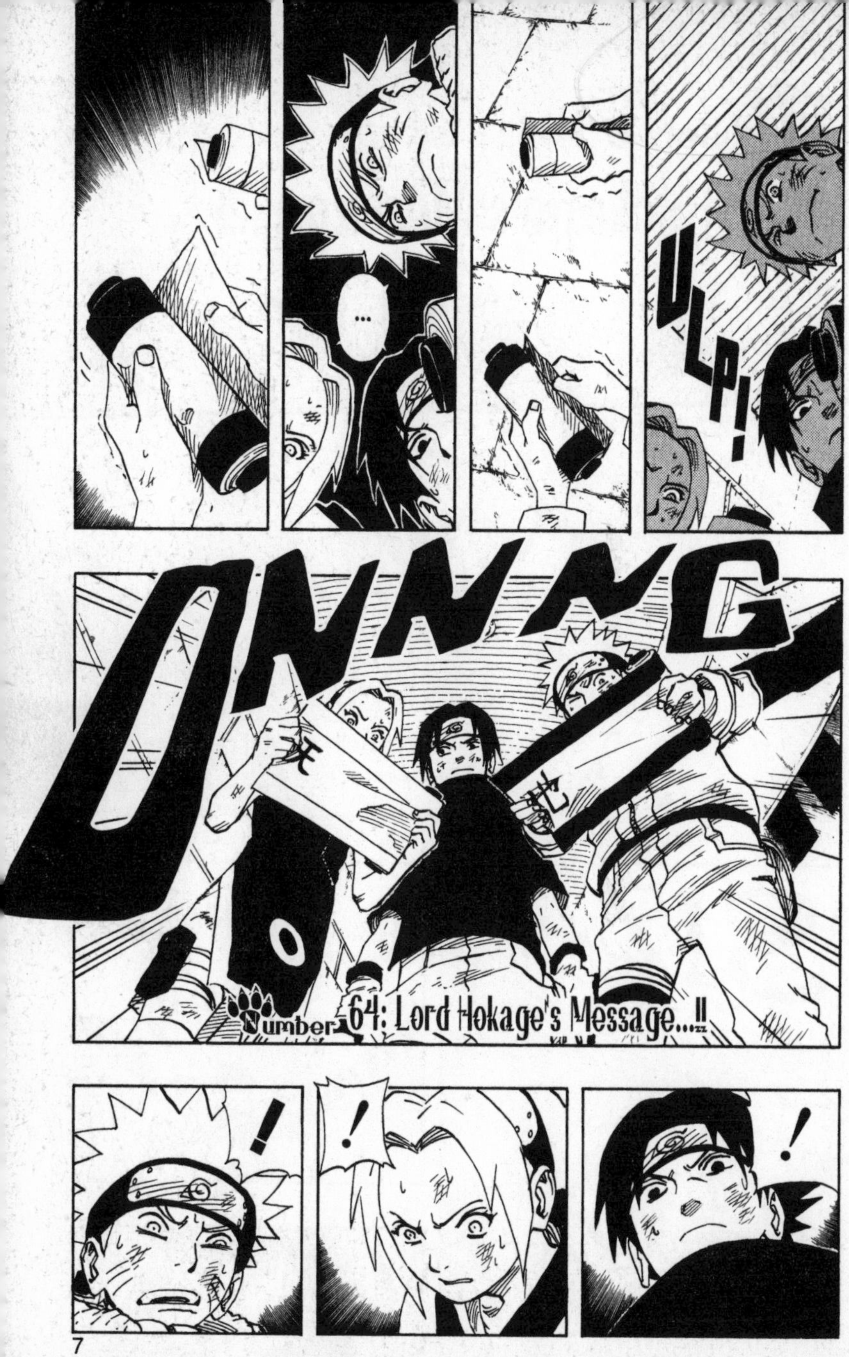

ULP!
...
DNNNG
Number 64: Lord Hokage's Message...!!
!
!
!

Number 64: Lord Hokage's Message...!!

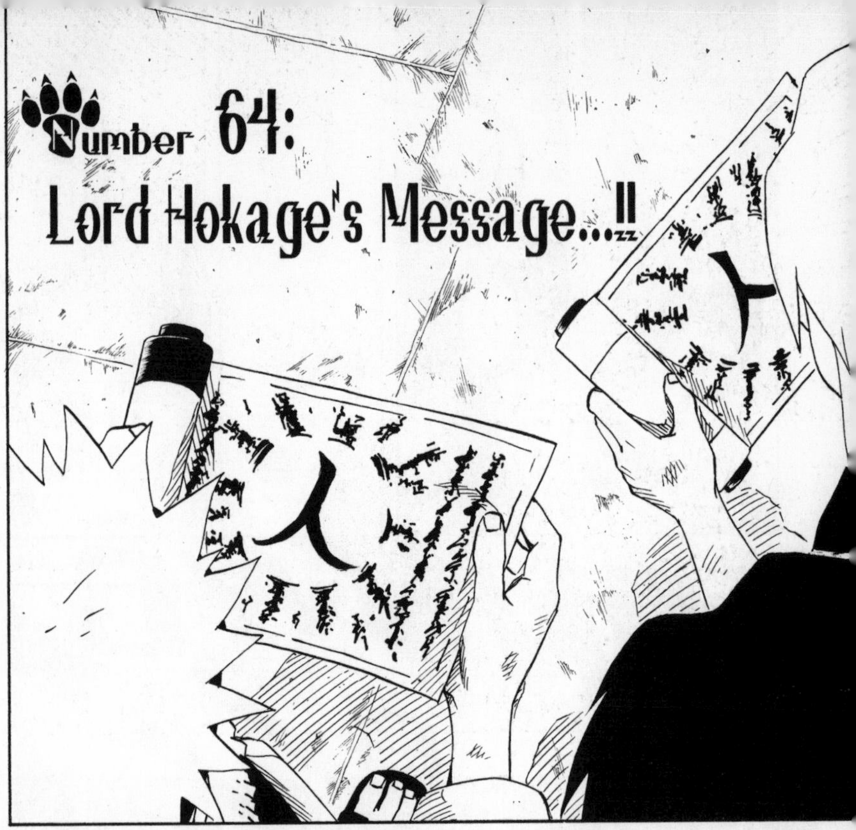

*THE CHARACTER IN THE CENTER OF THE SCROLLS MEANS "PERSON" OR "HUMANITY."

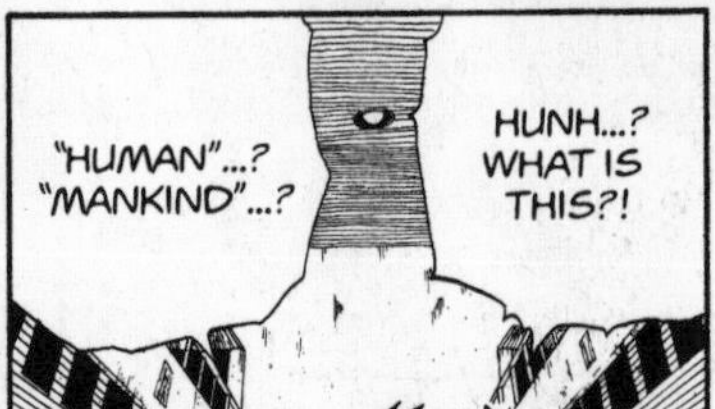
HUNH...? WHAT IS THIS?!
"HUMAN"...? "MANKIND"...?

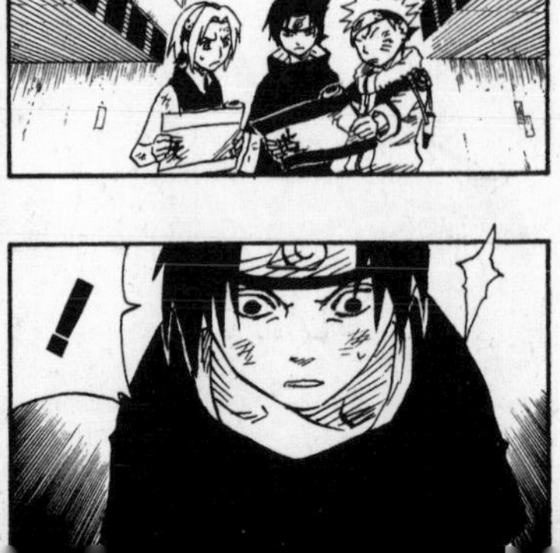
!

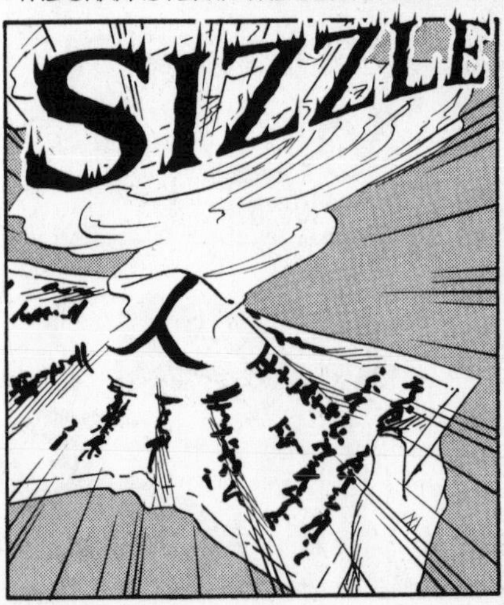
SIZZLE

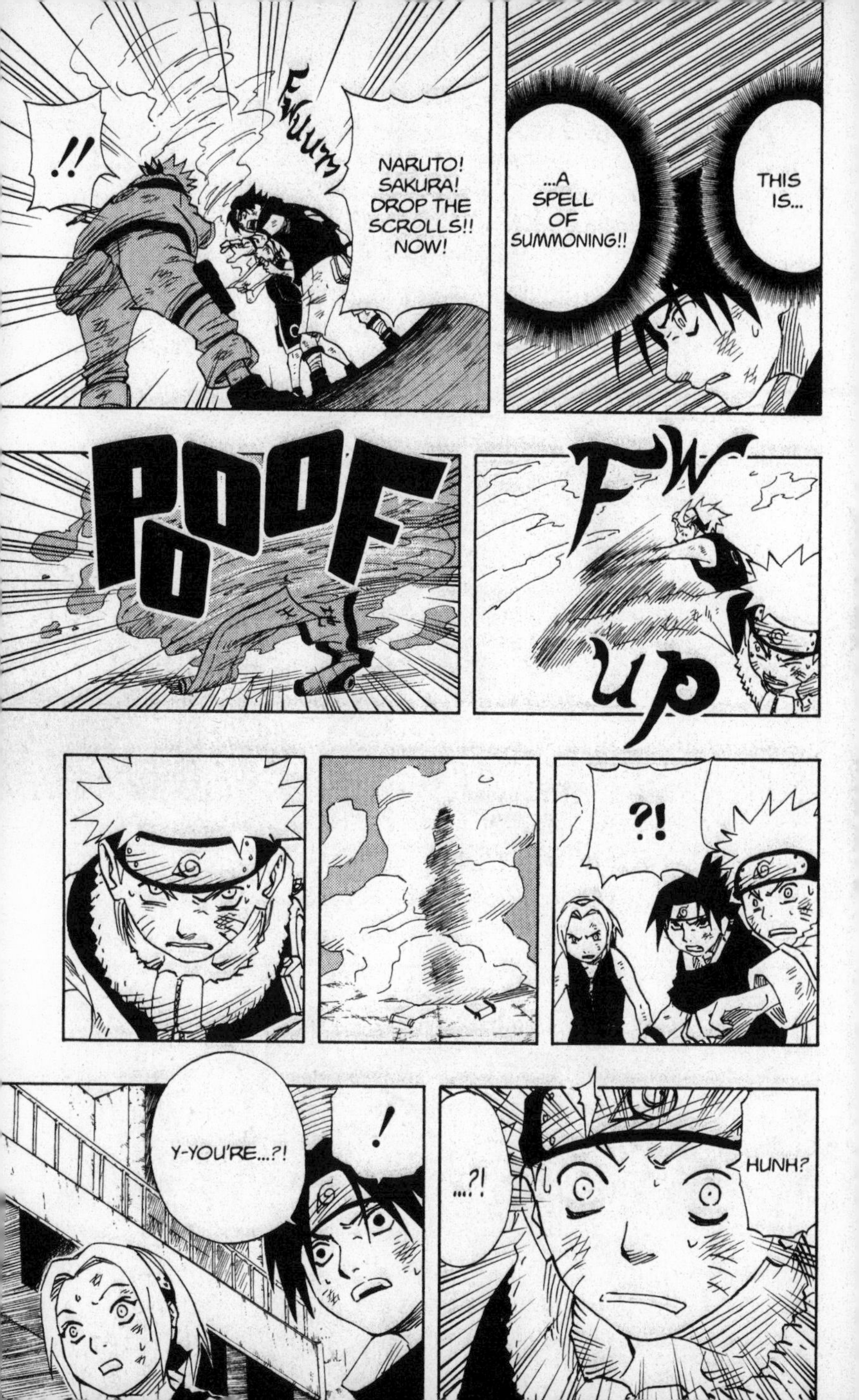
THIS IS...
...A SPELL OF SUMMONING!!
NARUTO! SAKURA! DROP THE SCROLLS!! NOW!
FWUUM
!!
FWUP
POOF
?!
HUNH?
...?!
!
Y-YOU'RE...?!

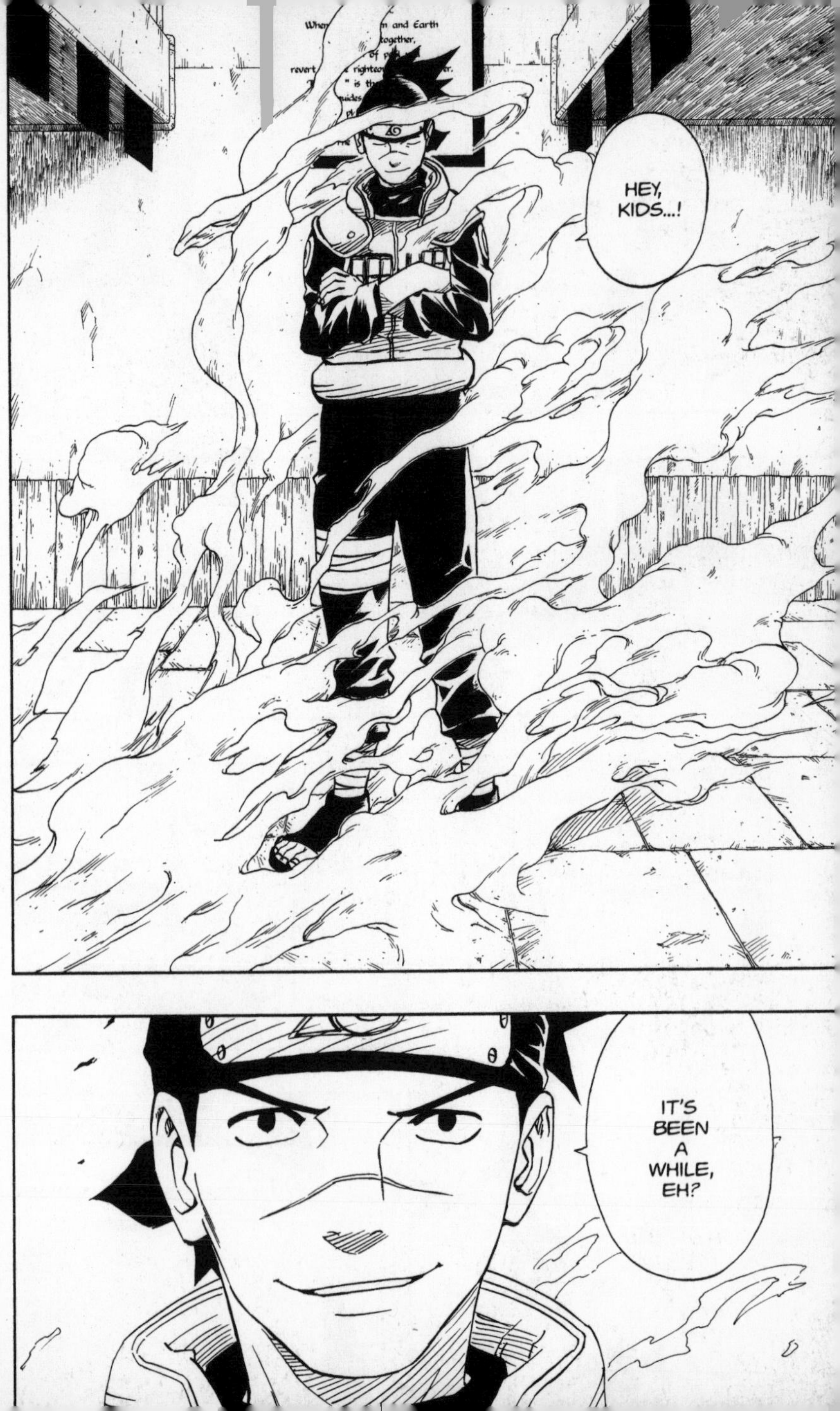
HEY, KIDS...!
IT'S BEEN A WHILE, EH?

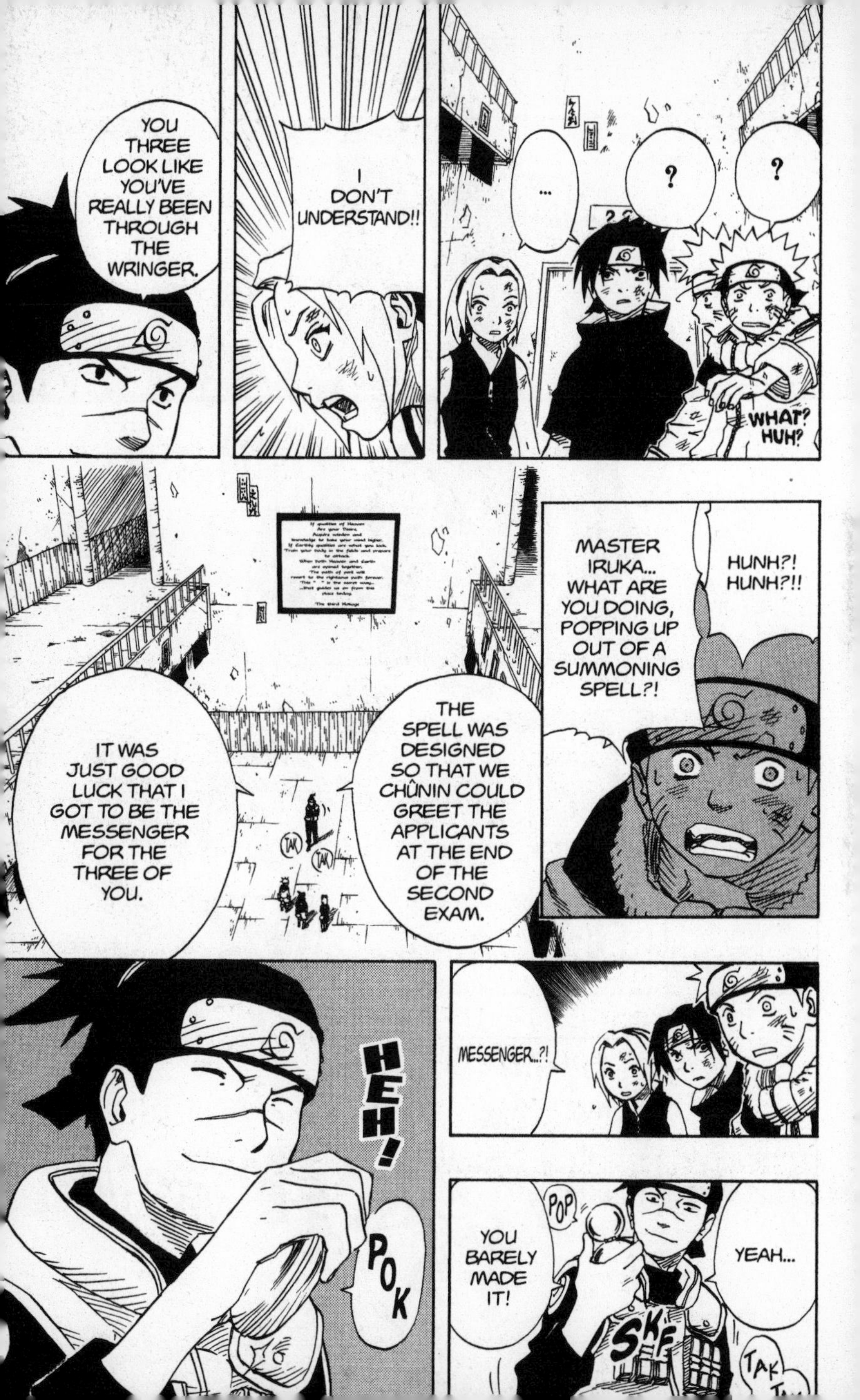
?
?
...
WHAT? HUH?
I DON'T UNDERSTAND!!
YOU THREE LOOK LIKE YOU'VE REALLY BEEN THROUGH THE WRINGER.
HUNH?! HUNH?!!
MASTER IRUKA... WHAT ARE YOU DOING, POPPING UP OUT OF A SUMMONING SPELL?!
THE SPELL WAS DESIGNED SO THAT WE CHÛNIN COULD GREET THE APPLICANTS AT THE END OF THE SECOND EXAM.
TAK
TAK
IT WAS JUST GOOD LUCK THAT I GOT TO BE THE MESSENGER FOR THE THREE OF YOU.
MESSENGER...?!
YEAH...
POP
YOU BARELY MADE IT!
SK'F
TAK
HEH!
POK

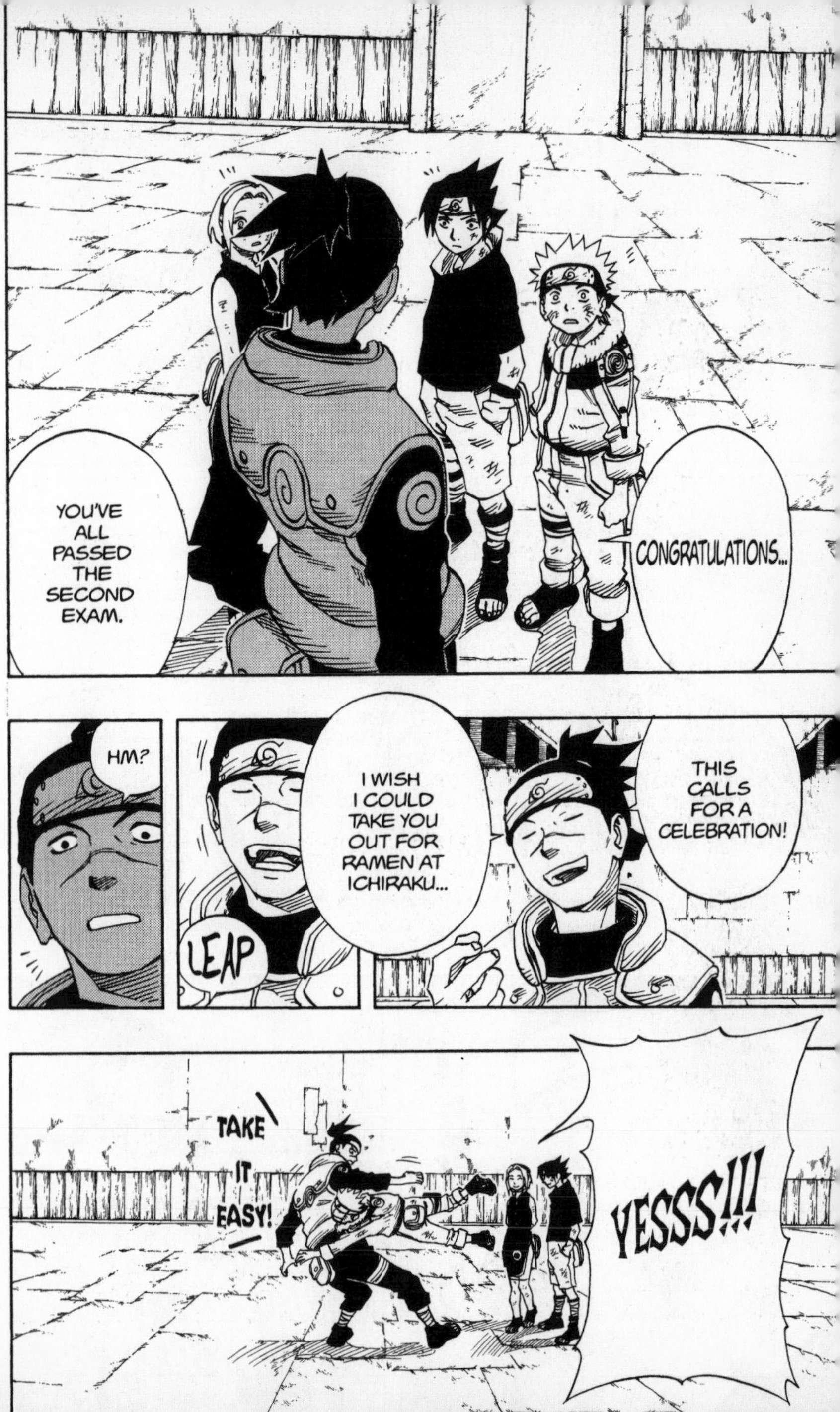
CONGRATULATIONS...
YOU'VE ALL PASSED THE SECOND EXAM.
THIS CALLS FOR A CELEBRATION!
I WISH I COULD TAKE YOU OUT FOR RAMEN AT ICHIRAKU...
LEAP
HM?
YESSS!!!
TAKE IT EASY!

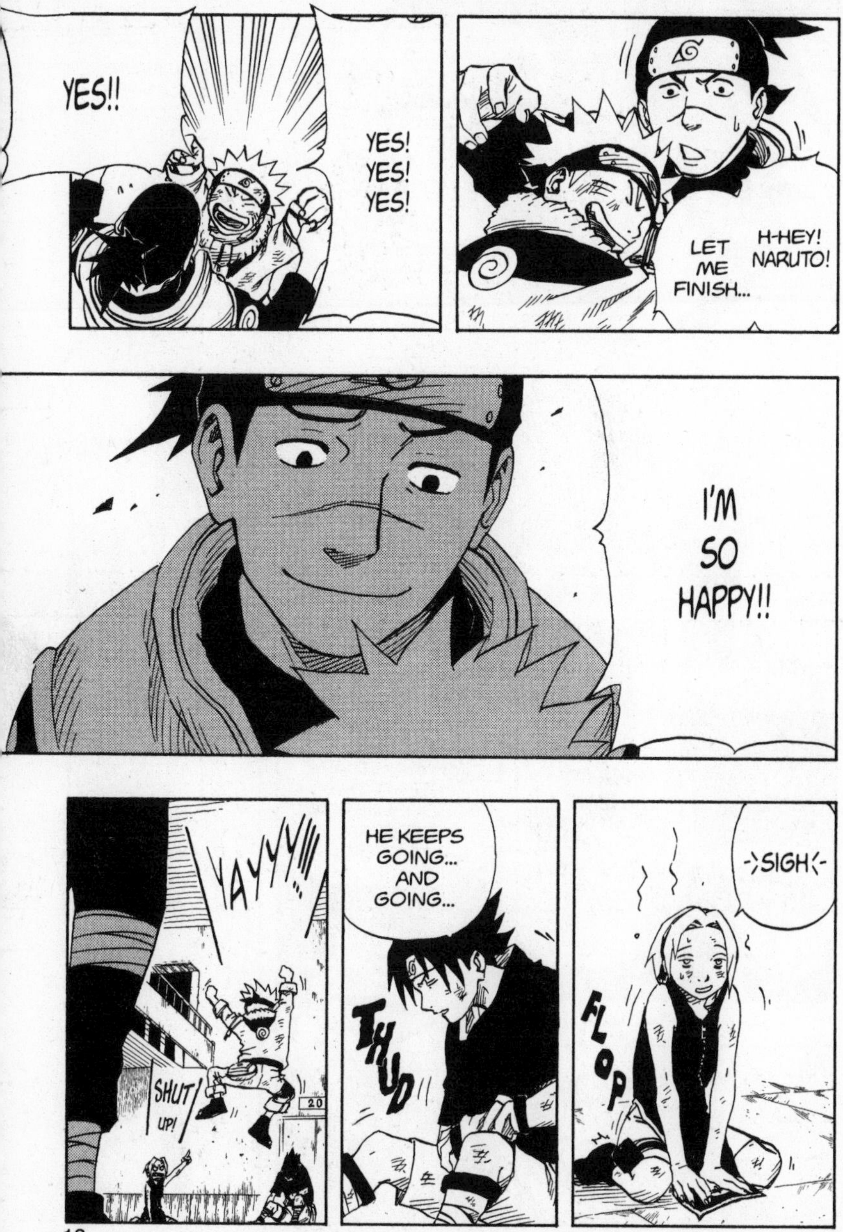
H-HEY! NARUTO!
LET ME FINISH...
YES! YES! YES!
YES!!
I'M SO HAPPY!!
-SIGH-
FLOP
HE KEEPS GOING... AND GOING...
THUD
YAYYY!!!
SHUT UP!

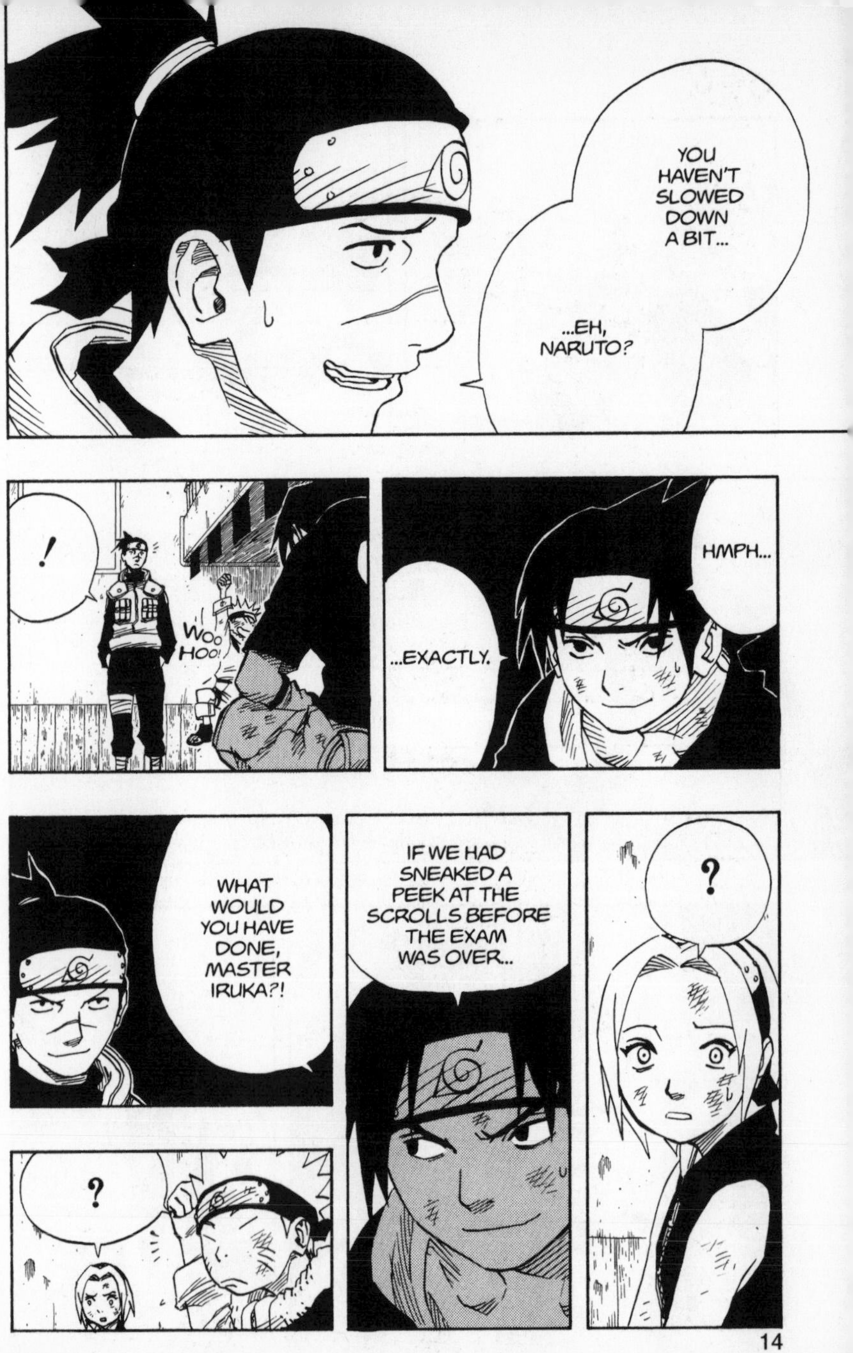
YOU HAVEN'T SLOWED DOWN A BIT...
...EH, NARUTO?
HMPH...
...EXACTLY.
!
WOO HOO!
?
IF WE HAD SNEAKED A PEEK AT THE SCROLLS BEFORE THE EXAM WAS OVER...
WHAT WOULD YOU HAVE DONE, MASTER IRUKA?!
?

READ THIS WAY

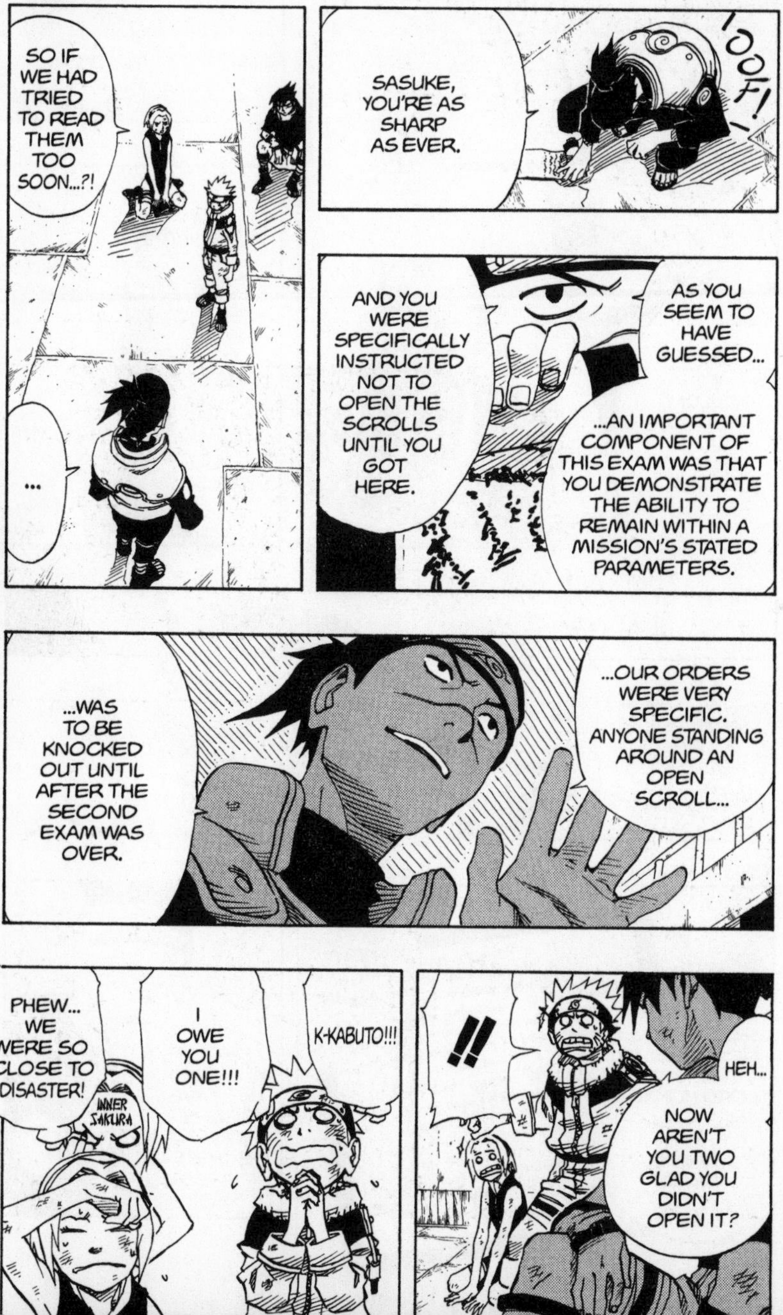

OOF!
SASUKE, YOU'RE AS SHARP AS EVER.
AS YOU SEEM TO HAVE GUESSED...
...AN IMPORTANT COMPONENT OF THIS EXAM WAS THAT YOU DEMONSTRATE THE ABILITY TO REMAIN WITHIN A MISSION'S STATED PARAMETERS.
AND YOU WERE SPECIFICALLY INSTRUCTED NOT TO OPEN THE SCROLLS UNTIL YOU GOT HERE.
SO IF WE HAD TRIED TO READ THEM TOO SOON...?!
...
...OUR ORDERS WERE VERY SPECIFIC. ANYONE STANDING AROUND AN OPEN SCROLL...
...WAS TO BE KNOCKED OUT UNTIL AFTER THE SECOND EXAM WAS OVER.
!!
HEH...
NOW AREN'T YOU TWO GLAD YOU DIDN'T OPEN IT?
K-KABUTO!!!
I OWE YOU ONE!!!
PHEW... WE WERE SO CLOSE TO DISASTER!
INNER SAKURA

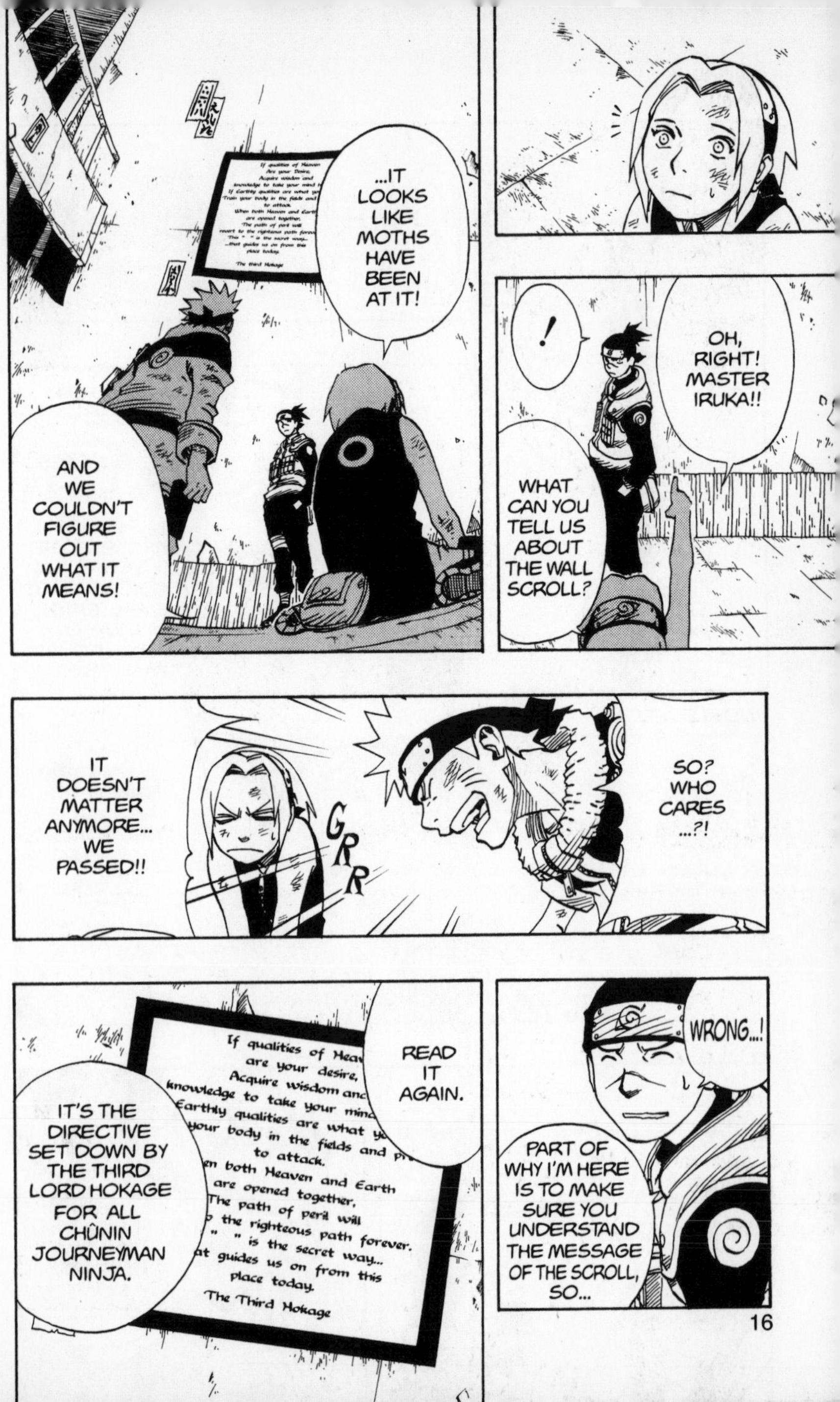
OH, RIGHT! MASTER IRUKA!!
!
WHAT CAN YOU TELL US ABOUT THE WALL SCROLL?
...IT LOOKS LIKE MOTHS HAVE BEEN AT IT!
AND WE COULDN'T FIGURE OUT WHAT IT MEANS!
SO? WHO CARES ...?!
GRR
IT DOESN'T MATTER ANYMORE... WE PASSED!!
WRONG...!
PART OF WHY I'M HERE IS TO MAKE SURE YOU UNDERSTAND THE MESSAGE OF THE SCROLL, SO...
READ IT AGAIN.
If qualities of Heav
are your desire,
Acquire wisdom and
knowledge to take your mind
Earthly qualities are what yo
your body in the fields and pr
to attack.
en both Heaven and Earth
are opened together,
The path of peril will
o the righteous path forever.
" " is the secret way...
at guides us on from this
place today.
The Third Hokage
IT'S THE DIRECTIVE SET DOWN BY THE THIRD LORD HOKAGE FOR ALL CHÛNIN JOURNEYMAN NINJA.

READ THIS WAY

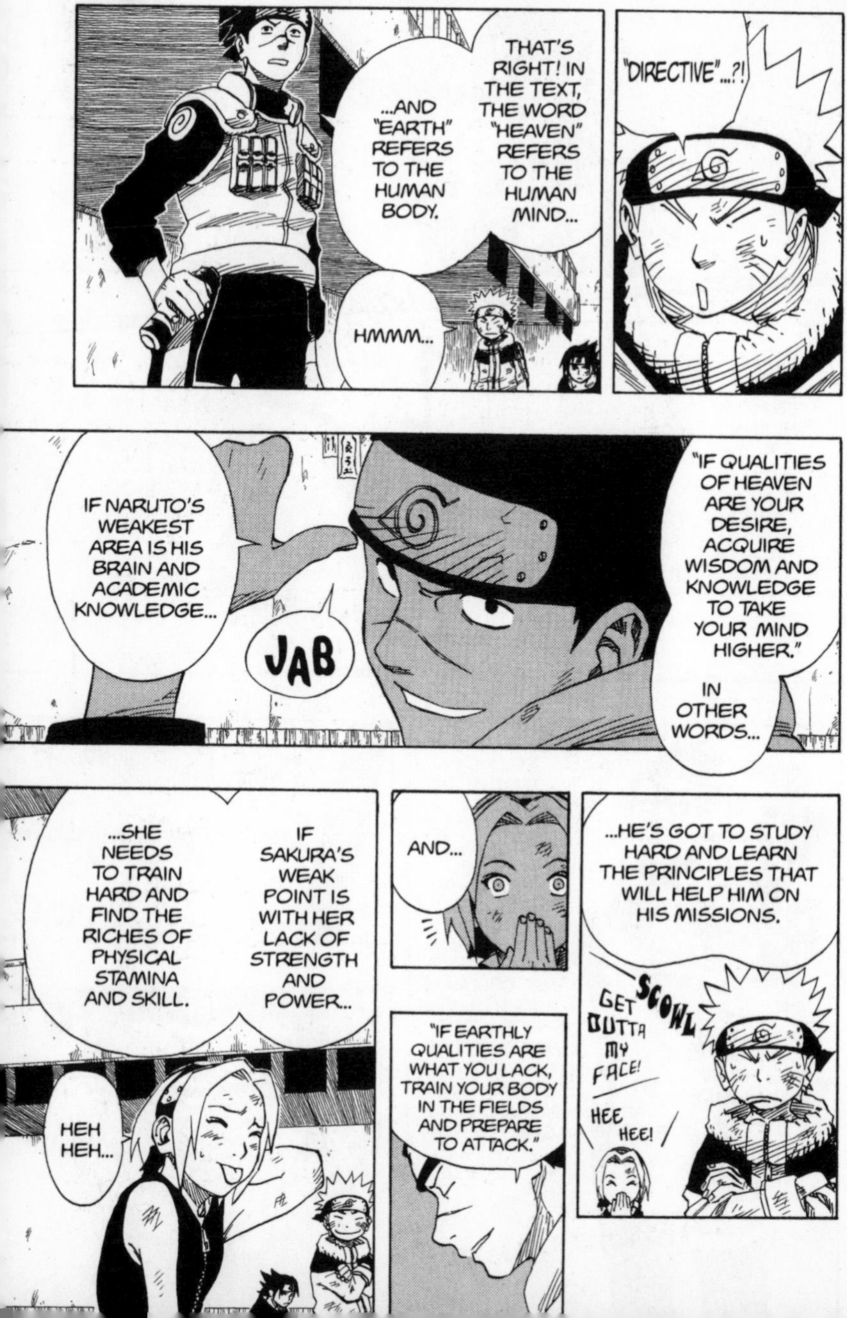
"DIRECTIVE"...?!
THAT'S RIGHT! IN THE TEXT, THE WORD "HEAVEN" REFERS TO THE HUMAN MIND...
...AND "EARTH" REFERS TO THE HUMAN BODY.
HMMM...
"IF QUALITIES OF HEAVEN ARE YOUR DESIRE, ACQUIRE WISDOM AND KNOWLEDGE TO TAKE YOUR MIND HIGHER."
IN OTHER WORDS...
JAB
IF NARUTO'S WEAKEST AREA IS HIS BRAIN AND ACADEMIC KNOWLEDGE...
...HE'S GOT TO STUDY HARD AND LEARN THE PRINCIPLES THAT WILL HELP HIM ON HIS MISSIONS.
SCOWL
GET OUTTA MY FACE!
HEE HEE!
AND...
"IF EARTHLY QUALITIES ARE WHAT YOU LACK, TRAIN YOUR BODY IN THE FIELDS AND PREPARE TO ATTACK."
IF SAKURA'S WEAK POINT IS WITH HER LACK OF STRENGTH AND POWER...
...SHE NEEDS TO TRAIN HARD AND FIND THE RICHES OF PHYSICAL STAMINA AND SKILL.
HEH HEH...

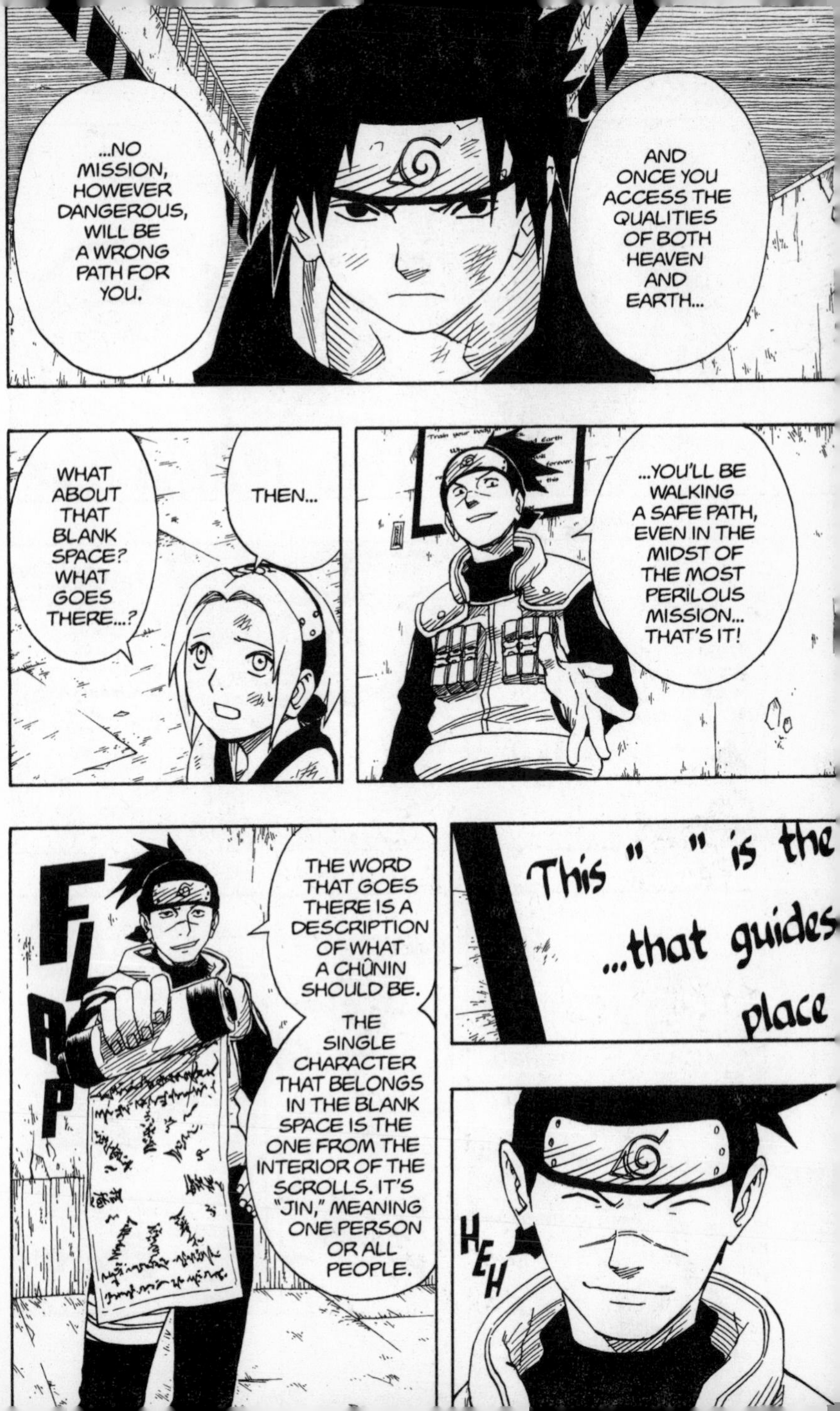
AND ONCE YOU ACCESS THE QUALITIES OF BOTH HEAVEN AND EARTH...
...NO MISSION, HOWEVER DANGEROUS, WILL BE A WRONG PATH FOR YOU.
...YOU'LL BE WALKING A SAFE PATH, EVEN IN THE MIDST OF THE MOST PERILOUS MISSION... THAT'S IT!
THEN...
WHAT ABOUT THAT BLANK SPACE? WHAT GOES THERE...?
This " " is the
...that guides
place
HEH
THE WORD THAT GOES THERE IS A DESCRIPTION OF WHAT A CHÛNIN SHOULD BE.
THE SINGLE CHARACTER THAT BELONGS IN THE BLANK SPACE IS THE ONE FROM THE INTERIOR OF THE SCROLLS. IT'S "JIN," MEANING ONE PERSON OR ALL PEOPLE.
FLAP

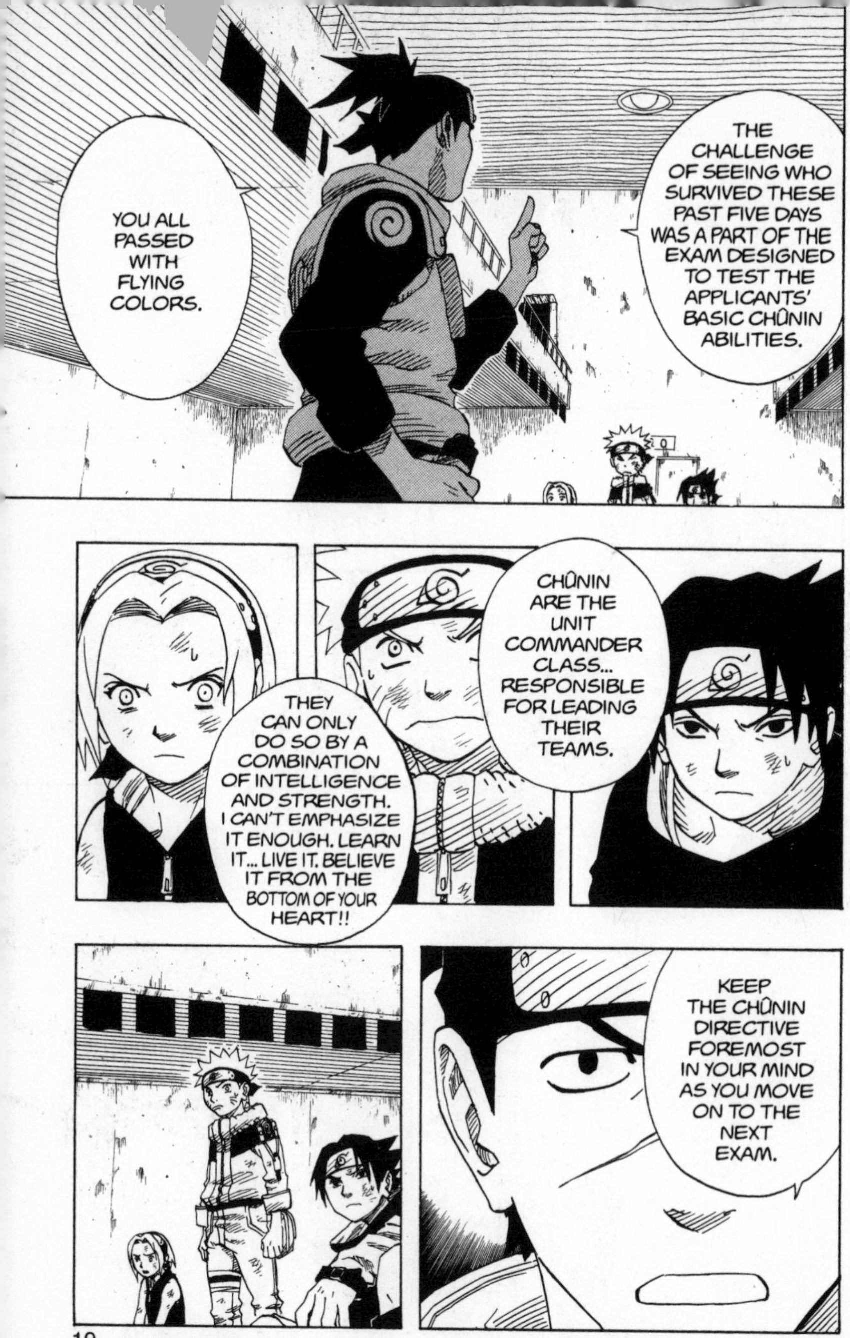
THE CHALLENGE OF SEEING WHO SURVIVED THESE PAST FIVE DAYS WAS A PART OF THE EXAM DESIGNED TO TEST THE APPLICANTS' BASIC CHÛNIN ABILITIES.
YOU ALL PASSED WITH FLYING COLORS.
CHÛNIN ARE THE UNIT COMMANDER CLASS... RESPONSIBLE FOR LEADING THEIR TEAMS.
THEY CAN ONLY DO SO BY A COMBINATION OF INTELLIGENCE AND STRENGTH. I CAN'T EMPHASIZE IT ENOUGH. LEARN IT... LIVE IT. BELIEVE IT FROM THE BOTTOM OF YOUR HEART!!
KEEP THE CHÛNIN DIRECTIVE FOREMOST IN YOUR MIND AS YOU MOVE ON TO THE NEXT EXAM.

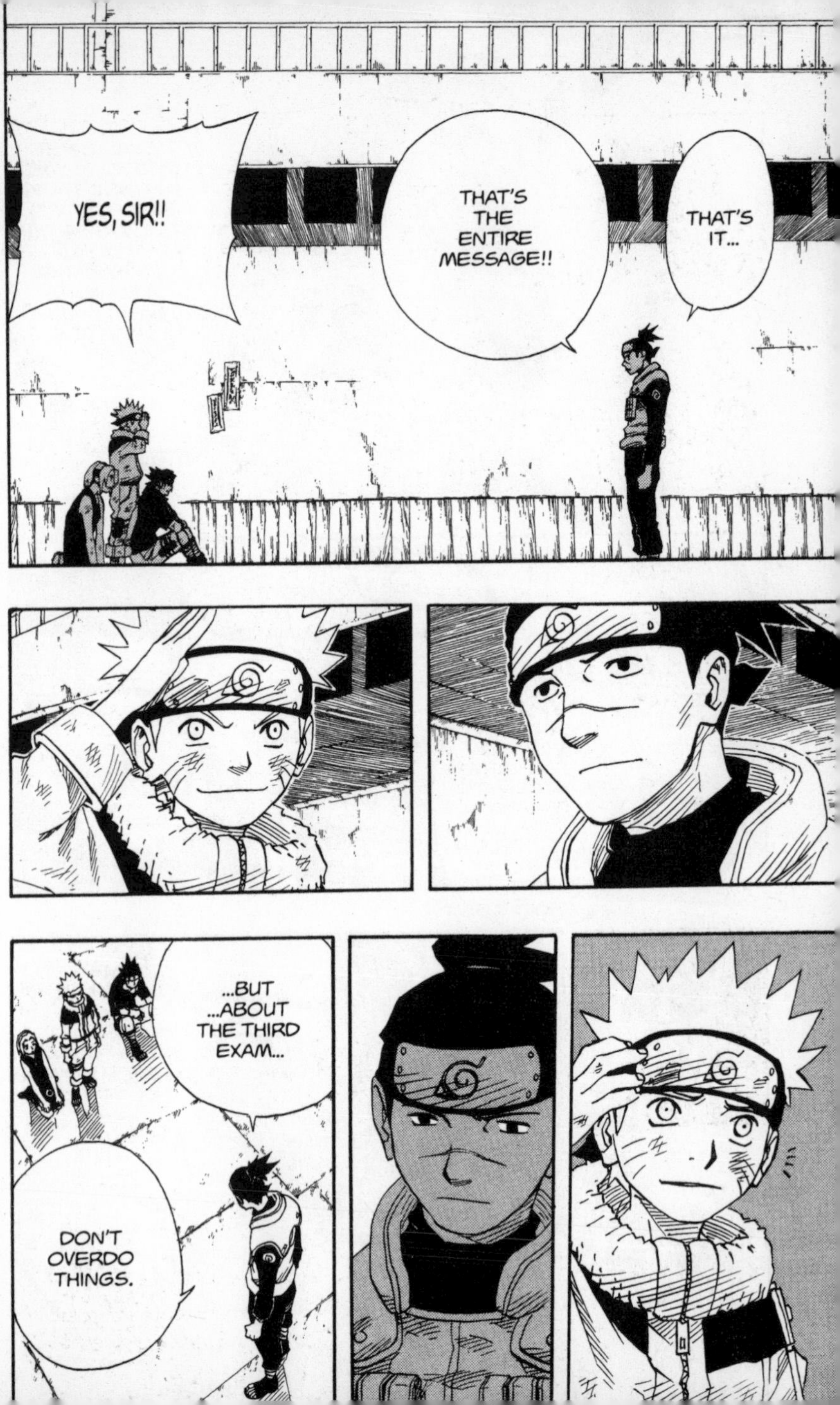
THAT'S IT...
THAT'S THE ENTIRE MESSAGE!!
YES, SIR!!
...BUT ...ABOUT THE THIRD EXAM...
DON'T OVERDO THINGS.

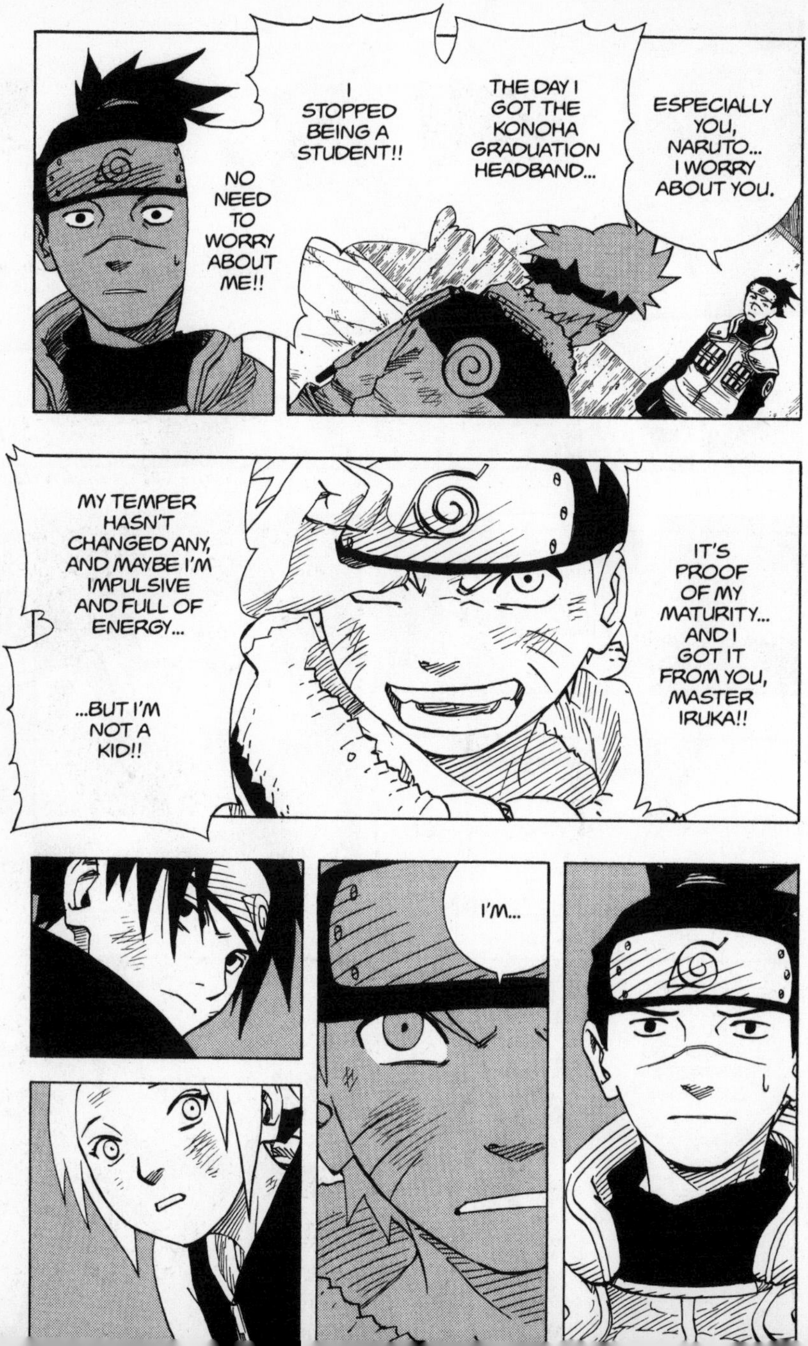
ESPECIALLY YOU, NARUTO... I WORRY ABOUT YOU.
THE DAY I GOT THE KONOHA GRADUATION HEADBAND...
I STOPPED BEING A STUDENT!!
NO NEED TO WORRY ABOUT ME!!
IT'S PROOF OF MY MATURITY... AND I GOT IT FROM YOU, MASTER IRUKA!!
MY TEMPER HASN'T CHANGED ANY, AND MAYBE I'M IMPULSIVE AND FULL OF ENERGY...
...BUT I'M NOT A KID!!
I'M...

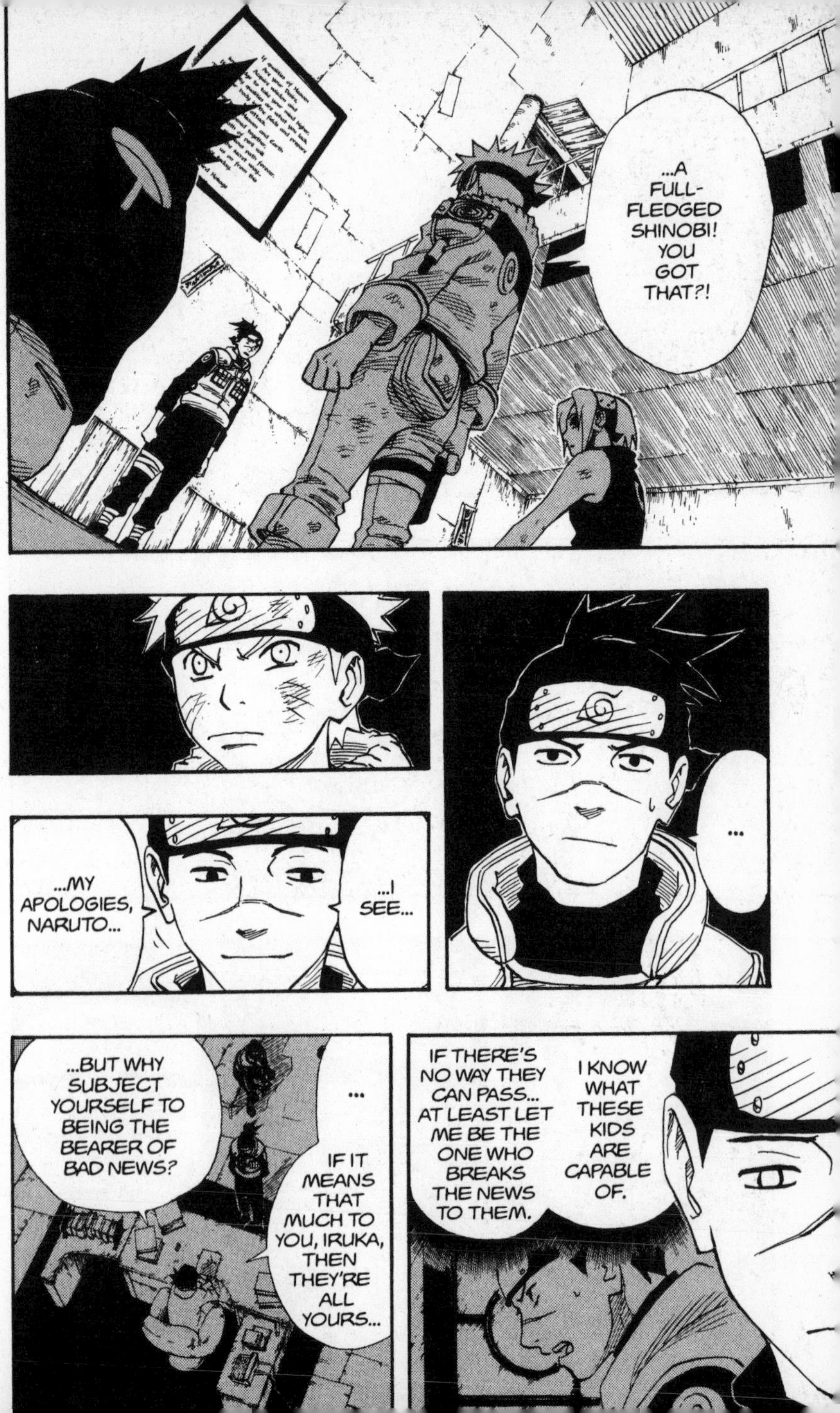
...A FULL-FLEDGED SHINOBI! YOU GOT THAT?!
...
...I SEE...
...MY APOLOGIES, NARUTO...
I KNOW WHAT THESE KIDS ARE CAPABLE OF.
IF THERE'S NO WAY THEY CAN PASS... AT LEAST LET ME BE THE ONE WHO BREAKS THE NEWS TO THEM.
...BUT WHY SUBJECT YOURSELF TO BEING THE BEARER OF BAD NEWS?
...
IF IT MEANS THAT MUCH TO YOU, IRUKA, THEN THEY'RE ALL YOURS...

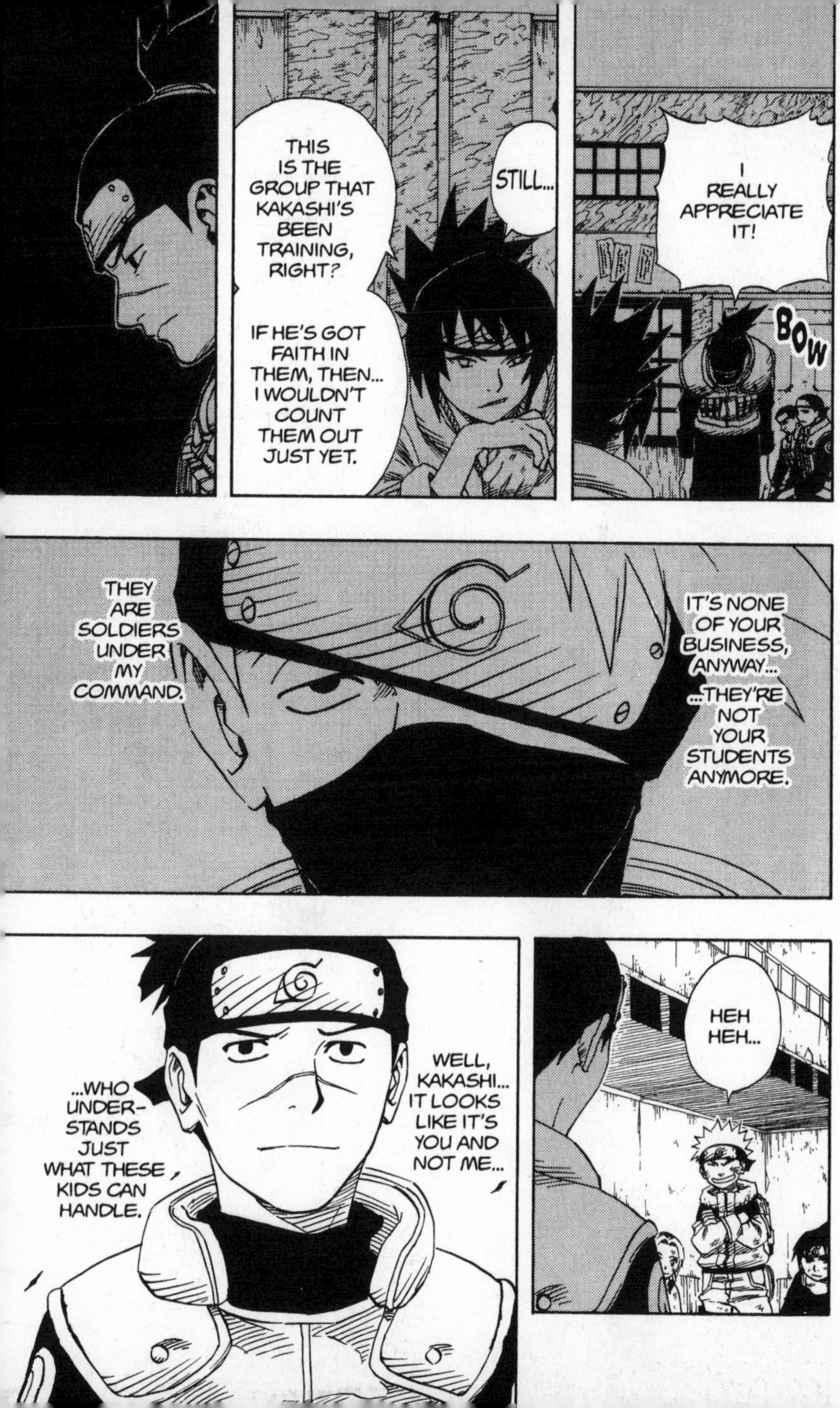
I REALLY APPRECIATE IT!
BOW
THIS IS THE GROUP THAT KAKASHI'S BEEN TRAINING, RIGHT?
STILL...
IF HE'S GOT FAITH IN THEM, THEN... I WOULDN'T COUNT THEM OUT JUST YET.
IT'S NONE OF YOUR BUSINESS, ANYWAY... ...THEY'RE NOT YOUR STUDENTS ANYMORE.
THEY ARE SOLDIERS UNDER MY COMMAND.
HEH HEH...
WELL, KAKASHI... IT LOOKS LIKE IT'S YOU AND NOT ME...
...WHO UNDERSTANDS JUST WHAT THESE KIDS CAN HANDLE.

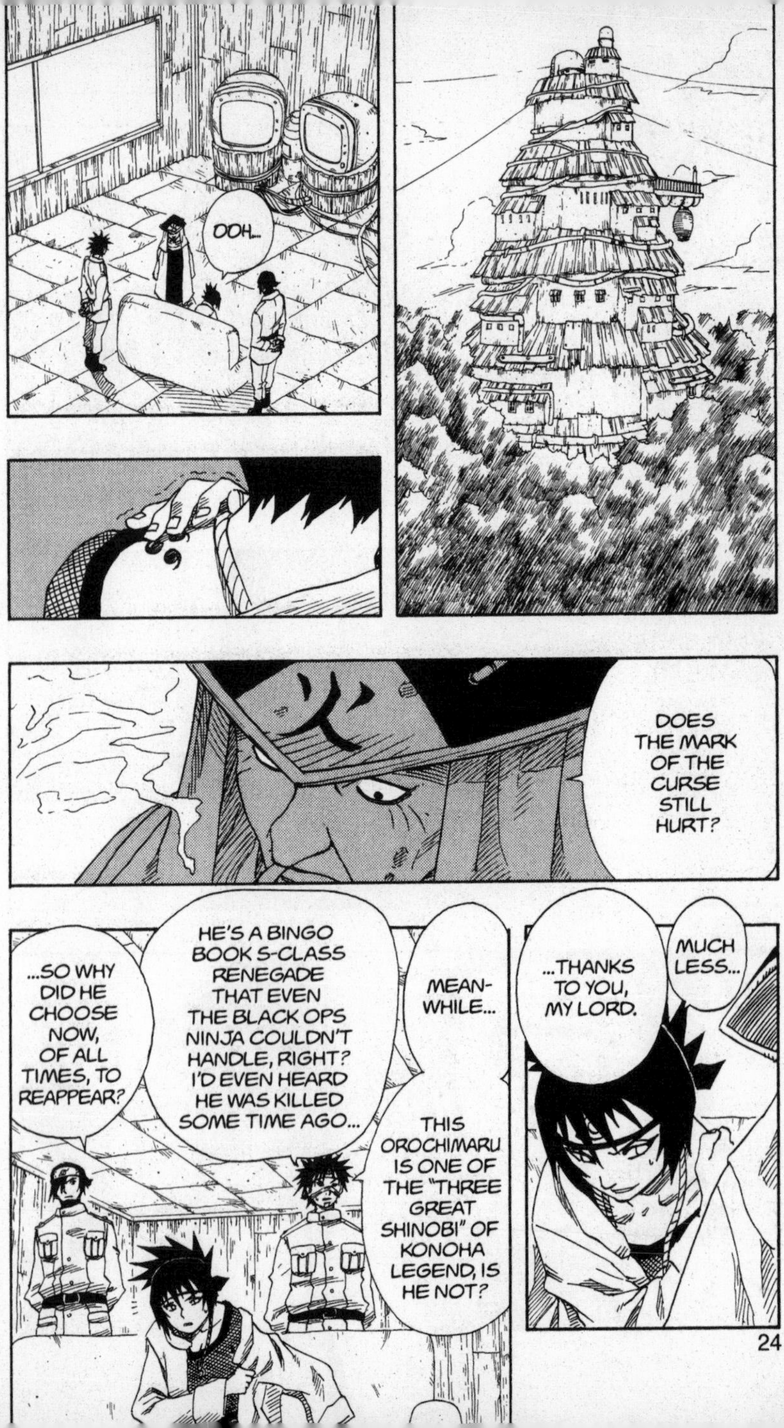
OOH...
DOES THE MARK OF THE CURSE STILL HURT?
MUCH LESS...
...THANKS TO YOU, MY LORD.
MEAN-WHILE...
THIS OROCHIMARU IS ONE OF THE "THREE GREAT SHINOBI" OF KONOHA LEGEND, IS HE NOT?
HE'S A BINGO BOOK S-CLASS RENEGADE THAT EVEN THE BLACK OPS NINJA COULDN'T HANDLE, RIGHT? I'D EVEN HEARD HE WAS KILLED SOME TIME AGO...
...SO WHY DID HE CHOOSE NOW, OF ALL TIMES, TO REAPPEAR?

READ THIS WAY

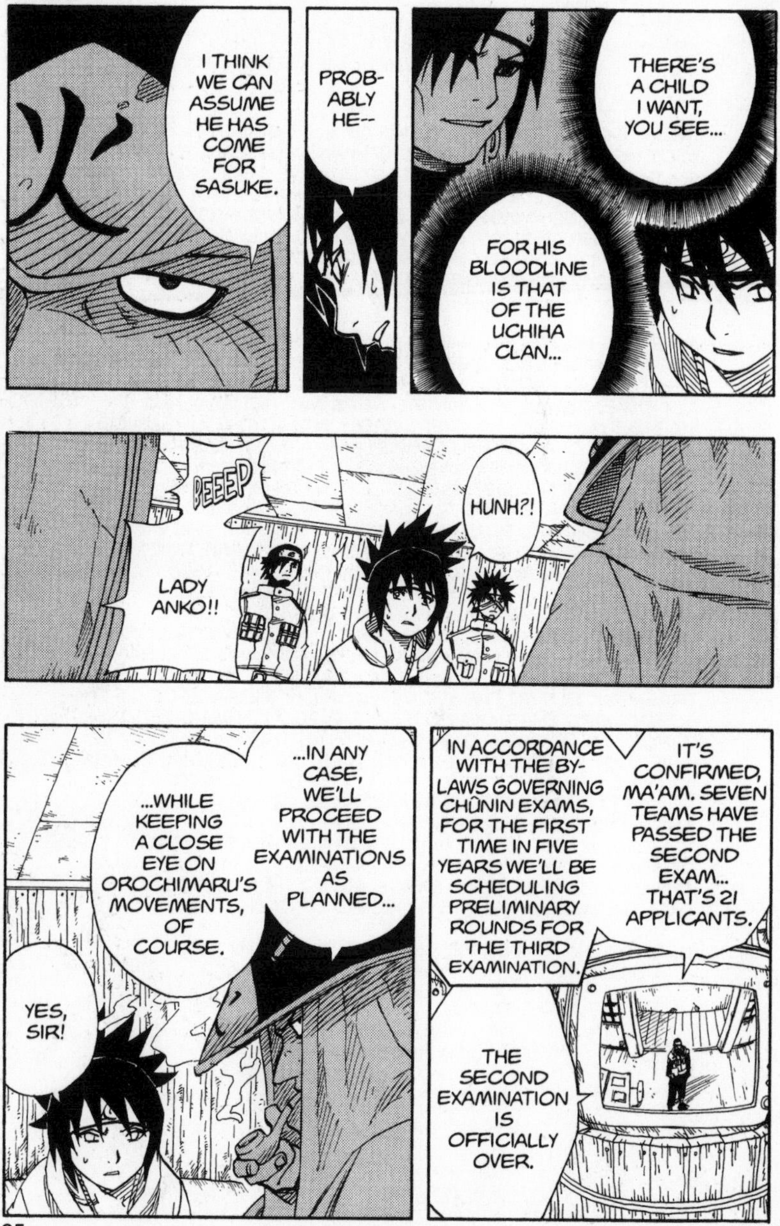

THERE'S A CHILD I WANT, YOU SEE...
FOR HIS BLOODLINE IS THAT OF THE UCHIHA CLAN...
PROB-ABLY HE--
I THINK WE CAN ASSUME HE HAS COME FOR SASUKE.
HUNH?!
BEEEP
LADY ANKO!!
IT'S CONFIRMED, MA'AM. SEVEN TEAMS HAVE PASSED THE SECOND EXAM... THAT'S 21 APPLICANTS.
IN ACCORDANCE WITH THE BY-LAWS GOVERNING CHÛNIN EXAMS, FOR THE FIRST TIME IN FIVE YEARS WE'LL BE SCHEDULING PRELIMINARY ROUNDS FOR THE THIRD EXAMINATION.
THE SECOND EXAMINATION IS OFFICIALLY OVER.
...IN ANY CASE, WE'LL PROCEED WITH THE EXAMINATIONS AS PLANNED...
...WHILE KEEPING A CLOSE EYE ON OROCHIMARU'S MOVEMENTS, OF COURSE.
YES, SIR!

THE WORLD OF KISHIMOTO MASASHI
MY PERSONAL HISTORY, PART 5

WHEN I GOT TO THE FINAL YEARS OF ELEMENTARY SCHOOL,
I GOT HOOKED ON *SHONEN JUMP* MANGA, THANKS TO THE
ANIMATED *DRAGON BALL* SERIES. BUT EVEN BEFORE
DRAGON BALL, I LOVED THE ANIME VERSION OF A *JUMP*
COMIC CALLED *KINNIKUMAN (ULTIMATE MUSCLE)* ON TV.
MY BROTHER AND I BOTH BECAME IDIOTICALLY OBSESSED
WITH IT, AND THE TWO OF US PLAYED AROUND A LOT, DESIGN-
ING OUR OWN SUPERHEROES.

MY LITTLE BROTHER'S FAVORITE CREATION WAS HIS KABUTO-
MUSHI (RHINOCEROS BEETLE) SUPERHERO KNOWN AS
"BEETLE MAN," AND SINCE I WAS A FANATIC FOR SPICES AND
CONDIMENTS, MY SPECIALTIES WERE "WASABI MAN" AND
"KARASHI MUSTARD MAN" (PROBABLY DUE TO THE INFLUENCE
OF A HERO CHARACTER IN *KINNIKUMAN* NAMED "CURRY COOK")...
AFTER DISCOVERING WHAT GREAT SUPERHEROES I COULD
MAKE OUT OF FOODSTUFFS, I ONLY HAD TO OPEN THE
REFRIGERATOR TO FIND ALL KINDS OF HOT NEW IDEAS FOR
ORIGINAL CHARACTERS. AND I REALLY THOUGHT THE VARIOUS
SPICE NAMES HAD A NICE RING TO THEM. BIZARRE, I KNOW...
BUT I TOOK IT VERY SERIOUSLY BACK THEN.

AROUND THE SAME TIME, I GOT MY FIRST LOOK AT THE
ANIMATED *FIST OF THE NORTH STAR*, AND I GOT TOTALLY INTO
IT. AT SCHOOL, WHEN MY GROUP GOT ASSIGNED TO CLEAN THE
CLASSROOM, IT WAS SO DIFFICULT TO CARRY THE HEAVY STEEL
TRASH CAN OUT TO THE INCINERATOR ON THE FAR SIDE OF THE
SCHOOLYARD THAT I DEVELOPED A TACTIC TO EVADE THE TASK.
I'D POKE MY FRIEND'S TEMPLES WITH MY THUMBS AND SAY, "I
HAVE JUST PRESSED ONE OF YOUR SECRET MERIDIAN POINTS.
YOU WILL NOW TAKE THE TRASH CAN TO THE INCINERATOR
TO EMPTY IT." MY FRIENDS WOULD RETALIATE BY RETORTING,
"I HAVE PRESSED THE SAME SECRET POINT" IN VERY SERIOUS
TONES, AND WE'D SPEND QUITE A WHILE PRESSING EACH
OTHER'S SECRET POINTS -- IN A COMPLETELY FRIENDLY WAY --
WHILE GETTING MASSIVE EXPOSURE TO THINGS LIKE DIOXINS
THAT THE WORLD HAD NEVER HEARD OF BACK THEN.

THOSE *JUMP* ANIME INSPIRED A LOT OF GOOD TIMES!

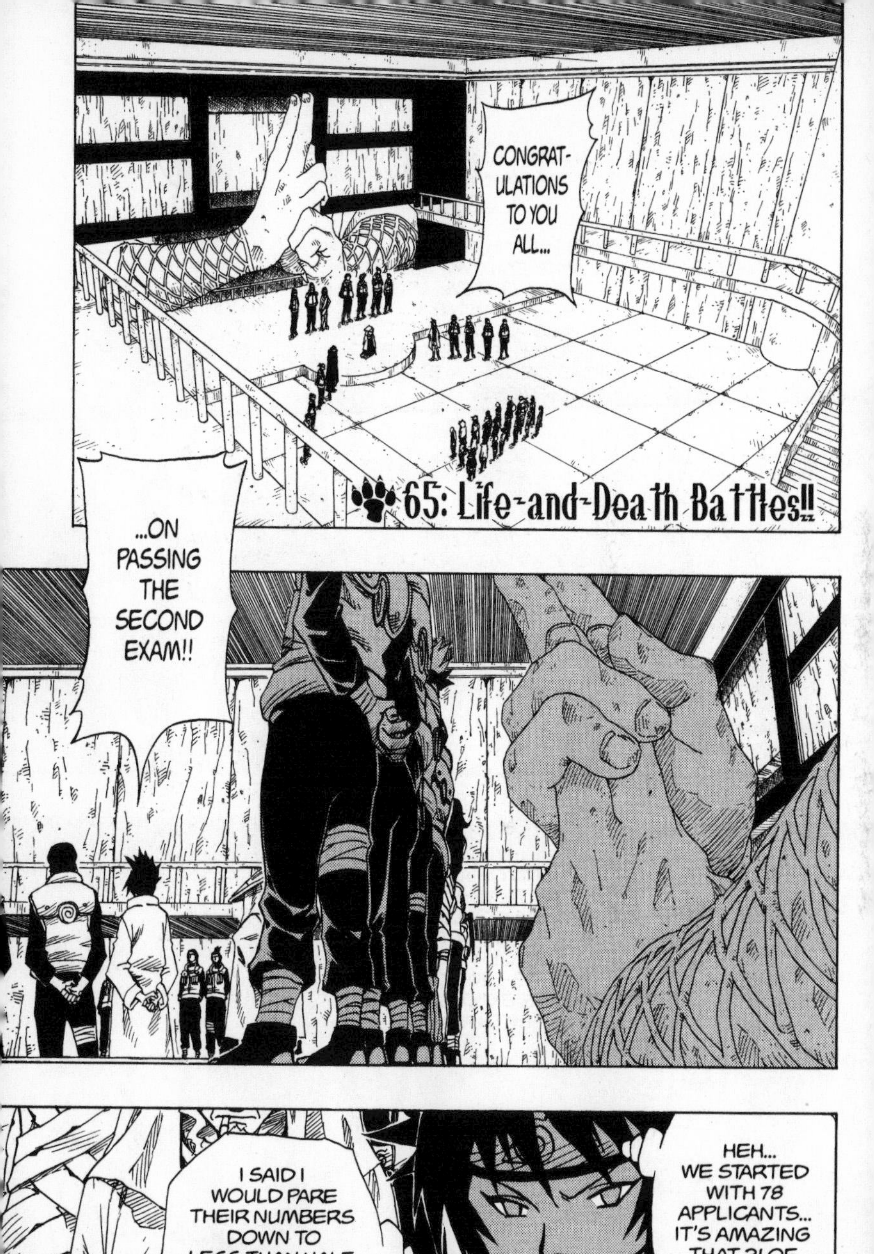
CONGRATULATIONS TO YOU ALL...
65: Life-and-Death Battles!!
...ON PASSING THE SECOND EXAM!!
HEH... WE STARTED WITH 78 APPLICANTS... IT'S AMAZING THAT 21 OF THEM ACTUALLY MADE IT.
I SAID I WOULD PARE THEIR NUMBERS DOWN TO LESS THAN HALF, BUT REALLY I WAS ONLY EXPECTING A SINGLE DIGIT FIGURE...

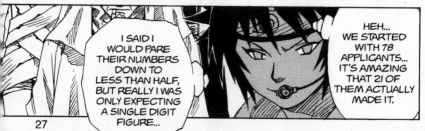

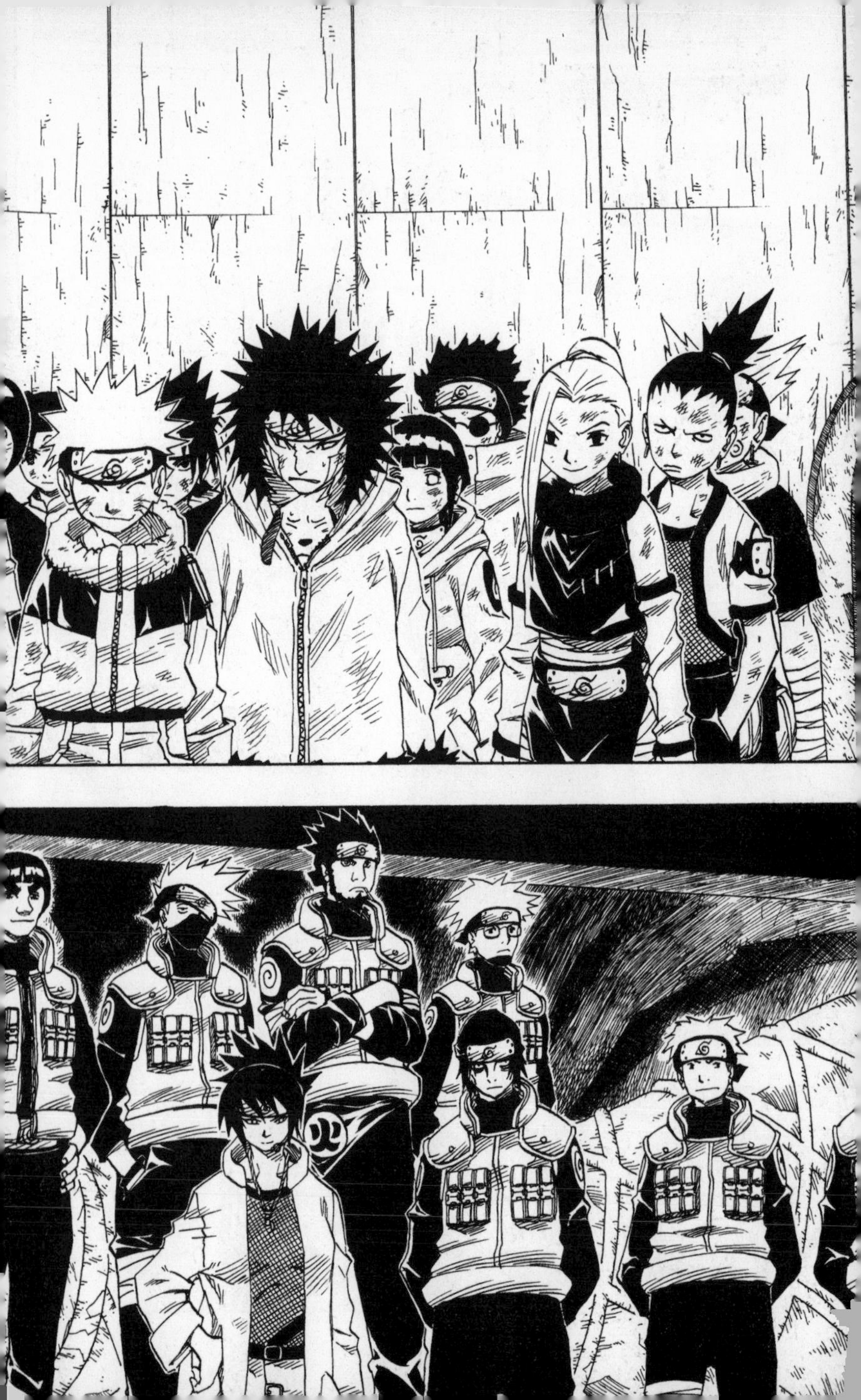

Number 65: Life-and-Death Battles!!

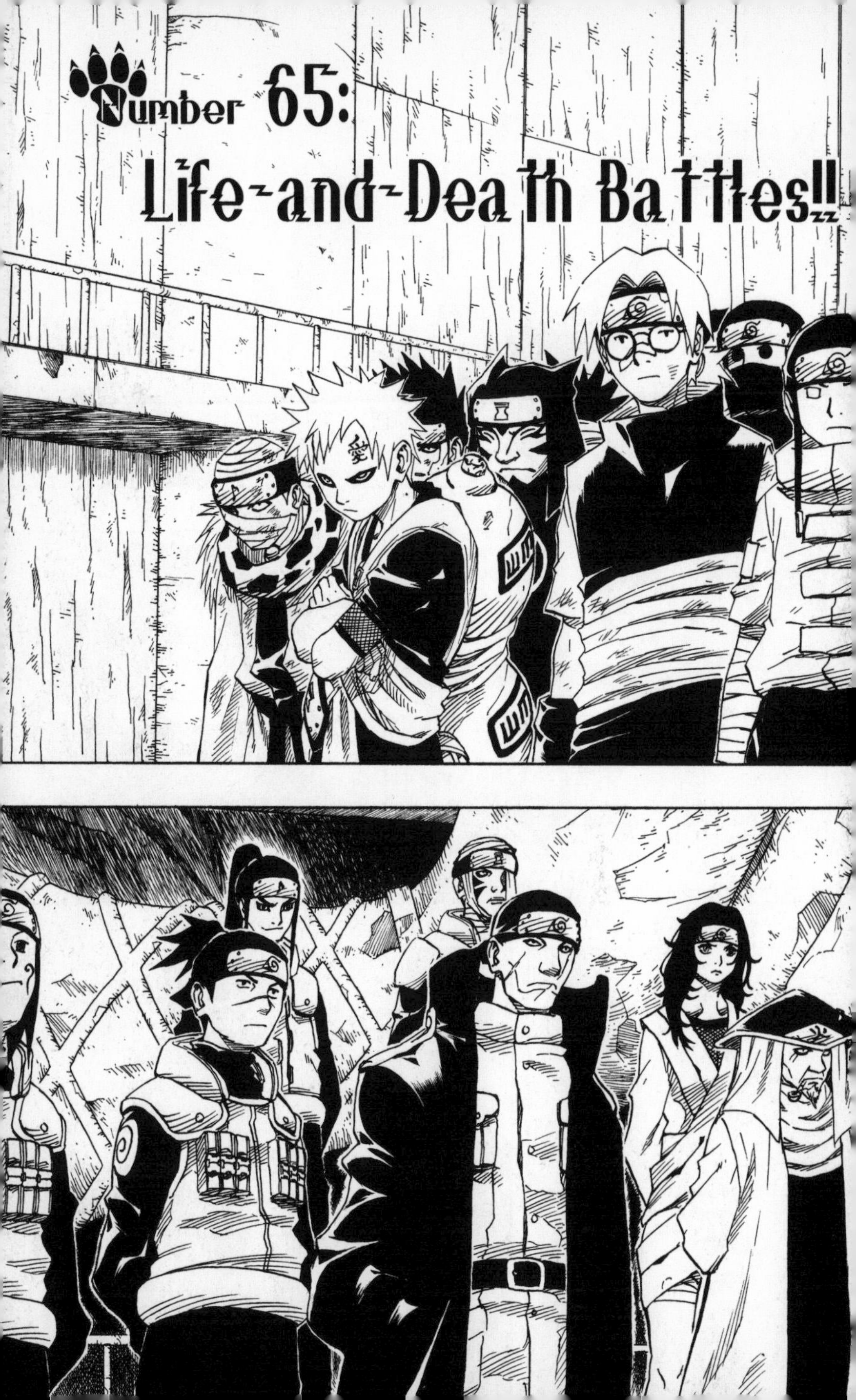

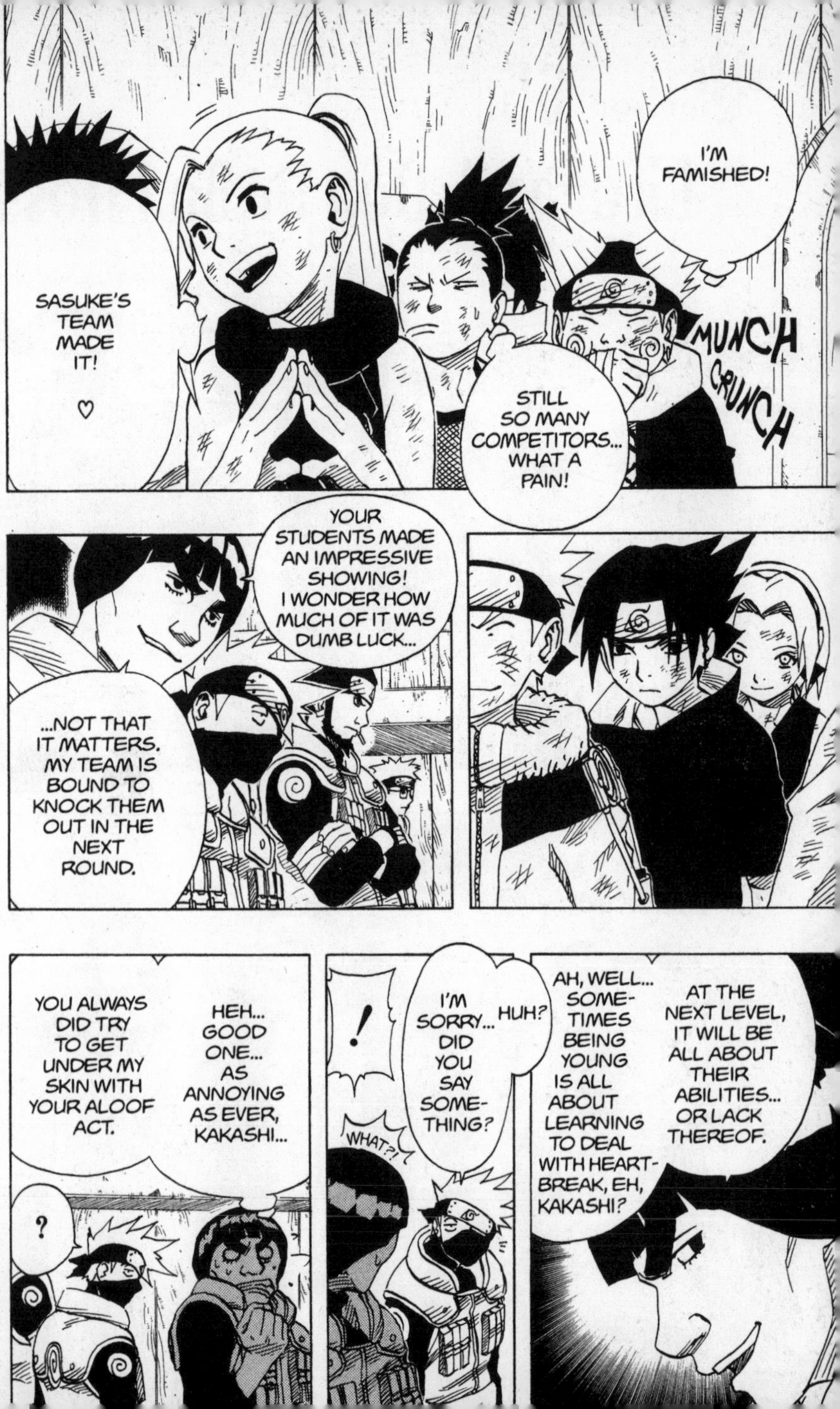

I'M FAMISHED!
MUNCH
CRUNCH
SASUKE'S TEAM MADE IT! ♡
STILL SO MANY COMPETITORS... WHAT A PAIN!
YOUR STUDENTS MADE AN IMPRESSIVE SHOWING! I WONDER HOW MUCH OF IT WAS DUMB LUCK...
...NOT THAT IT MATTERS. MY TEAM IS BOUND TO KNOCK THEM OUT IN THE NEXT ROUND.
AT THE NEXT LEVEL, IT WILL BE ALL ABOUT THEIR ABILITIES... OR LACK THEREOF.
AH, WELL... SOME-TIMES BEING YOUNG IS ALL ABOUT LEARNING TO DEAL WITH HEART-BREAK, EH, KAKASHI?
HUH?
I'M SORRY... DID YOU SAY SOME-THING?
!
WHAT?!
HEH... GOOD ONE... AS ANNOYING AS EVER, KAKASHI...
YOU ALWAYS DID TRY TO GET UNDER MY SKIN WITH YOUR ALOOF ACT.
?

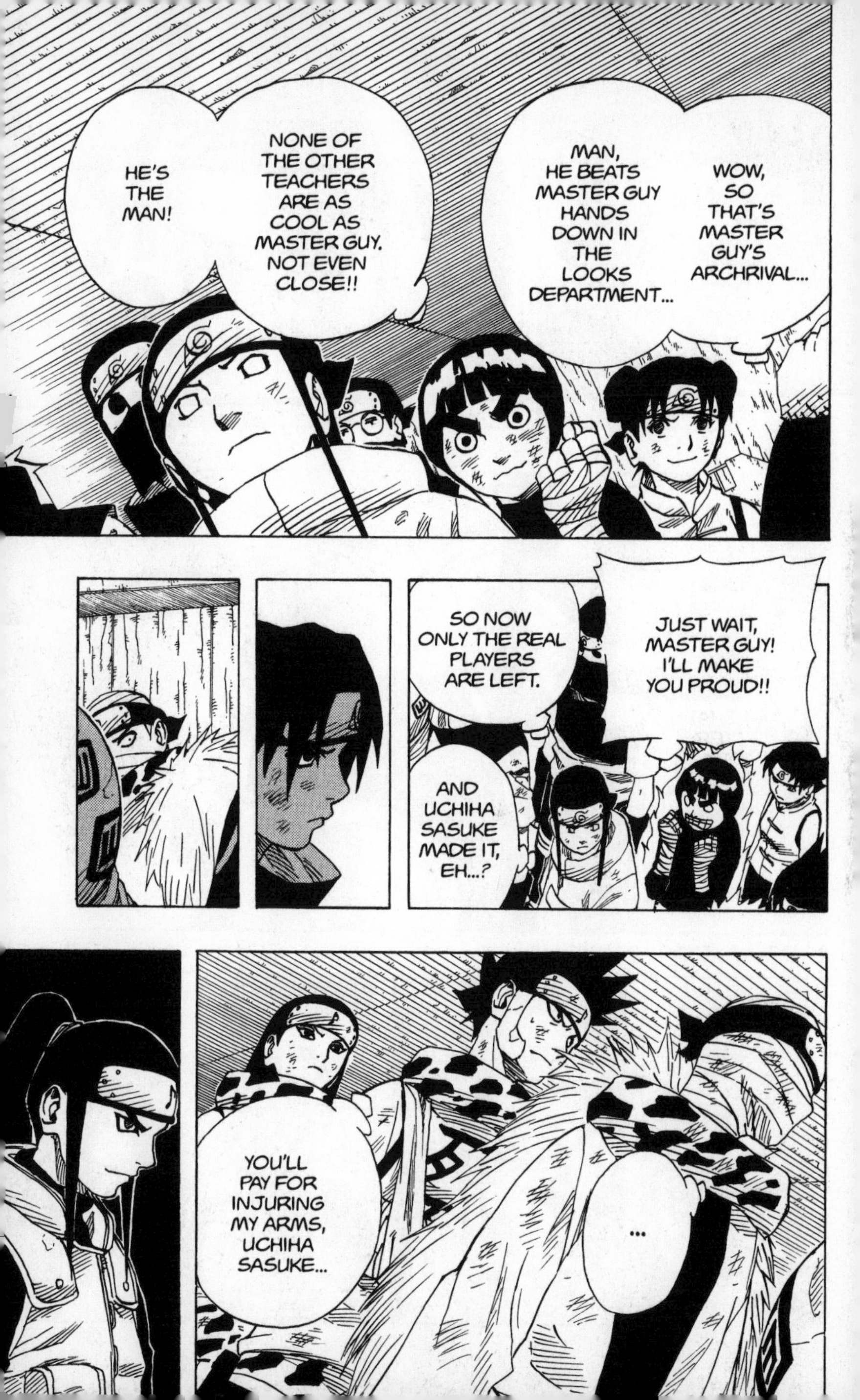
WOW, SO THAT'S MASTER GUY'S ARCHRIVAL...
MAN, HE BEATS MASTER GUY HANDS DOWN IN THE LOOKS DEPARTMENT...
NONE OF THE OTHER TEACHERS ARE AS COOL AS MASTER GUY. NOT EVEN CLOSE!!
HE'S THE MAN!
JUST WAIT, MASTER GUY! I'LL MAKE YOU PROUD!!
SO NOW ONLY THE REAL PLAYERS ARE LEFT.
AND UCHIHA SASUKE MADE IT, EH...?
...
YOU'LL PAY FOR INJURING MY ARMS, UCHIHA SASUKE...

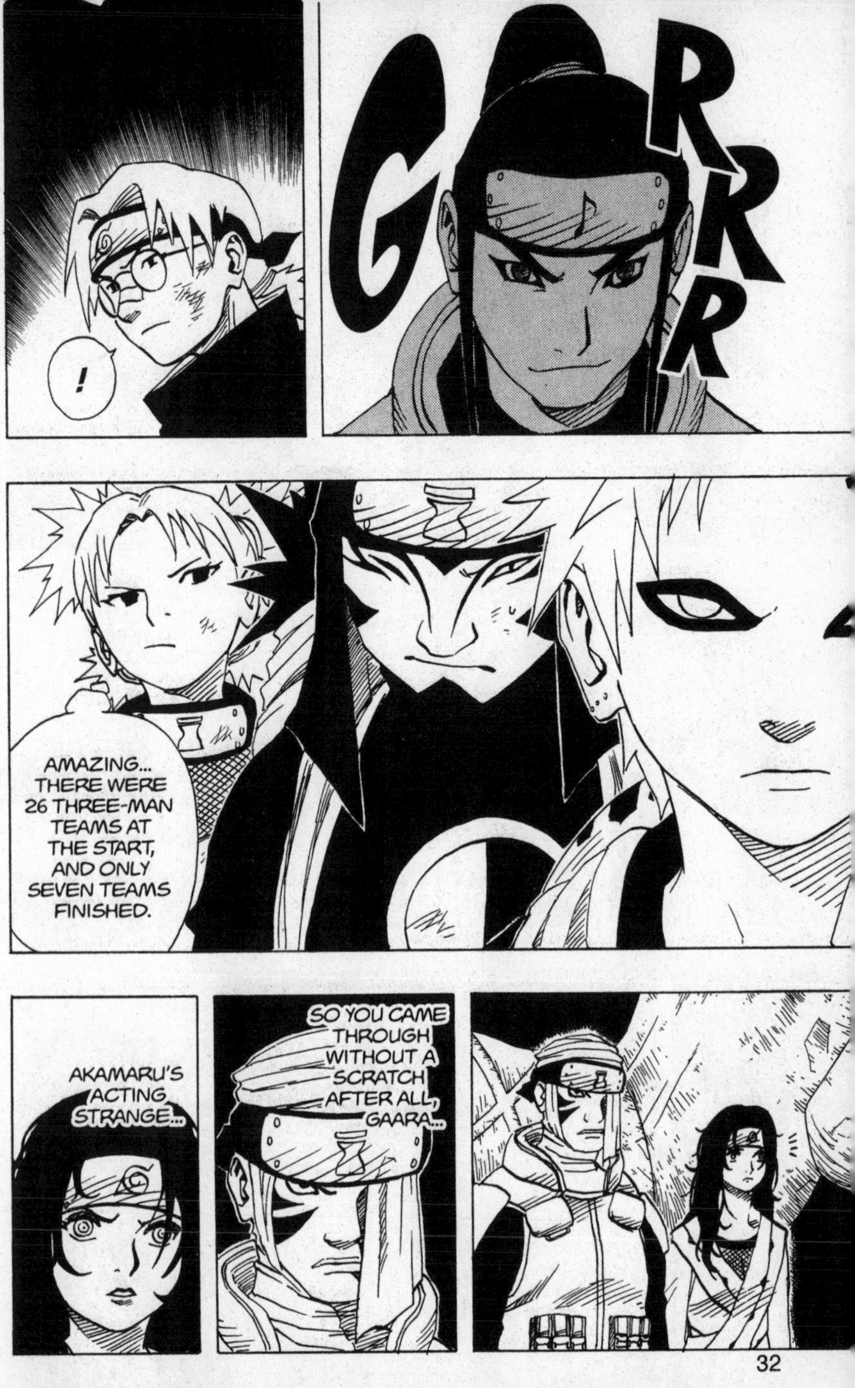
GRRRR
!
AMAZING... THERE WERE 26 THREE-MAN TEAMS AT THE START, AND ONLY SEVEN TEAMS FINISHED.
SO YOU CAME THROUGH WITHOUT A SCRATCH AFTER ALL, GAARA...
AKAMARU'S ACTING STRANGE...

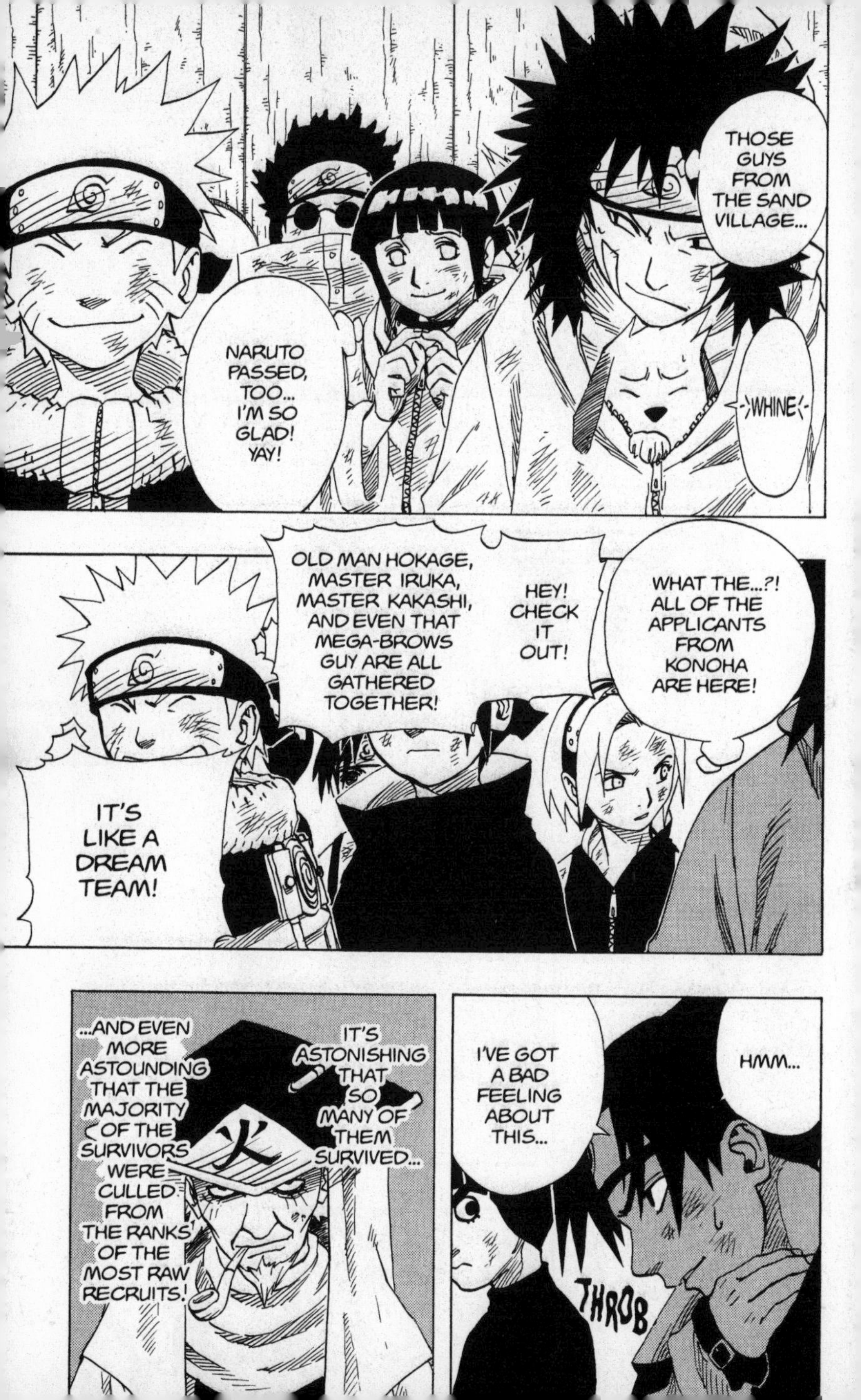
THOSE GUYS FROM THE SAND VILLAGE...
WHINE
NARUTO PASSED, TOO... I'M SO GLAD! YAY!
WHAT THE...?! ALL OF THE APPLICANTS FROM KONOHA ARE HERE!
HEY! CHECK IT OUT!
OLD MAN HOKAGE, MASTER IRUKA, MASTER KAKASHI, AND EVEN THAT MEGA-BROWS GUY ARE ALL GATHERED TOGETHER!
IT'S LIKE A DREAM TEAM!
HMM...
I'VE GOT A BAD FEELING ABOUT THIS...
THROB
IT'S ASTONISHING THAT SO MANY OF THEM SURVIVED...
...AND EVEN MORE ASTOUNDING THAT THE MAJORITY OF THE SURVIVORS WERE CULLED FROM THE RANKS OF THE MOST RAW RECRUITS!

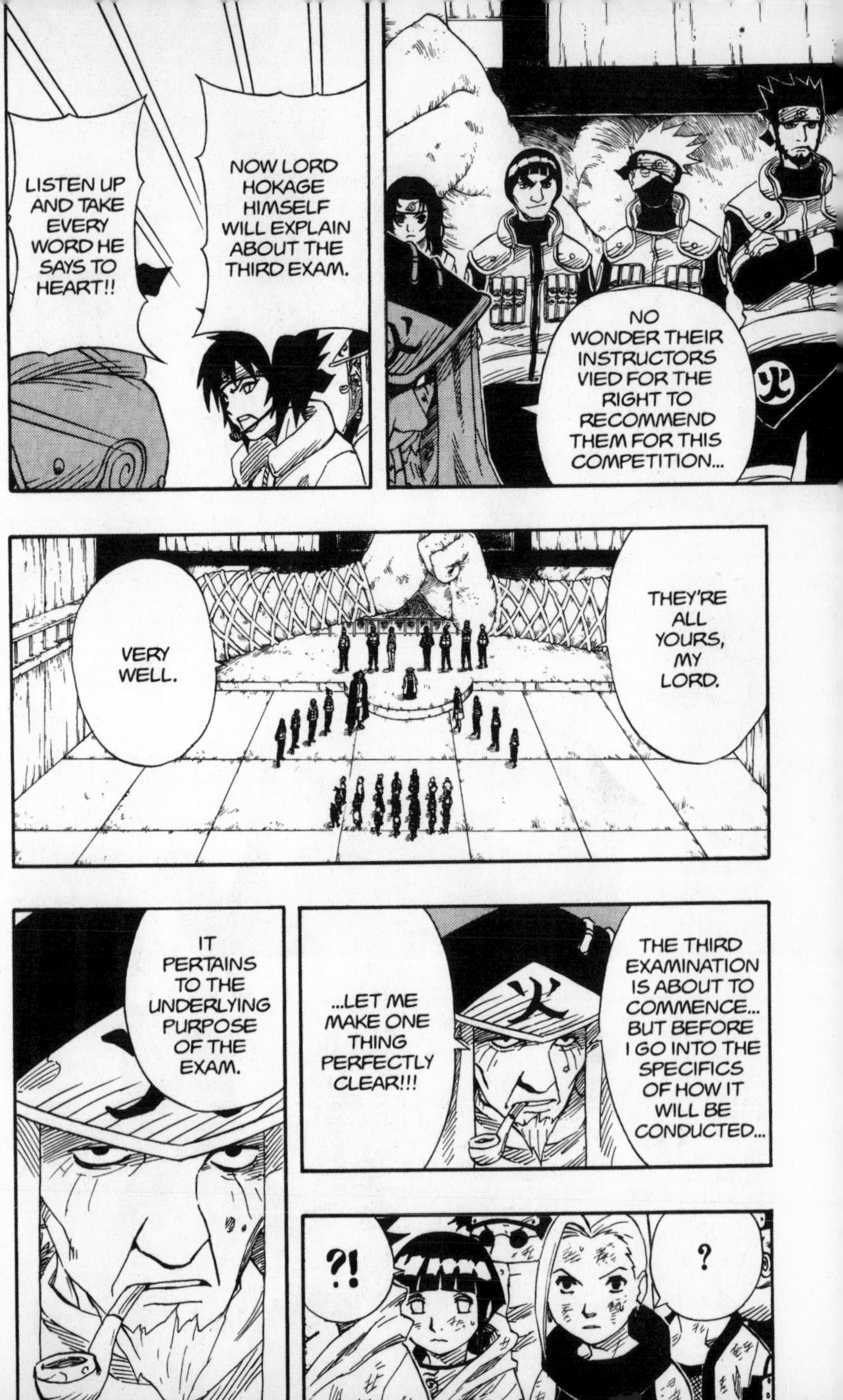
NO WONDER THEIR INSTRUCTORS VIED FOR THE RIGHT TO RECOMMEND THEM FOR THIS COMPETITION...
NOW LORD HOKAGE HIMSELF WILL EXPLAIN ABOUT THE THIRD EXAM.
LISTEN UP AND TAKE EVERY WORD HE SAYS TO HEART!!
THEY'RE ALL YOURS, MY LORD.
VERY WELL.
THE THIRD EXAMINATION IS ABOUT TO COMMENCE... BUT BEFORE I GO INTO THE SPECIFICS OF HOW IT WILL BE CONDUCTED...
...LET ME MAKE ONE THING PERFECTLY CLEAR!!!
?
?!
IT PERTAINS TO THE UNDERLYING PURPOSE OF THE EXAM.

READ THIS WAY

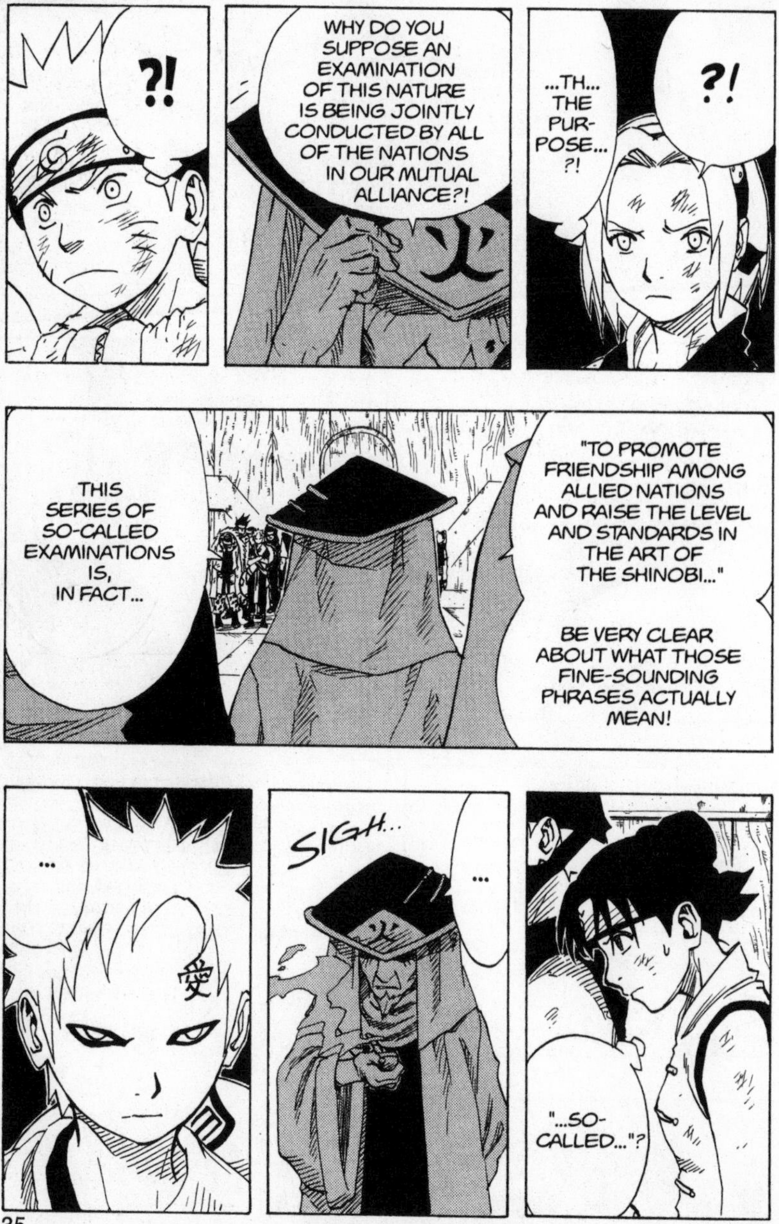
?!
...TH... THE PUR-POSE... ?!
WHY DO YOU SUPPOSE AN EXAMINATION OF THIS NATURE IS BEING JOINTLY CONDUCTED BY ALL OF THE NATIONS IN OUR MUTUAL ALLIANCE?!
?!
"TO PROMOTE FRIENDSHIP AMONG ALLIED NATIONS AND RAISE THE LEVEL AND STANDARDS IN THE ART OF THE SHINOBI..."
BE VERY CLEAR ABOUT WHAT THOSE FINE-SOUNDING PHRASES ACTUALLY MEAN!
THIS SERIES OF SO-CALLED EXAMINATIONS IS, IN FACT...
"...SO-CALLED..."?
...
SIGH...
...

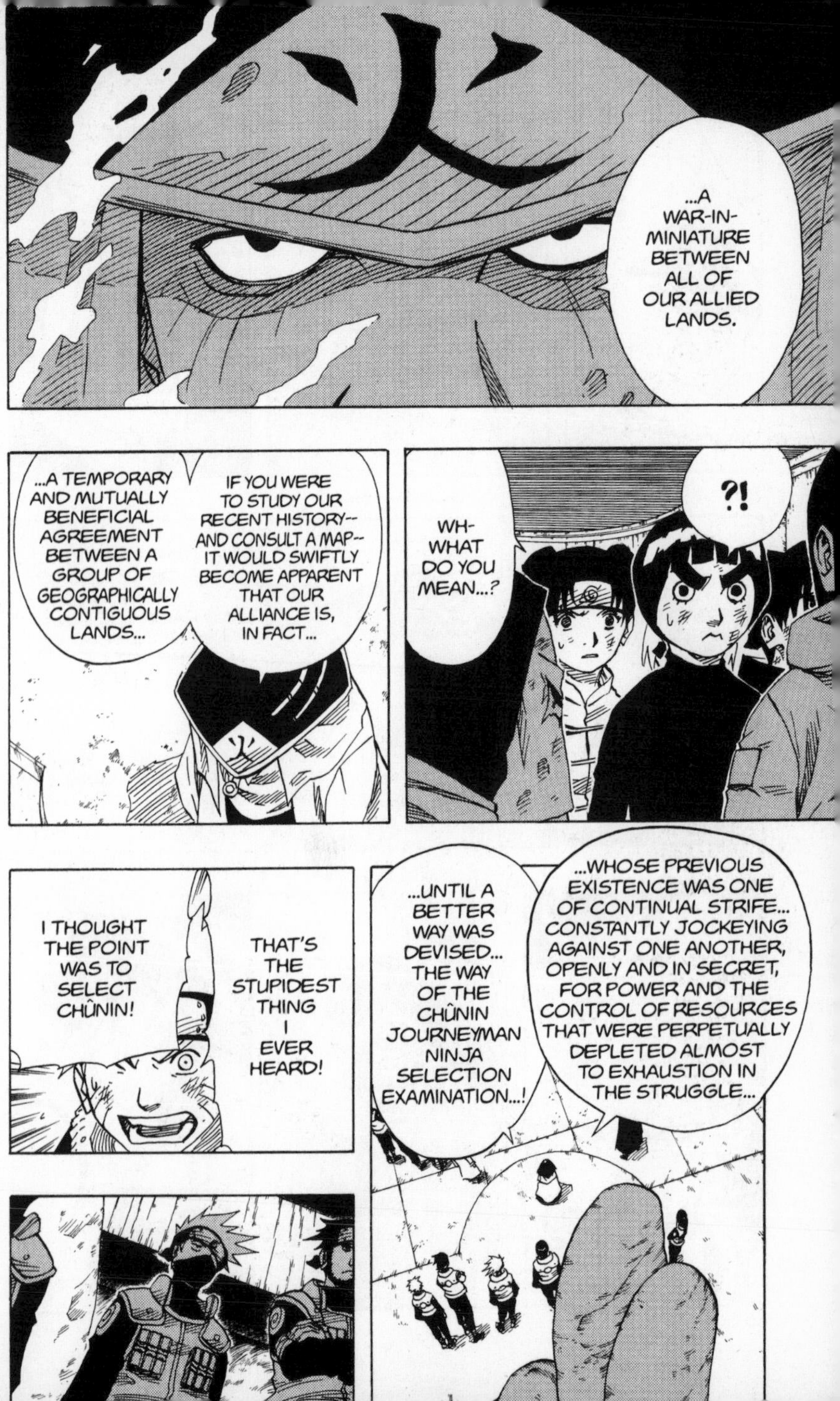
...A WAR-IN-MINIATURE BETWEEN ALL OF OUR ALLIED LANDS.
?!
WH-WHAT DO YOU MEAN...?
IF YOU WERE TO STUDY OUR RECENT HISTORY-- AND CONSULT A MAP-- IT WOULD SWIFTLY BECOME APPARENT THAT OUR ALLIANCE IS, IN FACT...
...A TEMPORARY AND MUTUALLY BENEFICIAL AGREEMENT BETWEEN A GROUP OF GEOGRAPHICALLY CONTIGUOUS LANDS...
...WHOSE PREVIOUS EXISTENCE WAS ONE OF CONTINUAL STRIFE... CONSTANTLY JOCKEYING AGAINST ONE ANOTHER, OPENLY AND IN SECRET, FOR POWER AND THE CONTROL OF RESOURCES THAT WERE PERPETUALLY DEPLETED ALMOST TO EXHAUSTION IN THE STRUGGLE...
...UNTIL A BETTER WAY WAS DEVISED... THE WAY OF THE CHÛNIN JOURNEYMAN NINJA SELECTION EXAMINATION...!
THAT'S THE STUPIDEST THING I EVER HEARD!
I THOUGHT THE POINT WAS TO SELECT CHÛNIN!

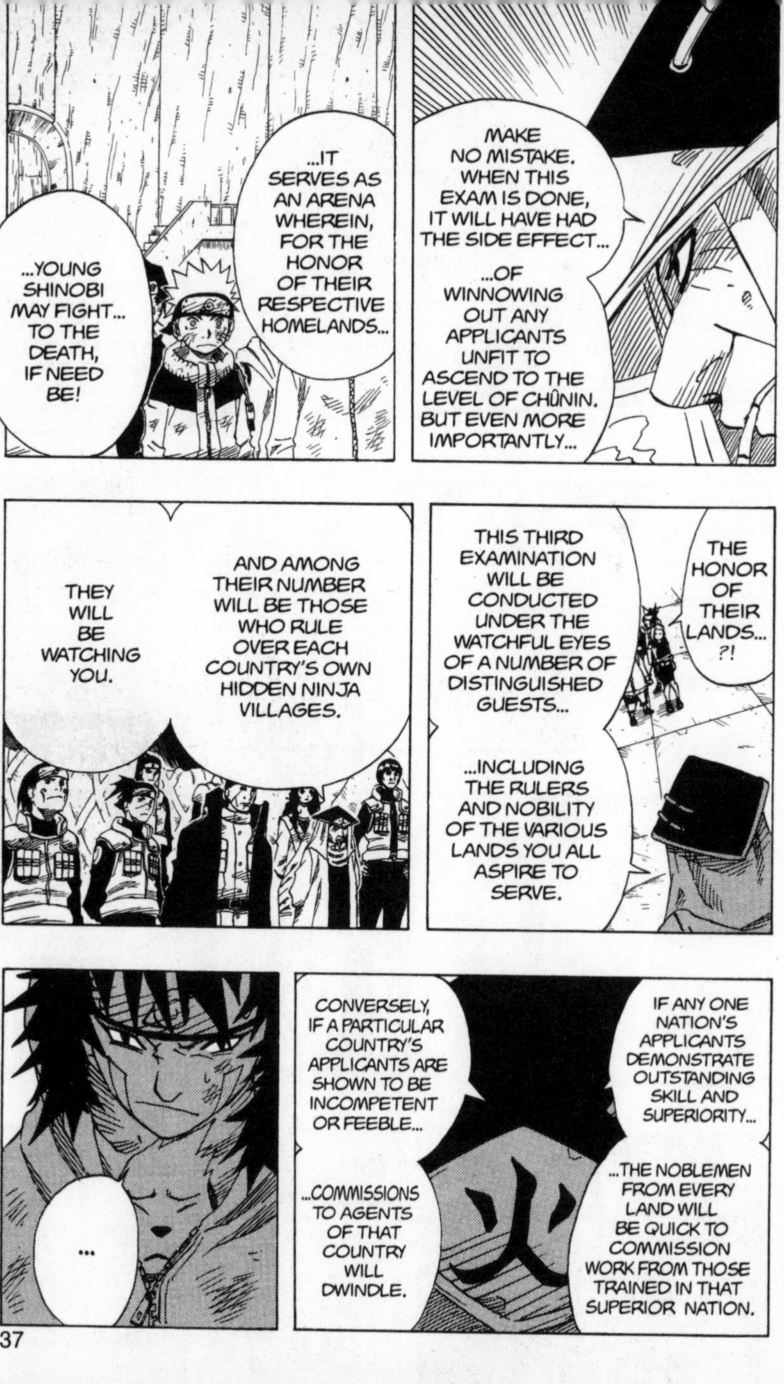
MAKE NO MISTAKE. WHEN THIS EXAM IS DONE, IT WILL HAVE HAD THE SIDE EFFECT...
...OF WINNOWING OUT ANY APPLICANTS UNFIT TO ASCEND TO THE LEVEL OF CHÛNIN. BUT EVEN MORE IMPORTANTLY...
...IT SERVES AS AN ARENA WHEREIN, FOR THE HONOR OF THEIR RESPECTIVE HOMELANDS...
...YOUNG SHINOBI MAY FIGHT... TO THE DEATH, IF NEED BE!
THE HONOR OF THEIR LANDS... ?!
THIS THIRD EXAMINATION WILL BE CONDUCTED UNDER THE WATCHFUL EYES OF A NUMBER OF DISTINGUISHED GUESTS...
...INCLUDING THE RULERS AND NOBILITY OF THE VARIOUS LANDS YOU ALL ASPIRE TO SERVE.
AND AMONG THEIR NUMBER WILL BE THOSE WHO RULE OVER EACH COUNTRY'S OWN HIDDEN NINJA VILLAGES.
THEY WILL BE WATCHING YOU.
IF ANY ONE NATION'S APPLICANTS DEMONSTRATE OUTSTANDING SKILL AND SUPERIORITY...
...THE NOBLEMEN FROM EVERY LAND WILL BE QUICK TO COMMISSION WORK FROM THOSE TRAINED IN THAT SUPERIOR NATION.
CONVERSELY, IF A PARTICULAR COUNTRY'S APPLICANTS ARE SHOWN TO BE INCOMPETENT OR FEEBLE...
...COMMISSIONS TO AGENTS OF THAT COUNTRY WILL DWINDLE.
...

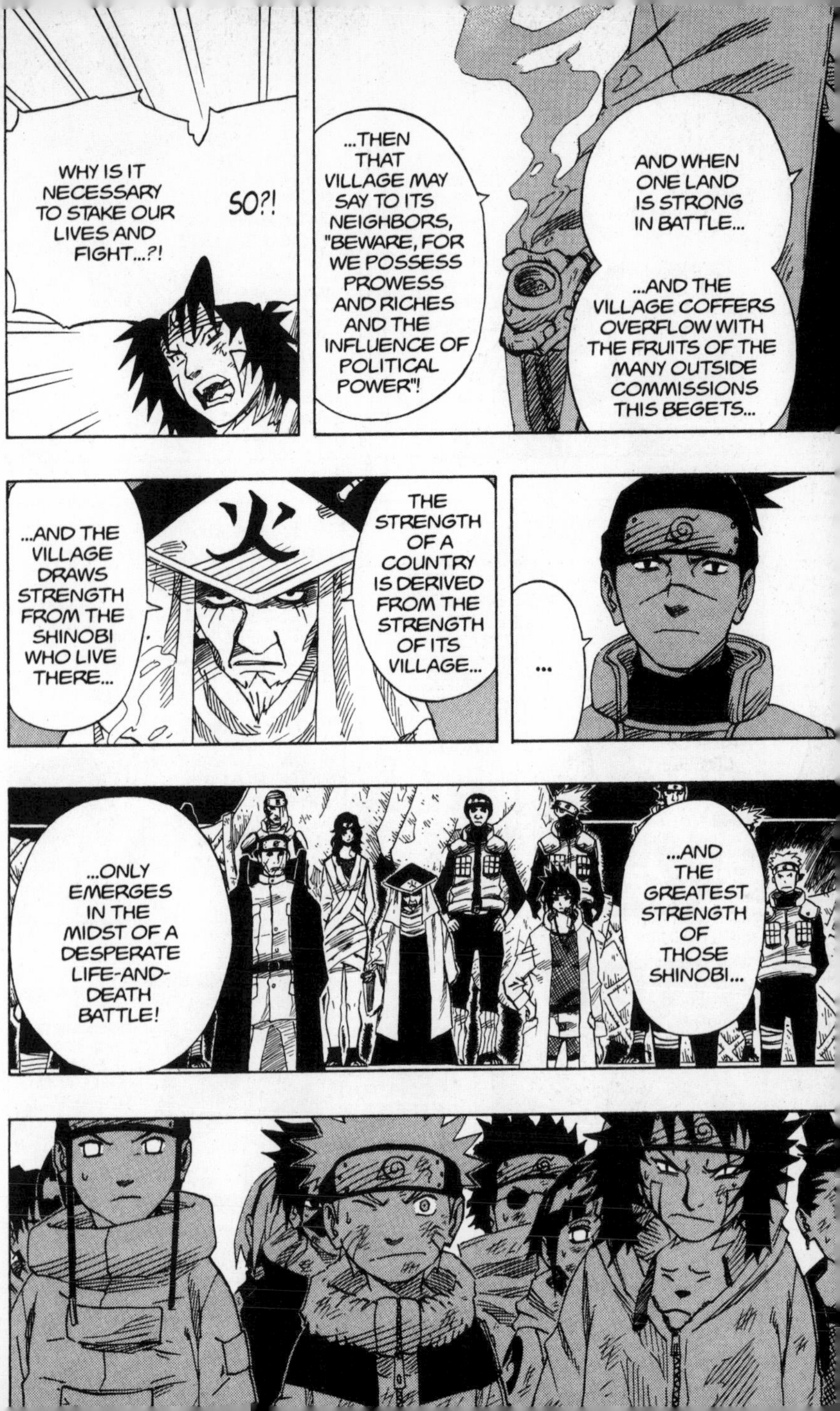
AND WHEN ONE LAND IS STRONG IN BATTLE...
...AND THE VILLAGE COFFERS OVERFLOW WITH THE FRUITS OF THE MANY OUTSIDE COMMISSIONS THIS BEGETS...
...THEN THAT VILLAGE MAY SAY TO ITS NEIGHBORS, "BEWARE, FOR WE POSSESS PROWESS AND RICHES AND THE INFLUENCE OF POLITICAL POWER"!
SO?!
WHY IS IT NECESSARY TO STAKE OUR LIVES AND FIGHT...?!
...
THE STRENGTH OF A COUNTRY IS DERIVED FROM THE STRENGTH OF ITS VILLAGE...
...AND THE VILLAGE DRAWS STRENGTH FROM THE SHINOBI WHO LIVE THERE...
...AND THE GREATEST STRENGTH OF THOSE SHINOBI...
...ONLY EMERGES IN THE MIDST OF A DESPERATE LIFE-AND-DEATH BATTLE!

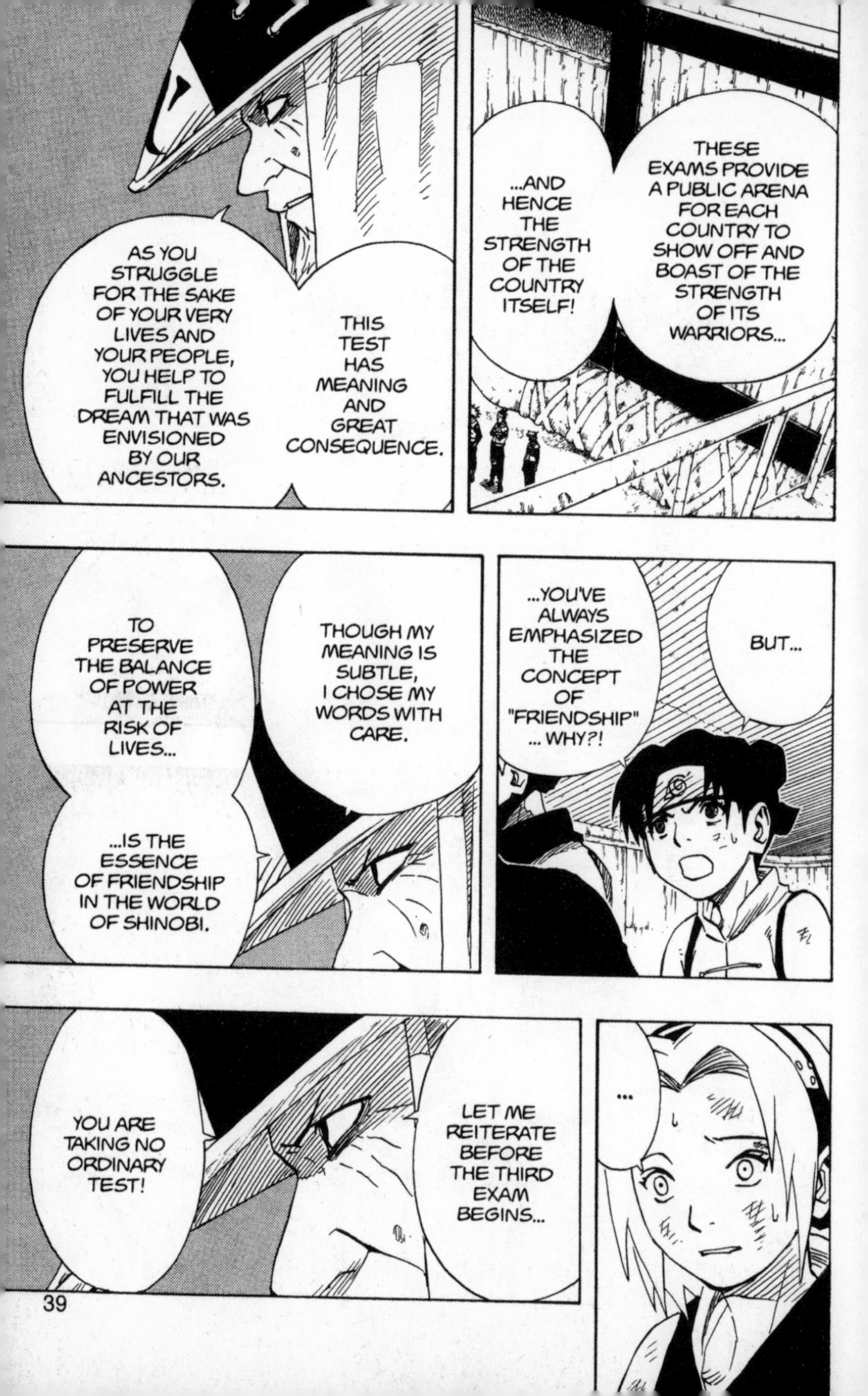
THESE EXAMS PROVIDE A PUBLIC ARENA FOR EACH COUNTRY TO SHOW OFF AND BOAST OF THE STRENGTH OF ITS WARRIORS...
...AND HENCE THE STRENGTH OF THE COUNTRY ITSELF!
THIS TEST HAS MEANING AND GREAT CONSEQUENCE.
AS YOU STRUGGLE FOR THE SAKE OF YOUR VERY LIVES AND YOUR PEOPLE, YOU HELP TO FULFILL THE DREAM THAT WAS ENVISIONED BY OUR ANCESTORS.
BUT...
...YOU'VE ALWAYS EMPHASIZED THE CONCEPT OF "FRIENDSHIP" ... WHY?!
THOUGH MY MEANING IS SUBTLE, I CHOSE MY WORDS WITH CARE.
TO PRESERVE THE BALANCE OF POWER AT THE RISK OF LIVES...
...IS THE ESSENCE OF FRIENDSHIP IN THE WORLD OF SHINOBI.
...
LET ME REITERATE BEFORE THE THIRD EXAM BEGINS...
YOU ARE TAKING NO ORDINARY TEST!

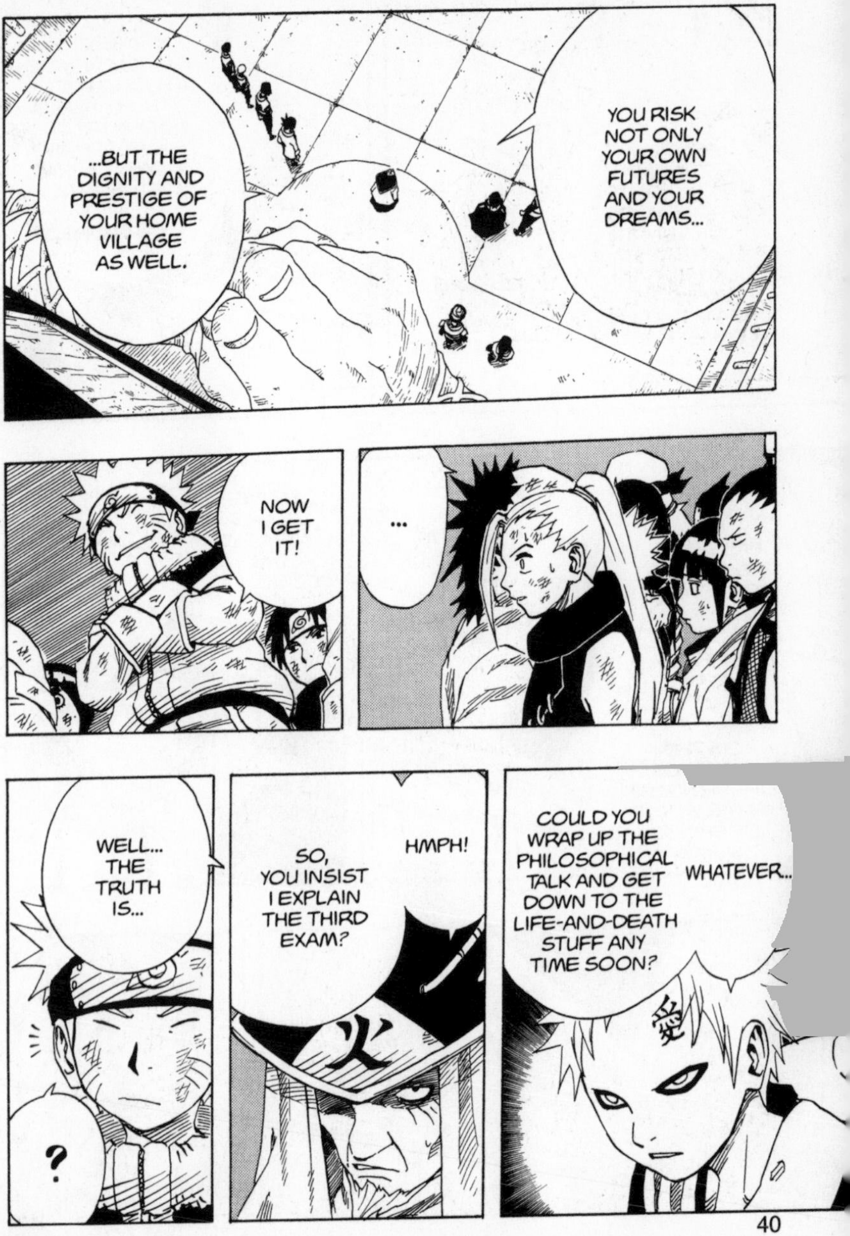
YOU RISK NOT ONLY YOUR OWN FUTURES AND YOUR DREAMS...
...BUT THE DIGNITY AND PRESTIGE OF YOUR HOME VILLAGE AS WELL.
...
NOW I GET IT!
WHATEVER...
COULD YOU WRAP UP THE PHILOSOPHICAL TALK AND GET DOWN TO THE LIFE-AND-DEATH STUFF ANY TIME SOON?
HMPH!
SO, YOU INSIST I EXPLAIN THE THIRD EXAM?
WELL... THE TRUTH IS...
?

READ THIS WAY

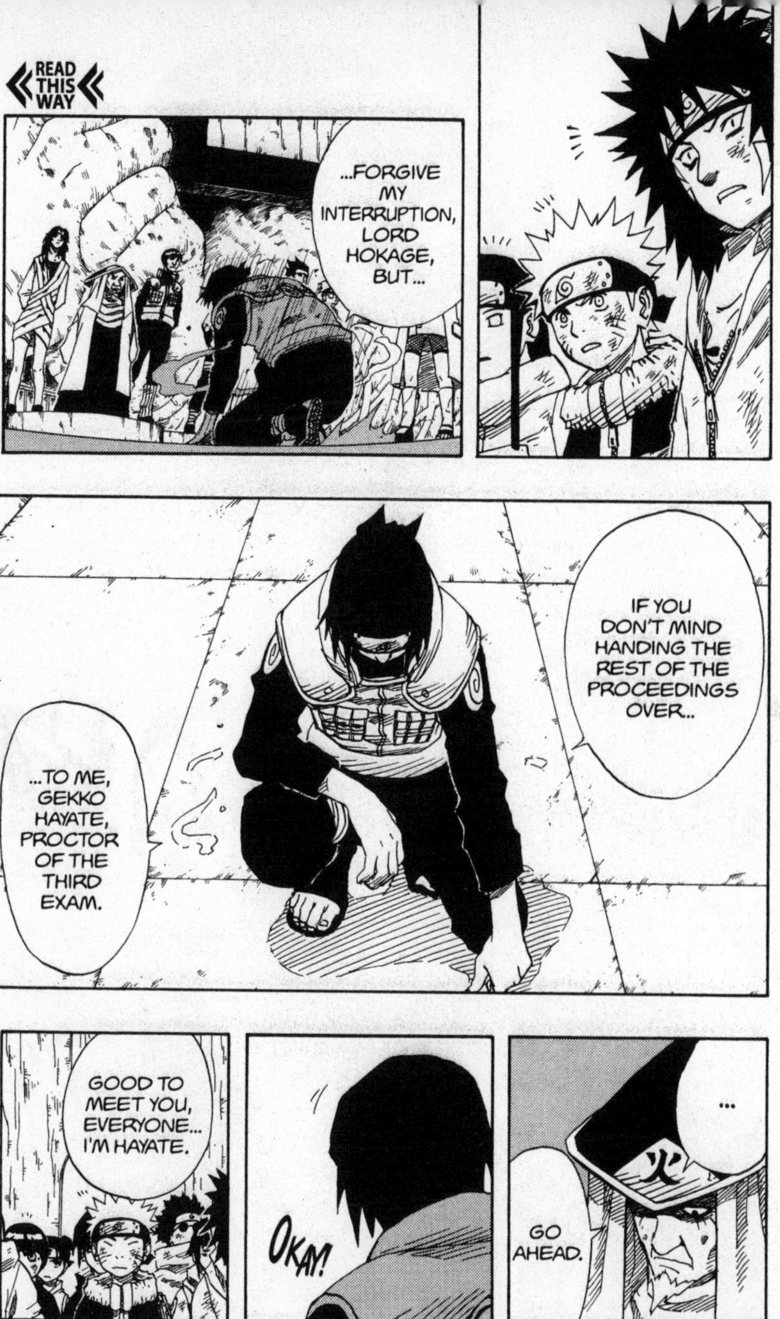
...FORGIVE MY INTERRUPTION, LORD HOKAGE, BUT...
IF YOU DON'T MIND HANDING THE REST OF THE PROCEEDINGS OVER...
...TO ME, GEKKO HAYATE, PROCTOR OF THE THIRD EXAM.
...
GO AHEAD.
OKAY!
GOOD TO MEET YOU, EVERYONE... I'M HAYATE.

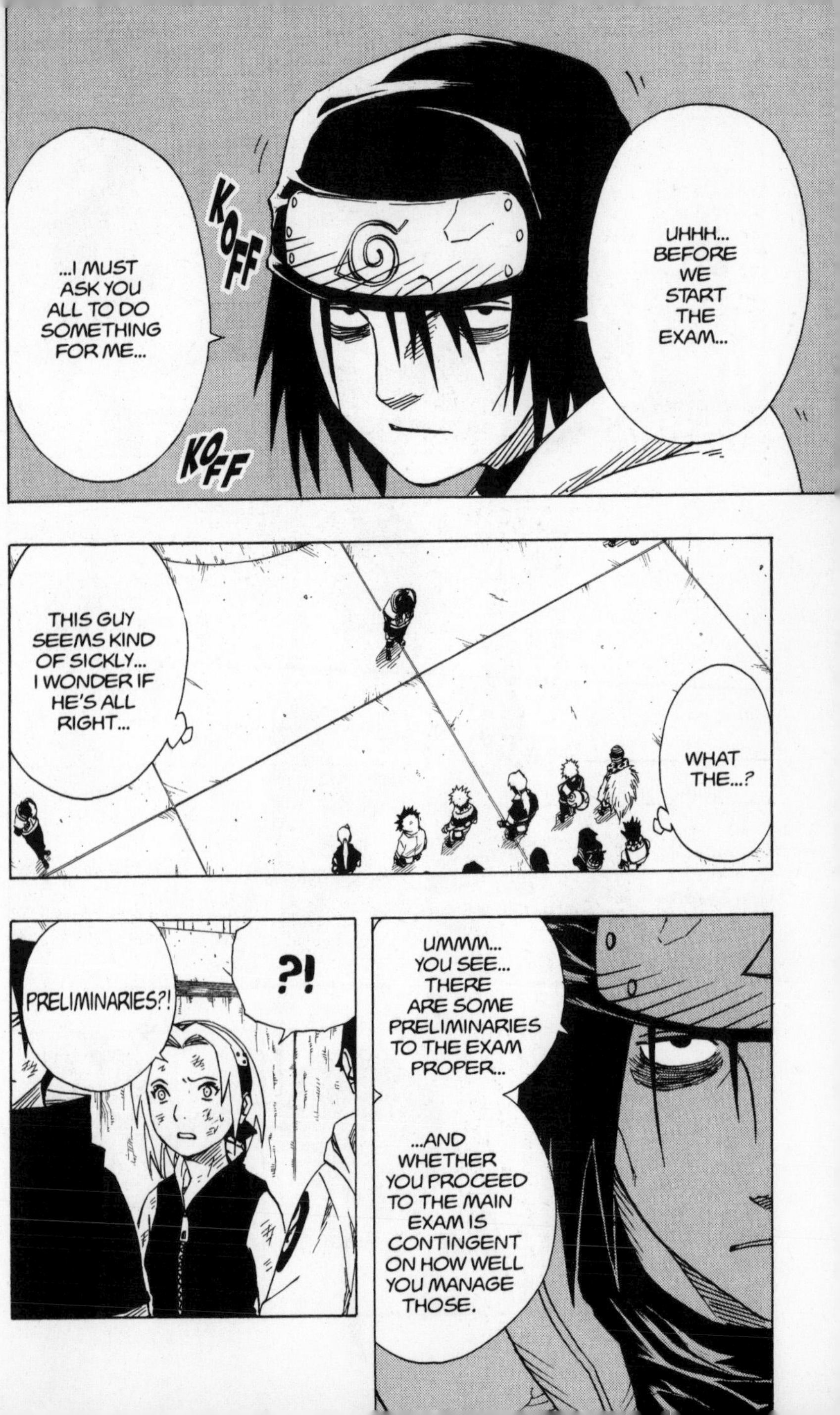
UHHH... BEFORE WE START THE EXAM...
KOFF
KOFF
...I MUST ASK YOU ALL TO DO SOMETHING FOR ME...
WHAT THE...?
THIS GUY SEEMS KIND OF SICKLY... I WONDER IF HE'S ALL RIGHT...
UMMM... YOU SEE... THERE ARE SOME PRELIMINARIES TO THE EXAM PROPER...
...AND WHETHER YOU PROCEED TO THE MAIN EXAM IS CONTINGENT ON HOW WELL YOU MANAGE THOSE.
?!
PRELIMINARIES?!

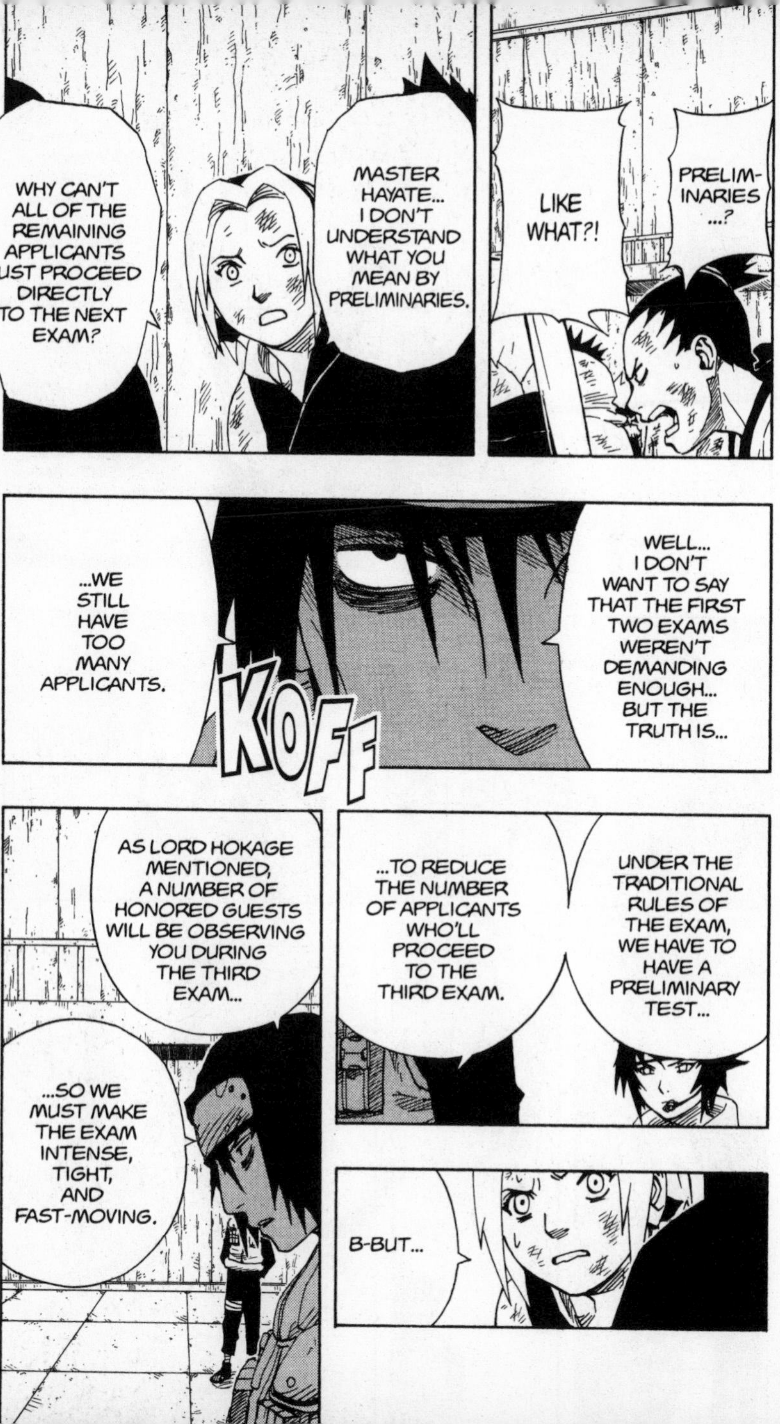
PRELIM-INARIES ...?
LIKE WHAT?!
MASTER HAYATE... I DON'T UNDERSTAND WHAT YOU MEAN BY PRELIMINARIES.
WHY CAN'T ALL OF THE REMAINING APPLICANTS JUST PROCEED DIRECTLY TO THE NEXT EXAM?
WELL... I DON'T WANT TO SAY THAT THE FIRST TWO EXAMS WEREN'T DEMANDING ENOUGH... BUT THE TRUTH IS...
KOFF
...WE STILL HAVE TOO MANY APPLICANTS.
UNDER THE TRADITIONAL RULES OF THE EXAM, WE HAVE TO HAVE A PRELIMINARY TEST...
...TO REDUCE THE NUMBER OF APPLICANTS WHO'LL PROCEED TO THE THIRD EXAM.
B-BUT...
AS LORD HOKAGE MENTIONED, A NUMBER OF HONORED GUESTS WILL BE OBSERVING YOU DURING THE THIRD EXAM...
...SO WE MUST MAKE THE EXAM INTENSE, TIGHT, AND FAST-MOVING.

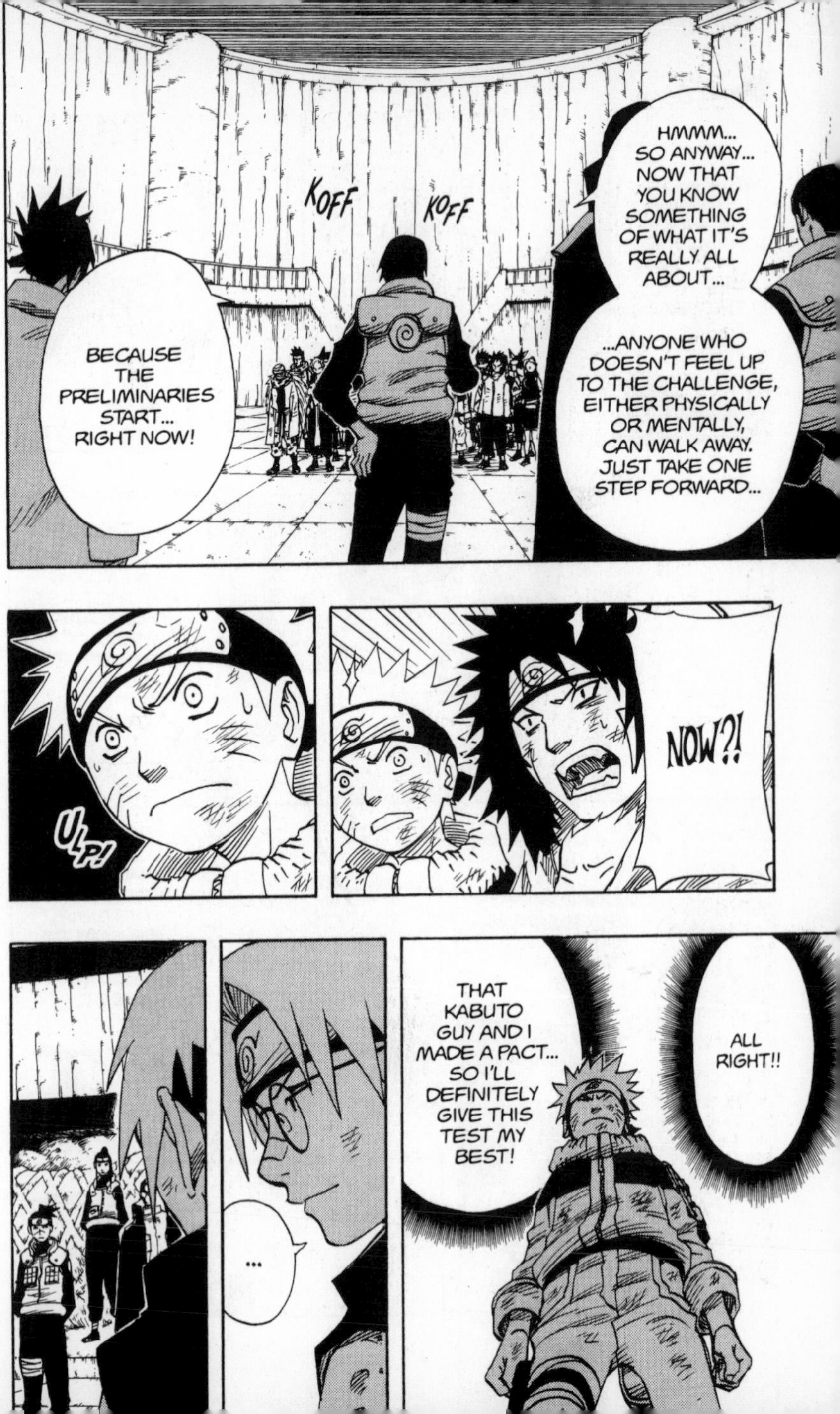
HMMM... SO ANYWAY... NOW THAT YOU KNOW SOMETHING OF WHAT IT'S REALLY ALL ABOUT...
...ANYONE WHO DOESN'T FEEL UP TO THE CHALLENGE, EITHER PHYSICALLY OR MENTALLY, CAN WALK AWAY. JUST TAKE ONE STEP FORWARD...
KOFF
KOFF
BECAUSE THE PRELIMINARIES START... RIGHT NOW!
NOW?!
ULP!
ALL RIGHT!!
THAT KABUTO GUY AND I MADE A PACT... SO I'LL DEFINITELY GIVE THIS TEST MY BEST!
...

READ THIS WAY

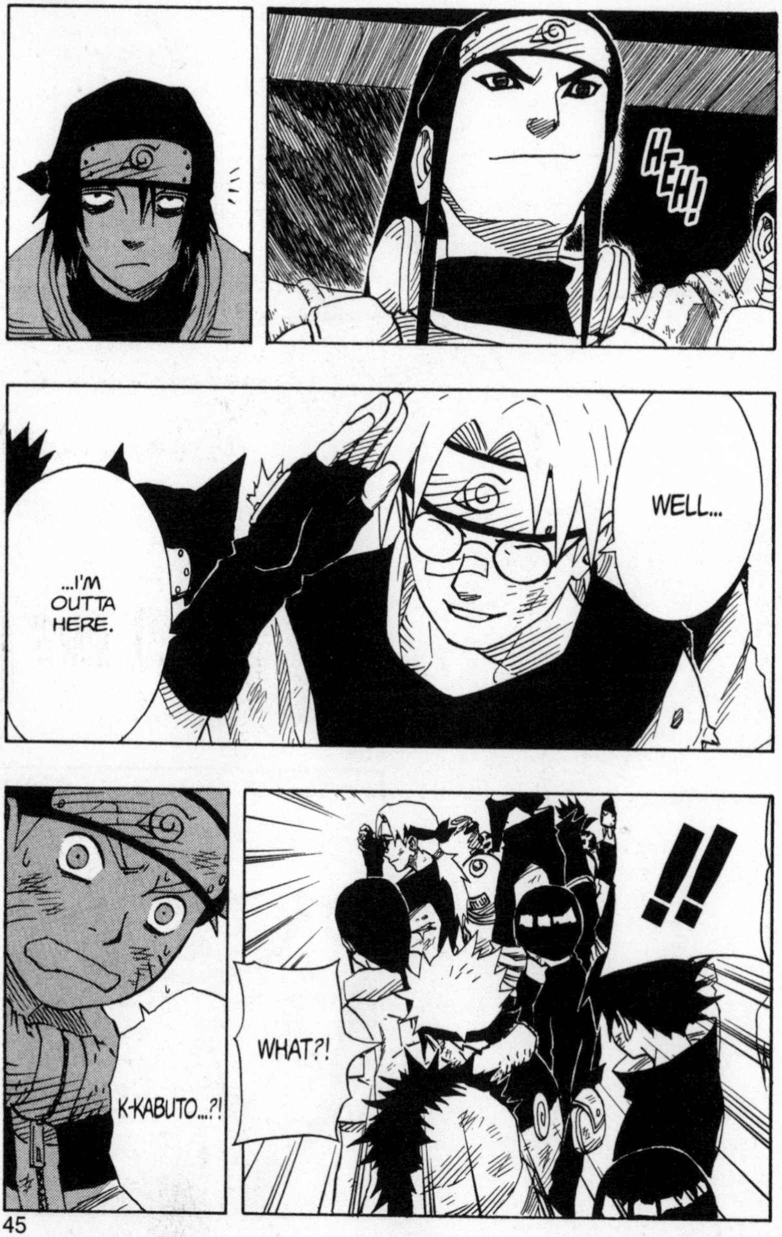
HEH!
WELL...
...I'M OUTTA HERE.
!!
WHAT?!
K-KABUTO...?!

Number 66: Sakura's Advice

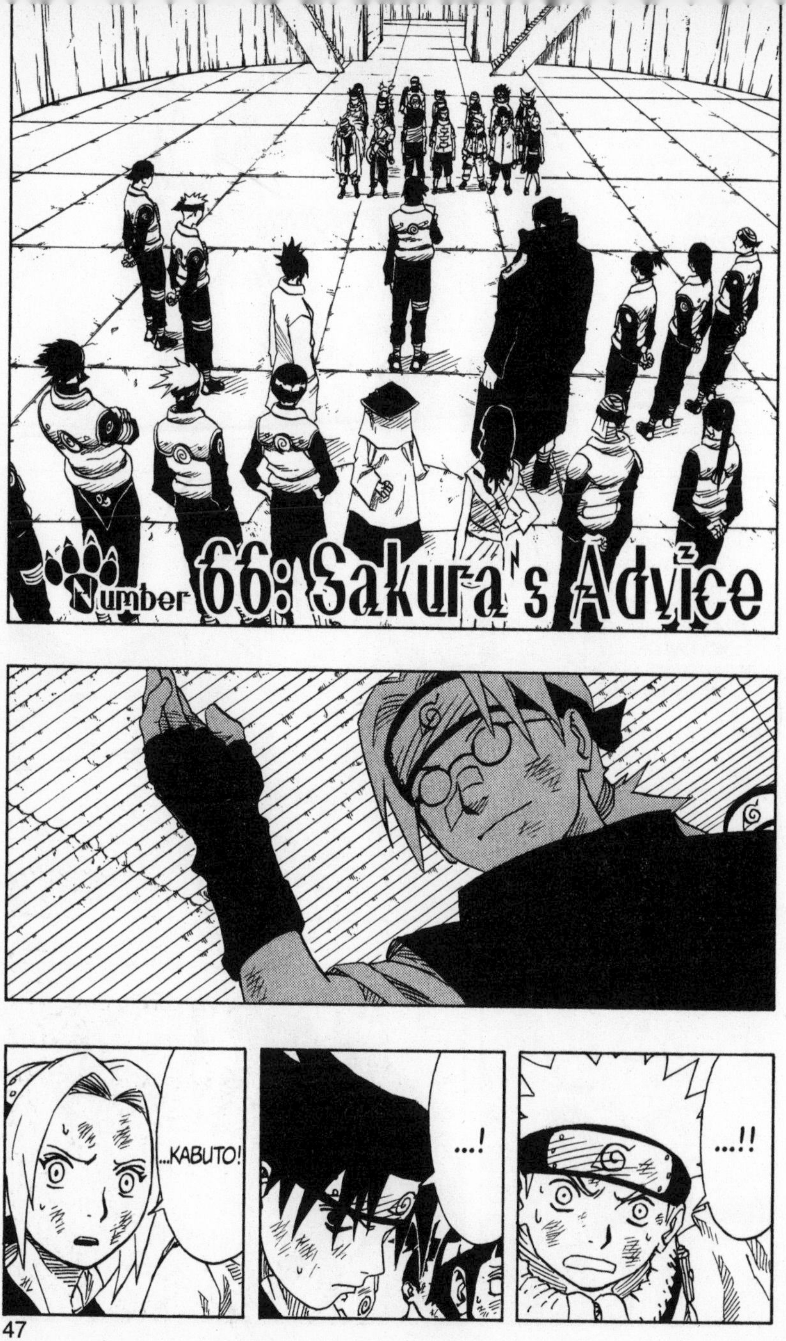
...!!
...!
...KABUTO!

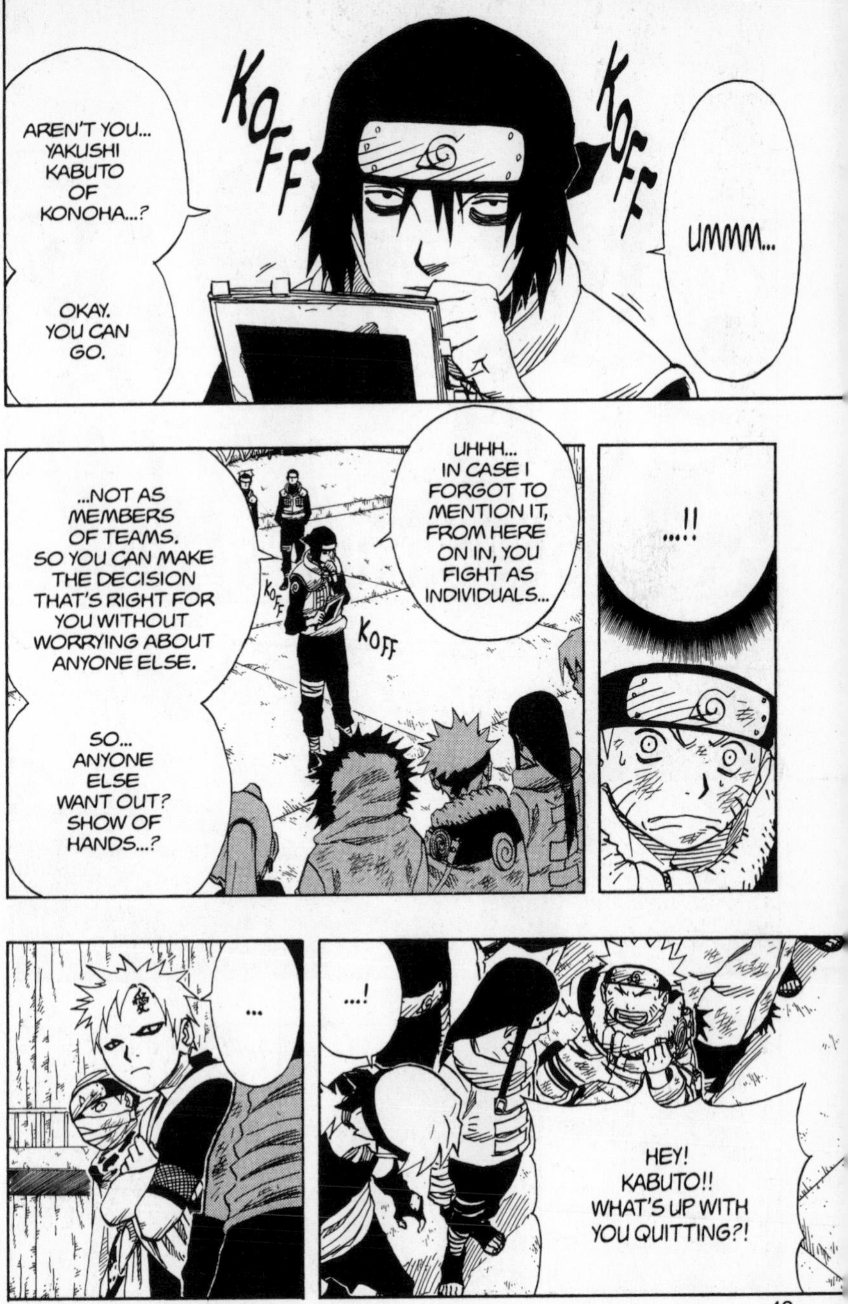
KOFF
UMMM...
KOFF
AREN'T YOU... YAKUSHI KABUTO OF KONOHA...?
OKAY. YOU CAN GO.
...!!
UHHH... IN CASE I FORGOT TO MENTION IT, FROM HERE ON IN, YOU FIGHT AS INDIVIDUALS...
...NOT AS MEMBERS OF TEAMS. SO YOU CAN MAKE THE DECISION THAT'S RIGHT FOR YOU WITHOUT WORRYING ABOUT ANYONE ELSE.
KOFF
KOFF
SO... ANYONE ELSE WANT OUT? SHOW OF HANDS...?
...!
HEY! KABUTO!! WHAT'S UP WITH YOU QUITTING?!
...

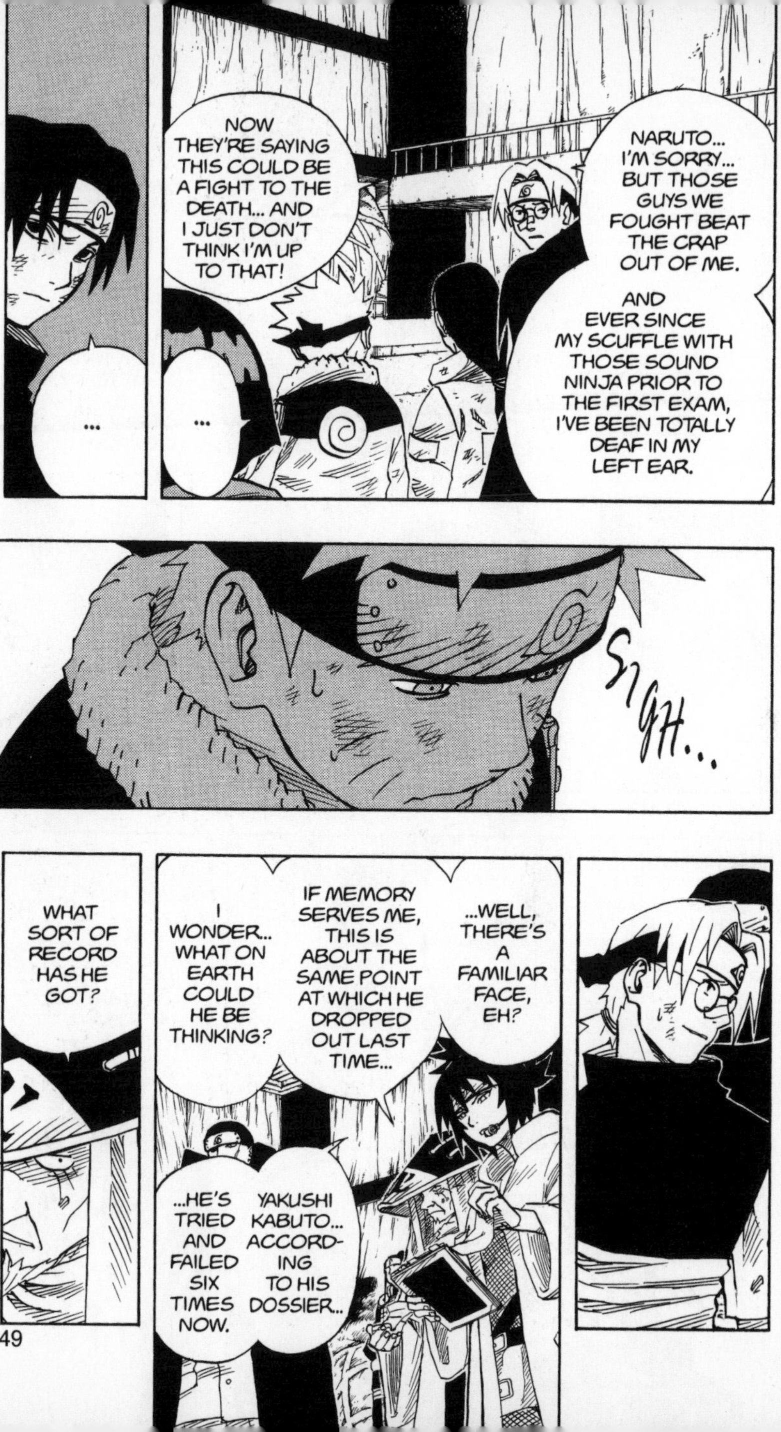
NARUTO... I'M SORRY... BUT THOSE GUYS WE FOUGHT BEAT THE CRAP OUT OF ME.
AND EVER SINCE MY SCUFFLE WITH THOSE SOUND NINJA PRIOR TO THE FIRST EXAM, I'VE BEEN TOTALLY DEAF IN MY LEFT EAR.
NOW THEY'RE SAYING THIS COULD BE A FIGHT TO THE DEATH... AND I JUST DON'T THINK I'M UP TO THAT!
...
...
SIGH...
...WELL, THERE'S A FAMILIAR FACE, EH?
IF MEMORY SERVES ME, THIS IS ABOUT THE SAME POINT AT WHICH HE DROPPED OUT LAST TIME...
I WONDER... WHAT ON EARTH COULD HE BE THINKING?
YAKUSHI KABUTO... ACCORDING TO HIS DOSSIER...
...HE'S TRIED AND FAILED SIX TIMES NOW.
WHAT SORT OF RECORD HAS HE GOT?

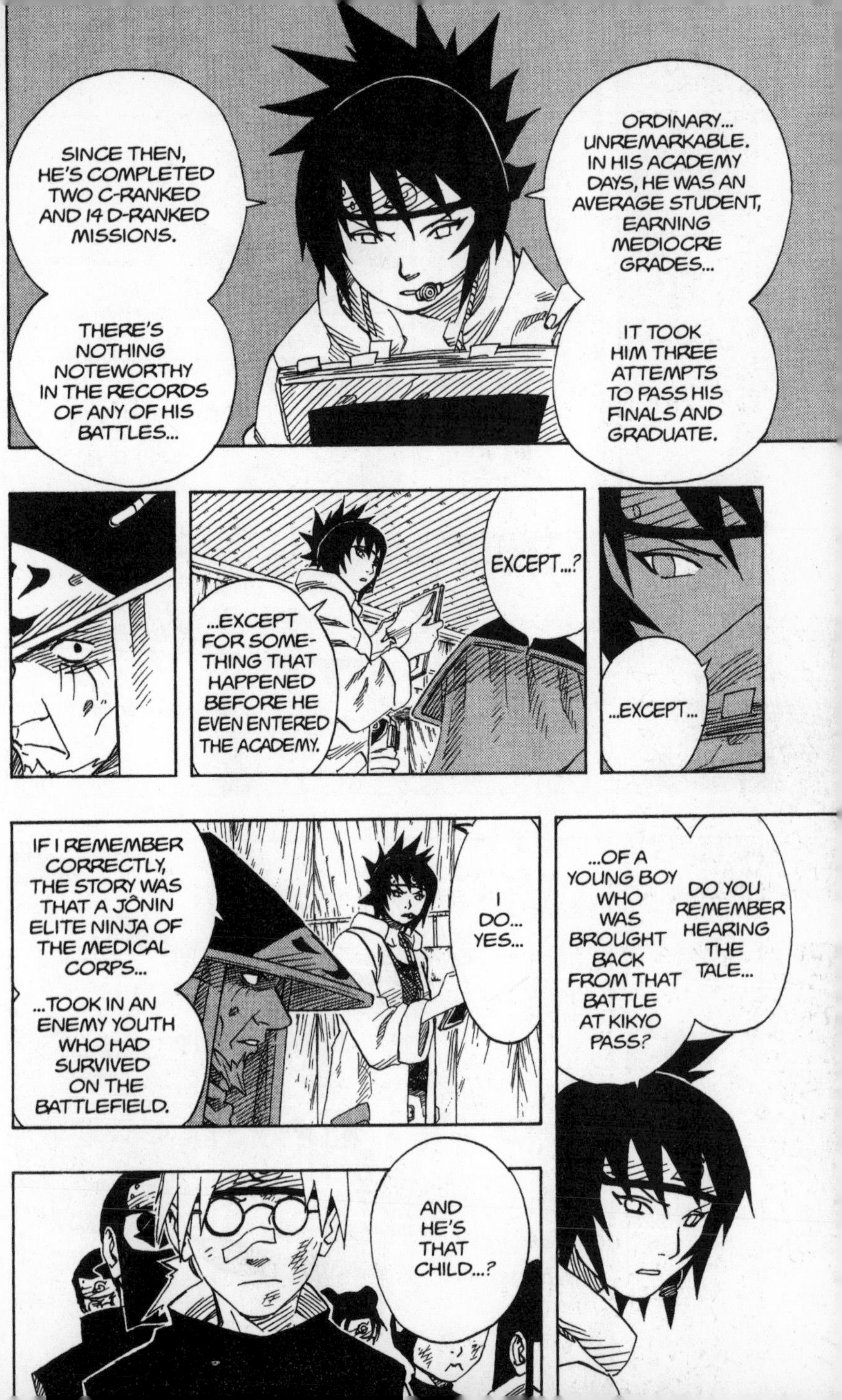
ORDINARY... UNREMARKABLE. IN HIS ACADEMY DAYS, HE WAS AN AVERAGE STUDENT, EARNING MEDIOCRE GRADES...
IT TOOK HIM THREE ATTEMPTS TO PASS HIS FINALS AND GRADUATE.
SINCE THEN, HE'S COMPLETED TWO C-RANKED AND 14 D-RANKED MISSIONS.
THERE'S NOTHING NOTEWORTHY IN THE RECORDS OF ANY OF HIS BATTLES...
...EXCEPT...
EXCEPT...?
...EXCEPT FOR SOME-THING THAT HAPPENED BEFORE HE EVEN ENTERED THE ACADEMY.
DO YOU REMEMBER HEARING THE TALE...
...OF A YOUNG BOY WHO WAS BROUGHT BACK FROM THAT BATTLE AT KIKYO PASS?
I DO... YES...
IF I REMEMBER CORRECTLY, THE STORY WAS THAT A JÔNIN ELITE NINJA OF THE MEDICAL CORPS...
...TOOK IN AN ENEMY YOUTH WHO HAD SURVIVED ON THE BATTLEFIELD.
AND HE'S THAT CHILD...?

READ THIS WAY

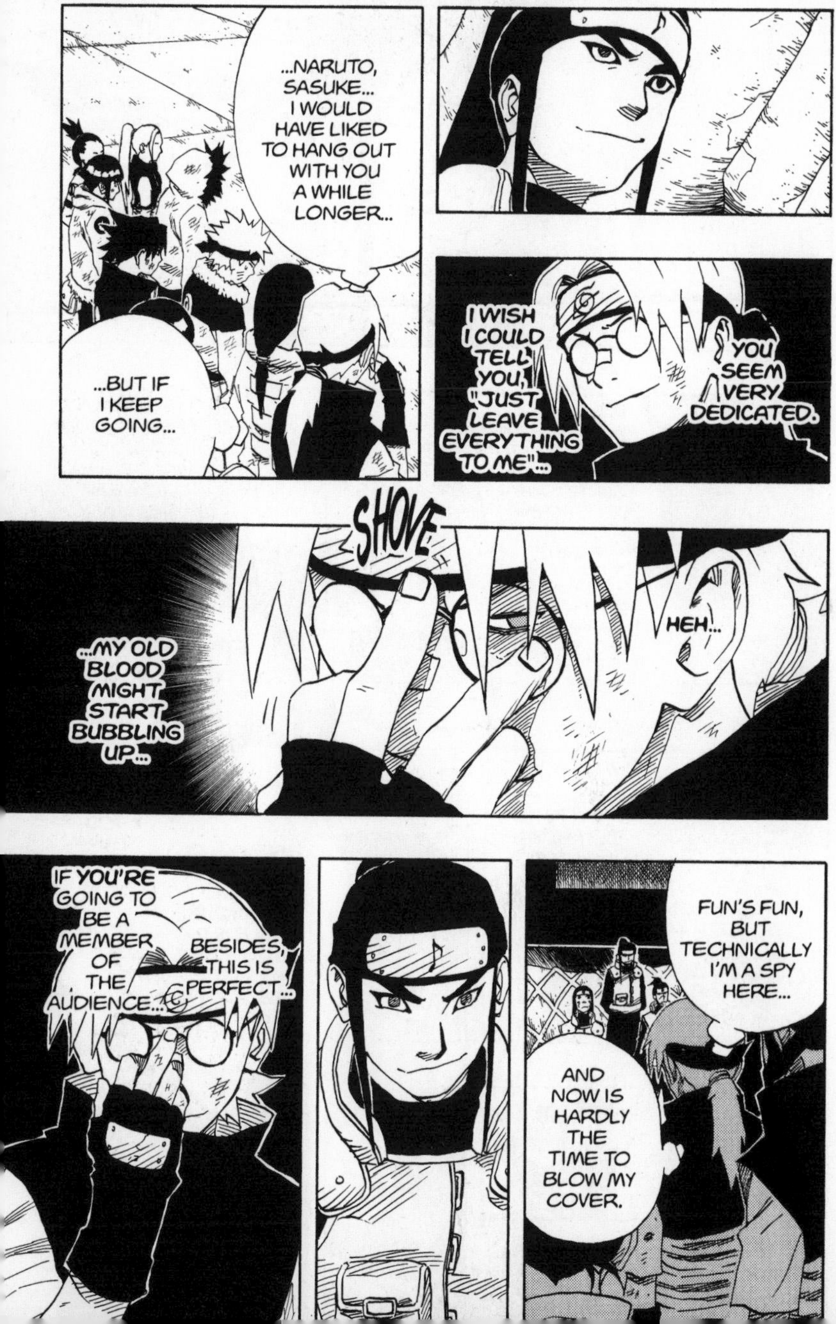
YOU SEEM VERY DEDICATED.
I WISH I COULD TELL YOU, "JUST LEAVE EVERYTHING TO ME"...
...NARUTO, SASUKE... I WOULD HAVE LIKED TO HANG OUT WITH YOU A WHILE LONGER...
...BUT IF I KEEP GOING...
SHOVE
HEH...
...MY OLD BLOOD MIGHT START BUBBLING UP...
FUN'S FUN, BUT TECHNICALLY I'M A SPY HERE...
AND NOW IS HARDLY THE TIME TO BLOW MY COVER.
BESIDES, THIS IS PERFECT...
IF YOU'RE GOING TO BE A MEMBER OF THE AUDIENCE...

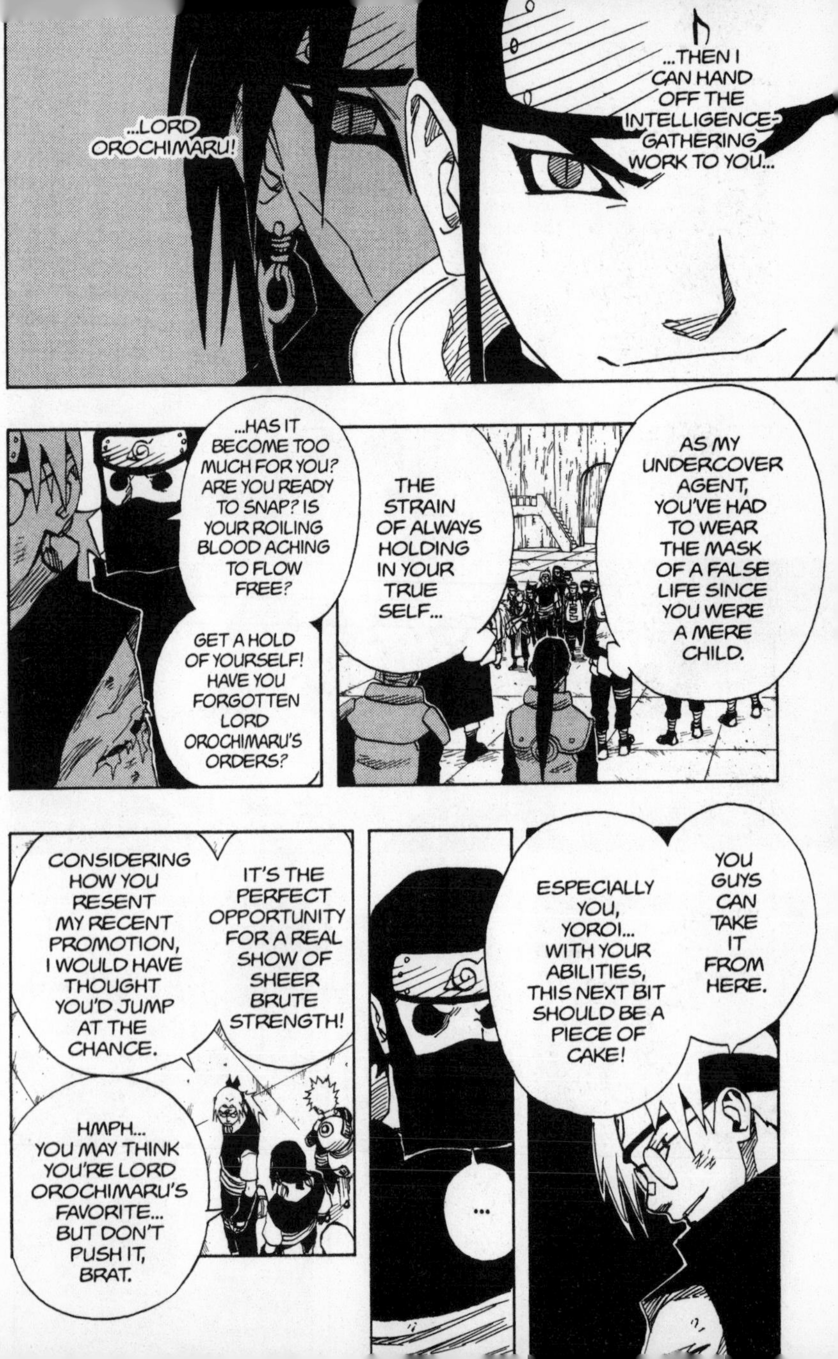
...THEN I CAN HAND OFF THE INTELLIGENCE-GATHERING WORK TO YOU...
...LORD OROCHIMARU!
AS MY UNDERCOVER AGENT, YOU'VE HAD TO WEAR THE MASK OF A FALSE LIFE SINCE YOU WERE A MERE CHILD.
THE STRAIN OF ALWAYS HOLDING IN YOUR TRUE SELF...
...HAS IT BECOME TOO MUCH FOR YOU? ARE YOU READY TO SNAP? IS YOUR ROILING BLOOD ACHING TO FLOW FREE?
GET A HOLD OF YOURSELF! HAVE YOU FORGOTTEN LORD OROCHIMARU'S ORDERS?
YOU GUYS CAN TAKE IT FROM HERE.
ESPECIALLY YOU, YOROI... WITH YOUR ABILITIES, THIS NEXT BIT SHOULD BE A PIECE OF CAKE!
...
IT'S THE PERFECT OPPORTUNITY FOR A REAL SHOW OF SHEER BRUTE STRENGTH!
CONSIDERING HOW YOU RESENT MY RECENT PROMOTION, I WOULD HAVE THOUGHT YOU'D JUMP AT THE CHANCE.
HMPH... YOU MAY THINK YOU'RE LORD OROCHIMARU'S FAVORITE... BUT DON'T PUSH IT, BRAT.

READ THIS WAY

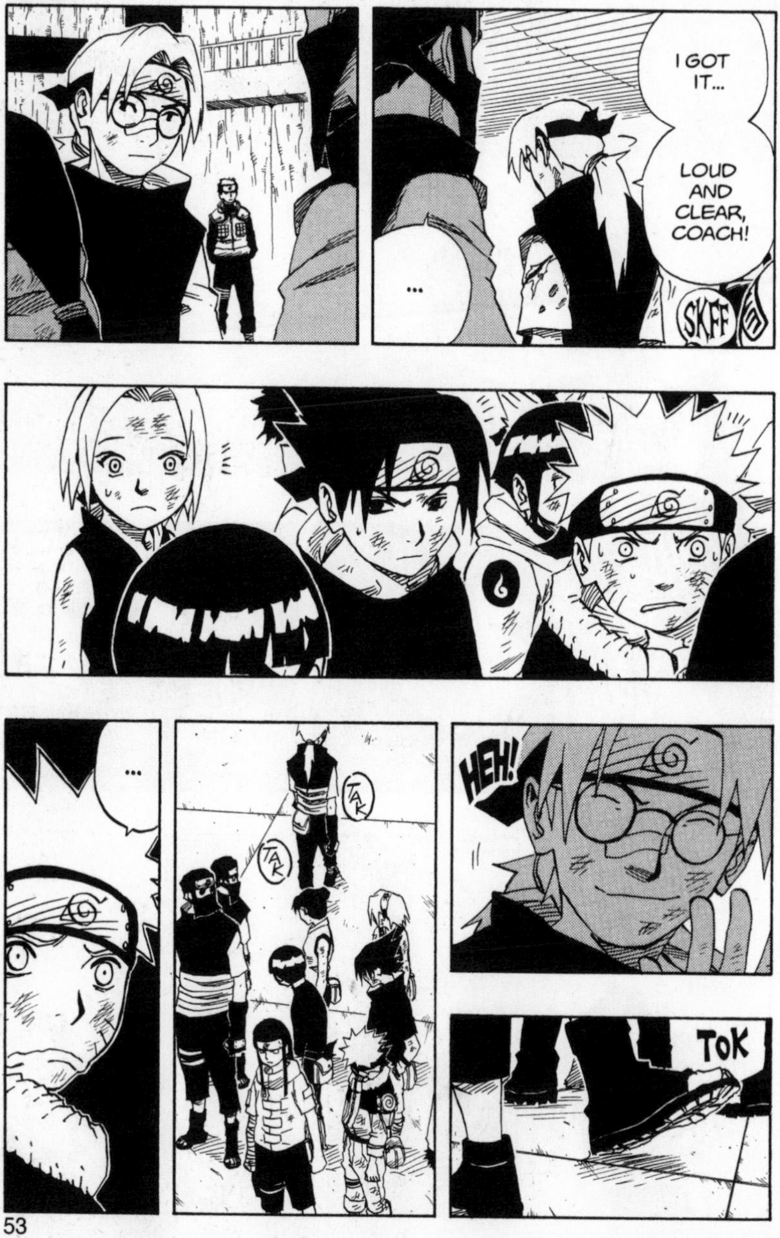

I GOT IT...
LOUD AND CLEAR, COACH!
...
SKFF
HEH!
TOK
TAK
TAK
...

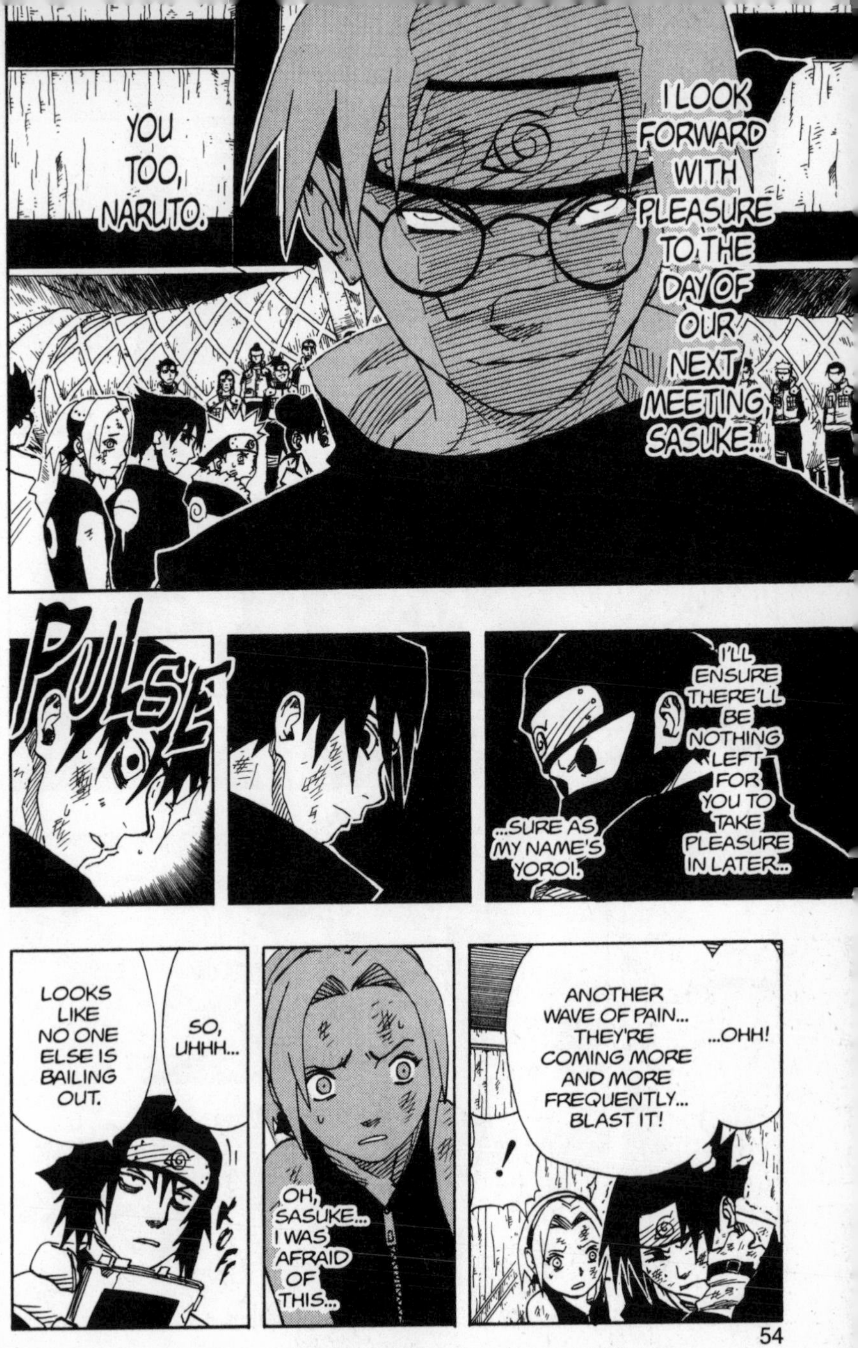
I LOOK FORWARD WITH PLEASURE TO THE DAY OF OUR NEXT MEETING, SASUKE...
YOU TOO, NARUTO.
PULSE
I'LL ENSURE THERE'LL BE NOTHING LEFT FOR YOU TO TAKE PLEASURE IN LATER...
...SURE AS MY NAME'S YOROI.
LOOKS LIKE NO ONE ELSE IS BAILING OUT.
SO, UHHH...
KOFF
OH, SASUKE... I WAS AFRAID OF THIS...
ANOTHER WAVE OF PAIN... THEY'RE COMING MORE AND MORE FREQUENTLY... BLAST IT!
...OHH!
!

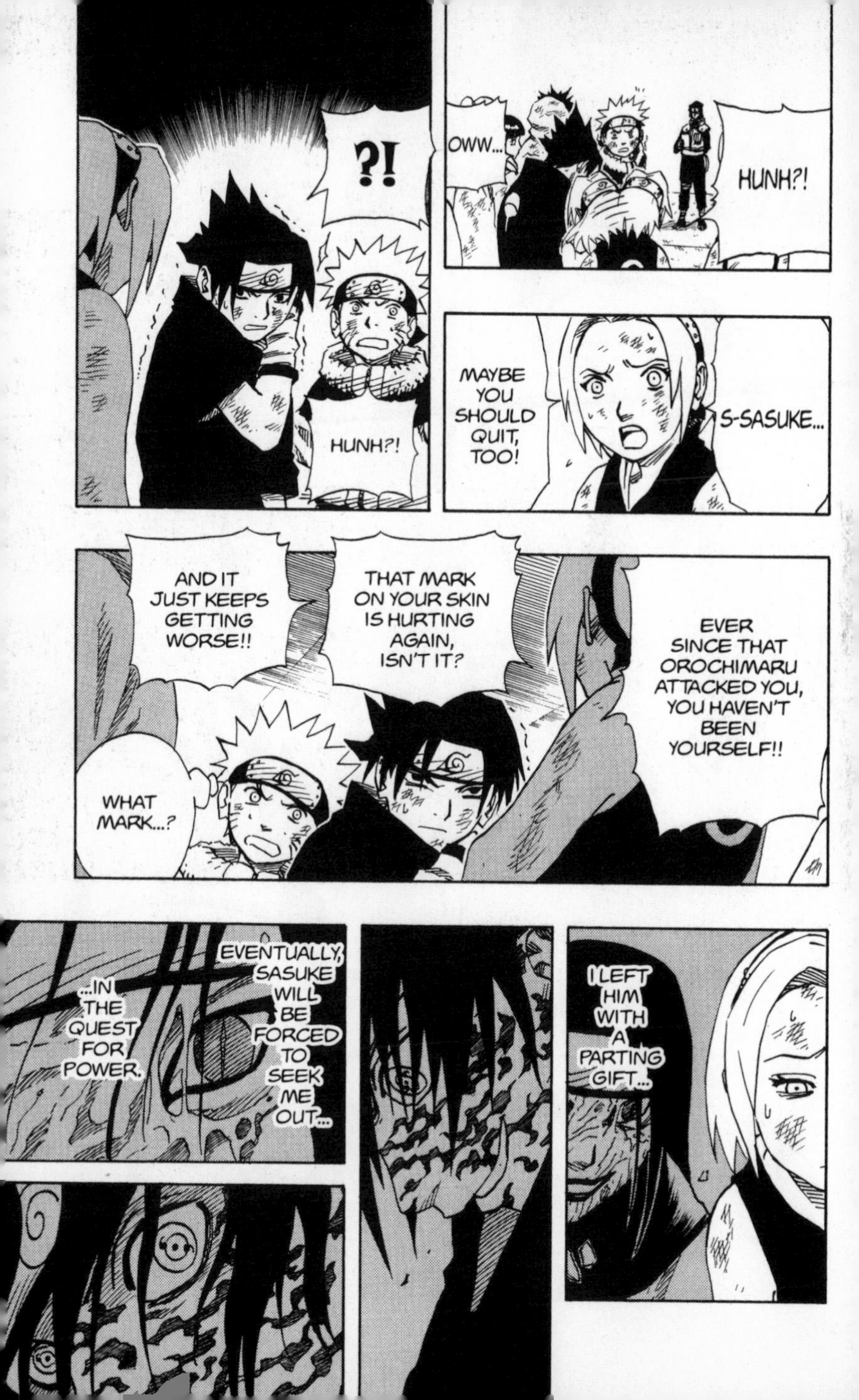
HUNH?!
OWW...
S-SASUKE...
MAYBE YOU SHOULD QUIT, TOO!
?!
HUNH?!
EVER SINCE THAT OROCHIMARU ATTACKED YOU, YOU HAVEN'T BEEN YOURSELF!!
THAT MARK ON YOUR SKIN IS HURTING AGAIN, ISN'T IT?
AND IT JUST KEEPS GETTING WORSE!!
WHAT MARK...?
I LEFT HIM WITH A PARTING GIFT...
EVENTUALLY, SASUKE WILL BE FORCED TO SEEK ME OUT...
...IN THE QUEST FOR POWER.

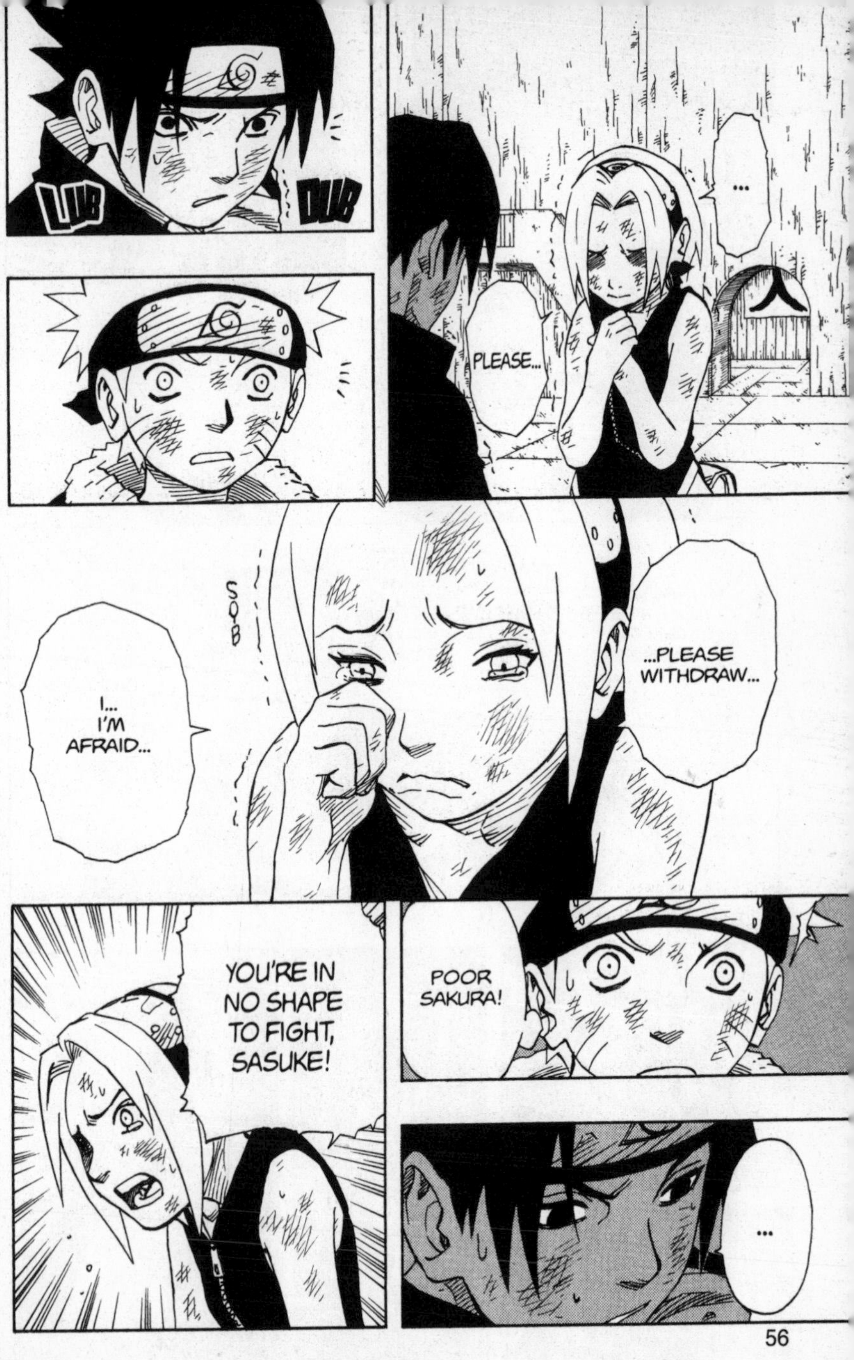
...
PLEASE...
LUB DUB
...PLEASE WITHDRAW...
SOB
I... I'M AFRAID...
POOR SAKURA!
...
YOU'RE IN NO SHAPE TO FIGHT, SASUKE!

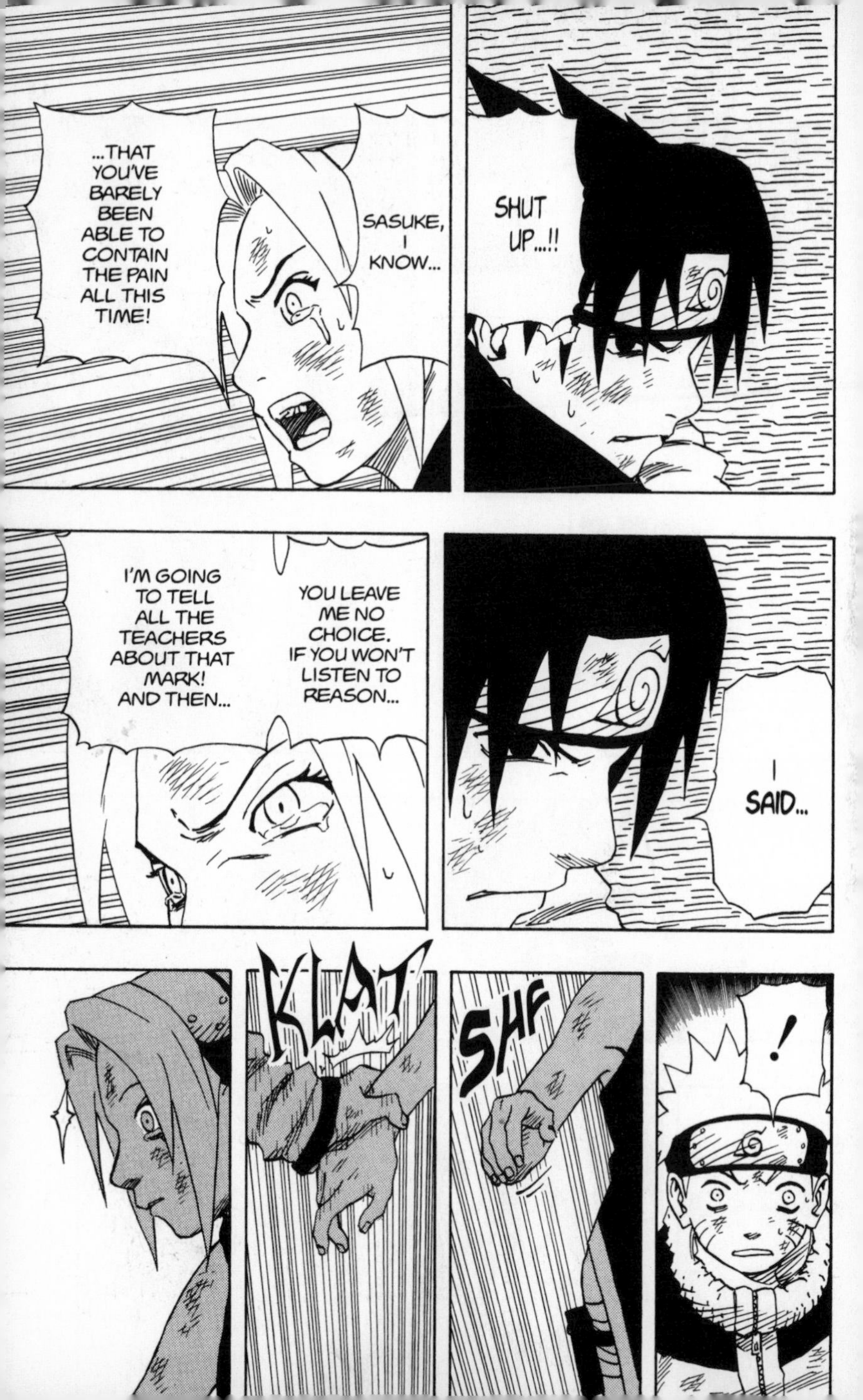
SHUT UP...!!
SASUKE, I KNOW...
...THAT YOU'VE BARELY BEEN ABLE TO CONTAIN THE PAIN ALL THIS TIME!
I SAID...
YOU LEAVE ME NO CHOICE. IF YOU WON'T LISTEN TO REASON...
I'M GOING TO TELL ALL THE TEACHERS ABOUT THAT MARK! AND THEN...
!
SHF
KLAT

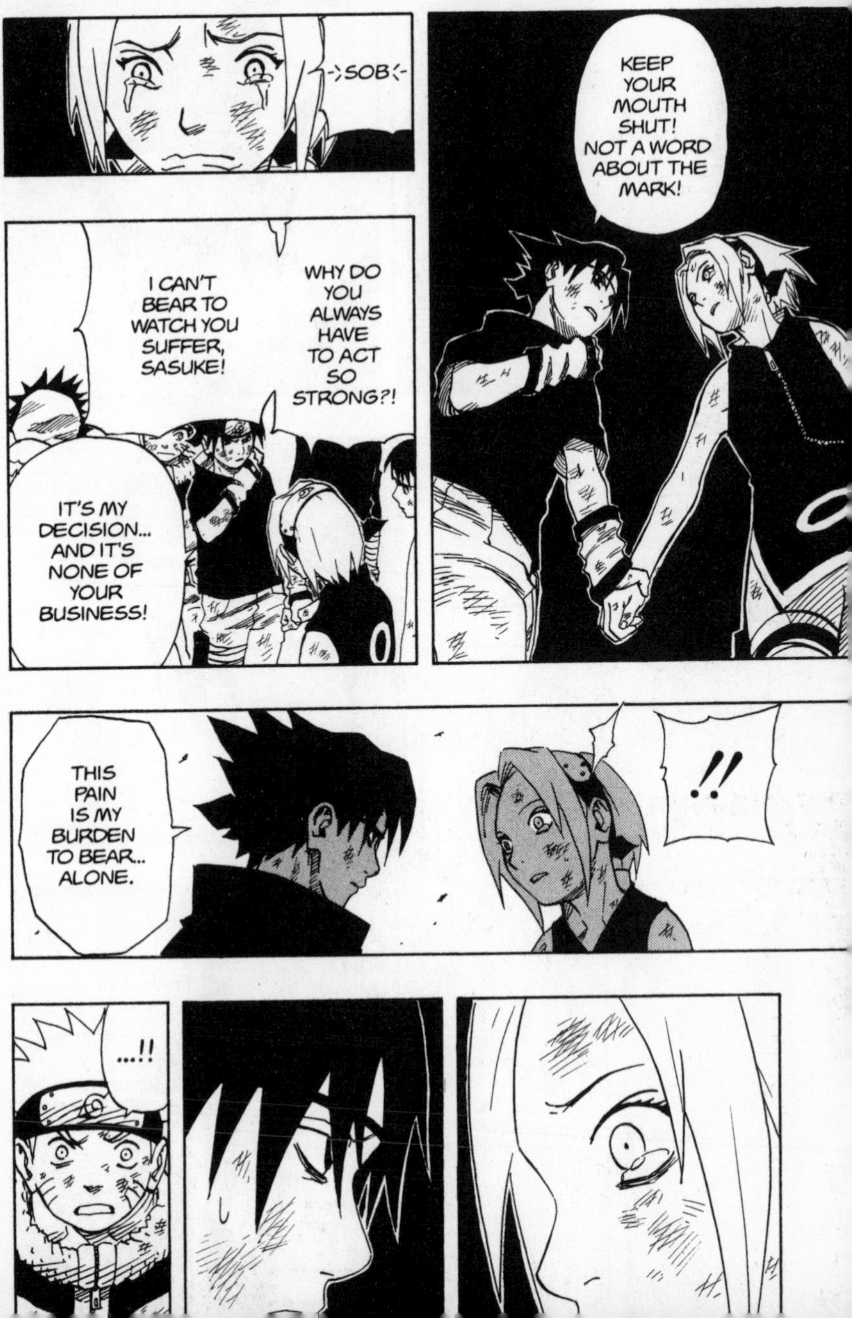
KEEP YOUR MOUTH SHUT! NOT A WORD ABOUT THE MARK!
SOB
WHY DO YOU ALWAYS HAVE TO ACT SO STRONG?!
I CAN'T BEAR TO WATCH YOU SUFFER, SASUKE!
IT'S MY DECISION... AND IT'S NONE OF YOUR BUSINESS!
!!
THIS PAIN IS MY BURDEN TO BEAR... ALONE.
...!!

READ THIS WAY

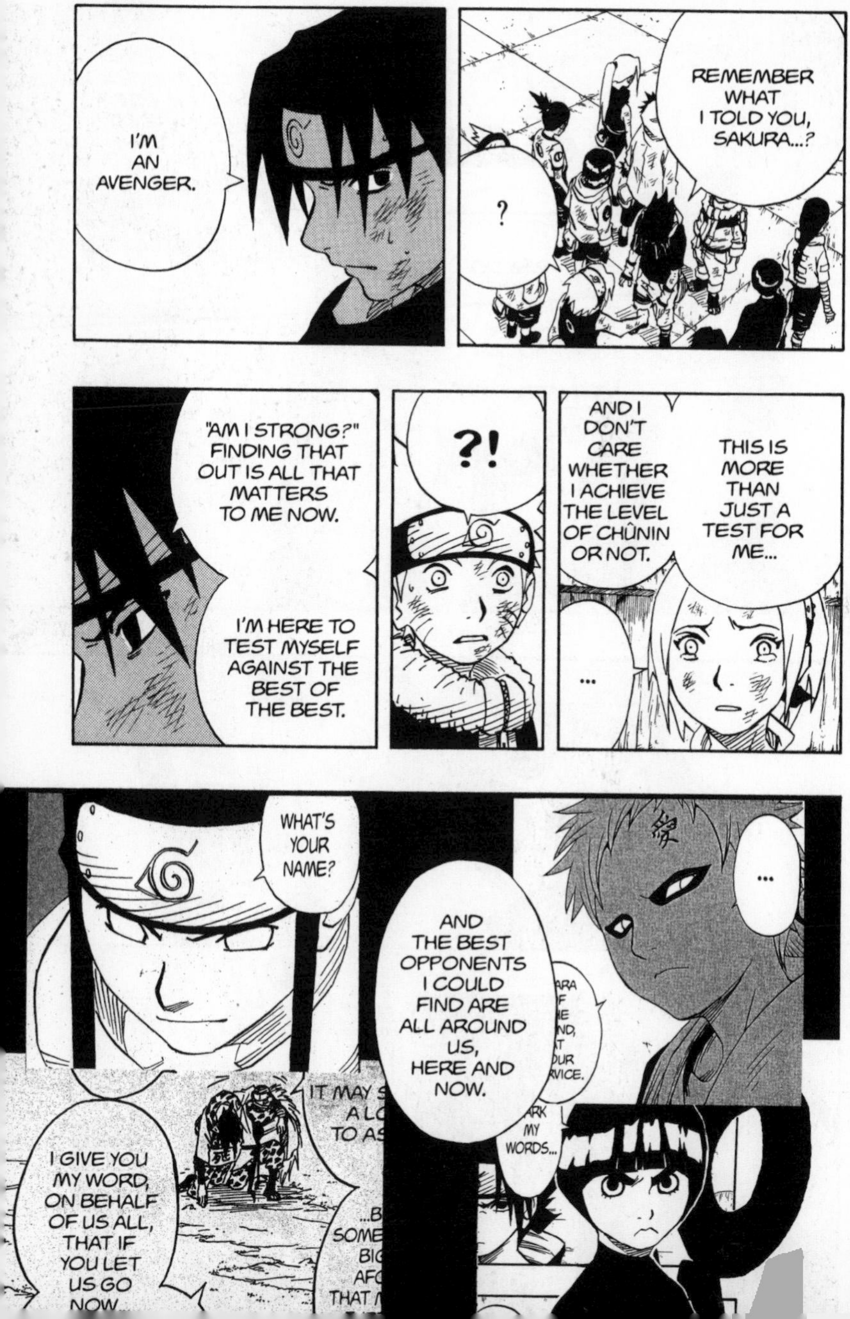
REMEMBER WHAT I TOLD YOU, SAKURA...?
?
I'M AN AVENGER.
THIS IS MORE THAN JUST A TEST FOR ME...
AND I DON'T CARE WHETHER I ACHIEVE THE LEVEL OF CHÛNIN OR NOT.
...
?!
"AM I STRONG?" FINDING THAT OUT IS ALL THAT MATTERS TO ME NOW.
I'M HERE TO TEST MYSELF AGAINST THE BEST OF THE BEST.
...
AND THE BEST OPPONENTS I COULD FIND ARE ALL AROUND US, HERE AND NOW.
WHAT'S YOUR NAME?
MY WORDS...
I GIVE YOU MY WORD, ON BEHALF OF US ALL, THAT IF YOU LET US GO

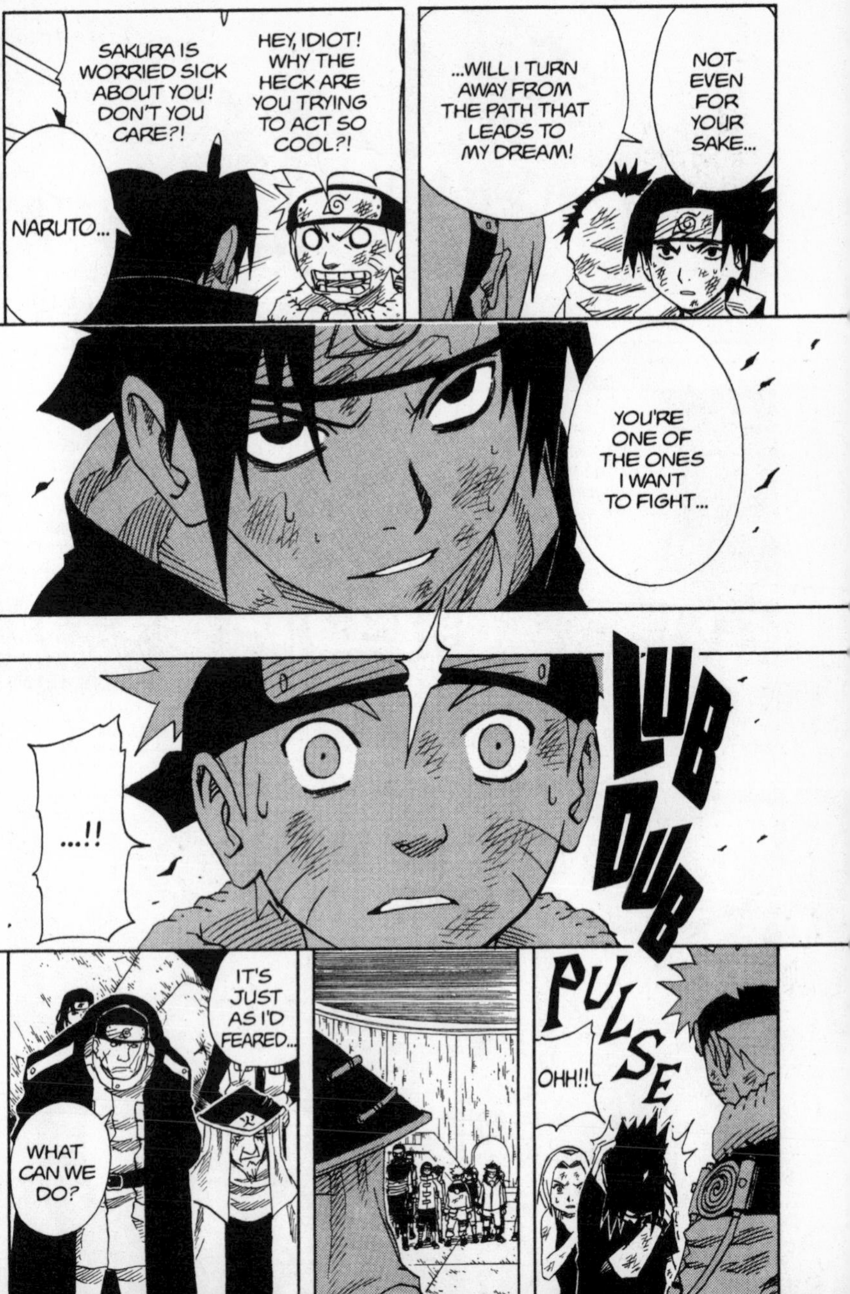
NOT EVEN FOR YOUR SAKE...
...WILL I TURN AWAY FROM THE PATH THAT LEADS TO MY DREAM!
HEY, IDIOT! WHY THE HECK ARE YOU TRYING TO ACT SO COOL?!
SAKURA IS WORRIED SICK ABOUT YOU! DON'T YOU CARE?!
NARUTO...
YOU'RE ONE OF THE ONES I WANT TO FIGHT...
LUB DUB
...!!
PULSE
OHH!!
IT'S JUST AS I'D FEARED...
WHAT CAN WE DO?

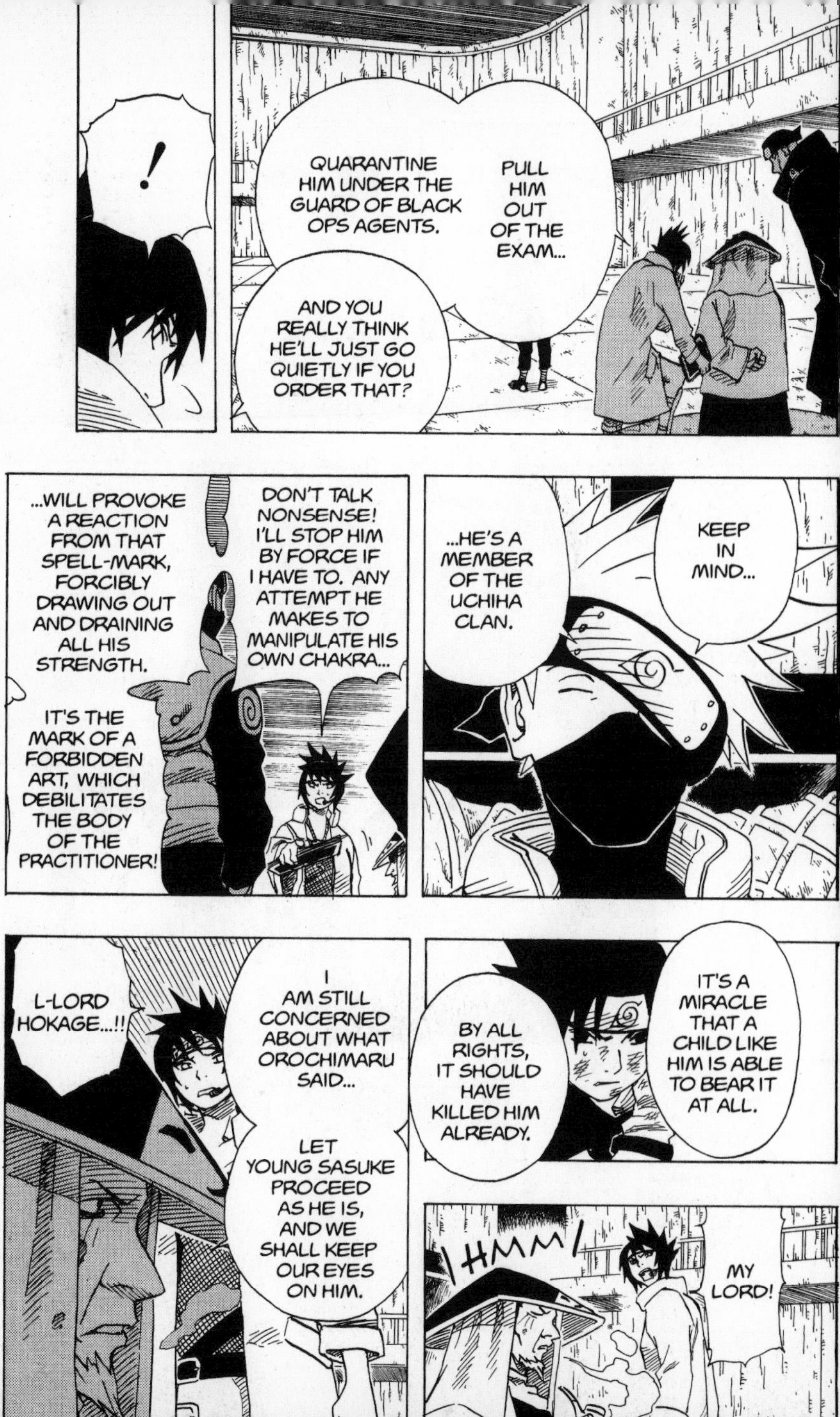
PULL HIM OUT OF THE EXAM...
QUARANTINE HIM UNDER THE GUARD OF BLACK OPS AGENTS.
AND YOU REALLY THINK HE'LL JUST GO QUIETLY IF YOU ORDER THAT?
!
KEEP IN MIND...
...HE'S A MEMBER OF THE UCHIHA CLAN.
DON'T TALK NONSENSE! I'LL STOP HIM BY FORCE IF I HAVE TO. ANY ATTEMPT HE MAKES TO MANIPULATE HIS OWN CHAKRA...
...WILL PROVOKE A REACTION FROM THAT SPELL-MARK, FORCIBLY DRAWING OUT AND DRAINING ALL HIS STRENGTH.
IT'S THE MARK OF A FORBIDDEN ART, WHICH DEBILITATES THE BODY OF THE PRACTITIONER!
IT'S A MIRACLE THAT A CHILD LIKE HIM IS ABLE TO BEAR IT AT ALL.
BY ALL RIGHTS, IT SHOULD HAVE KILLED HIM ALREADY.
MY LORD!
HMM!
I AM STILL CONCERNED ABOUT WHAT OROCHIMARU SAID...
L-LORD HOKAGE...!!
LET YOUNG SASUKE PROCEED AS HE IS, AND WE SHALL KEEP OUR EYES ON HIM.

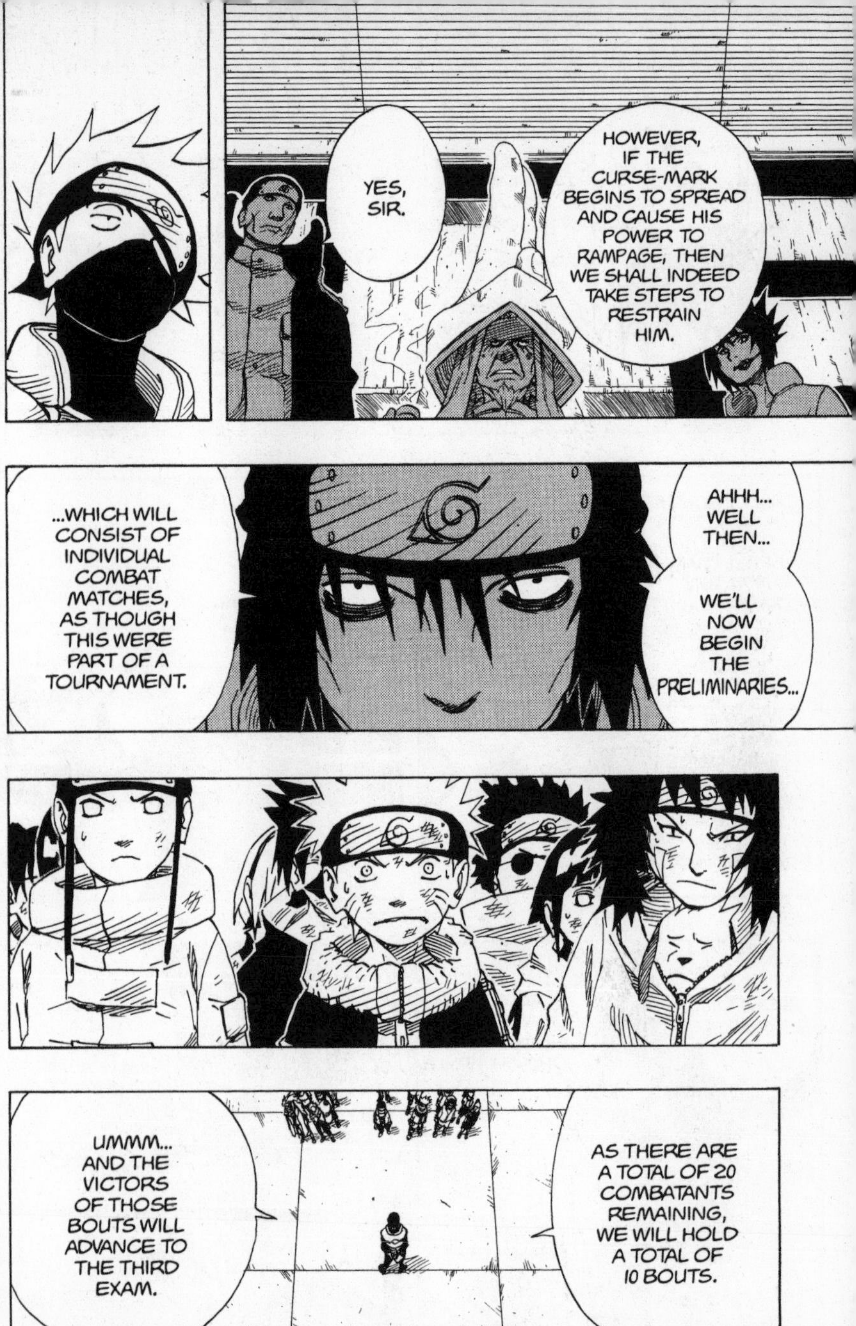
HOWEVER, IF THE CURSE-MARK BEGINS TO SPREAD AND CAUSE HIS POWER TO RAMPAGE, THEN WE SHALL INDEED TAKE STEPS TO RESTRAIN HIM.
YES, SIR.
AHHH... WELL THEN...
WE'LL NOW BEGIN THE PRELIMINARIES...
...WHICH WILL CONSIST OF INDIVIDUAL COMBAT MATCHES, AS THOUGH THIS WERE PART OF A TOURNAMENT.
AS THERE ARE A TOTAL OF 20 COMBATANTS REMAINING, WE WILL HOLD A TOTAL OF 10 BOUTS.
UMMM... AND THE VICTORS OF THOSE BOUTS WILL ADVANCE TO THE THIRD EXAM.

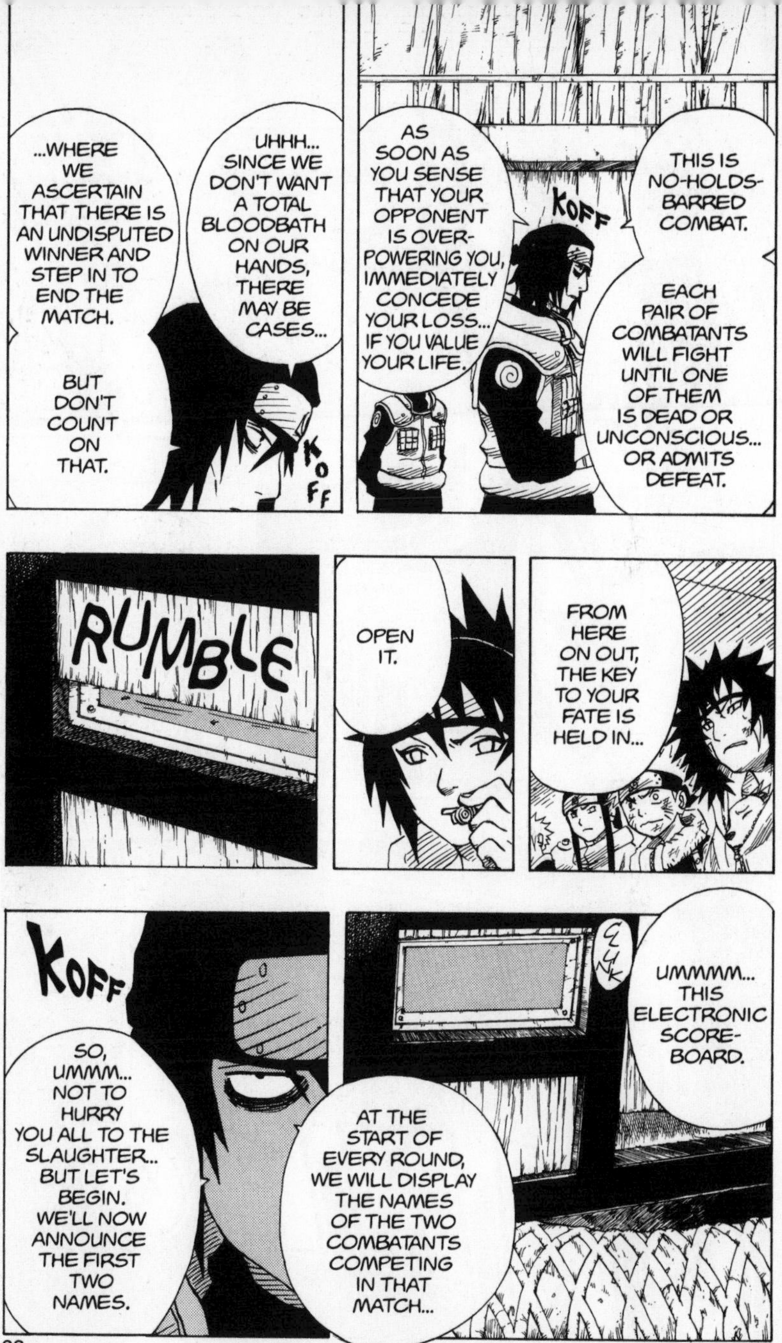
THIS IS NO-HOLDS-BARRED COMBAT.
EACH PAIR OF COMBATANTS WILL FIGHT UNTIL ONE OF THEM IS DEAD OR UNCONSCIOUS... OR ADMITS DEFEAT.
KOFF
AS SOON AS YOU SENSE THAT YOUR OPPONENT IS OVER-POWERING YOU, IMMEDIATELY CONCEDE YOUR LOSS... IF YOU VALUE YOUR LIFE.
UHHH... SINCE WE DON'T WANT A TOTAL BLOODBATH ON OUR HANDS, THERE MAY BE CASES...
...WHERE WE ASCERTAIN THAT THERE IS AN UNDISPUTED WINNER AND STEP IN TO END THE MATCH.
BUT DON'T COUNT ON THAT.
KOFF
FROM HERE ON OUT, THE KEY TO YOUR FATE IS HELD IN...
OPEN IT.
RUMBLE
CLUNK
UMMMM... THIS ELECTRONIC SCORE-BOARD.
AT THE START OF EVERY ROUND, WE WILL DISPLAY THE NAMES OF THE TWO COMBATANTS COMPETING IN THAT MATCH...
KOFF
SO, UMMM... NOT TO HURRY YOU ALL TO THE SLAUGHTER... BUT LET'S BEGIN. WE'LL NOW ANNOUNCE THE FIRST TWO NAMES.

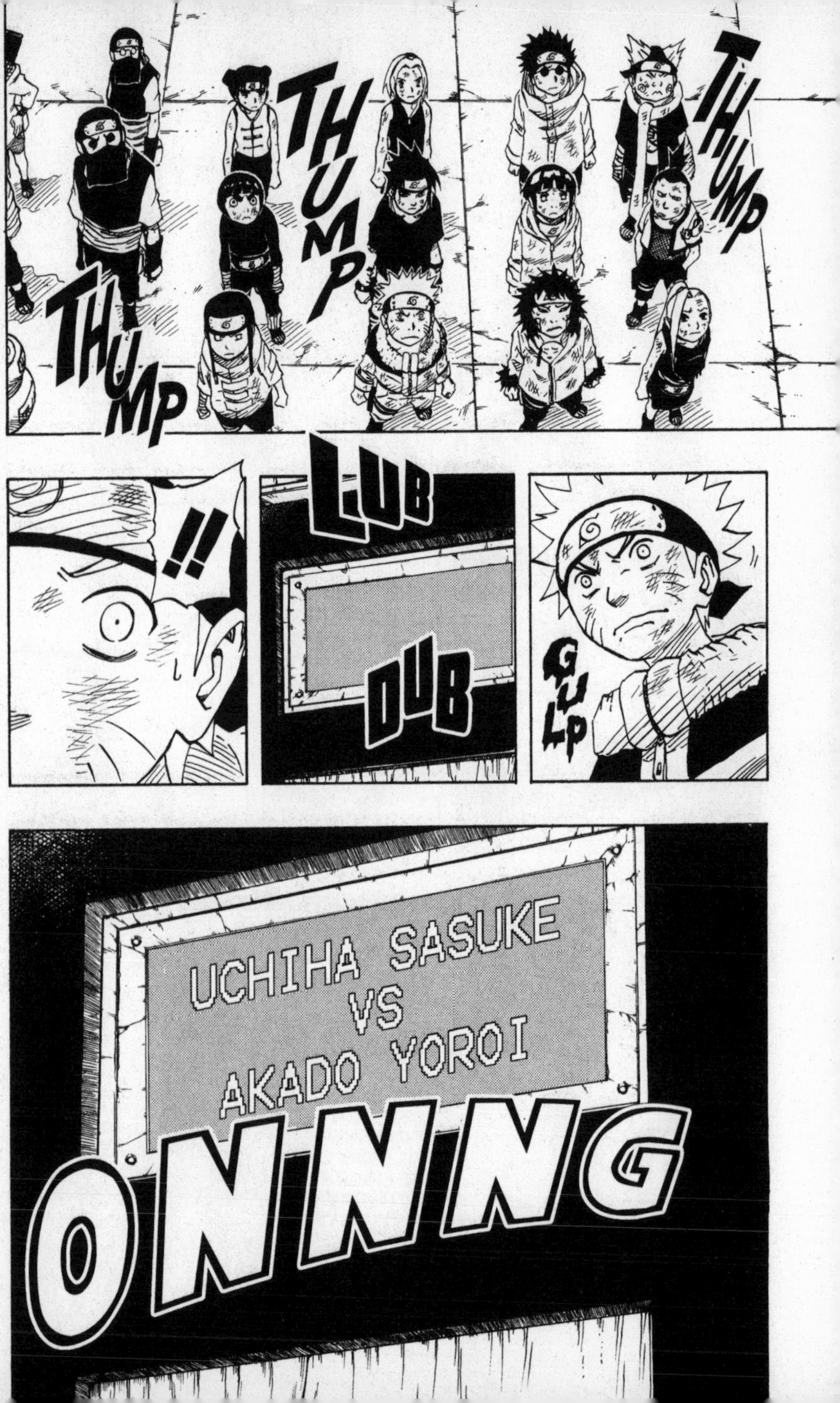
THUMP
THUMP
THUMP
GULP
LUB
DUB
!!
UCHIHA SASUKE
VS
AKADO YOROI
ONNNG

READ THIS WAY

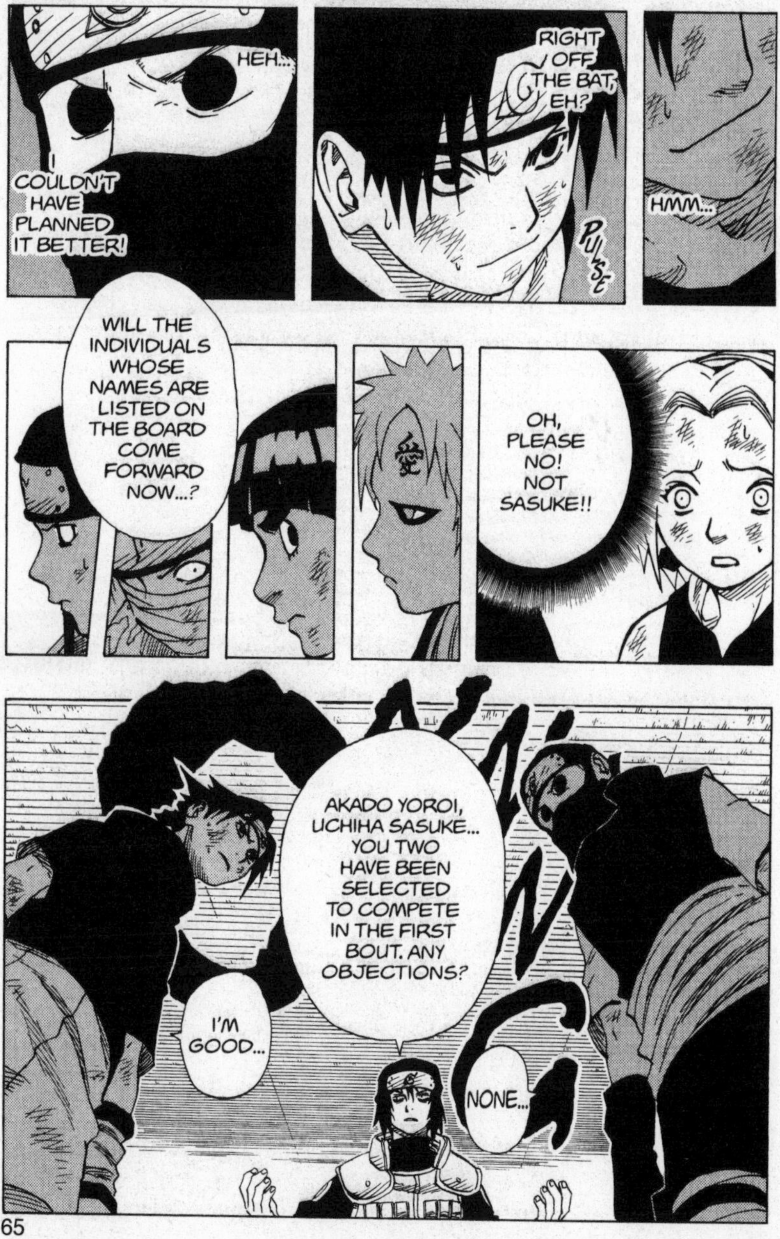
HMM...
RIGHT OFF THE BAT, EH?
PULSE
HEH...
COULDN'T HAVE PLANNED IT BETTER!
OH, PLEASE NO! NOT SASUKE!!
WILL THE INDIVIDUALS WHOSE NAMES ARE LISTED ON THE BOARD COME FORWARD NOW...?
AKADO YOROI, UCHIHA SASUKE... YOU TWO HAVE BEEN SELECTED TO COMPETE IN THE FIRST BOUT. ANY OBJECTIONS?
NONE...
I'M GOOD...

THE WORLD OF KISHIMOTO MASASHI
MY PERSONAL HISTORY, PART 6

DURING MY LAST FEW YEARS OF ELEMENTARY SCHOOL, I WAS
COMPLETELY ADDICTED TO *DRAGON BALL*. I HAD NEVER BEEN
SO INTO ANYTHING BEFORE, AND I REVERED TORIYAMA AKIRA
LIKE A GOD. AT EVERY OPPORTUNITY THAT AROSE, I WOULD
TRACE AND DRAW ALL OF THE CHARACTERS FROM *DRAGON
BALL* AND PORE OVER MY FRIENDS' COPIES OF *SHONEN JUMP*,
ALL SO I COULD SEE MORE *DRAGON BALL*. I WASN'T GETTING A
SINGLE YEN IN ALLOWANCE AT THAT TIME -- THE ONLY MONEY I
HAD WAS THE GIFTS OF CASH I'D GET ON NEW YEAR'S -- SO BUY-
ING MY OWN COPIES WAS OUT OF THE QUESTION. BEING FORCED
TO STRETCH OUT MY NEW YEAR'S MONEY TO LAST AN ENTIRE
YEAR DIDN'T LEAVE ME ANY FUNDS FOR A WEEKLY PUBLICATION,
EVEN ONE THAT ONLY COST 190 YEN PER ISSUE.

AT FIRST, *DRAGON BALL* WAS MY SOLE REASON FOR READING
JUMP, BUT EVENTUALLY I BEGAN TO REALIZE HOW INTERESTING
A NUMBER OF THE OTHER TITLES IN THE ANTHOLOGY WERE.
I STARTED FOLLOWING *JOJO'S BIZARRE ADVENTURE*, *SAINT
SEIYA (KNIGHTS OF THE ZODIAC)*, *HIGH SCHOOL KIMENGUMI*
AND OTHERS, AND BECAME A FAN OF *JUMP* ITSELF. ONCE I
REALIZED HOW FUNNY MANGA WERE AND HOW MUCH I LIKED
THEM, I BEGAN TO ASPIRE TO BECOME A MANGA ARTIST...
AND TO CREATE A SERIAL OF MY OWN THAT COULD APPEAR
IN *JUMP*. AND I CLEARLY RECALL THAT THE FIRST MANGA I
EVER DREW WAS "HIATARI-KUN," A SERIES ABOUT THE ADVEN-
TURES OF A MYSTERIOUS YOUNG NINJA.

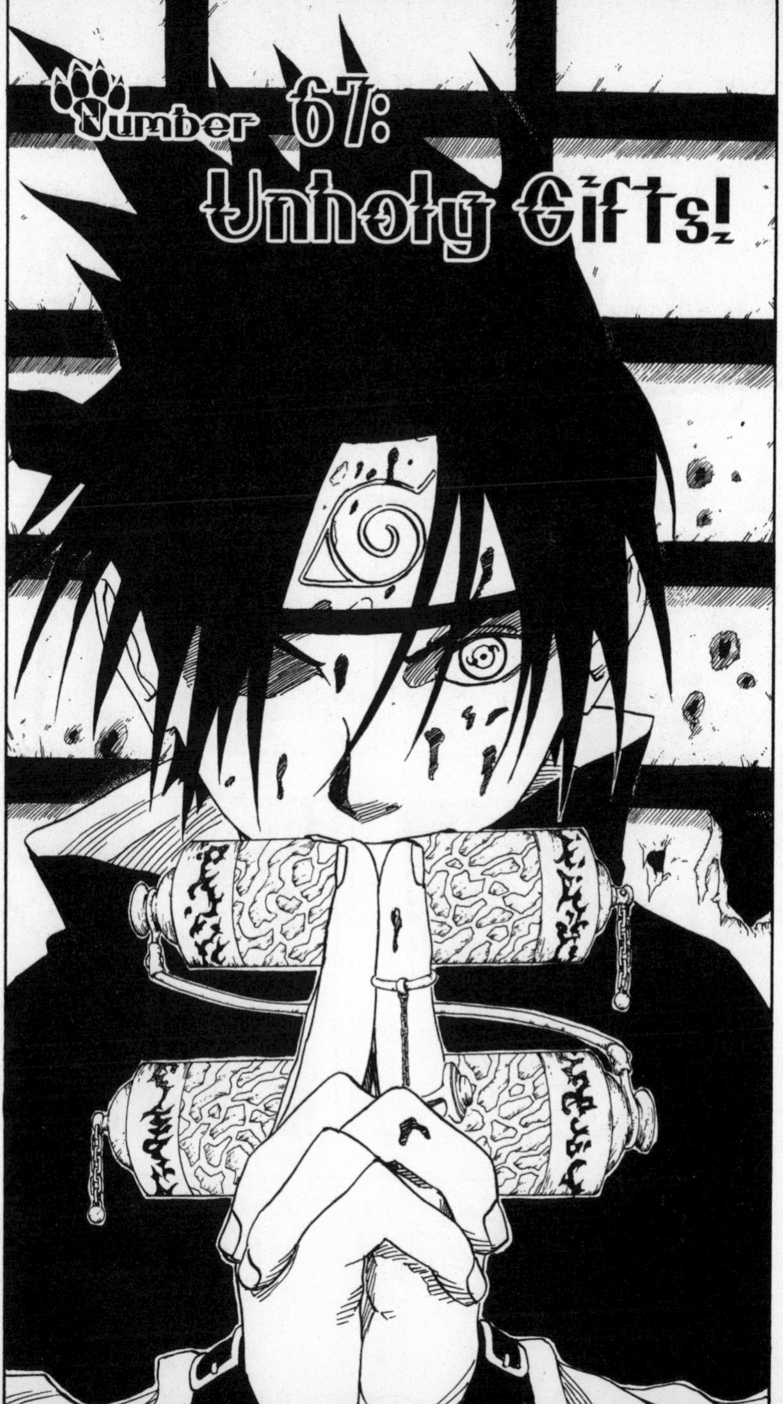
Number 67:
Unholy Gifts!

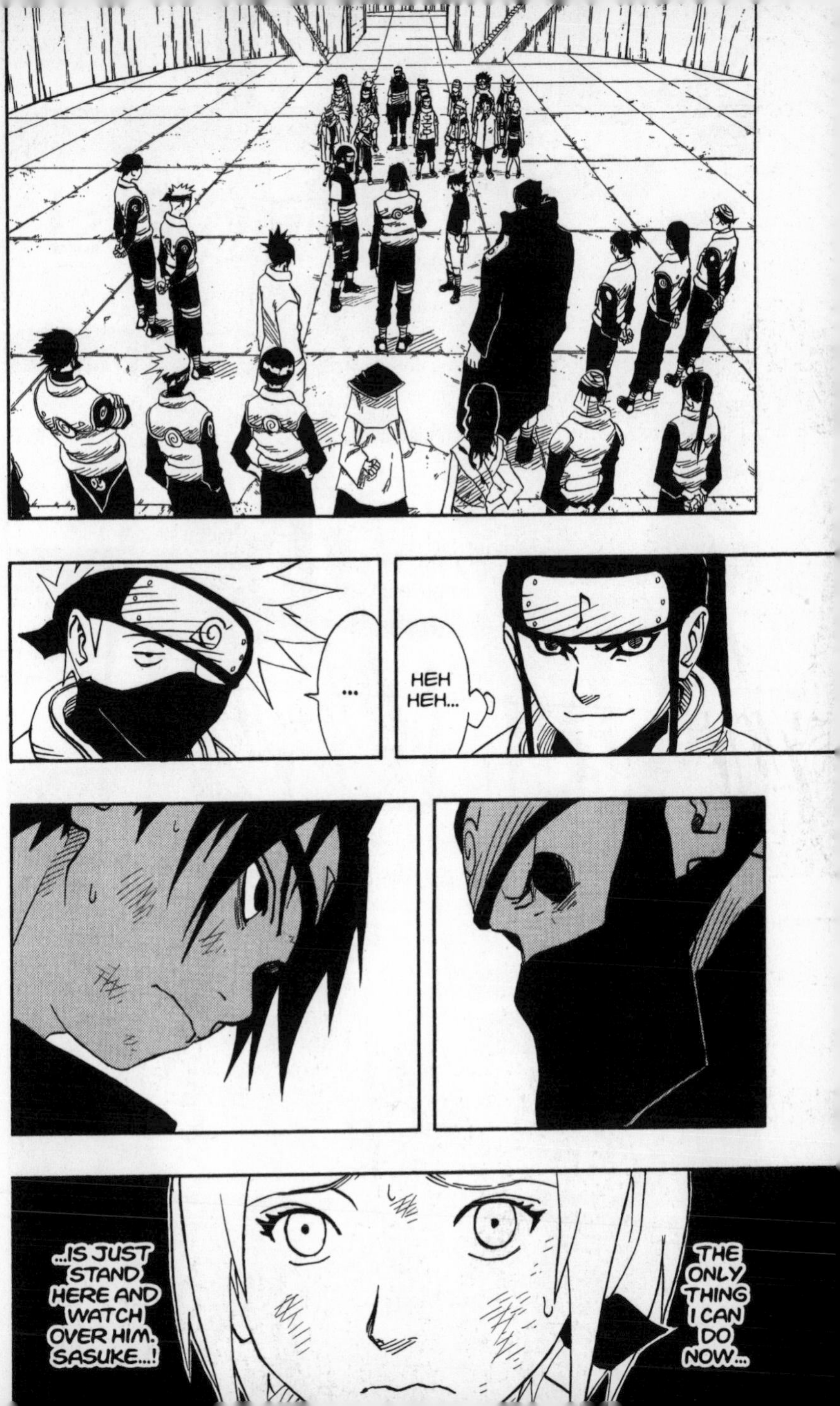
HEH HEH...
...
THE ONLY THING I CAN DO NOW...
...IS JUST STAND HERE AND WATCH OVER HIM. SASUKE...!

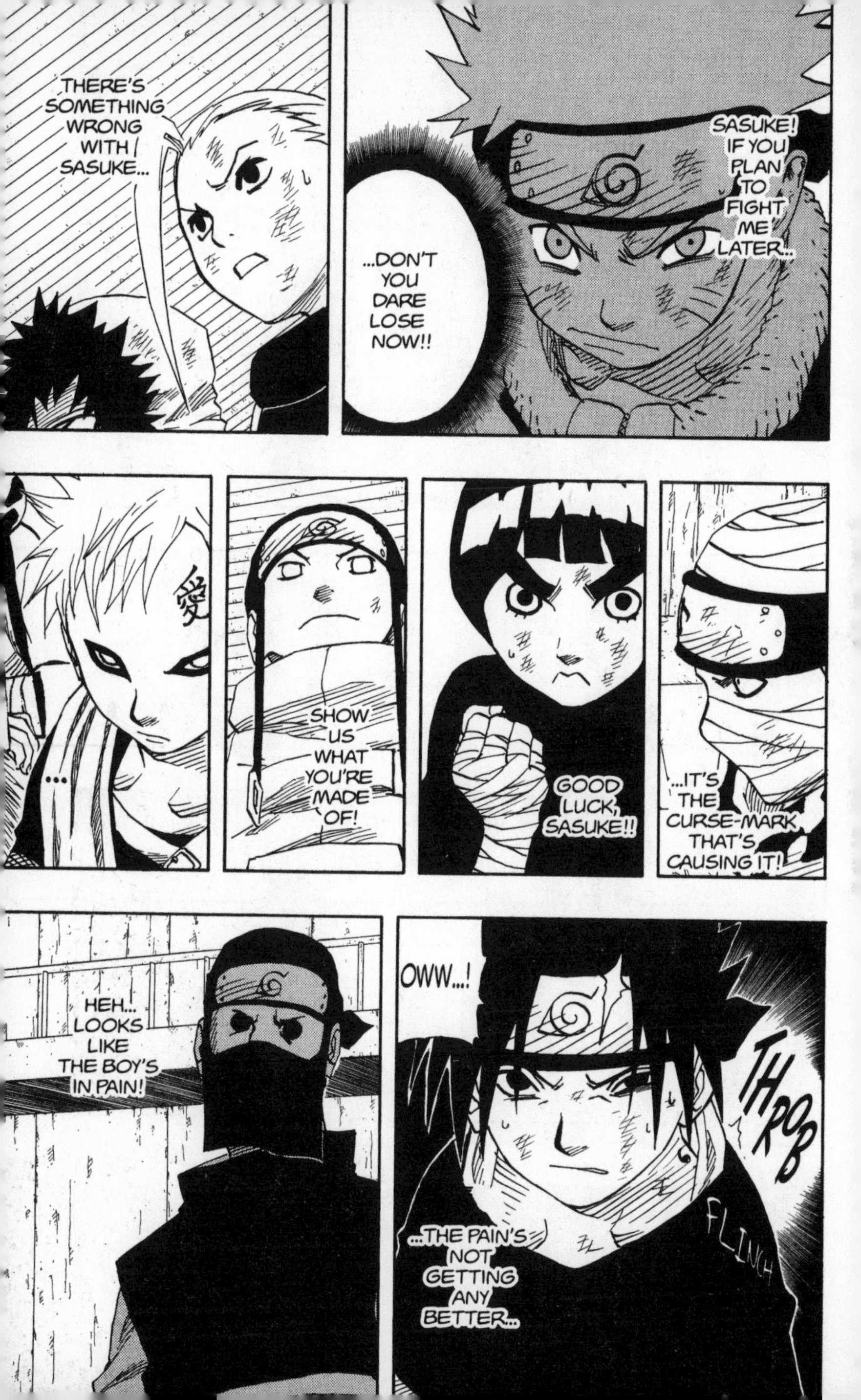
SASUKE! IF YOU PLAN TO FIGHT ME LATER...
...DON'T YOU DARE LOSE NOW!!
THERE'S SOMETHING WRONG WITH SASUKE...
...IT'S THE CURSE-MARK THAT'S CAUSING IT!
GOOD LUCK, SASUKE!!
SHOW US WHAT YOU'RE MADE OF!
...
OWW...!
THROB
FLINCH
...THE PAIN'S NOT GETTING ANY BETTER...
HEH... LOOKS LIKE THE BOY'S IN PAIN!

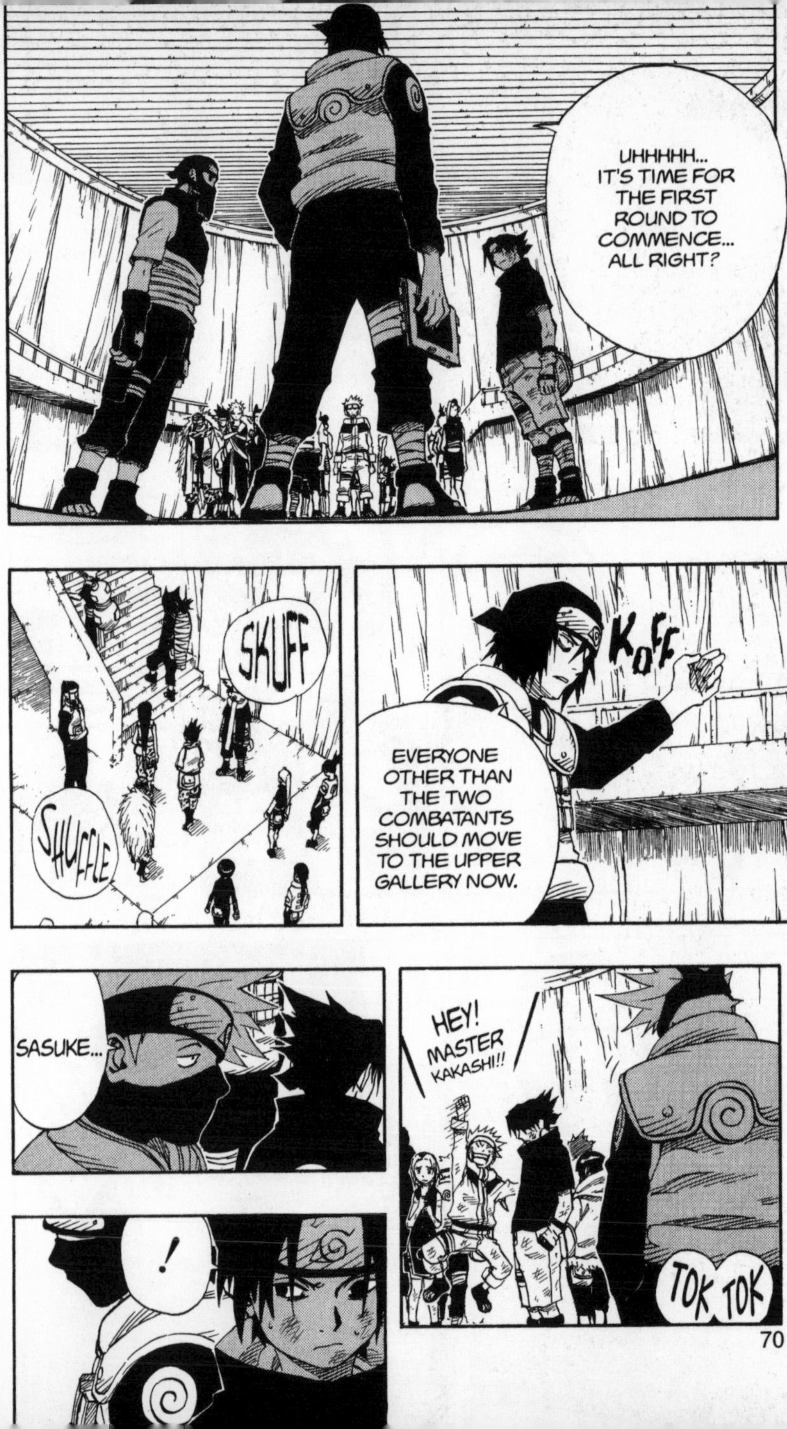
UHHHHH... IT'S TIME FOR THE FIRST ROUND TO COMMENCE... ALL RIGHT?
KOFF
EVERYONE OTHER THAN THE TWO COMBATANTS SHOULD MOVE TO THE UPPER GALLERY NOW.
SKUFF
SHUFFLE
HEY! MASTER KAKASHI!!
TOK TOK
SASUKE...
!

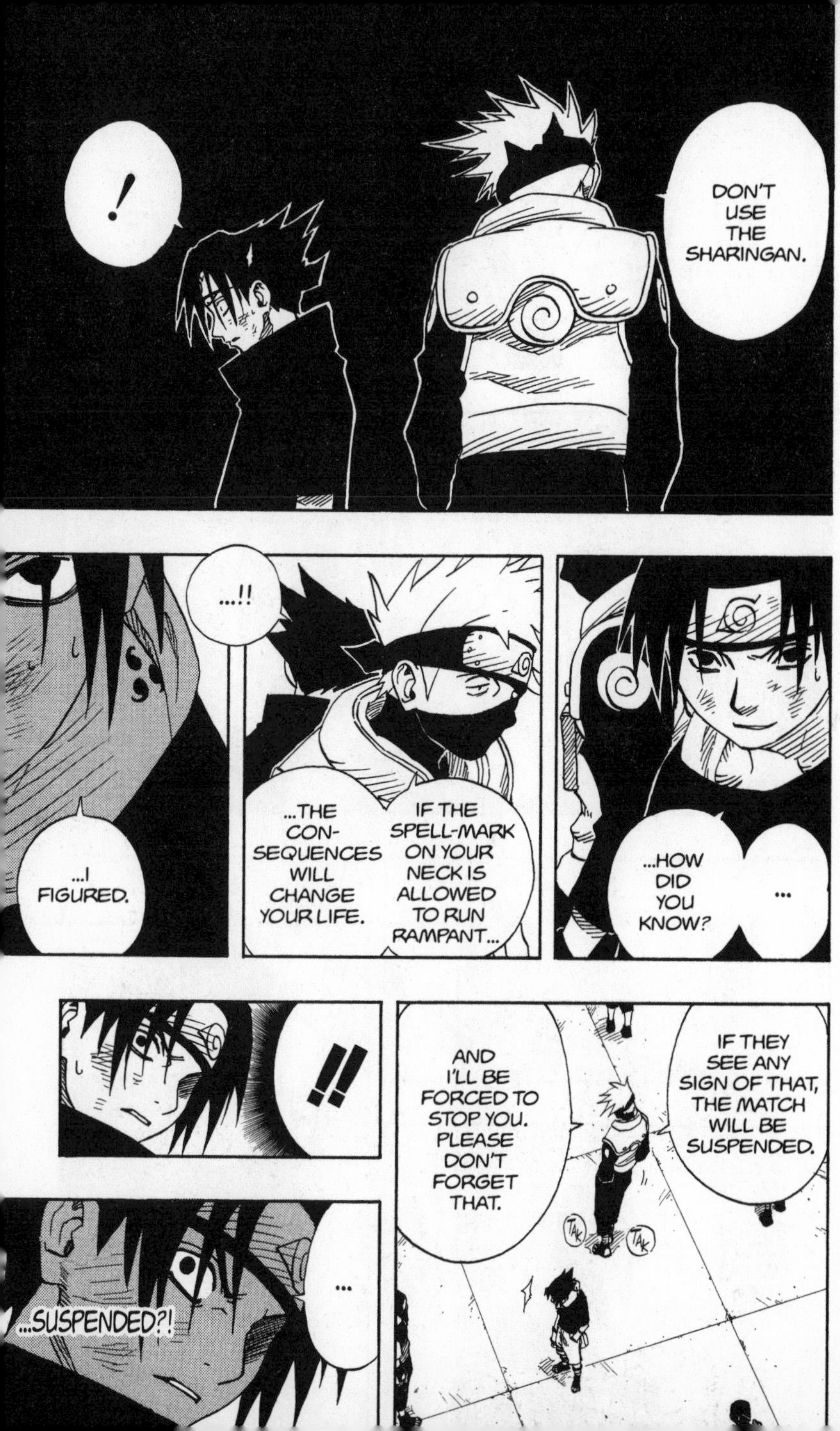
DON'T USE THE SHARINGAN.
!
...
...HOW DID YOU KNOW?
...!!
IF THE SPELL-MARK ON YOUR NECK IS ALLOWED TO RUN RAMPANT...
...THE CON-SEQUENCES WILL CHANGE YOUR LIFE.
...I FIGURED.
IF THEY SEE ANY SIGN OF THAT, THE MATCH WILL BE SUSPENDED.
AND I'LL BE FORCED TO STOP YOU. PLEASE DON'T FORGET THAT.
TAK
TAK
!!
...
...SUSPENDED?!

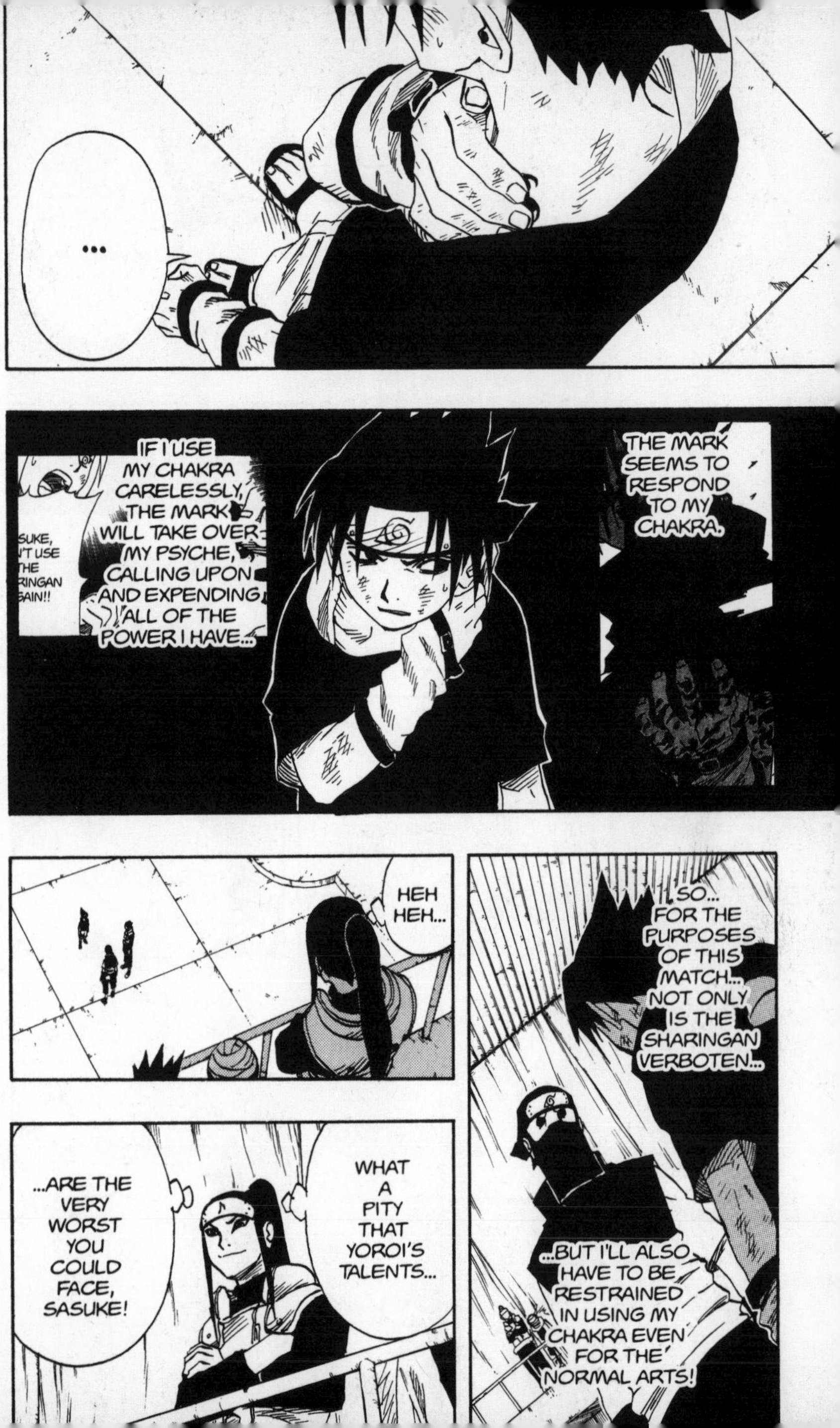
...
THE MARK SEEMS TO RESPOND TO MY CHAKRA.
IF I USE MY CHAKRA CARELESSLY, THE MARK WILL TAKE OVER MY PSYCHE, CALLING UPON AND EXPENDING ALL OF THE POWER I HAVE...
SUKE, N'T USE THE RINGAN AIN!!
SO... FOR THE PURPOSES OF THIS MATCH... NOT ONLY IS THE SHARINGAN VERBOTEN...
...BUT I'LL ALSO HAVE TO BE RESTRAINED IN USING MY CHAKRA EVEN FOR THE NORMAL ARTS!
HEH HEH...
WHAT A PITY THAT YOROI'S TALENTS...
...ARE THE VERY WORST YOU COULD FACE, SASUKE!

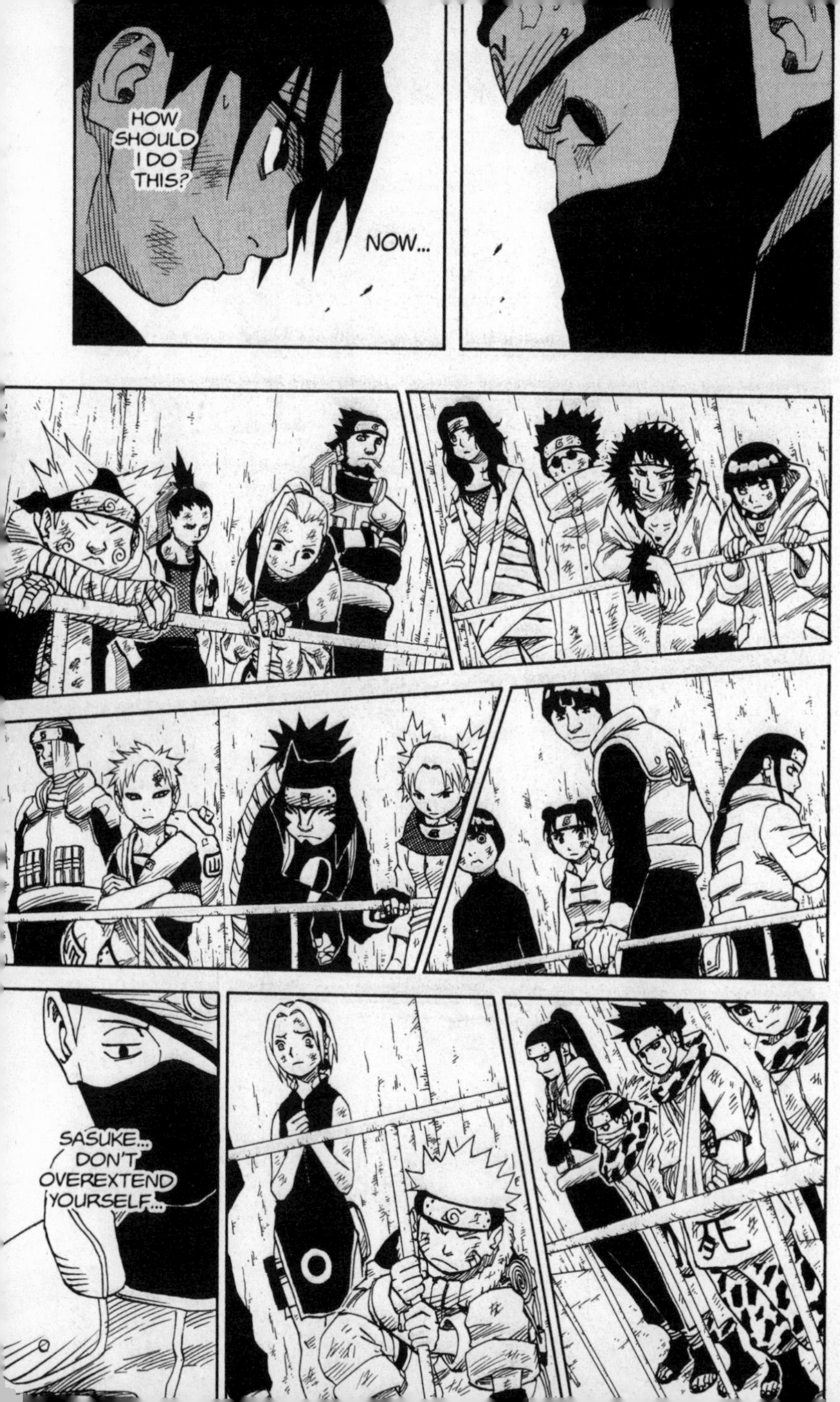
NOW...
HOW SHOULD I DO THIS?
SASUKE... DON'T OVEREXTEND YOURSELF...

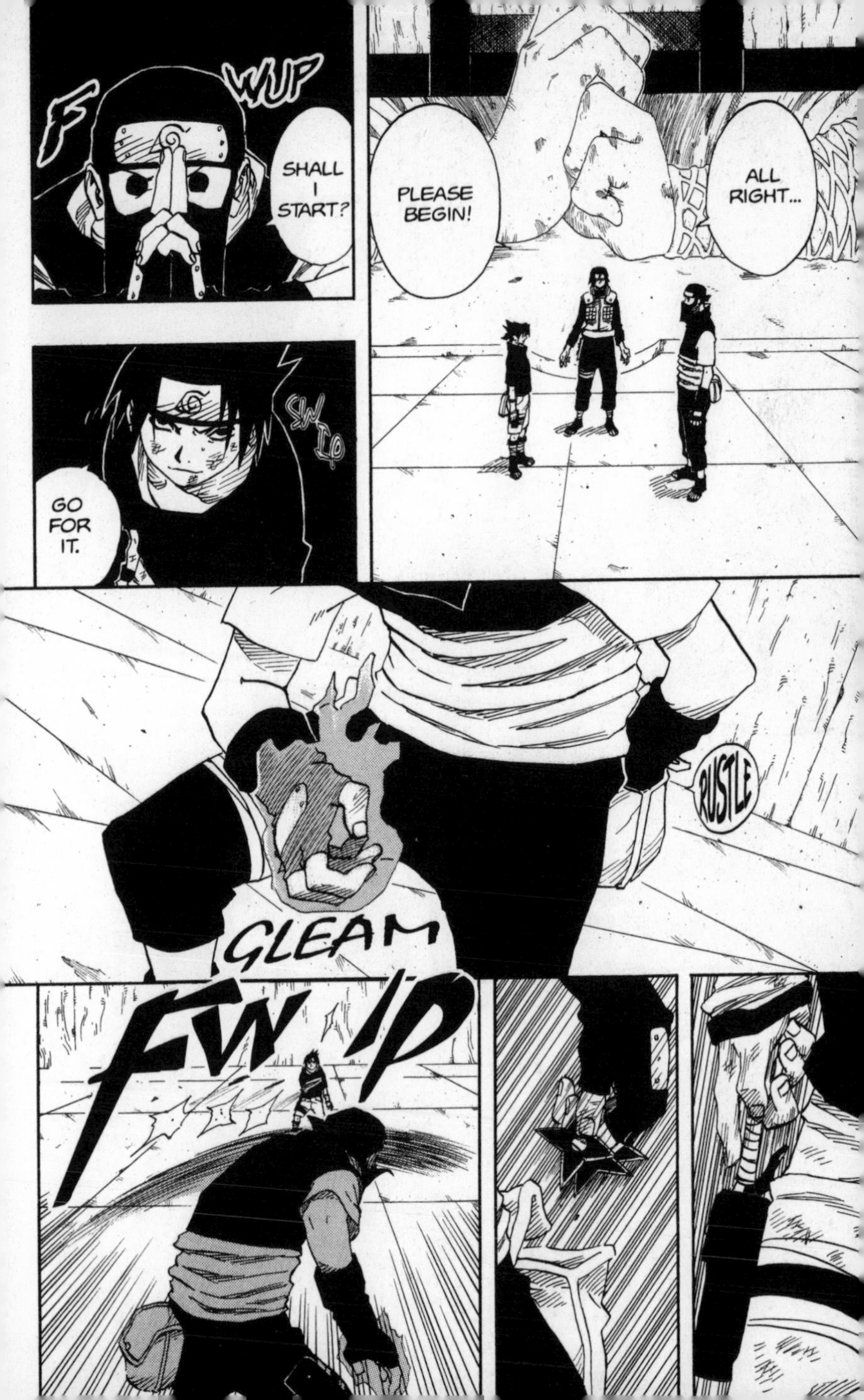
ALL RIGHT...
PLEASE BEGIN!
F WUP
SHALL I START?
SWIP
GO FOR IT.
RUSTLE
GLEAM
FWIP

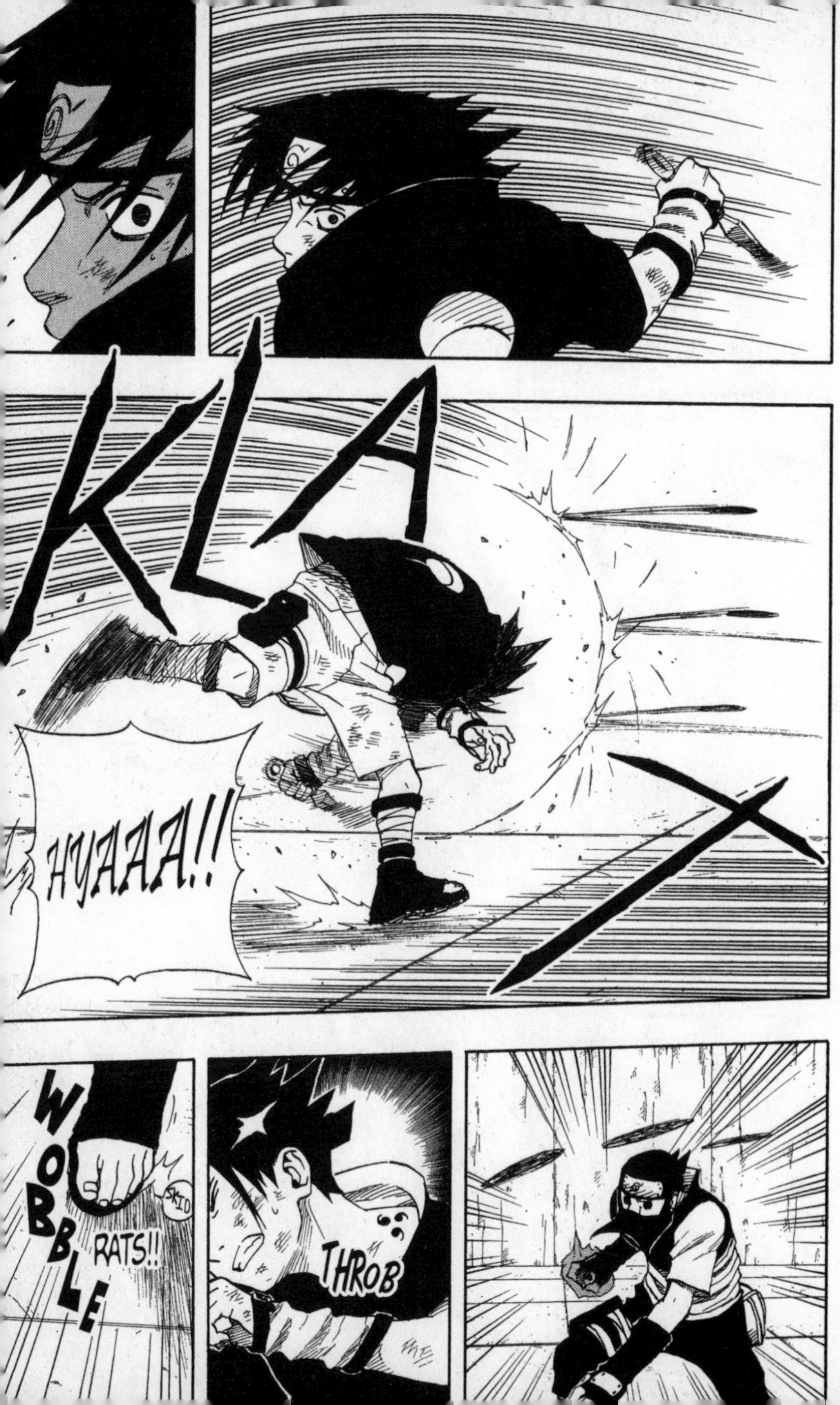
KLA
HYAAA!!
THROB
WOBBLE
SKID
RATS!!

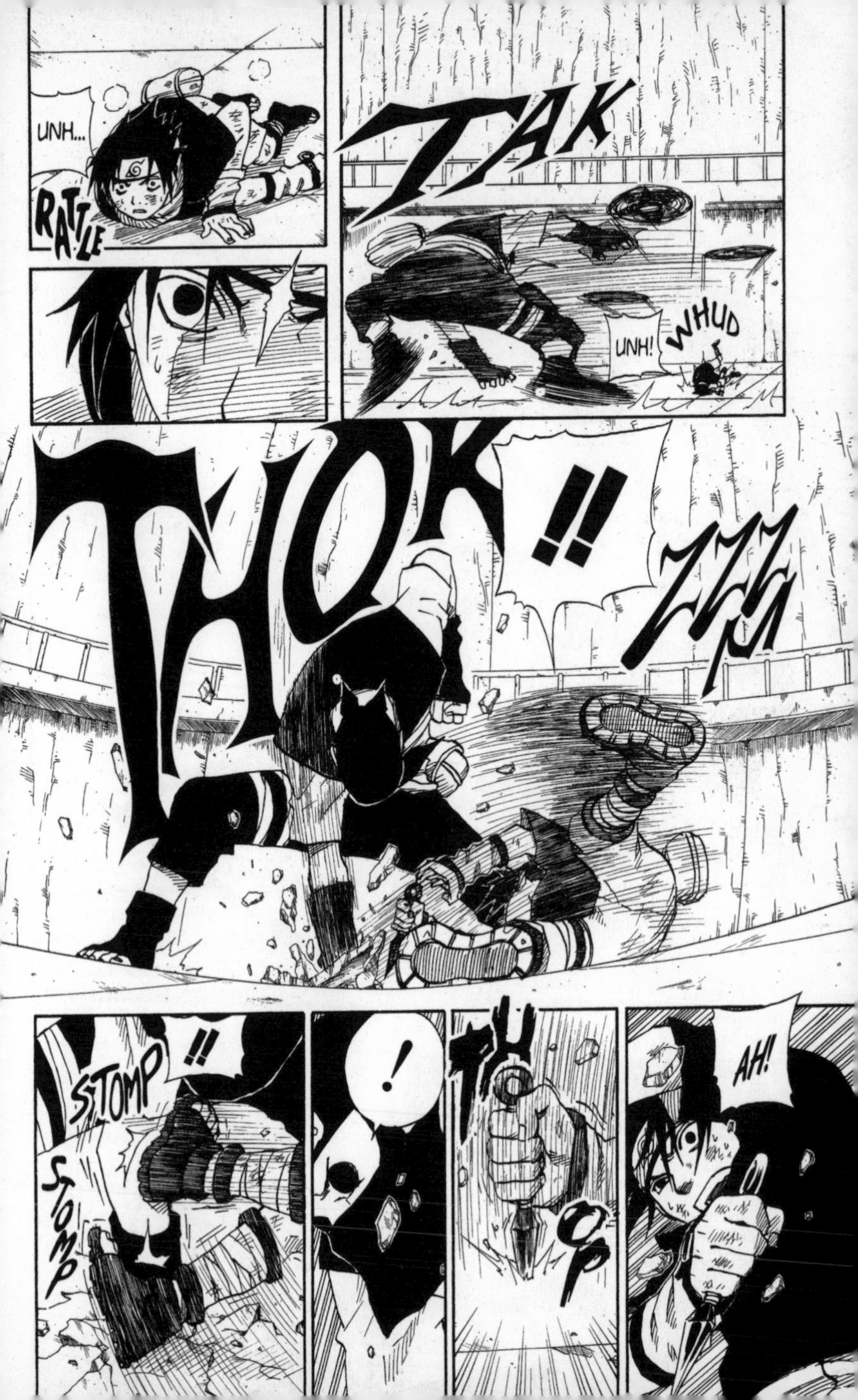

TAK
UNH!
WHUD
UNH...
RATTLE
THOK!!
AH!
!
STOMP !!
STOMP

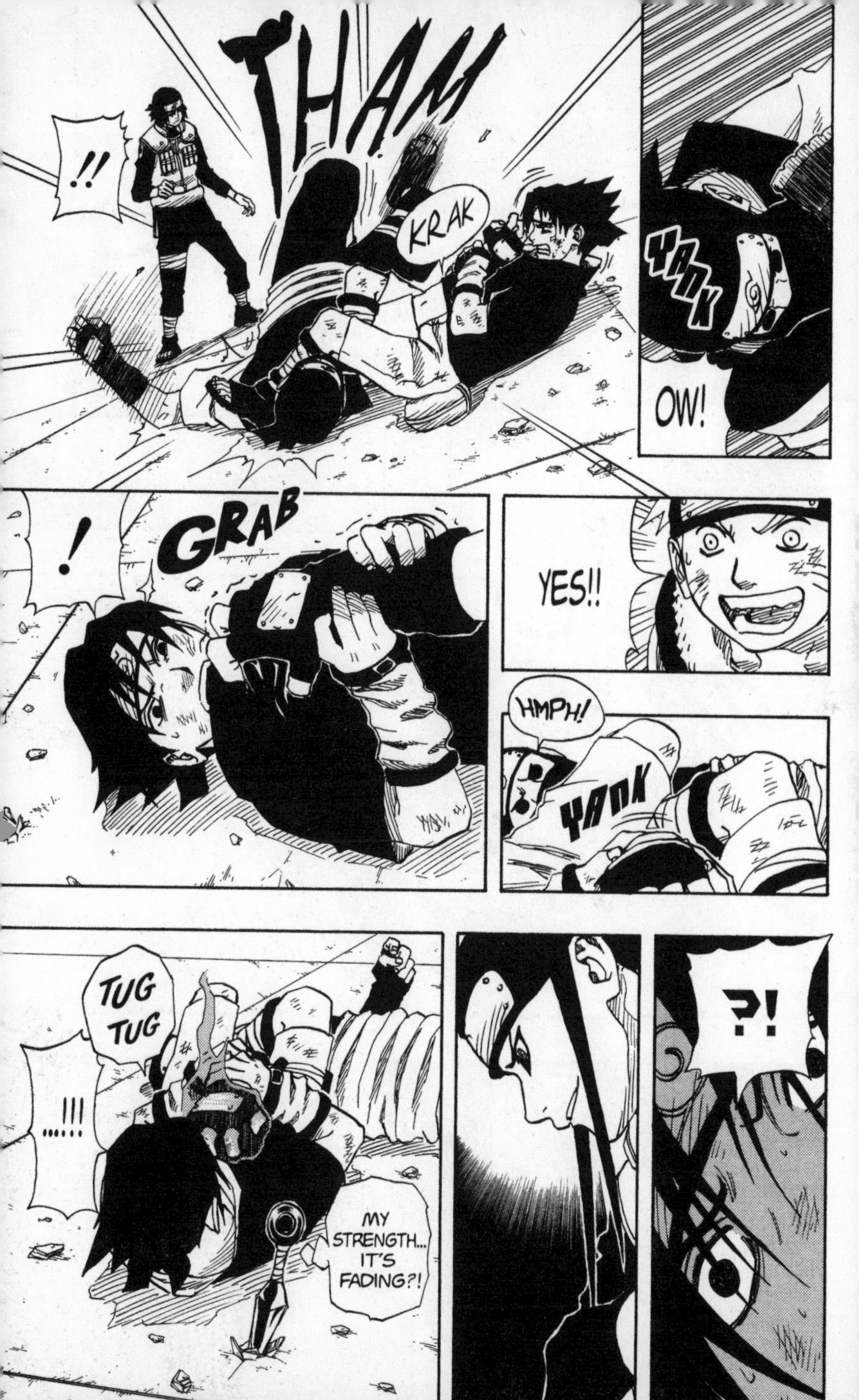
YANK
OW!
THAM
!!
KRAK
YES!!
HMPH!
YANK
GRAB
!
?!
TUG TUG
...!!!
MY STRENGTH... IT'S FADING?!

POW

AAHH!!

SHIVER

SLAP

SHIVER SHAKE

SHAKE

CRUNCH

?!

SHAKE SHAKE

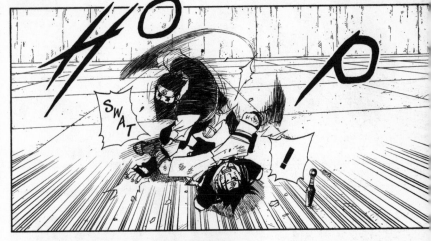

HOP

SWAT

!

TAK

TWITCH TWITCH

UNNH...

WH-WHY...?
WHERE
DID
ALL MY
STRENGTH
GO?

TWITCH

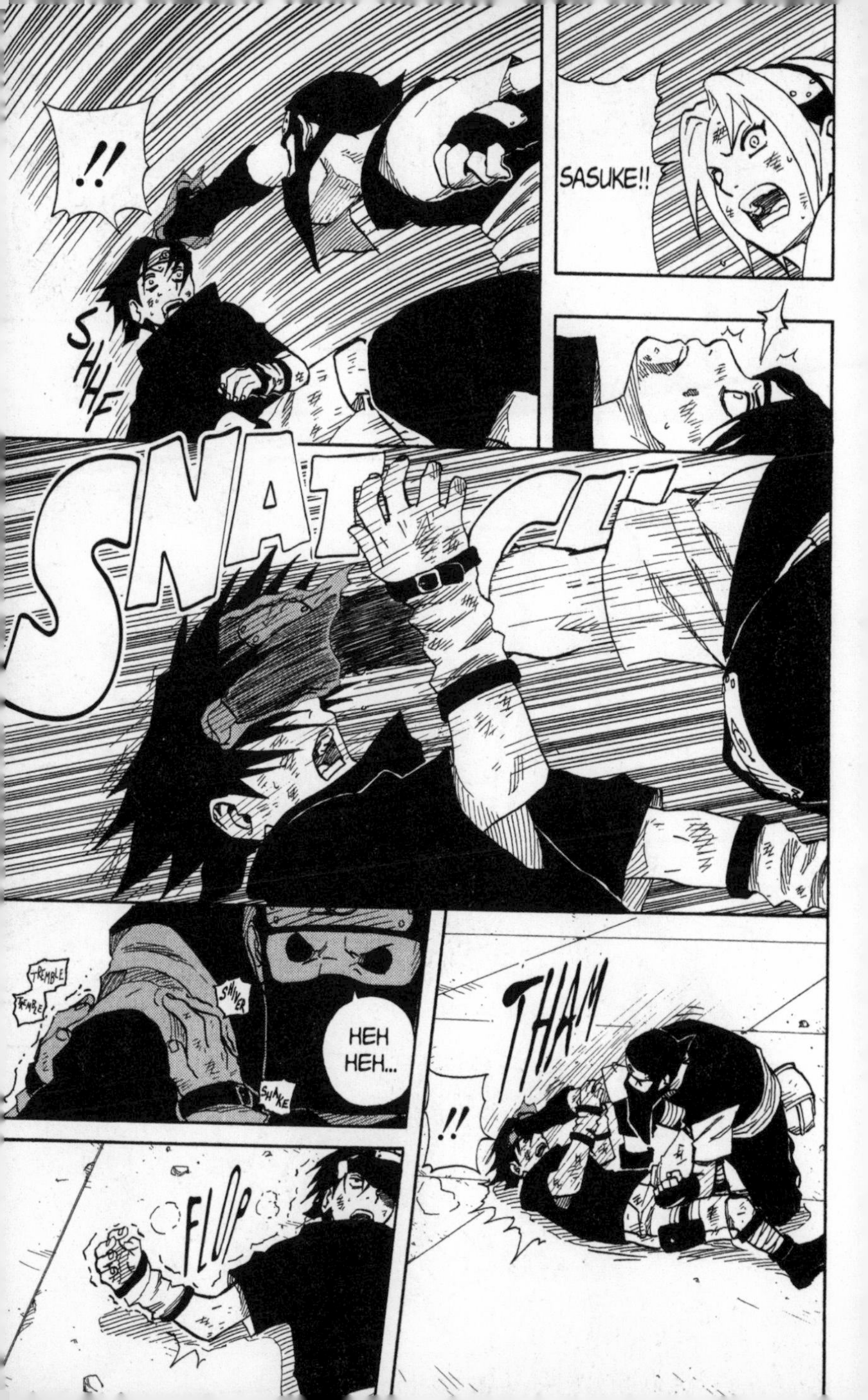
SASUKE!!
!!
SHHF
SNATCH
THAM
!!
TREMBLE
TREMBLE
SHIVER
HEH HEH...
SHAKE
FLOP

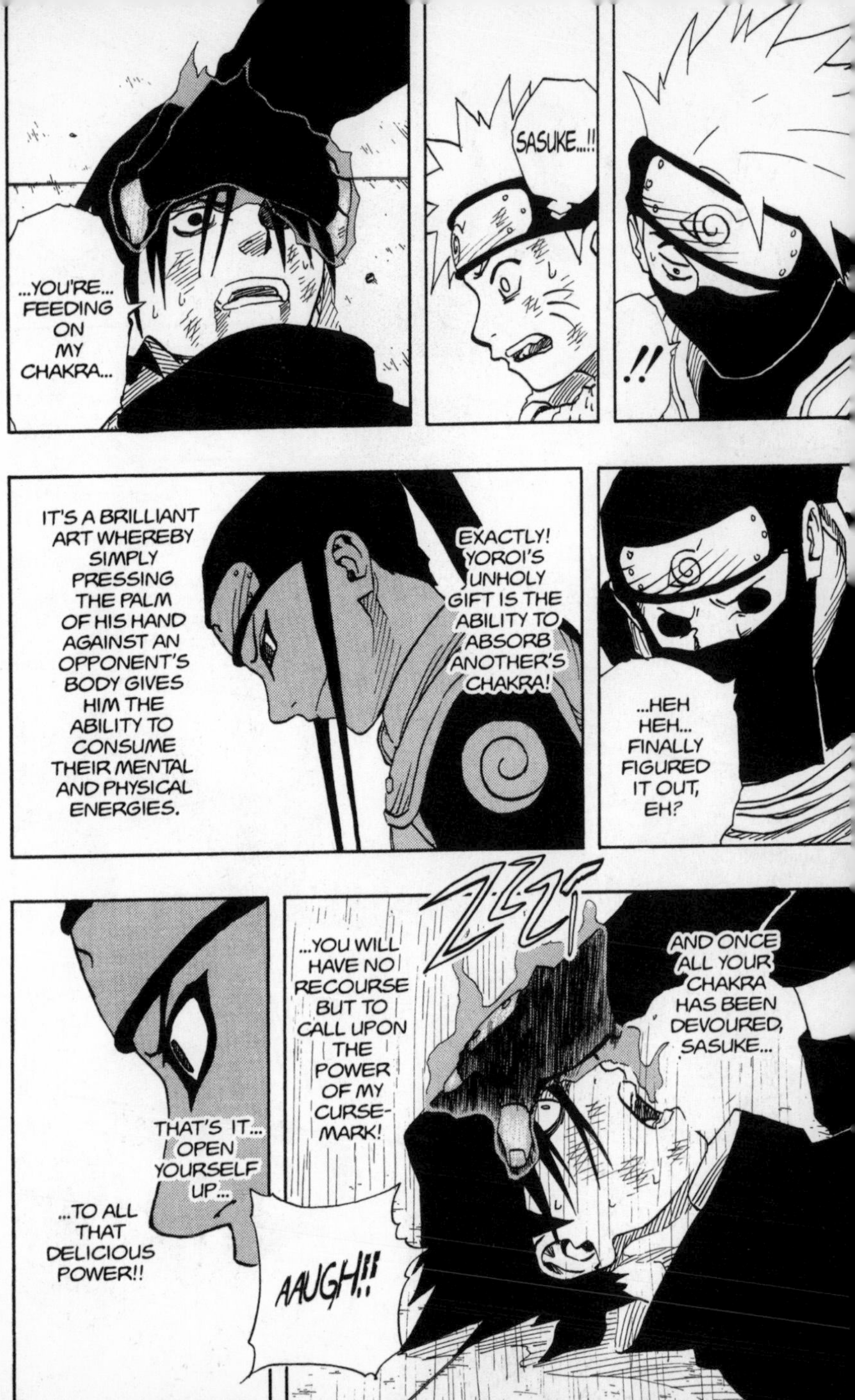
!!
SASUKE...!!
...YOU'RE... FEEDING ON MY CHAKRA...
...HEH HEH... FINALLY FIGURED IT OUT, EH?
EXACTLY! YOROI'S UNHOLY GIFT IS THE ABILITY TO ABSORB ANOTHER'S CHAKRA!
IT'S A BRILLIANT ART WHEREBY SIMPLY PRESSING THE PALM OF HIS HAND AGAINST AN OPPONENT'S BODY GIVES HIM THE ABILITY TO CONSUME THEIR MENTAL AND PHYSICAL ENERGIES.
ZZZ
AND ONCE ALL YOUR CHAKRA HAS BEEN DEVOURED, SASUKE...
...YOU WILL HAVE NO RECOURSE BUT TO CALL UPON THE POWER OF MY CURSE-MARK!
AAUGH!!
THAT'S IT... OPEN YOURSELF UP...
...TO ALL THAT DELICIOUS POWER!!

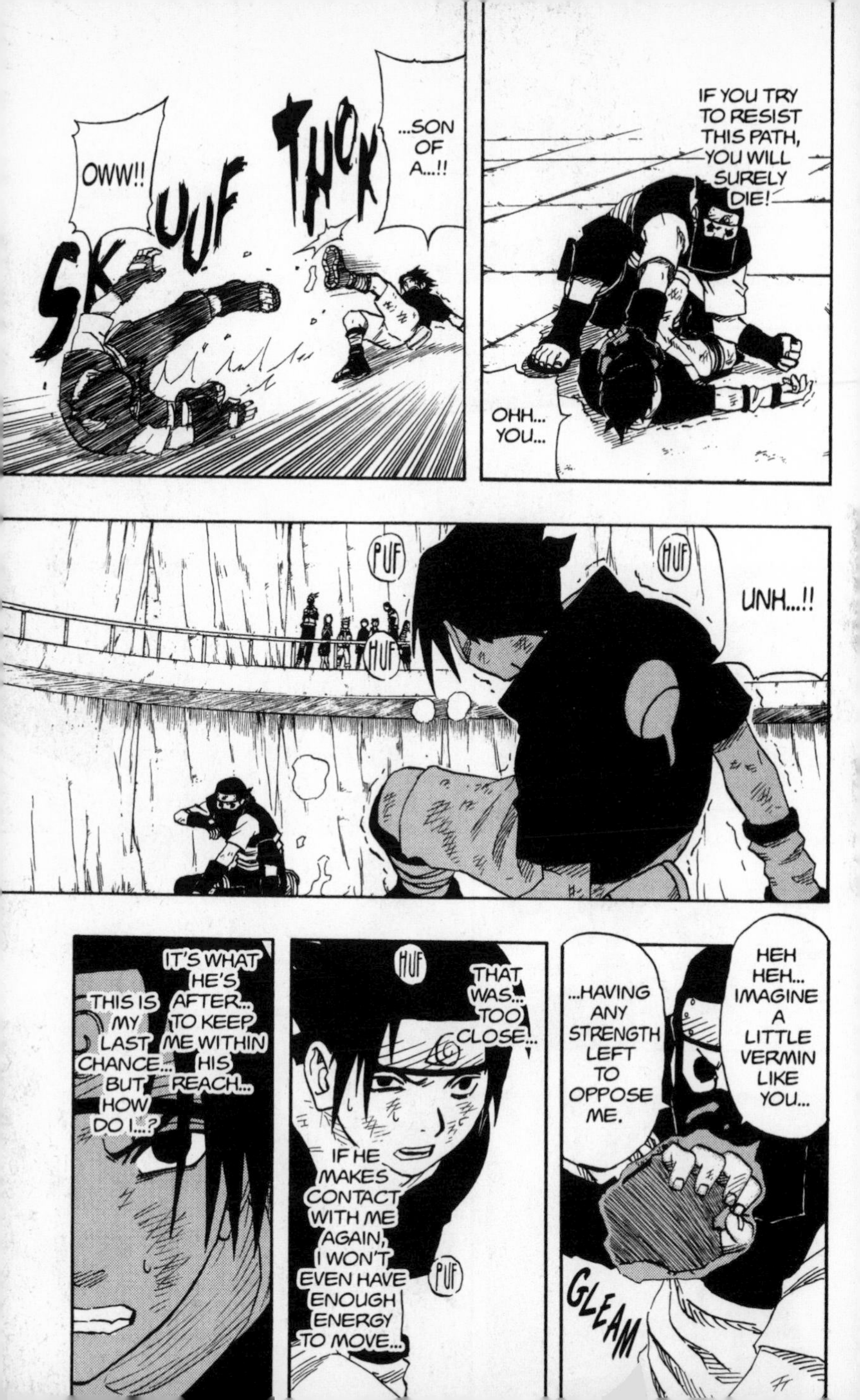

IF YOU TRY TO RESIST THIS PATH, YOU WILL SURELY DIE!
OHH... YOU...
...SON OF A...!!
THOCK
UUF
OWW!!
SK
HUF
UNH...!!
PUF
HUF
HEH HEH... IMAGINE A LITTLE VERMIN LIKE YOU...
...HAVING ANY STRENGTH LEFT TO OPPOSE ME.
GLEAM
HUF
THAT WAS... TOO CLOSE...
IF HE MAKES CONTACT WITH ME AGAIN, I WON'T EVEN HAVE ENOUGH ENERGY TO MOVE...
PUF
IT'S WHAT HE'S AFTER... TO KEEP ME WITHIN HIS REACH...
THIS IS MY LAST CHANCE... BUT HOW DO I...?

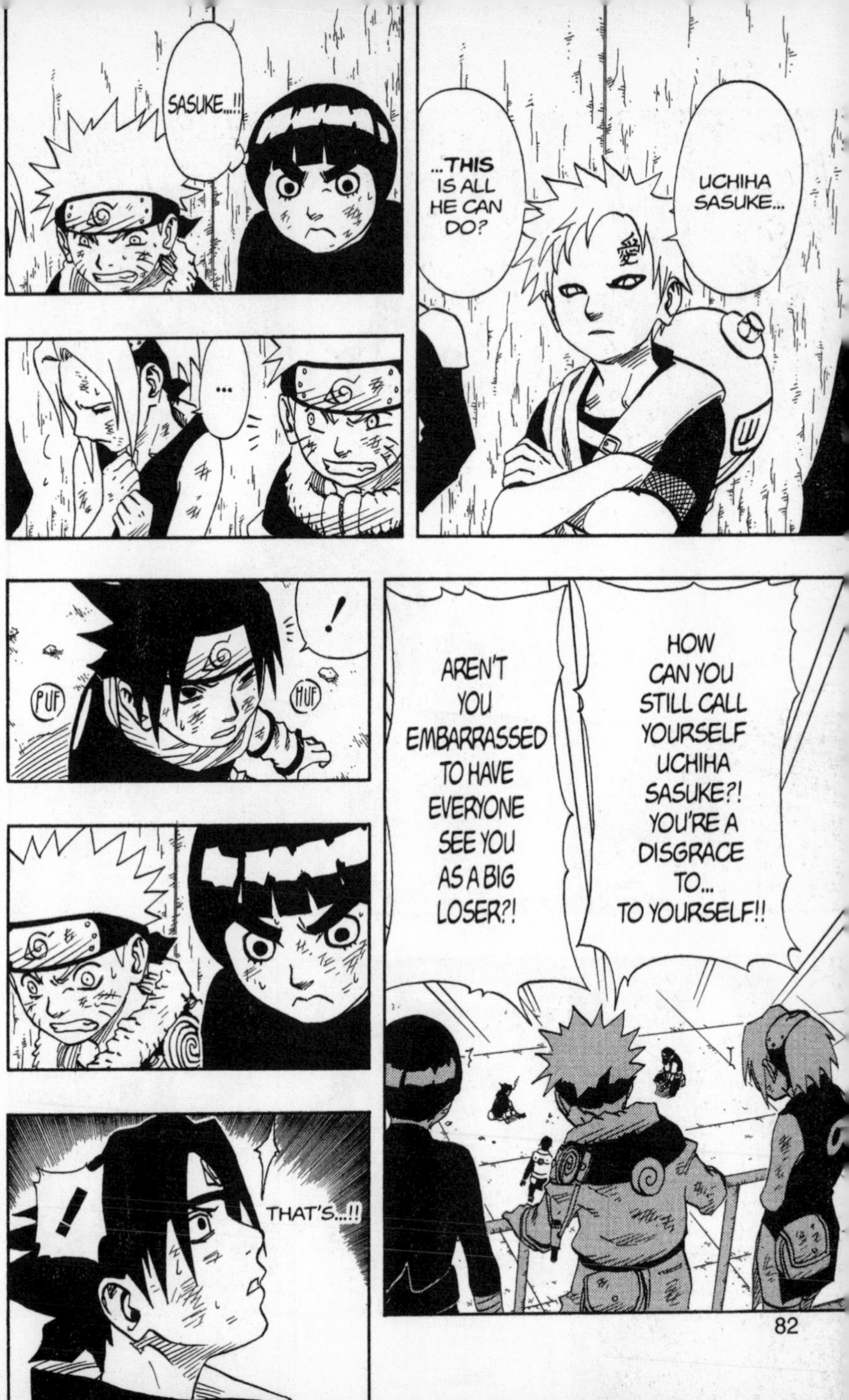
UCHIHA SASUKE...
...THIS IS ALL HE CAN DO?
SASUKE...!!
...
HOW CAN YOU STILL CALL YOURSELF UCHIHA SASUKE?! YOU'RE A DISGRACE TO... TO YOURSELF!!
AREN'T YOU EMBARRASSED TO HAVE EVERYONE SEE YOU AS A BIG LOSER?!
!
HUF
PUF
THAT'S...!!
!

READ THIS WAY

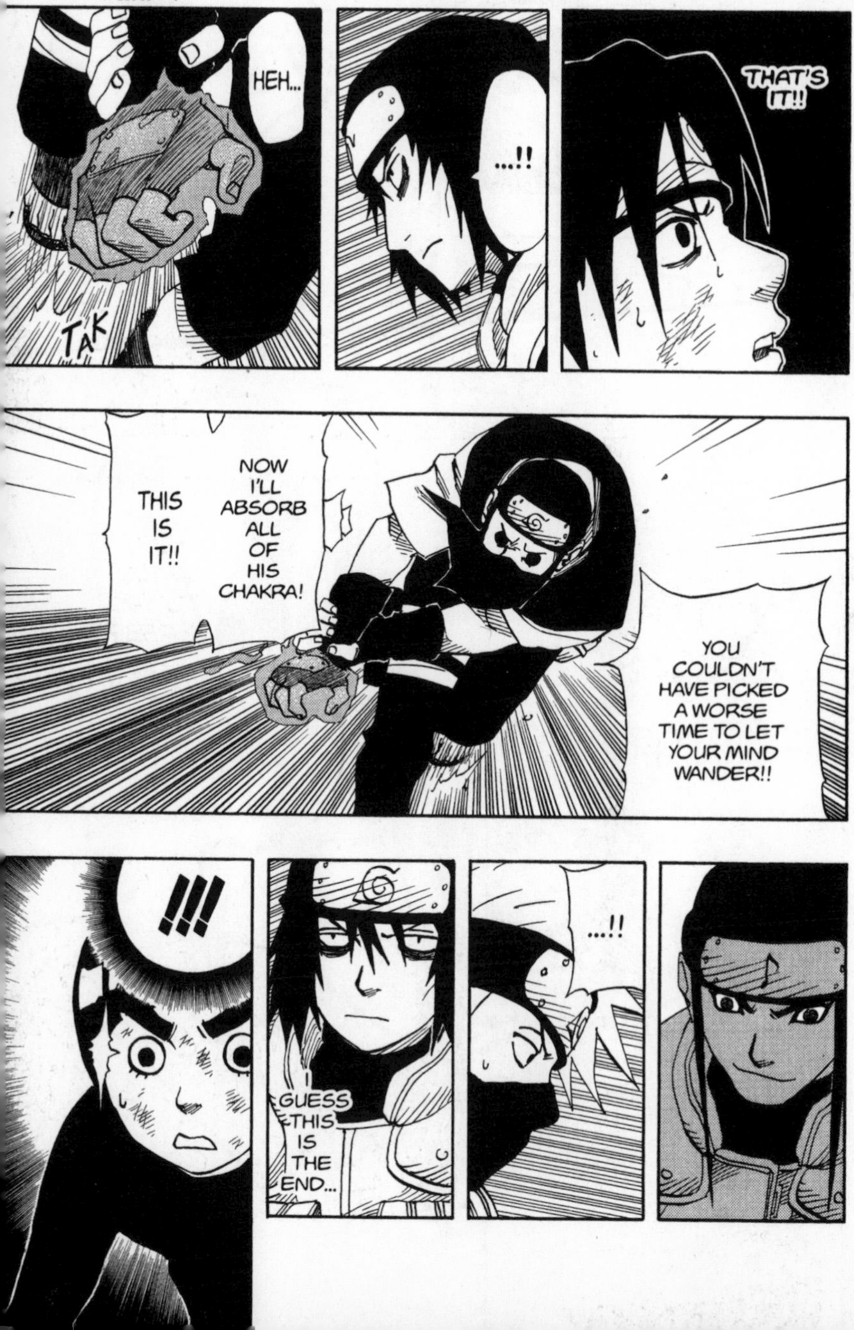
THAT'S IT!!
...!!
HEH...
TAK
YOU COULDN'T HAVE PICKED A WORSE TIME TO LET YOUR MIND WANDER!!
NOW I'LL ABSORB ALL OF HIS CHAKRA!
THIS IS IT!!
...!!
GUESS THIS IS THE END...
!!!

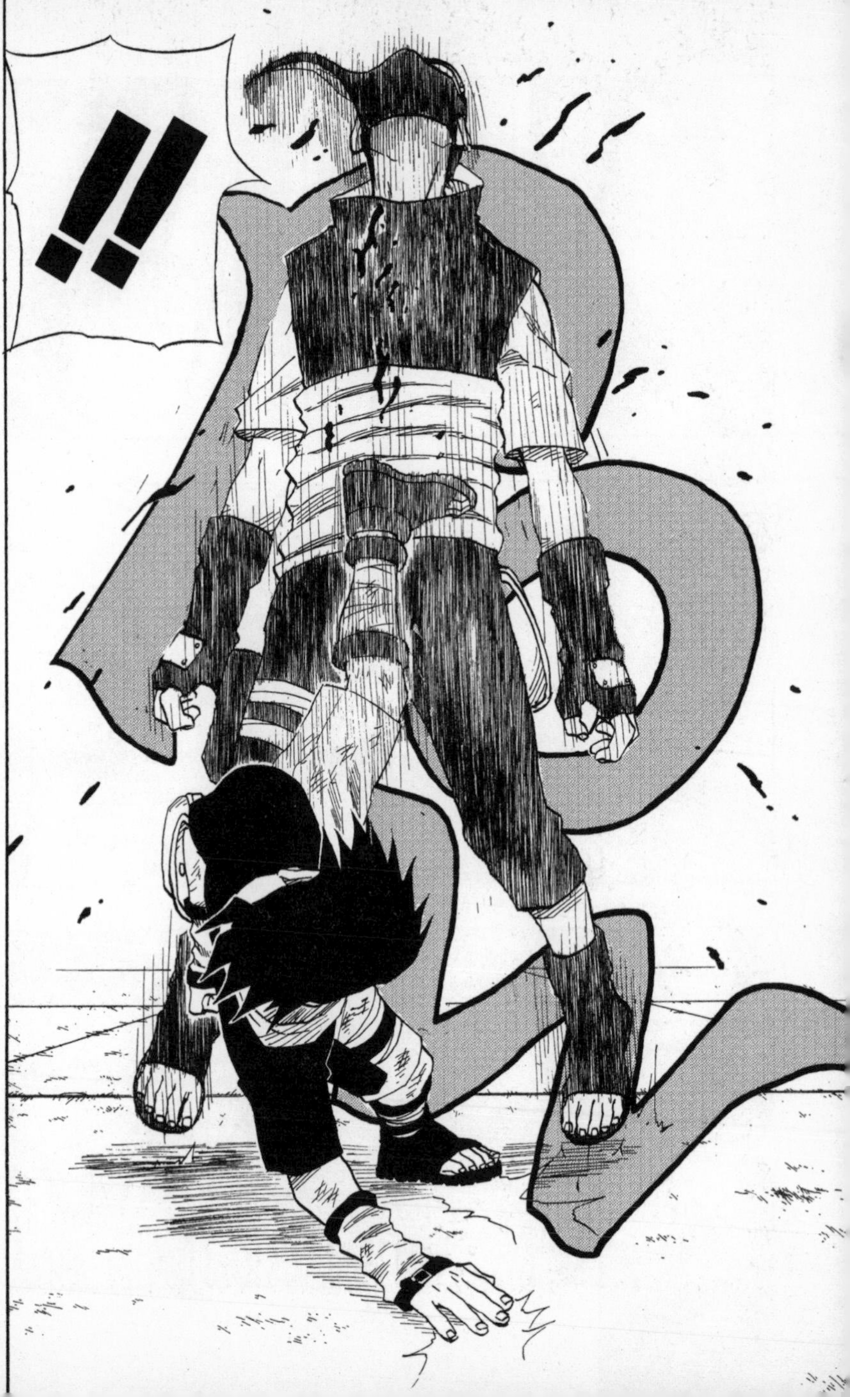
!!

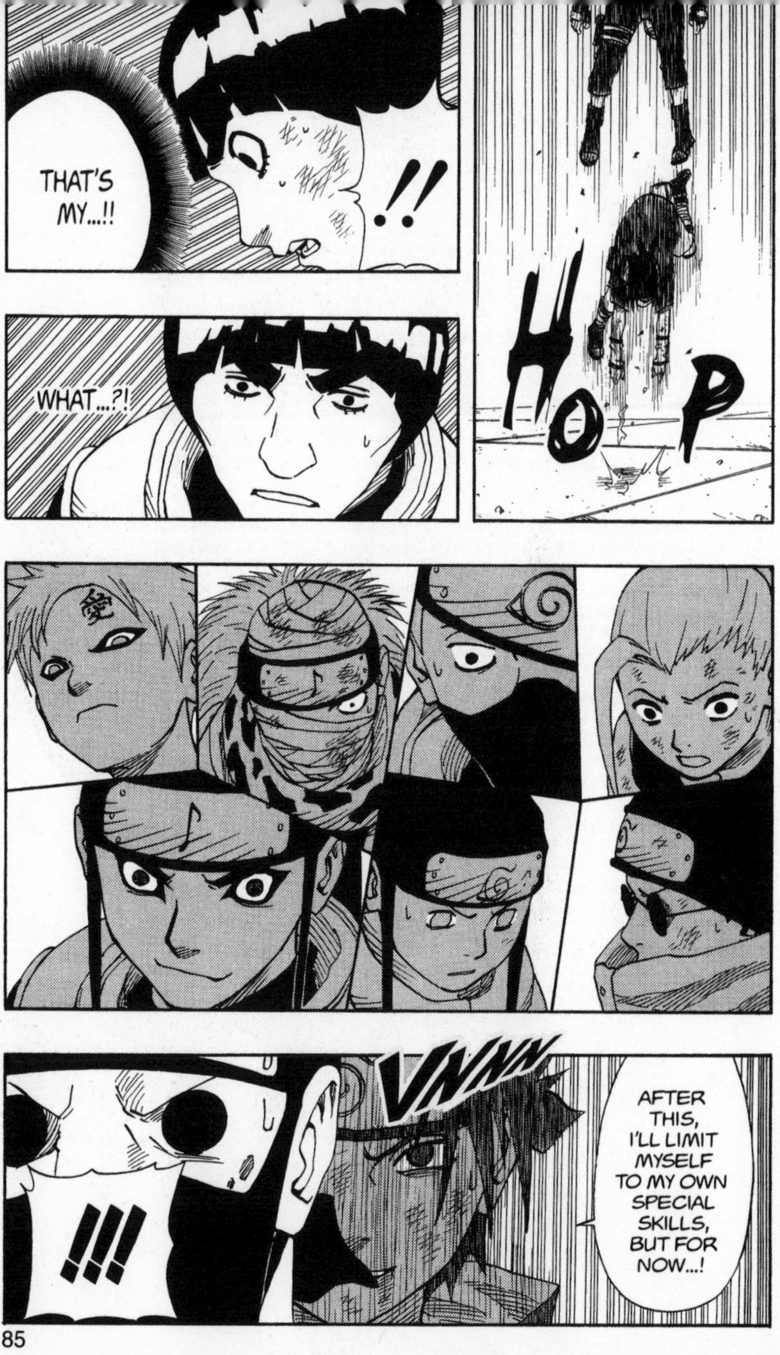
HOP
THAT'S MY...!!
!!
WHAT...?!
VNNN
AFTER THIS, I'LL LIMIT MYSELF TO MY OWN SPECIAL SKILLS, BUT FOR NOW...!
!!!

THE WORLD OF KISHIMOTO MASASHI
MY PERSONAL HISTORY, PART 7.1

SO MUCH HAPPENED DURING MY FINAL YEARS OF ELEMEN-
TARY SCHOOL THAT THERE'S STILL A LOT TO WRITE ABOUT,
SO I'LL CONTINUE...

I'D BECOME SO OBSESSED WITH *DRAGON BALL* THAT, BE-
FORE I HAD EVEN REALIZED IT, MY OWN ART HAD BEGUN TO
SO COMPLETELY MIMIC THE STYLE OF TORIYAMA AKIRA'S
ARTWORK THAT MY DRAWINGS LOOKED JUST LIKE HIS.

AROUND THAT TIME, LOOKING AT THE VIDEO GAME NEWS IN
SHONEN JUMP'S GAME GUIDE INSERT, I SAW ILLUSTRATIONS
THAT LOOKED JUST LIKE MR. TORIYAMA'S.

"WHATEVER IT IS, THIS GAME LOOKS AWESOME!" I THOUGHT,
AND WHEN I PERUSED THE COLUMN MORE CLOSELY AND
REALIZED THAT MR. TORIYAMA HAD DESIGNED THE CHARAC-
TERS, I GOT VERY EXCITED. THAT GAME, NEEDLESS TO SAY,
WAS *DRAGON QUEST*. I REALLY WANTED TO PLAY IT, BUT BACK
THEN THAT WAS AN UNREACHABLE DREAM FOR ME. AT THAT
TIME, I DIDN'T EVEN HAVE A FAMICOM ("FAMILY COMPUTER"--
THE ORIGINAL NINTENDO GAME SYSTEM) THOUGH MOST OF
MY CLASSMATES DID OWN ONE.

BEGGING MY PARENTS WOULDN'T HAVE WORKED, BECAUSE
MY FATHER WAS VERY STRICT. IF I SO MUCH AS BREATHED THE
WORD "GAME," HE'D LECTURE ME AND TELL ME TO GO STUDY.
THAT'S WHEN MY LITTLE TWIN BROTHER HAD AN INCREDIBLE
EPIPHANY AND SAID, "OUR ONLY HOPE IS TO HAVE SOMEONE
GIVE US A FAMICOM!!" AND HE STARTED NEGOTIATING WITH
SOME OF OUR FRIENDS WHO HE THOUGHT WERE LIKELY
PROSPECTS. I DOUBTED THAT ANY OF THOSE KIDS WOULD
JUST GIVE AWAY SOMETHING THAT COST OVER 10,000 YEN
(ABOUT 100 U.S. DOLLARS)... UNTIL... VOILA! ONE OF OUR
FRIENDS ACTUALLY PRESENTED US WITH HIS FAMICOM!
IN THAT MOMENT, THAT KID'S GENEROSITY MADE HIM SEEM
LIKE A GOD TO ME!

Number 68: Blood of the Uchiha

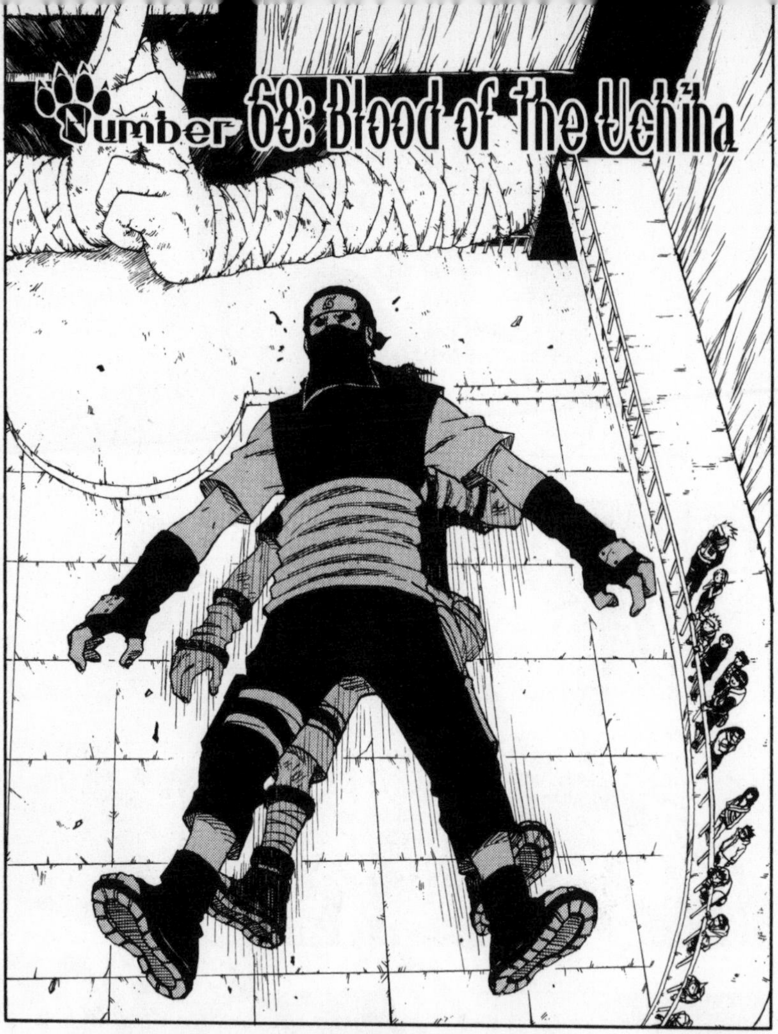

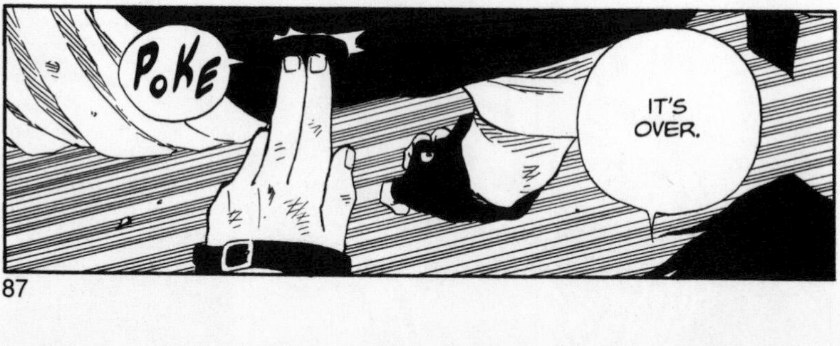
IT'S OVER.
POKE

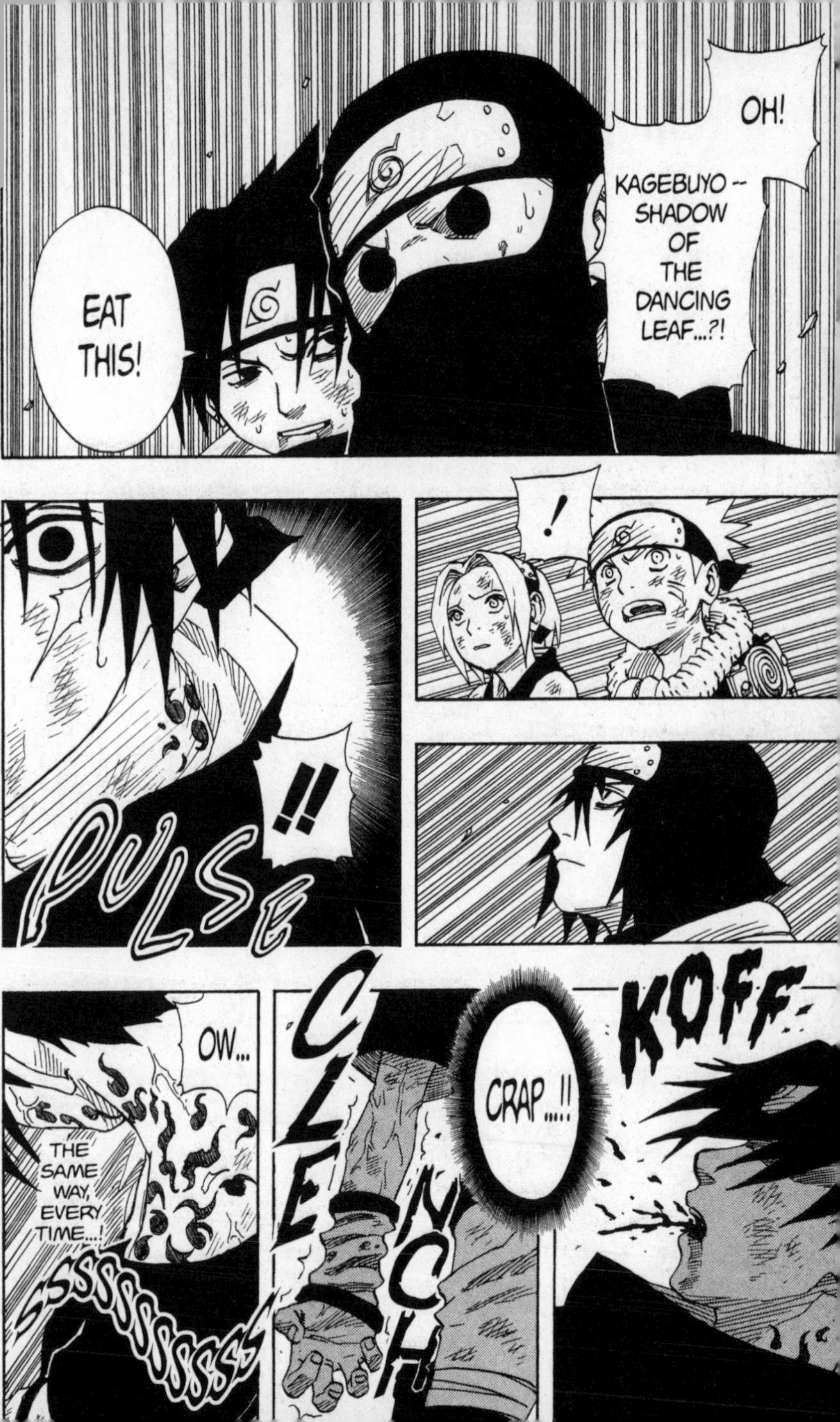
OH!
KAGEBUYO -- SHADOW OF THE DANCING LEAF...?!
EAT THIS!
!
!!
PULSE
KOFF
CRAP...!!
CLENCH
OW...
THE SAME WAY, EVERY TIME...!
SSSSSSSSSSSSS

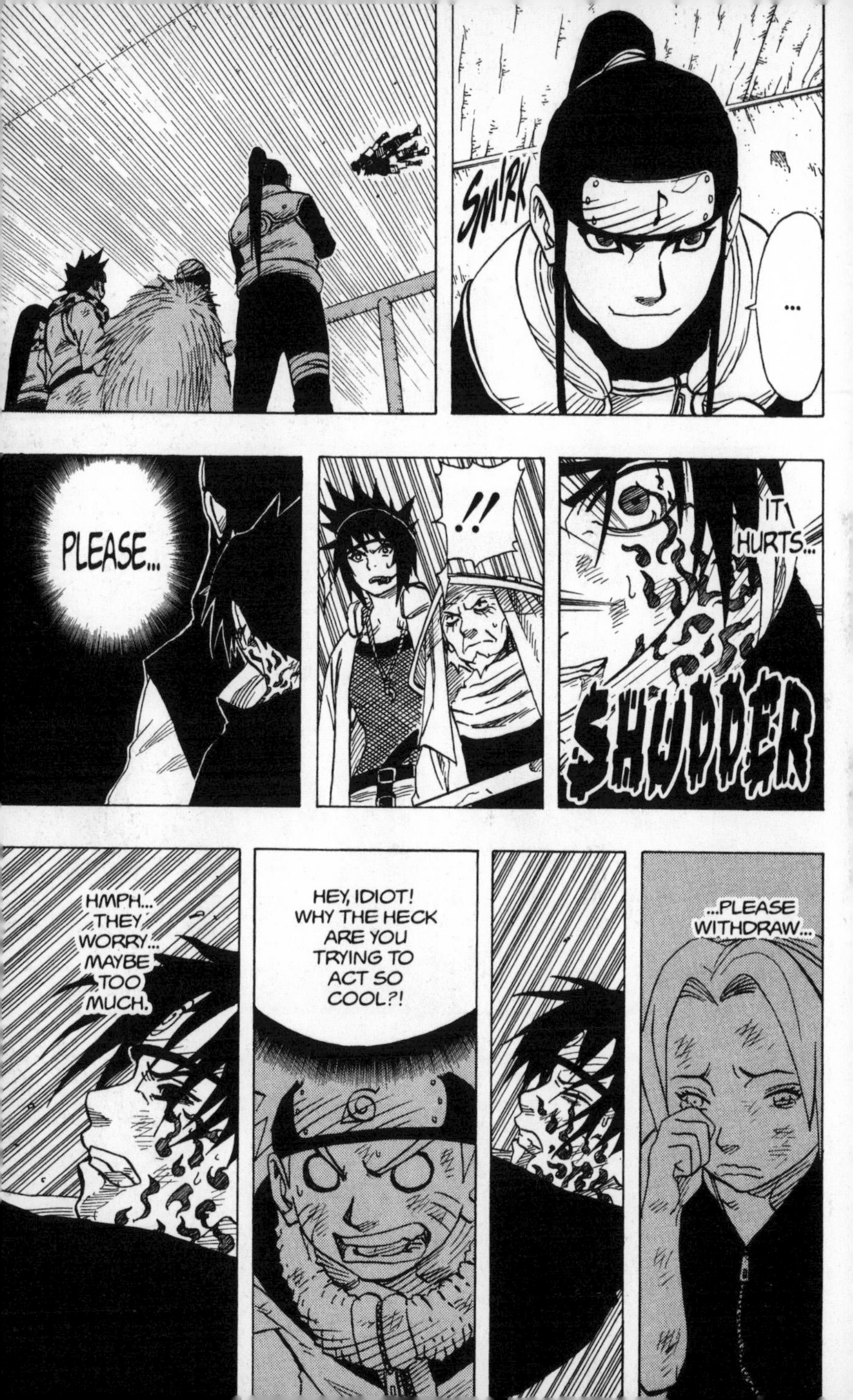
SMIRK
...
IT HURTS...
SHUDDER
!!
PLEASE...
...PLEASE WITHDRAW...
HEY, IDIOT! WHY THE HECK ARE YOU TRYING TO ACT SO COOL?!
HMPH... THEY WORRY... MAYBE TOO MUCH.

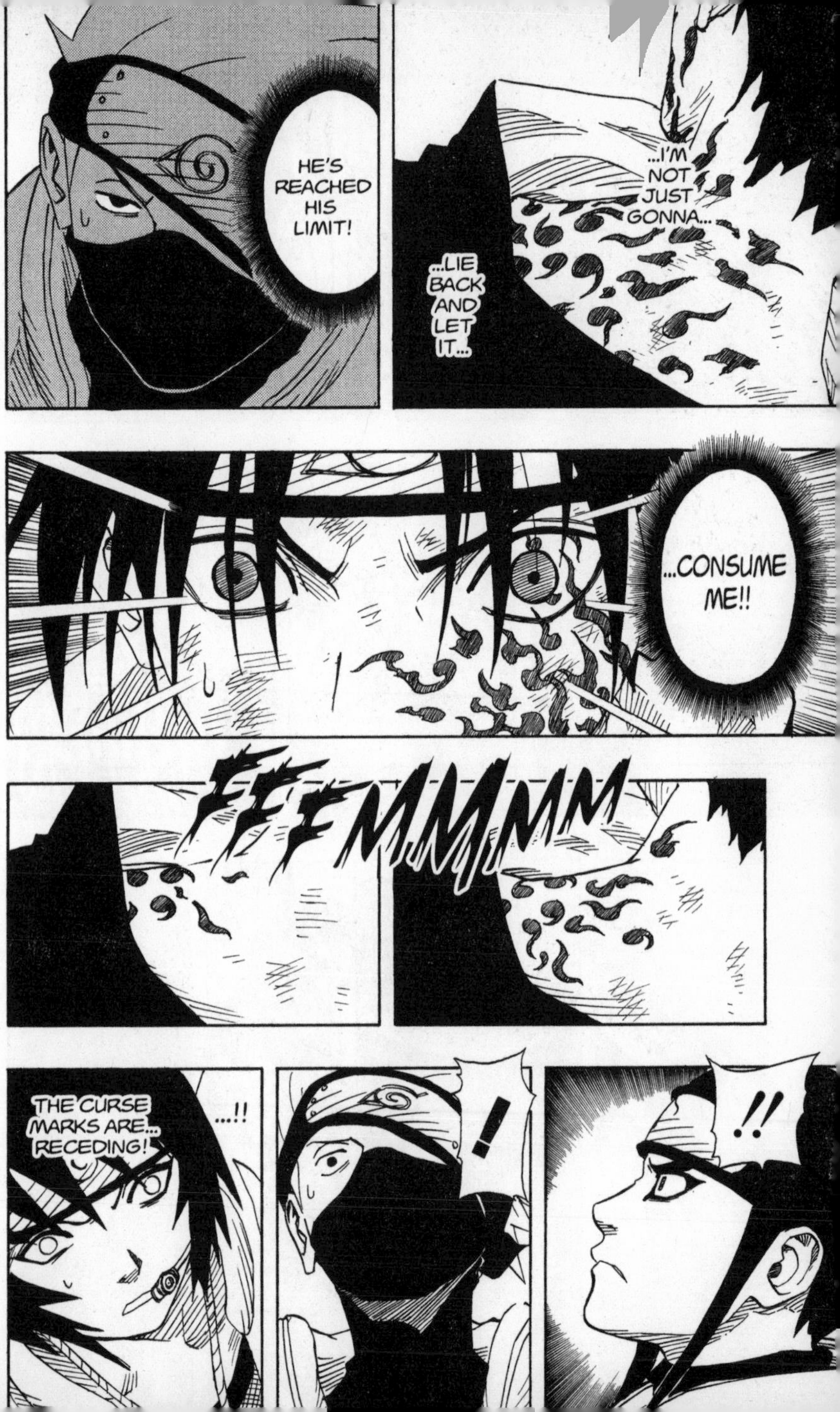

...I'M NOT JUST GONNA...
...LIE BACK AND LET IT...
HE'S REACHED HIS LIMIT!
...CONSUME ME!!
FFFMMMMM
!!
!
...!!
THE CURSE MARKS ARE... RECEDING!

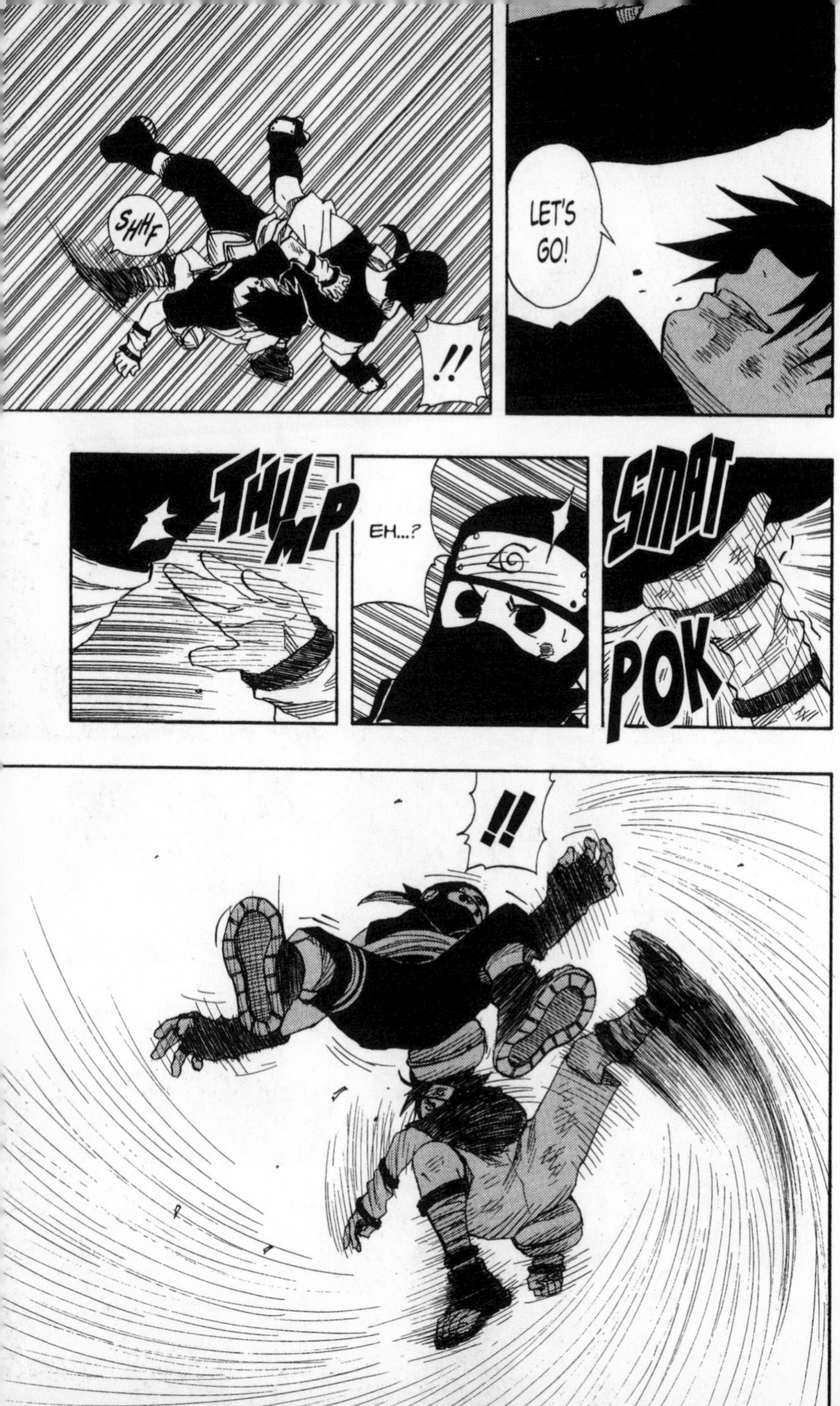
LET'S GO!
SHHF
!!
SMAT
POK
EH...?
THUMP
!!

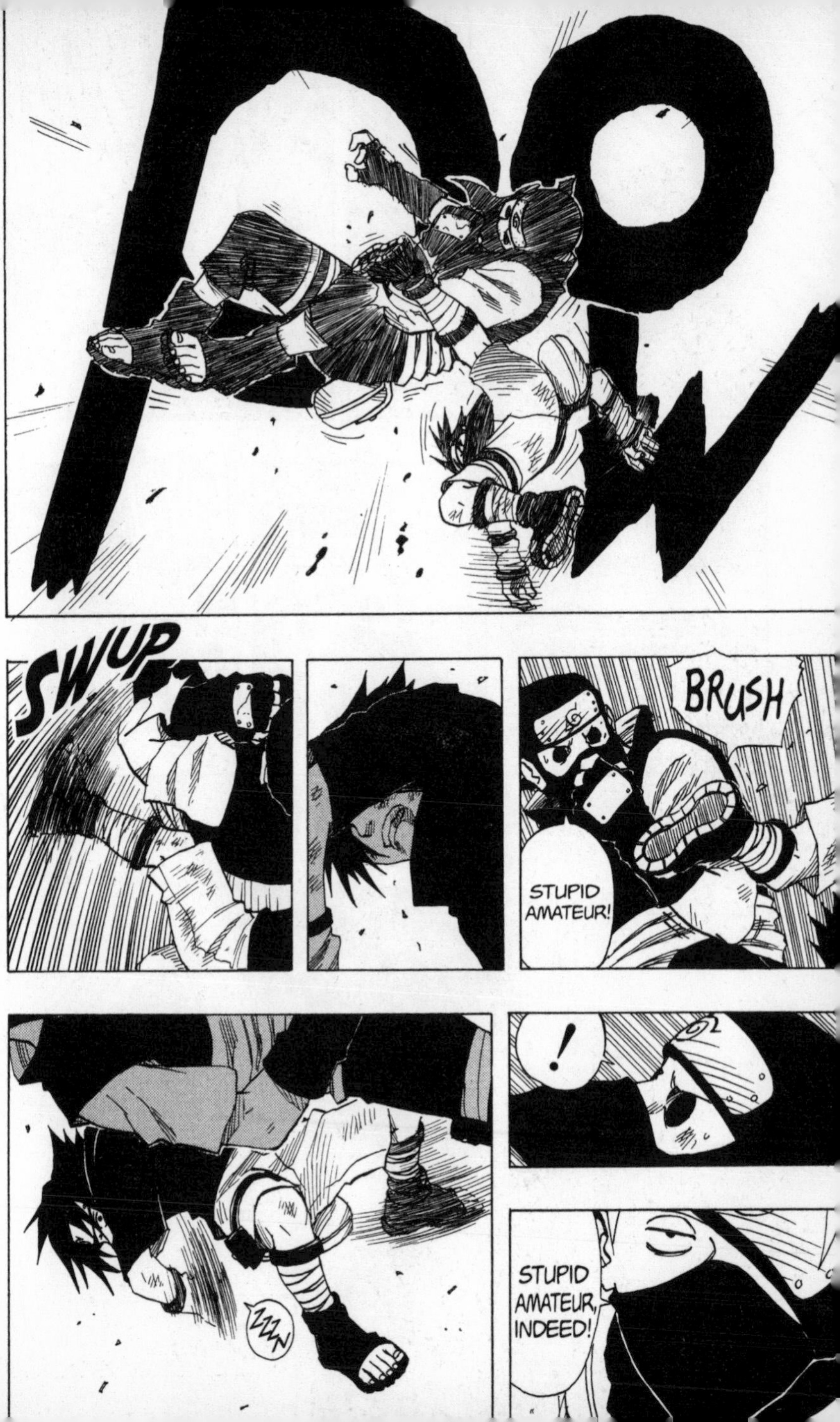
POW
BRUSH
STUPID AMATEUR!
SWUP
!
STUPID AMATEUR, INDEED!

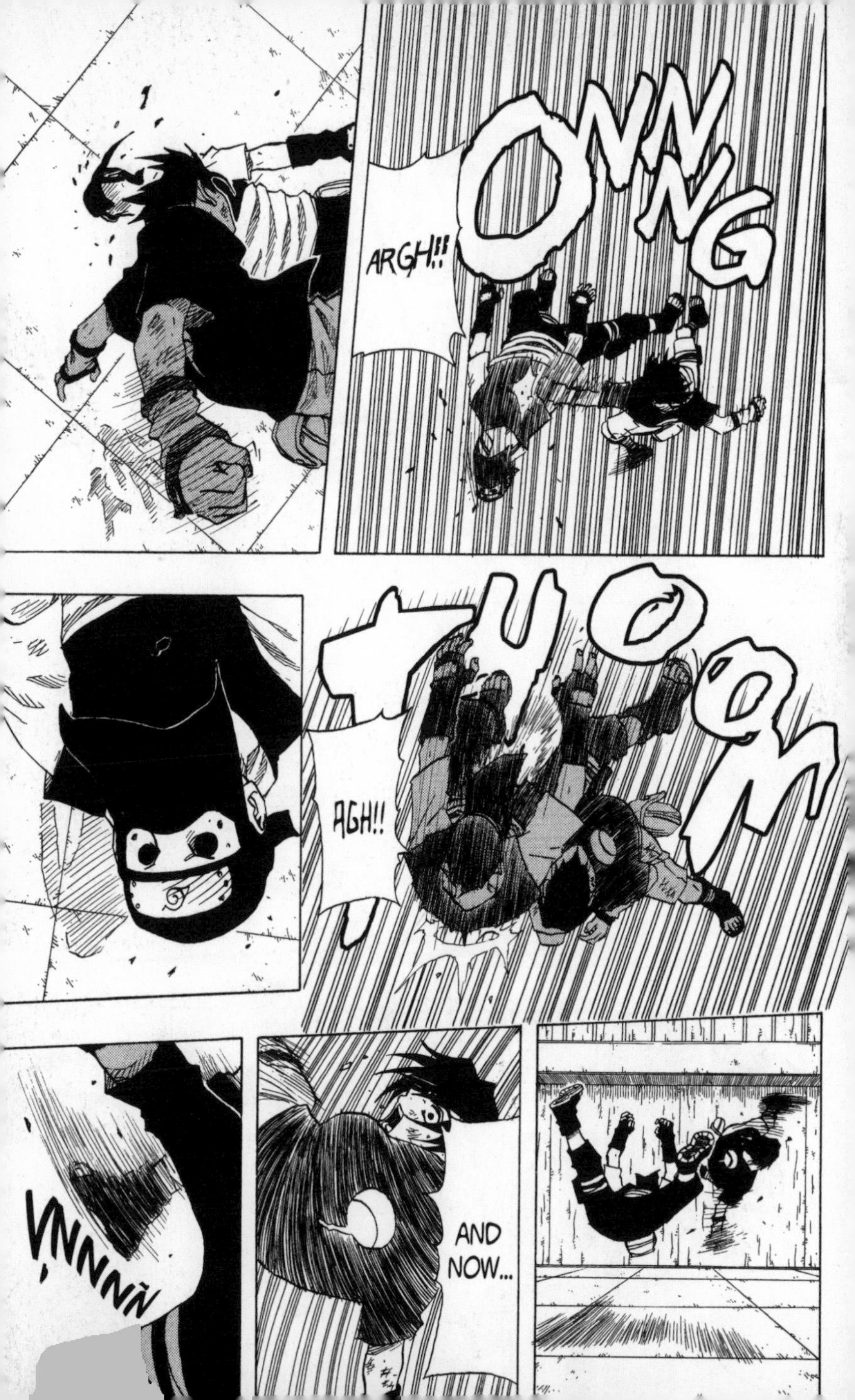
ARGH!!
AGH!!
AND NOW...

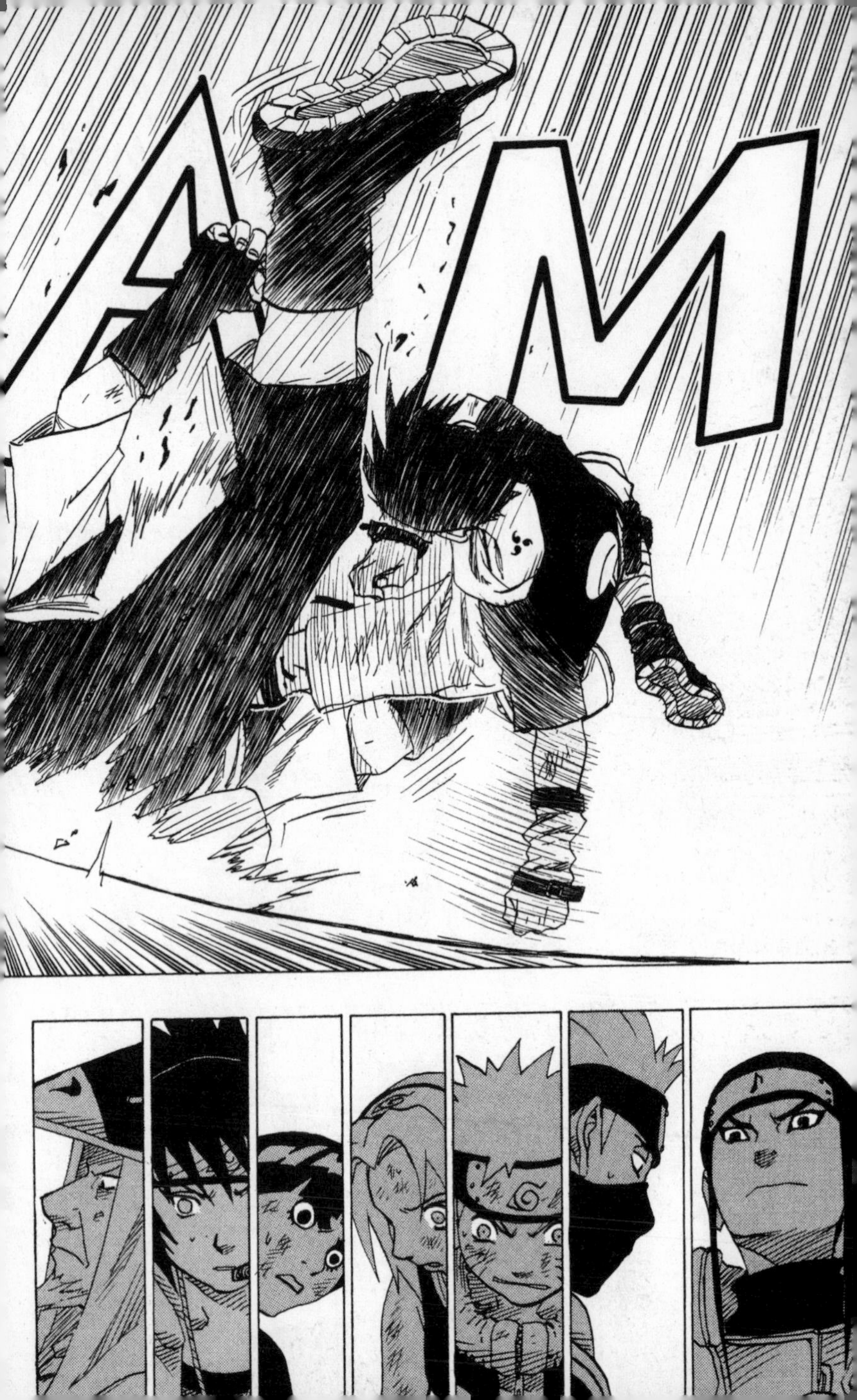
AM

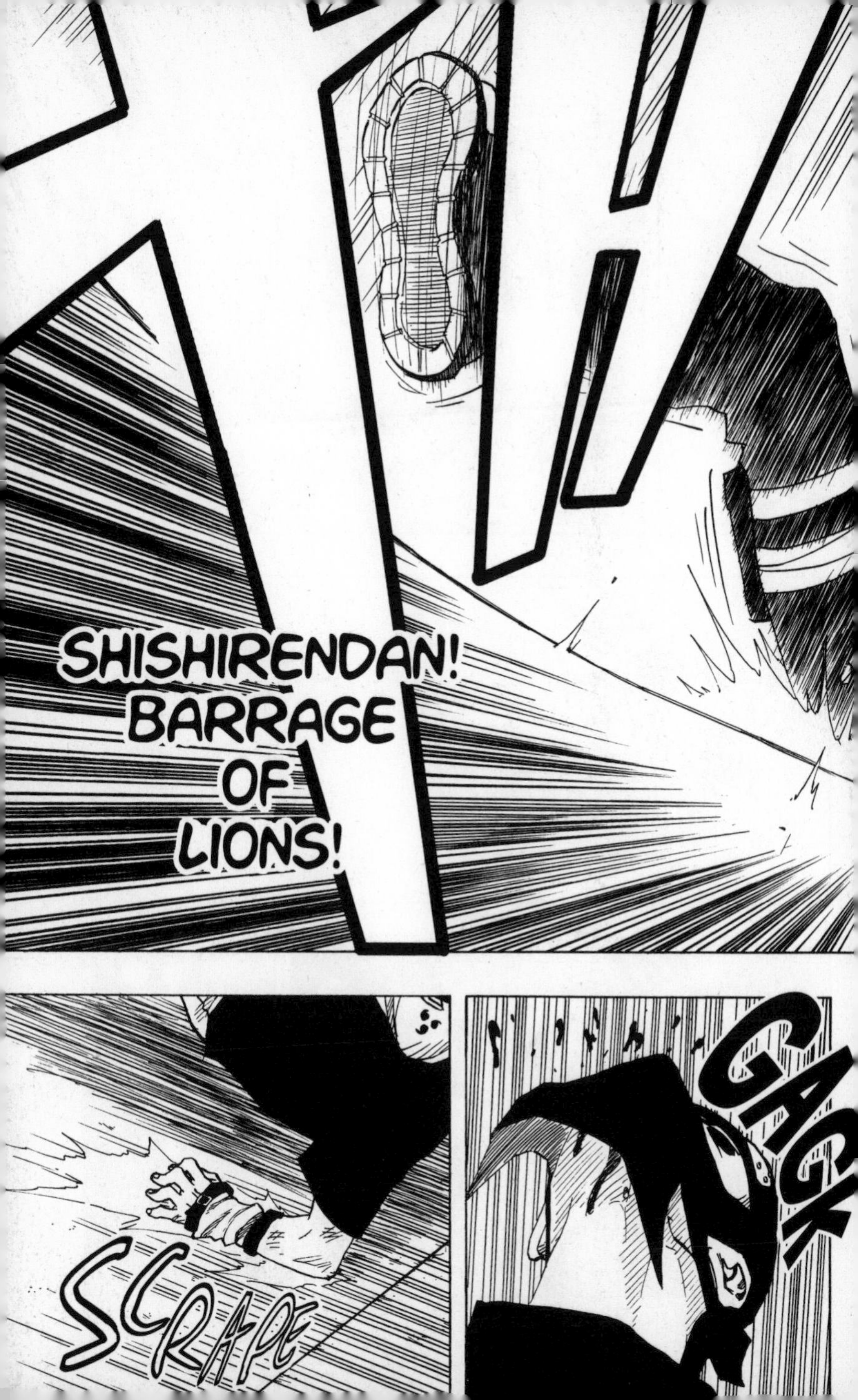
SHISHIRENDAN! BARRAGE OF LIONS!
GACK
SCRAPE

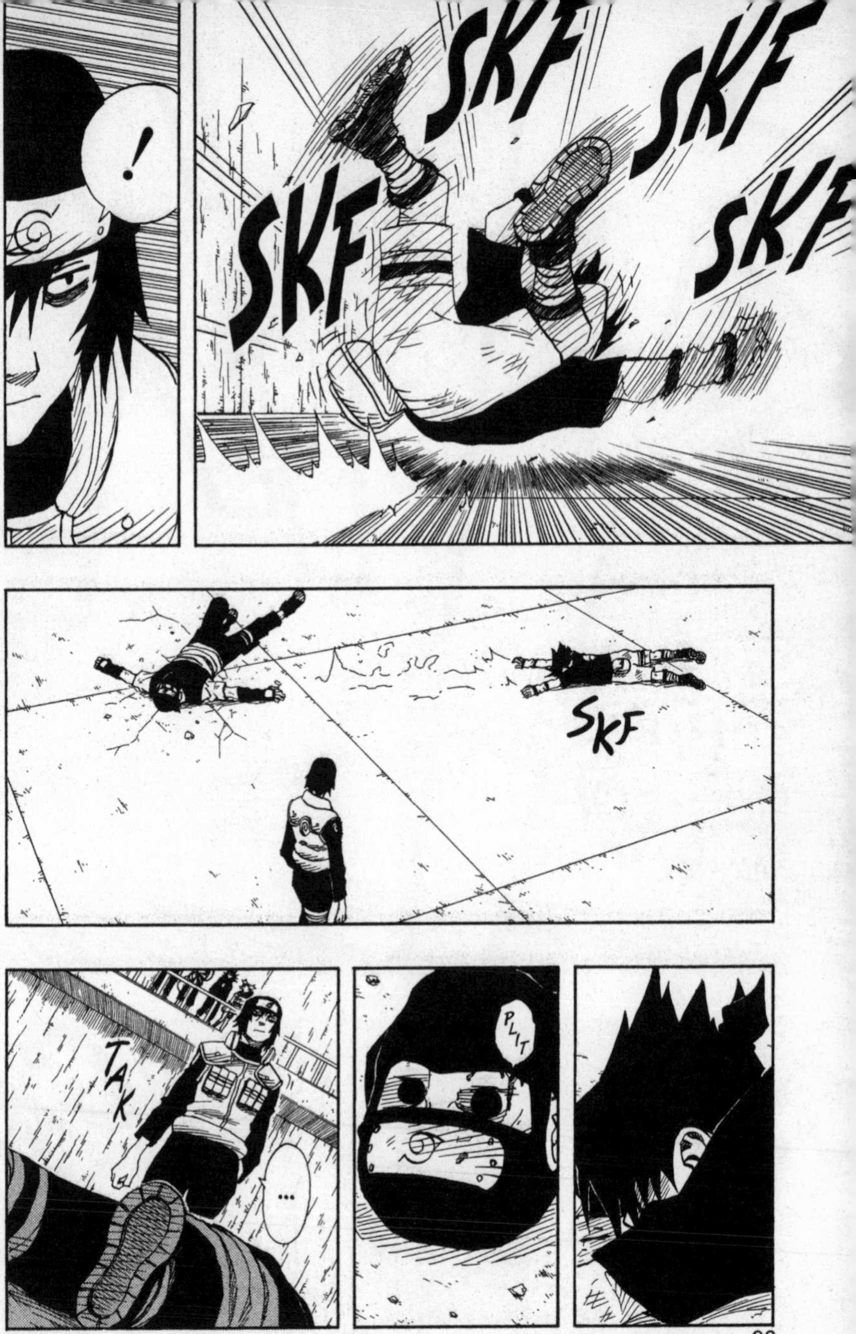
SKF
SKF
SKF
SKF
SKF
!
SKF
PLIT
TAK
...

READ THIS WAY

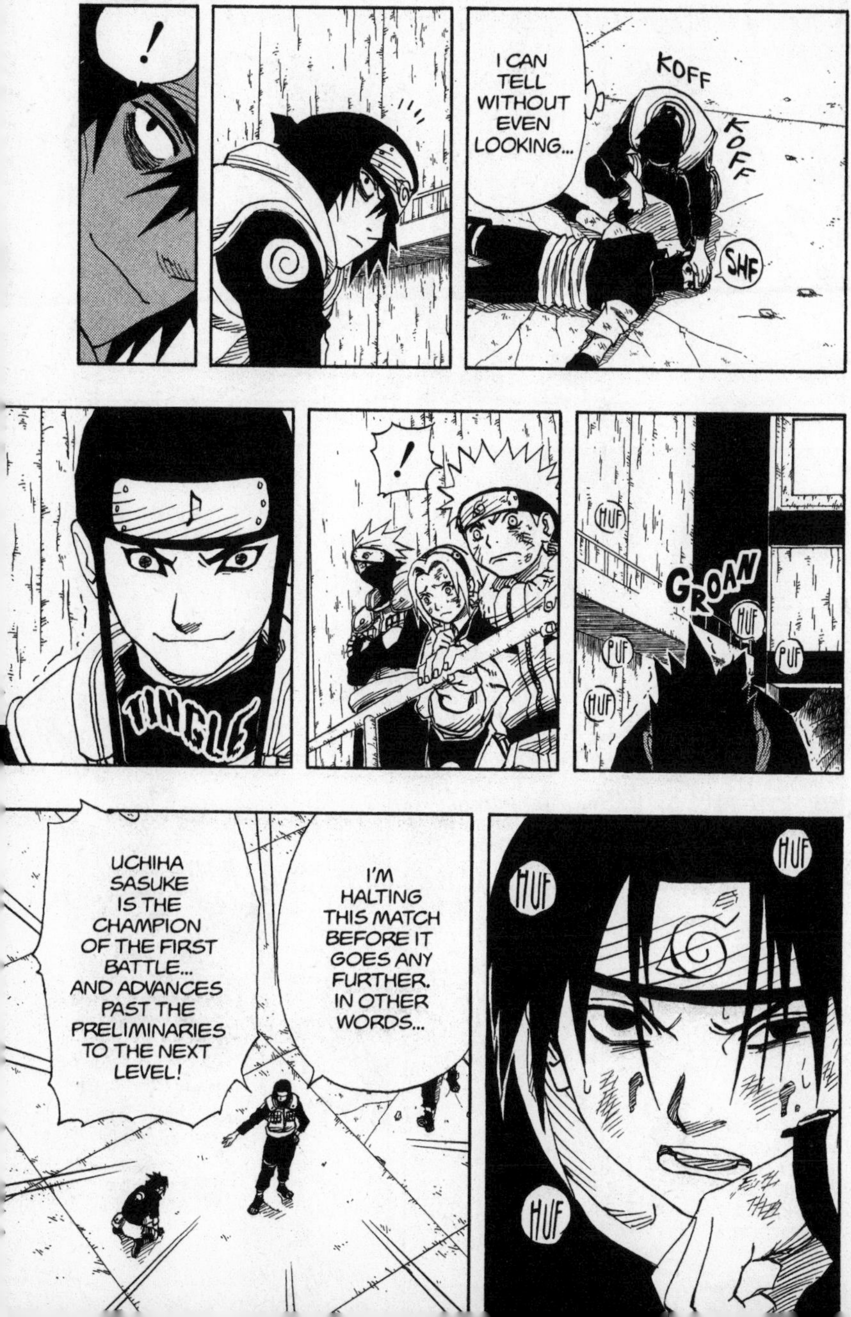
I CAN TELL WITHOUT EVEN LOOKING...
KOFF
KOFF
SHF
!
HUF
GROAN
HUF
PUF
PUF
HUF
!
TINGLE
HUF
HUF
HUF
I'M HALTING THIS MATCH BEFORE IT GOES ANY FURTHER. IN OTHER WORDS...
UCHIHA SASUKE IS THE CHAMPION OF THE FIRST BATTLE... AND ADVANCES PAST THE PRELIMINARIES TO THE NEXT LEVEL!

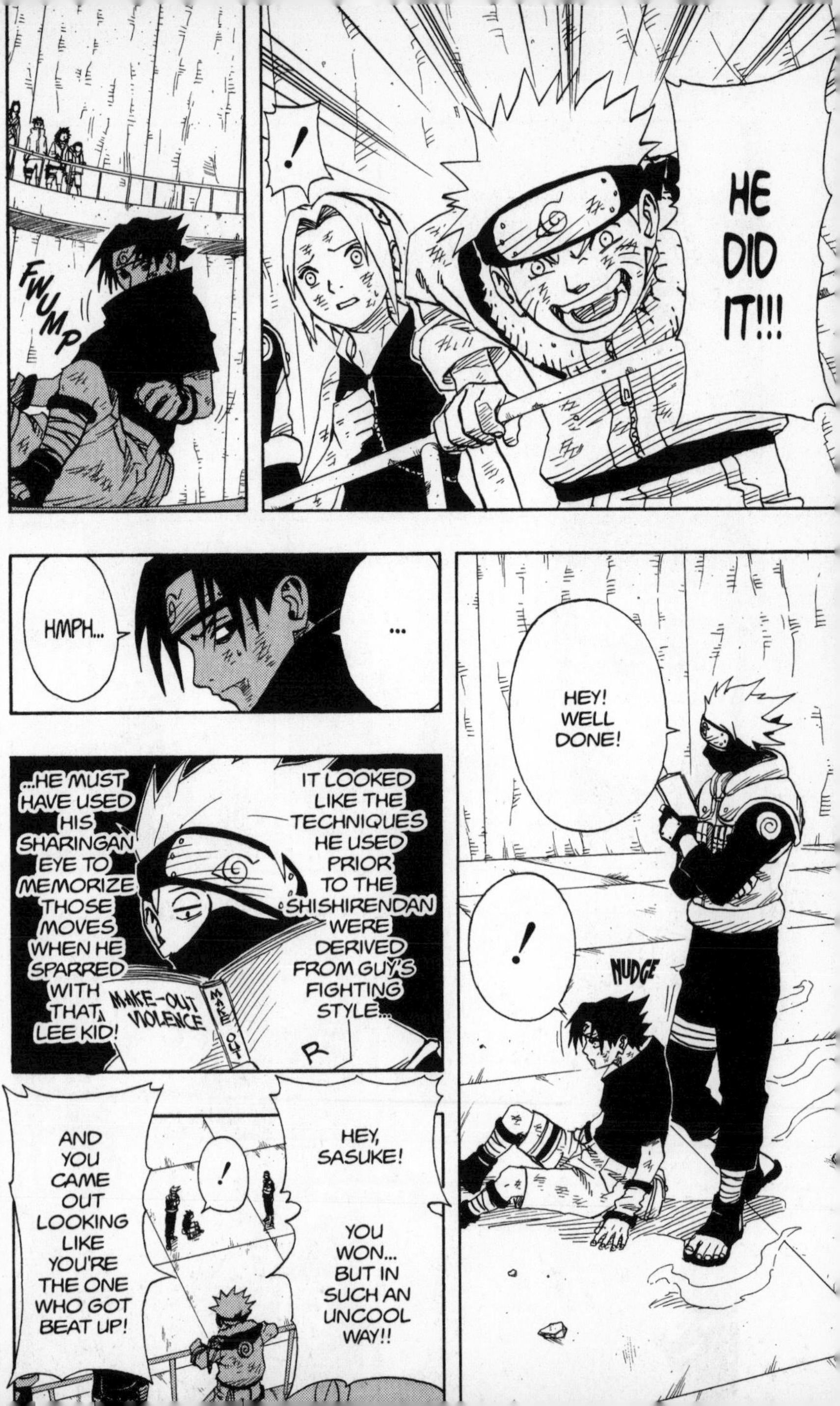
HE DID IT!!!
!
FWUMP
HEY! WELL DONE!
!
NUDGE
...
HMPH...
IT LOOKED LIKE THE TECHNIQUES HE USED PRIOR TO THE SHISHIRENDAN WERE DERIVED FROM GUY'S FIGHTING STYLE...
...HE MUST HAVE USED HIS SHARINGAN EYE TO MEMORIZE THOSE MOVES WHEN HE SPARRED WITH THAT LEE KID!
MAKE-OUT VIOLENCE
MAKE OUT
HEY, SASUKE!
YOU WON... BUT IN SUCH AN UNCOOL WAY!!
!
AND YOU CAME OUT LOOKING LIKE YOU'RE THE ONE WHO GOT BEAT UP!

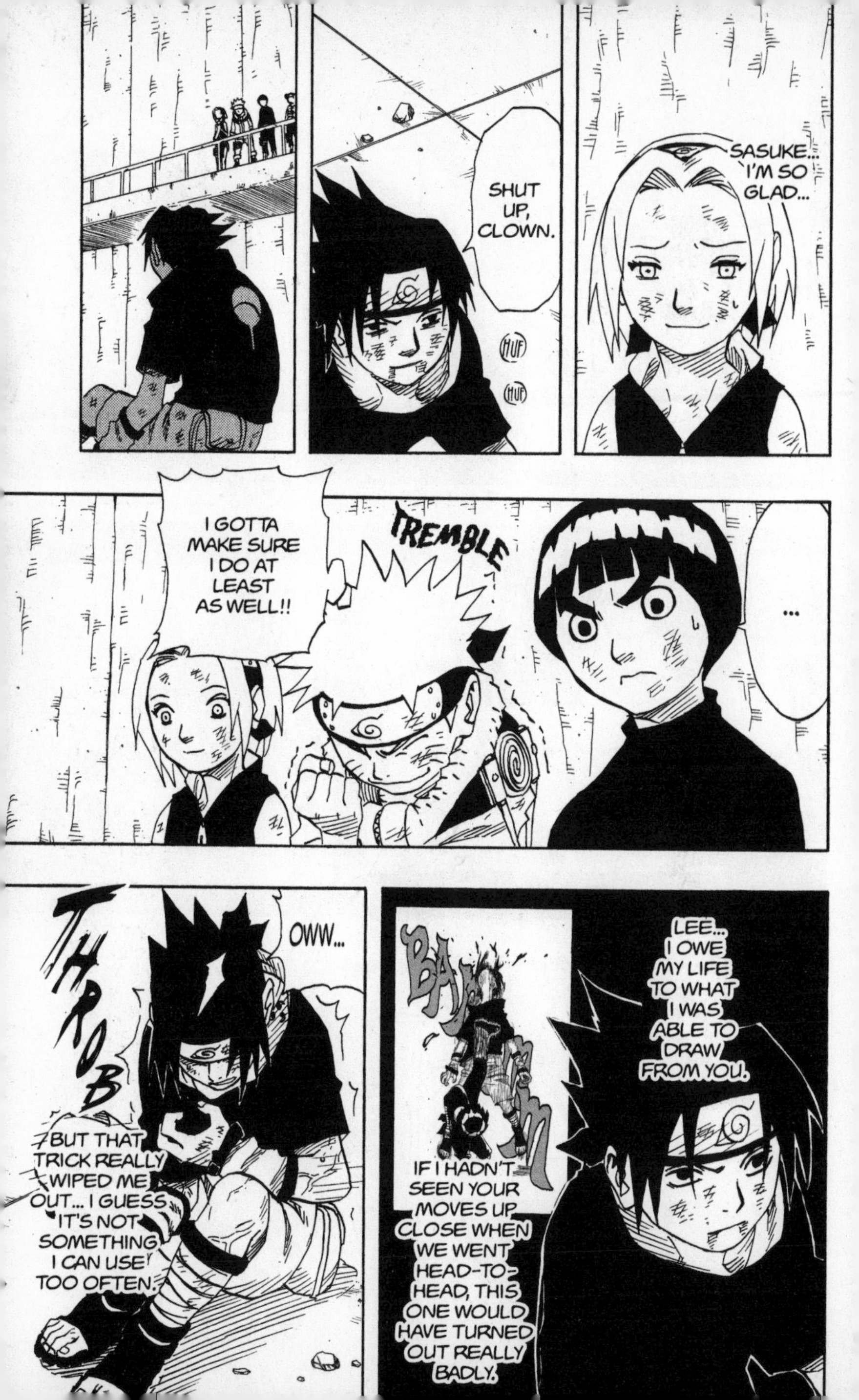
SASUKE... I'M SO GLAD...
SHUT UP, CLOWN.
HUF
HUF
...
TREMBLE
I GOTTA MAKE SURE I DO AT LEAST AS WELL!!
LEE... I OWE MY LIFE TO WHAT I WAS ABLE TO DRAW FROM YOU.
IF I HADN'T SEEN YOUR MOVES UP CLOSE WHEN WE WENT HEAD-TO-HEAD, THIS ONE WOULD HAVE TURNED OUT REALLY BADLY.
OWW...
THROB
BUT THAT TRICK REALLY WIPED ME OUT... I GUESS IT'S NOT SOMETHING I CAN USE TOO OFTEN.

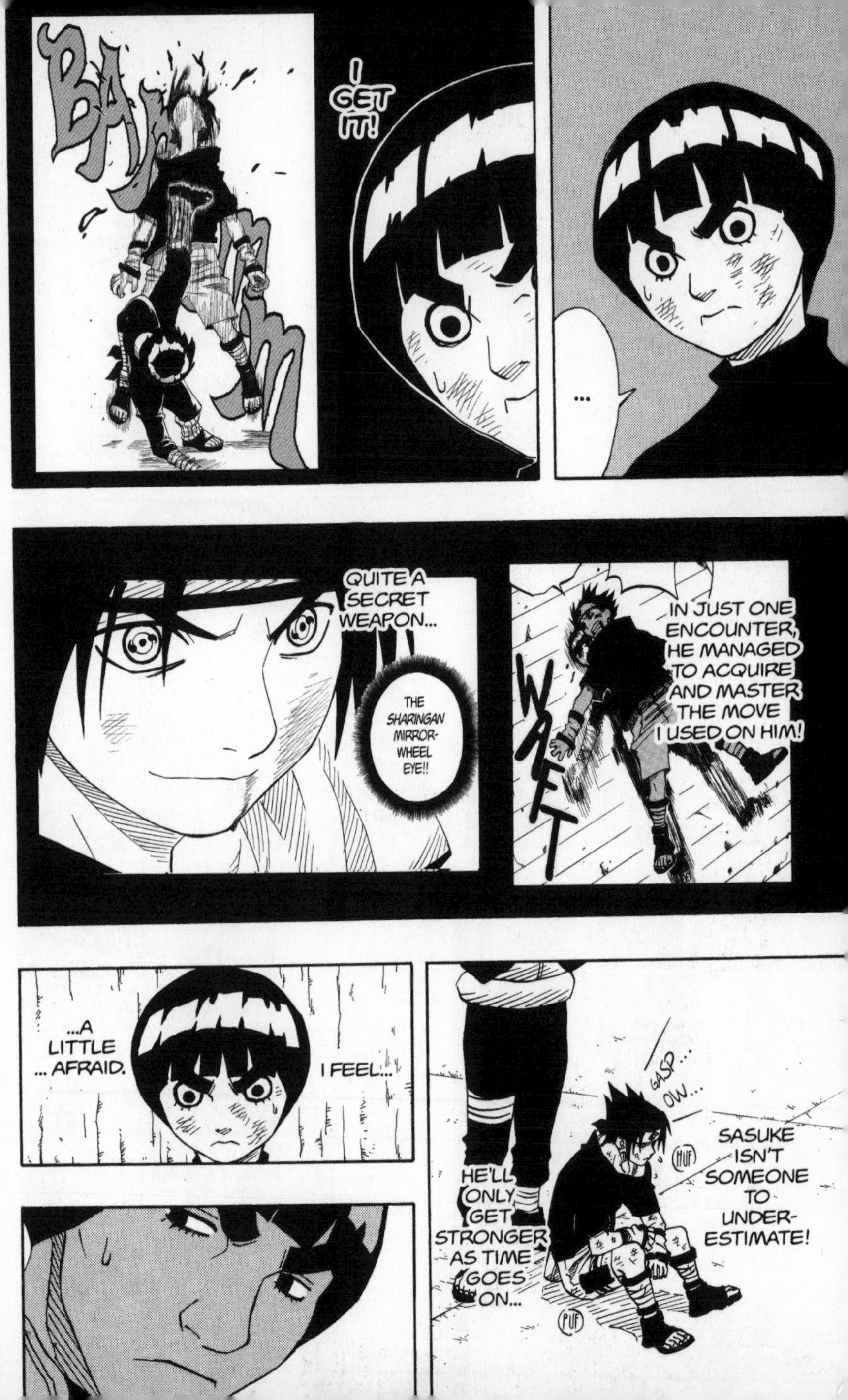
...
I GET IT!
BAM
IN JUST ONE ENCOUNTER, HE MANAGED TO ACQUIRE AND MASTER THE MOVE I USED ON HIM!
QUITE A SECRET WEAPON...
THE SHARINGAN MIRROR-WHEEL EYE!!
GASP... OW...
SASUKE ISN'T SOMEONE TO UNDER-ESTIMATE!
HUF
HE'LL ONLY GET STRONGER AS TIME GOES ON...
PUF
I FEEL...
...A LITTLE ... AFRAID.

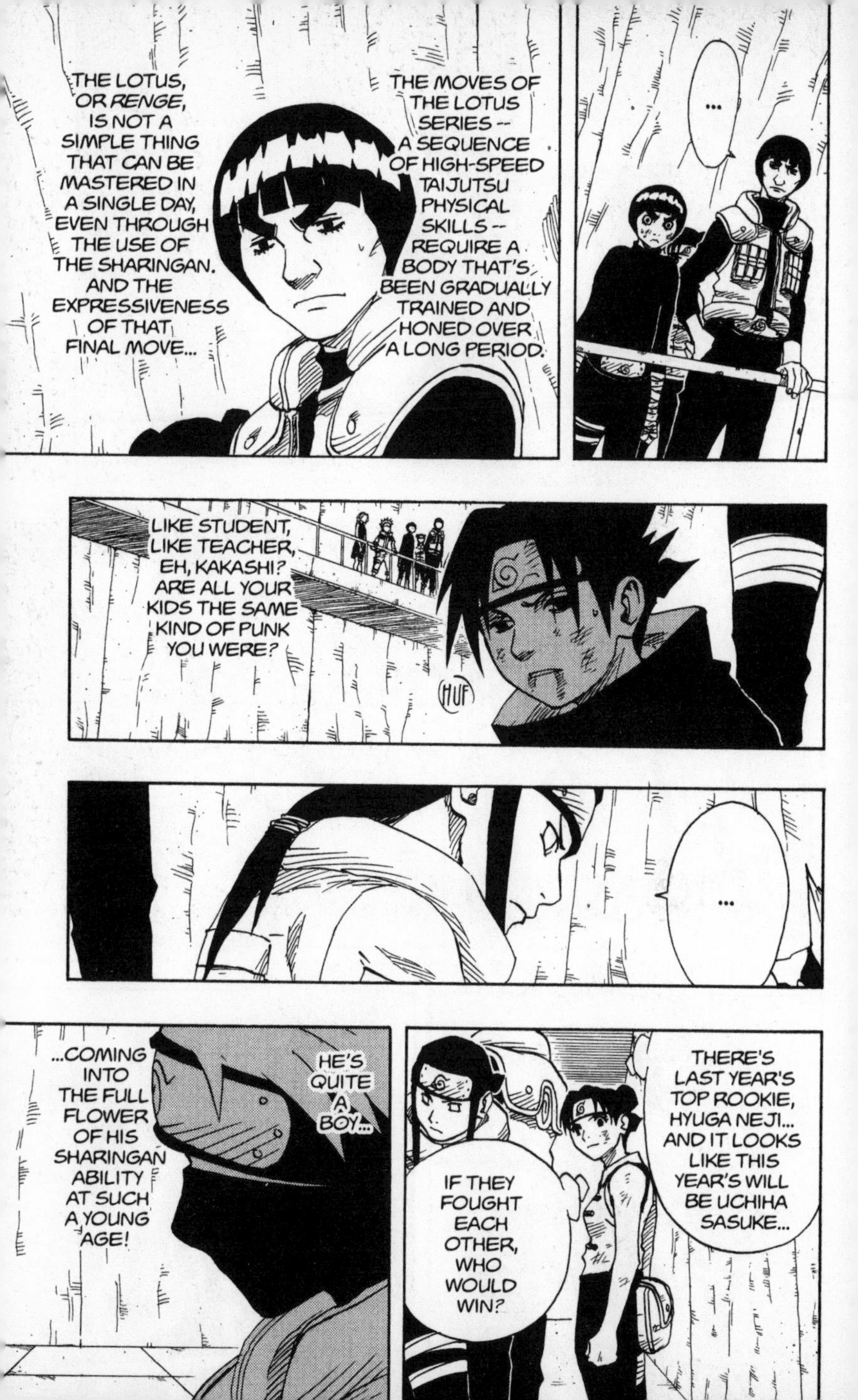
...
THE MOVES OF THE LOTUS SERIES -- A SEQUENCE OF HIGH-SPEED TAIJUTSU PHYSICAL SKILLS -- REQUIRE A BODY THAT'S BEEN GRADUALLY TRAINED AND HONED OVER A LONG PERIOD.
THE LOTUS, OR RENGE, IS NOT A SIMPLE THING THAT CAN BE MASTERED IN A SINGLE DAY, EVEN THROUGH THE USE OF THE SHARINGAN. AND THE EXPRESSIVENESS OF THAT FINAL MOVE...
LIKE STUDENT, LIKE TEACHER, EH, KAKASHI? ARE ALL YOUR KIDS THE SAME KIND OF PUNK YOU WERE?
HUF
...
THERE'S LAST YEAR'S TOP ROOKIE, HYUGA NEJI... AND IT LOOKS LIKE THIS YEAR'S WILL BE UCHIHA SASUKE...
IF THEY FOUGHT EACH OTHER, WHO WOULD WIN?
HE'S QUITE A BOY...
...COMING INTO THE FULL FLOWER OF HIS SHARINGAN ABILITY AT SUCH A YOUNG AGE!

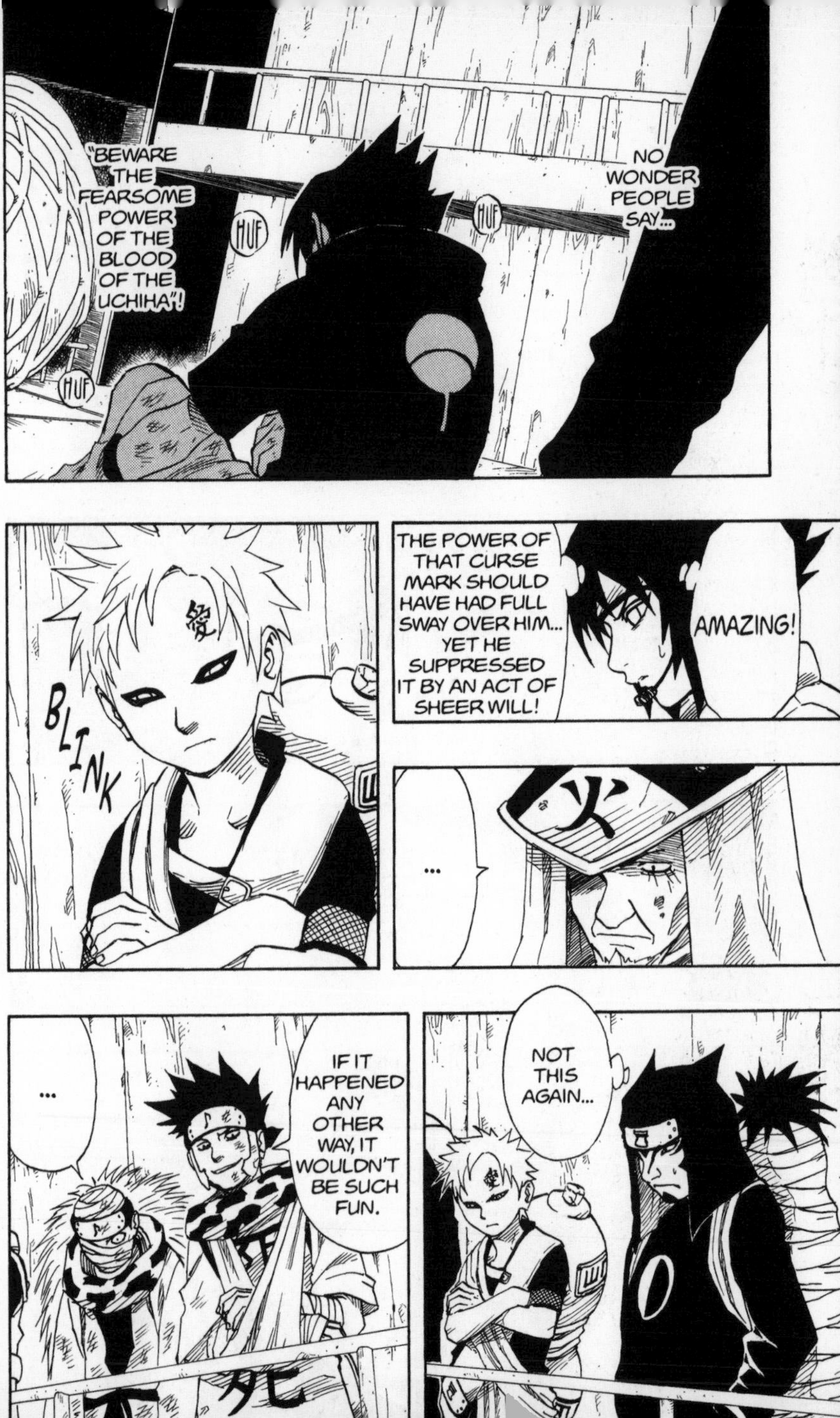
NO WONDER PEOPLE SAY...
HUF
HUF
"BEWARE THE FEARSOME POWER OF THE BLOOD OF THE UCHIHA"!
HUF
AMAZING!
THE POWER OF THAT CURSE MARK SHOULD HAVE HAD FULL SWAY OVER HIM... YET HE SUPPRESSED IT BY AN ACT OF SHEER WILL!
...
BLINK
NOT THIS AGAIN...
IF IT HAPPENED ANY OTHER WAY, IT WOULDN'T BE SUCH FUN.
...

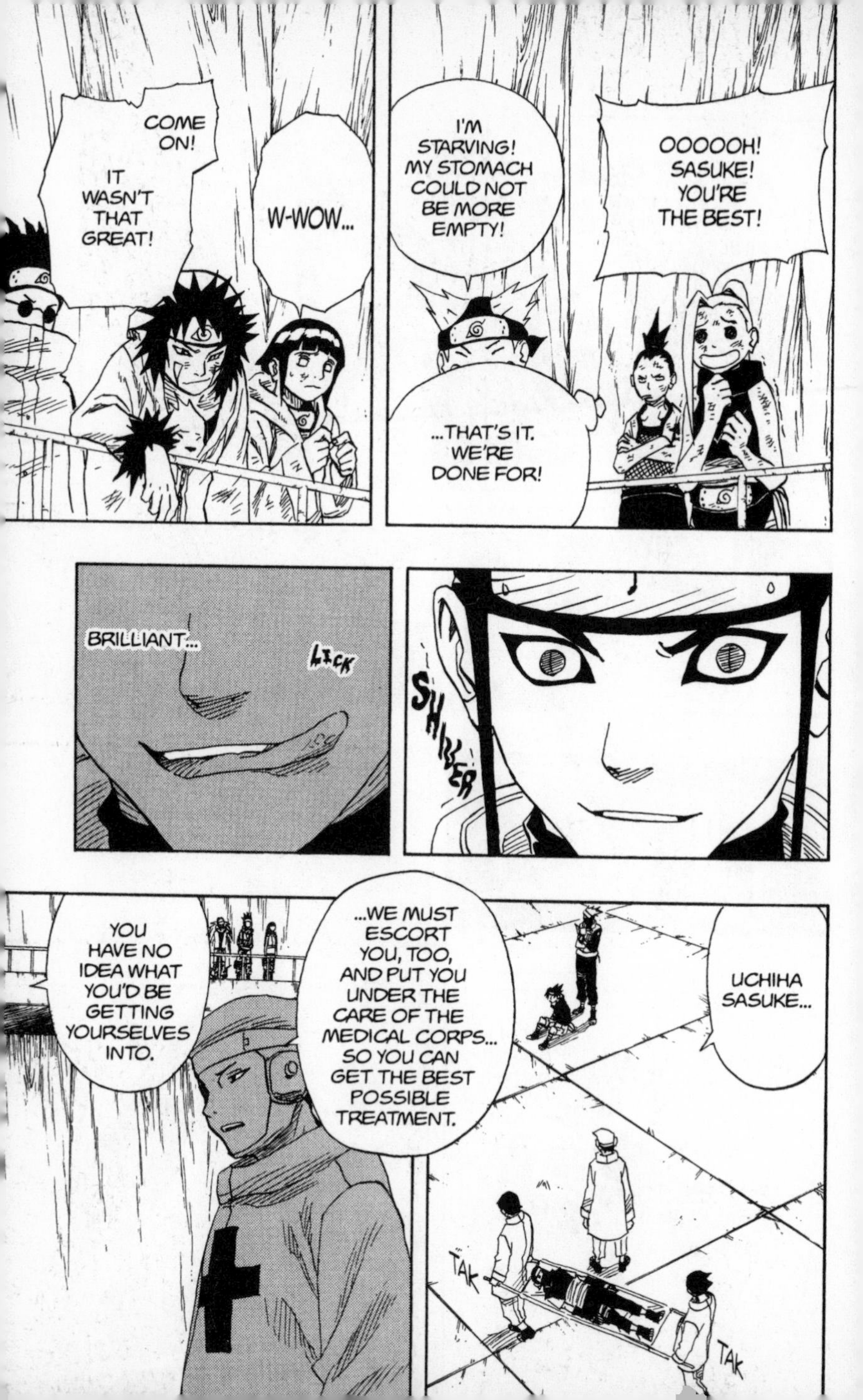
OOOOOH! SASUKE! YOU'RE THE BEST!
I'M STARVING! MY STOMACH COULD NOT BE MORE EMPTY!
...THAT'S IT. WE'RE DONE FOR!
W-WOW...
COME ON!
IT WASN'T THAT GREAT!
SHIVER
LICK
BRILLIANT...
UCHIHA SASUKE...
...WE MUST ESCORT YOU, TOO, AND PUT YOU UNDER THE CARE OF THE MEDICAL CORPS... SO YOU CAN GET THE BEST POSSIBLE TREATMENT.
TAK
TAK
YOU HAVE NO IDEA WHAT YOU'D BE GETTING YOURSELVES INTO.

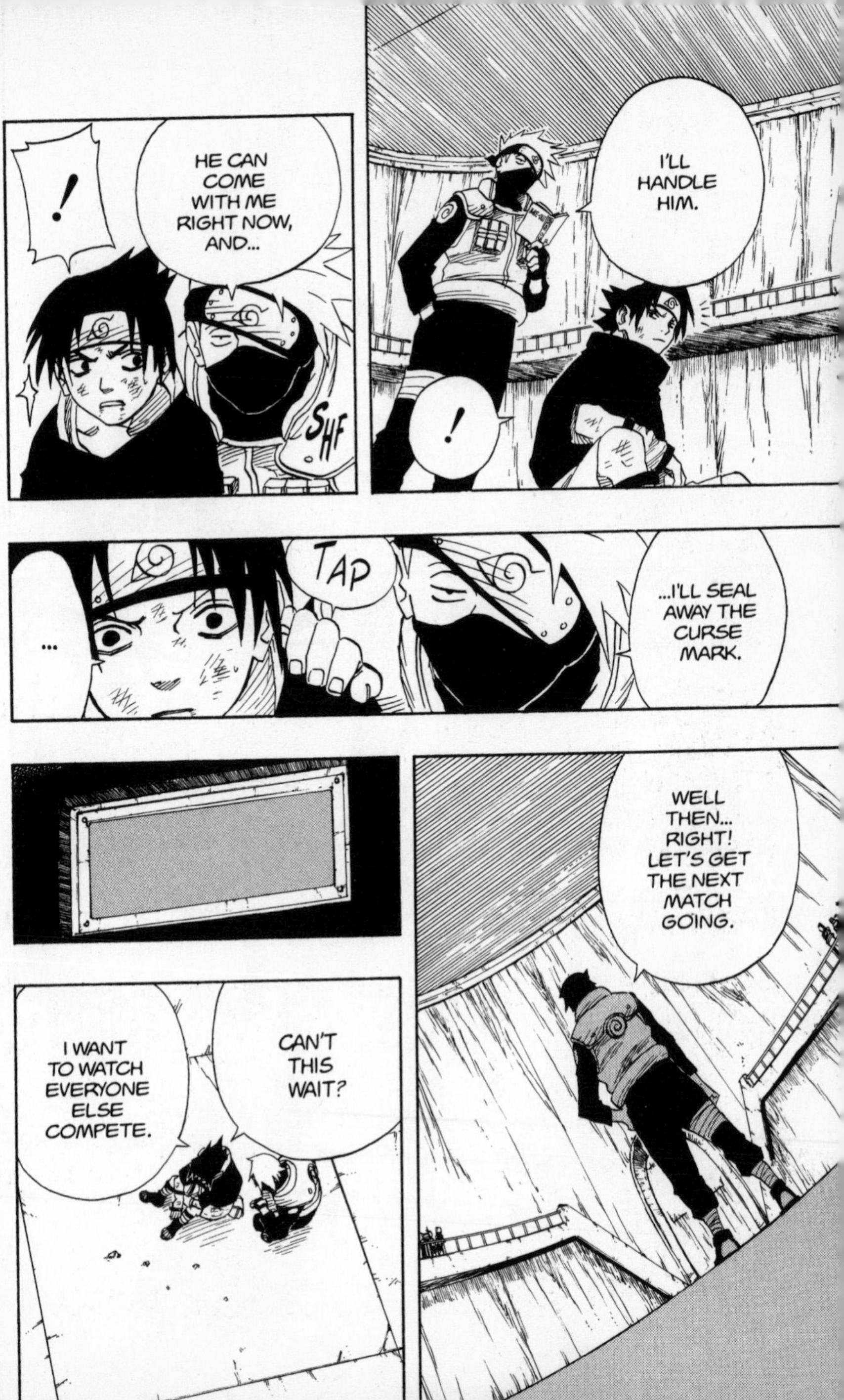
I'LL HANDLE HIM.
!
HE CAN COME WITH ME RIGHT NOW, AND...
!
SHF
...I'LL SEAL AWAY THE CURSE MARK.
TAP
...
WELL THEN... RIGHT! LET'S GET THE NEXT MATCH GOING.
CAN'T THIS WAIT?
I WANT TO WATCH EVERYONE ELSE COMPETE.

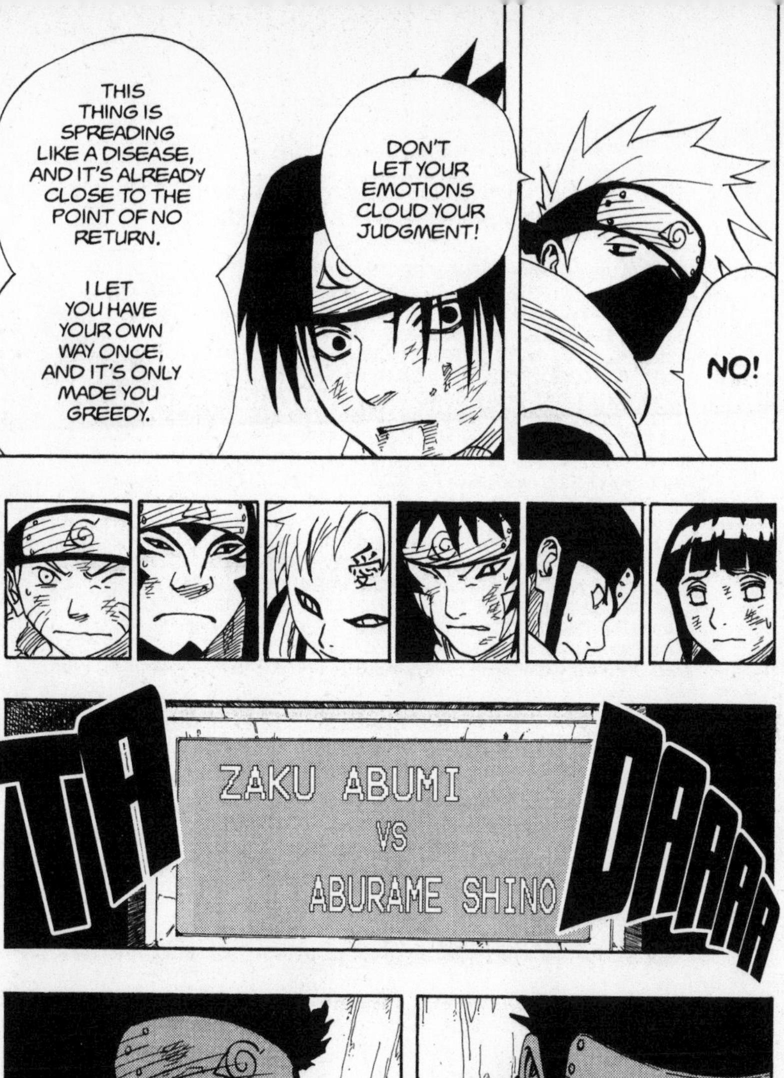
NO!
DON'T LET YOUR EMOTIONS CLOUD YOUR JUDGMENT!
THIS THING IS SPREADING LIKE A DISEASE, AND IT'S ALREADY CLOSE TO THE POINT OF NO RETURN.
I LET YOU HAVE YOUR OWN WAY ONCE, AND IT'S ONLY MADE YOU GREEDY.
TA
ZAKU ABUMI
VS
ABURAME SHINO
DAAAA
WHO'S THAT LOSER?
...

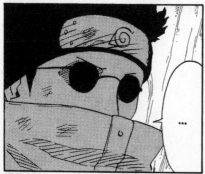

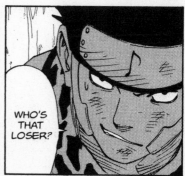

THE WORLD OF KISHIMOTO MASASHI
MY PERSONAL HISTORY, PART 7.2

WE HARASSED MY FATHER RELENTLESSLY UNTIL HE CAVED
AND FINALLY LET US BUY *DRAGON QUEST*. IN FACT, IT WAS THE
FIRST SOFTWARE I EVER PURCHASED. EVERYTHING ABOUT
THE EXPERIENCE WAS NEW AND DIFFERENT. IT WAS THE FIRST
ROLE-PLAYING GAME INTRODUCED FOR THE NINTENDO FAMI-
COM ("FAMILY COMPUTER") GAMING SYSTEM... AND I WAS
COMPLETELY AT SEA ABOUT A LOT OF HOW IT WORKED, EVEN
AFTER STUDYING THE MANUAL. THERE I'D BE, LOCKED IN
BATTLE WITH SLIME, AND UP WOULD POP A MESSAGE
CONGRATULATING ME ON HAVING MASTERED THE HOIMI
HEALING SPELL NEEDED TO COMBAT IT. BUT I DIDN'T HAVE A
CLUE WHAT TO DO WITH IT. ACCORDING TO THE MANUAL, YOU
WERE SUPPOSED TO CHANT THE HOIMI AND ALL OF YOUR "HIT
POINTS" WOULD BE RESTORED, BUT THERE WAS NO HINT OF
HOW TO DO THAT. LUCKILY, SOMEHOW MY LITTLE BROTHER
HAD SOME KIND OF FLASH OF INSIGHT AND FIGURED OUT
THAT WE SHOULD FLIP THE SWITCH ON THE BUILT-IN MICRO-
PHONE IN THE SECOND CONTROLLER. AS SOON AS HE HAD IT
TURNED ON, MY BROTHER YELLED "HOIMI!!" RIGHT INTO THE
SECONDARY CONTROLLER'S MIKE!!

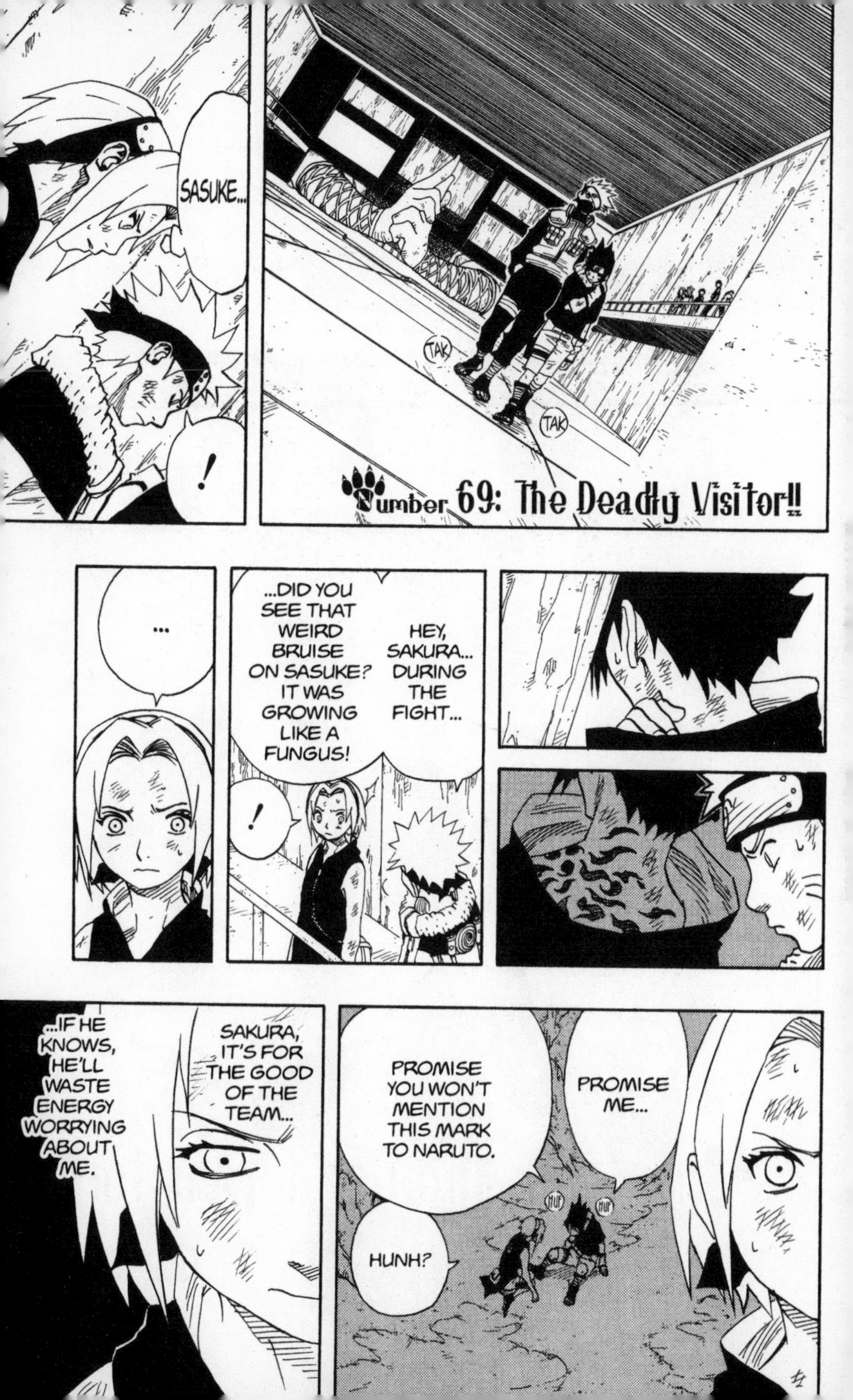
TAK
TAK
Number 69: The Deadly Visitor!!
SASUKE...
!
HEY, SAKURA... DURING THE FIGHT...
...DID YOU SEE THAT WEIRD BRUISE ON SASUKE? IT WAS GROWING LIKE A FUNGUS!
!
...
PROMISE ME...
PROMISE YOU WON'T MENTION THIS MARK TO NARUTO.
HUF
HUF
HUNH?
SAKURA, IT'S FOR THE GOOD OF THE TEAM...
...IF HE KNOWS, HE'LL WASTE ENERGY WORRYING ABOUT ME.

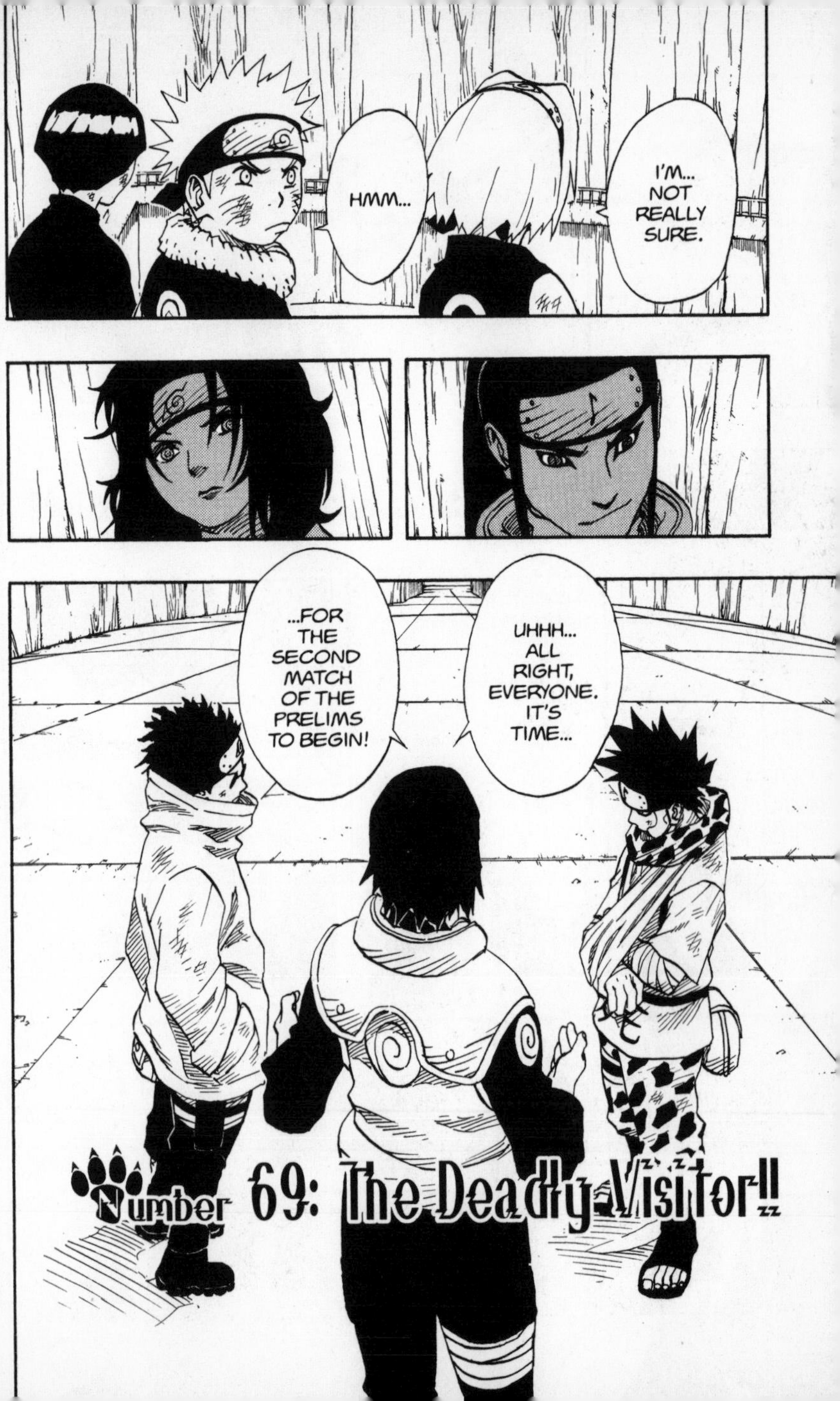
I'M... NOT REALLY SURE.
HMM...
UHHH... ALL RIGHT, EVERYONE. IT'S TIME...
...FOR THE SECOND MATCH OF THE PRELIMS TO BEGIN!
Number 69: The Deadly Visitor!!

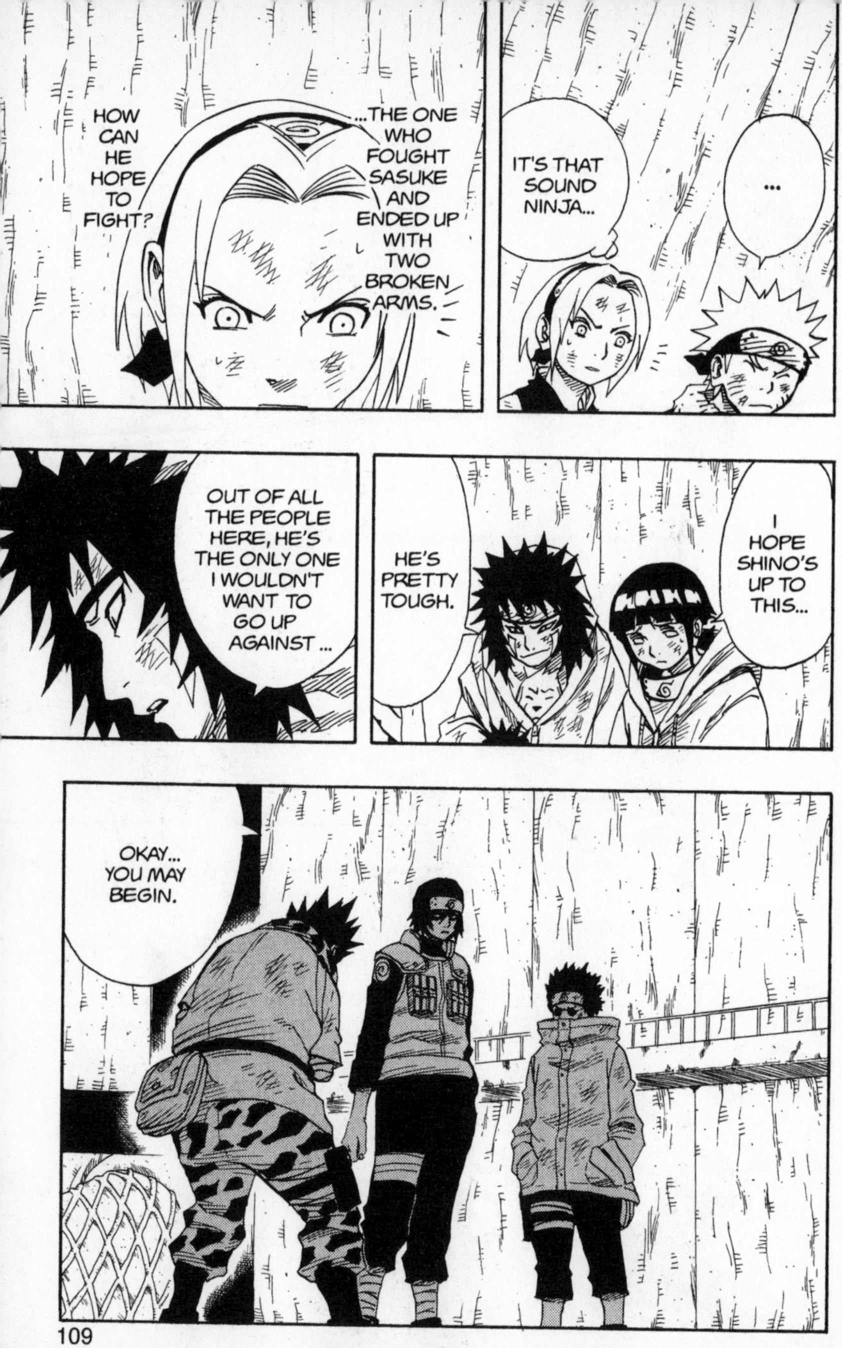
...
IT'S THAT SOUND NINJA...
...THE ONE WHO FOUGHT SASUKE AND ENDED UP WITH TWO BROKEN ARMS.
HOW CAN HE HOPE TO FIGHT?
I HOPE SHINO'S UP TO THIS...
HE'S PRETTY TOUGH.
OUT OF ALL THE PEOPLE HERE, HE'S THE ONLY ONE I WOULDN'T WANT TO GO UP AGAINST ...
OKAY... YOU MAY BEGIN.

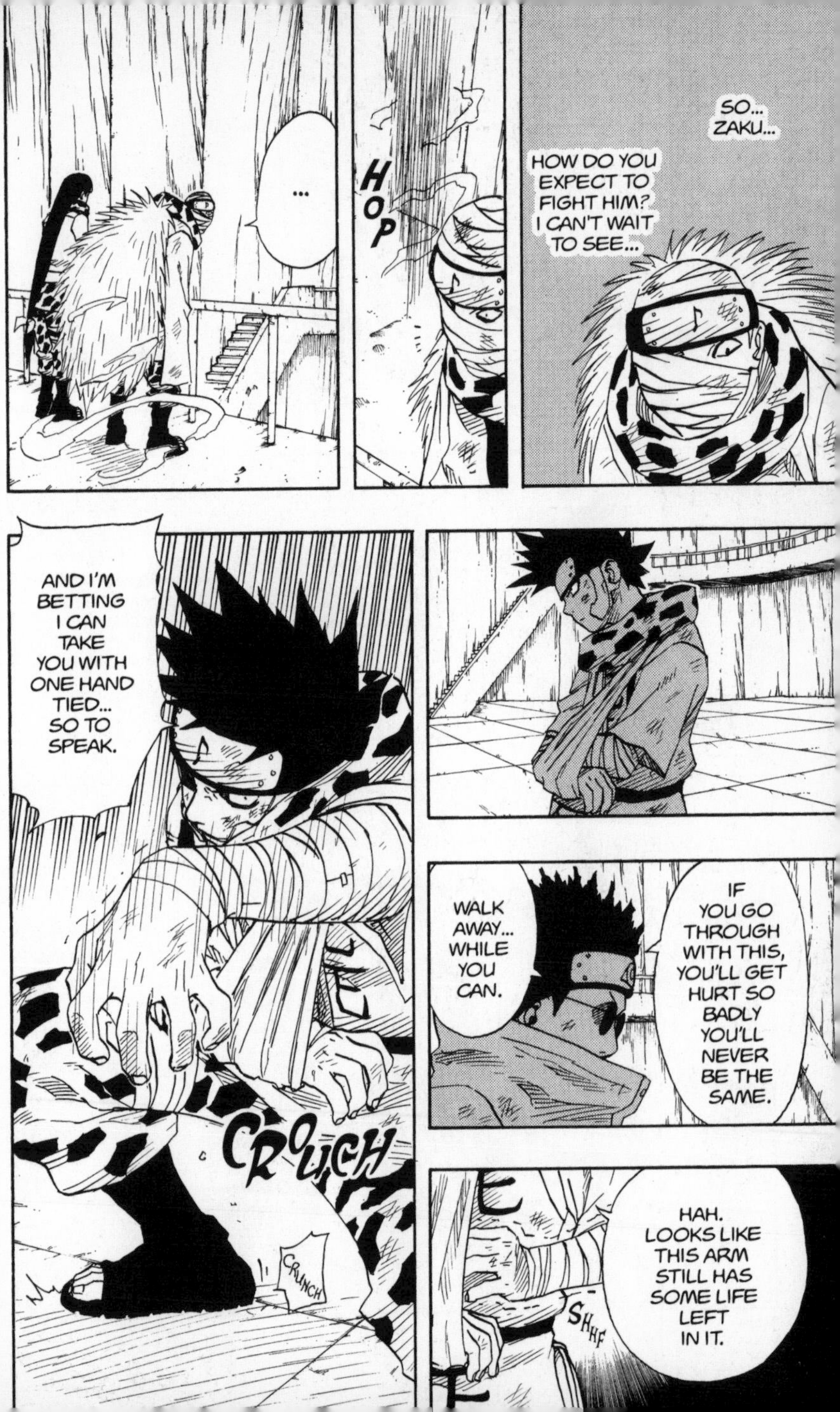
SO... ZAKU...
HOW DO YOU EXPECT TO FIGHT HIM? I CAN'T WAIT TO SEE...
HOP
...
IF YOU GO THROUGH WITH THIS, YOU'LL GET HURT SO BADLY YOU'LL NEVER BE THE SAME.
WALK AWAY... WHILE YOU CAN.
HAH. LOOKS LIKE THIS ARM STILL HAS SOME LIFE LEFT IN IT.
SHHF
AND I'M BETTING I CAN TAKE YOU WITH ONE HAND TIED... SO TO SPEAK.
CRUNCH
CRUNCH

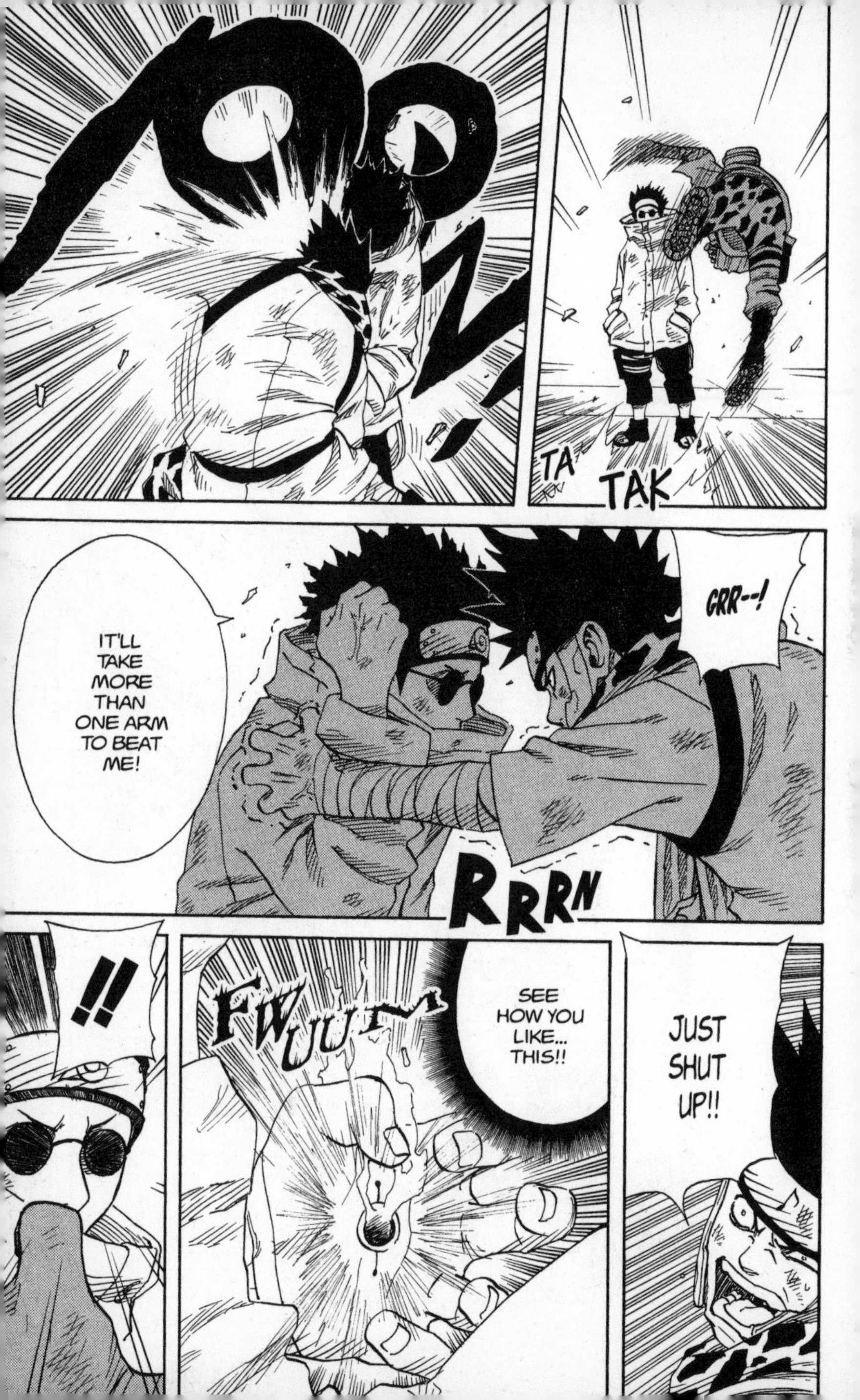
TA
TAK
GRR--!
IT'LL TAKE MORE THAN ONE ARM TO BEAT ME!
RRRN
JUST SHUT UP!!
SEE HOW YOU LIKE... THIS!!
FWUUM
!!

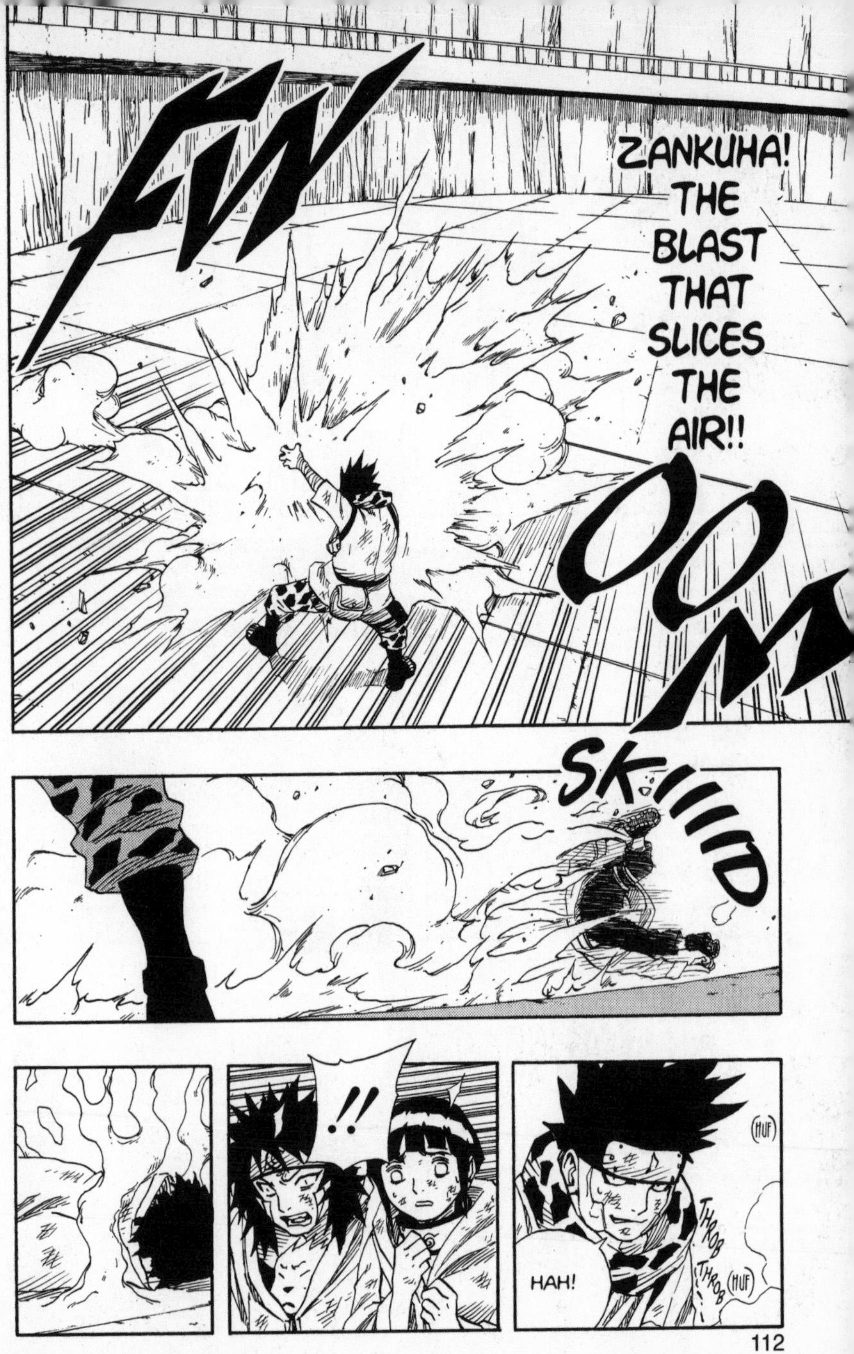
FW
ZANKUHA! THE BLAST THAT SLICES THE AIR!!
OOM
SKIIIID
(HUF)
THROB THROB
(HUF)
HAH!
!!

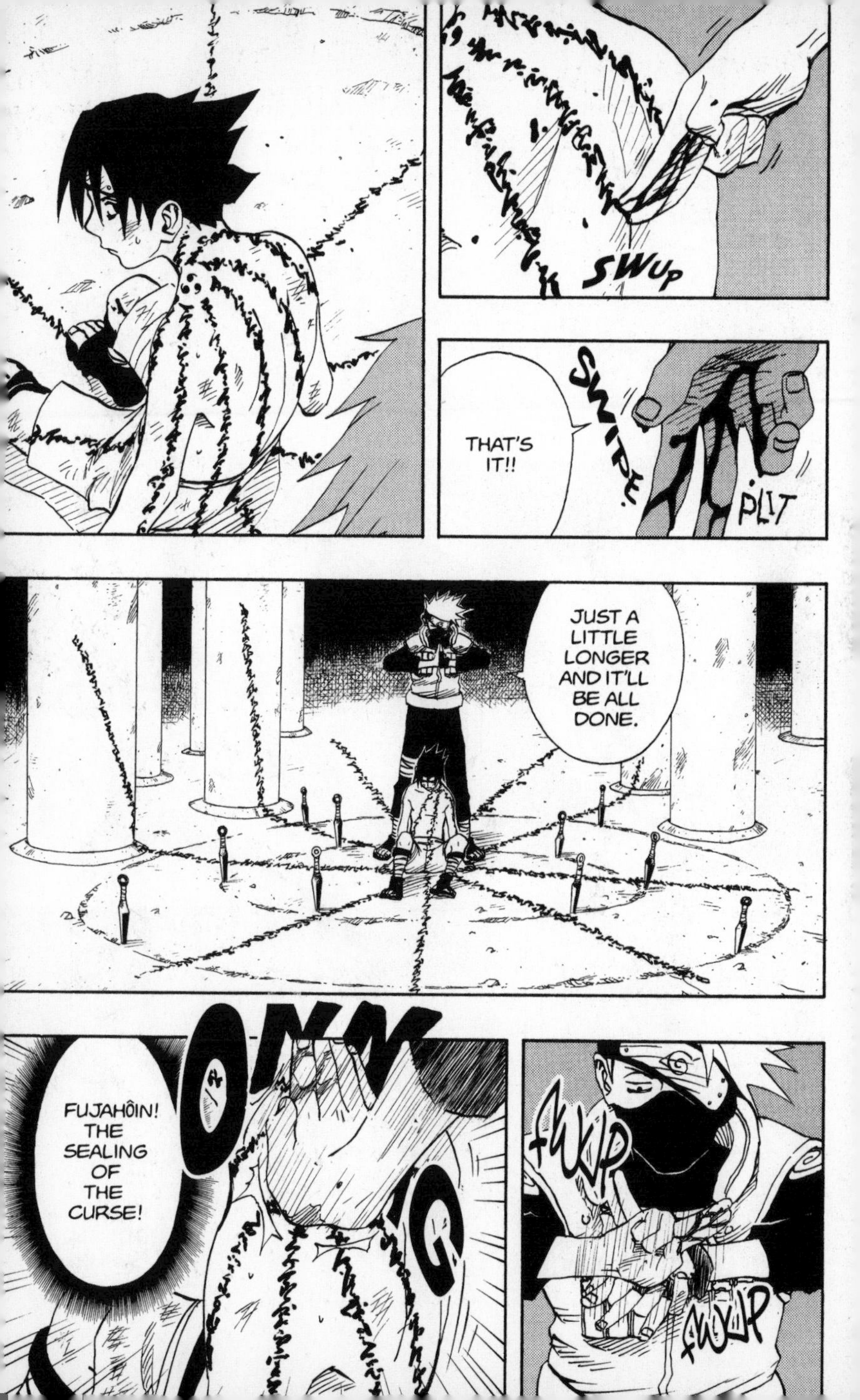
SWUP
SWIPE
THAT'S IT!!
PLIT
JUST A LITTLE LONGER AND IT'LL BE ALL DONE.
FWUP
FWUP
ONN
G
FUJAHÔIN! THE SEALING OF THE CURSE!

OWW!

AAA—!

THROB

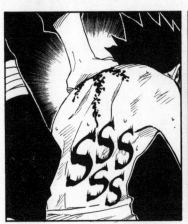

SSS SS

AGH!

SSSSS

HMM...

HUF

FWUMP

HUF

HUF

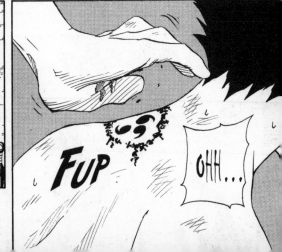

FUP

OHH...

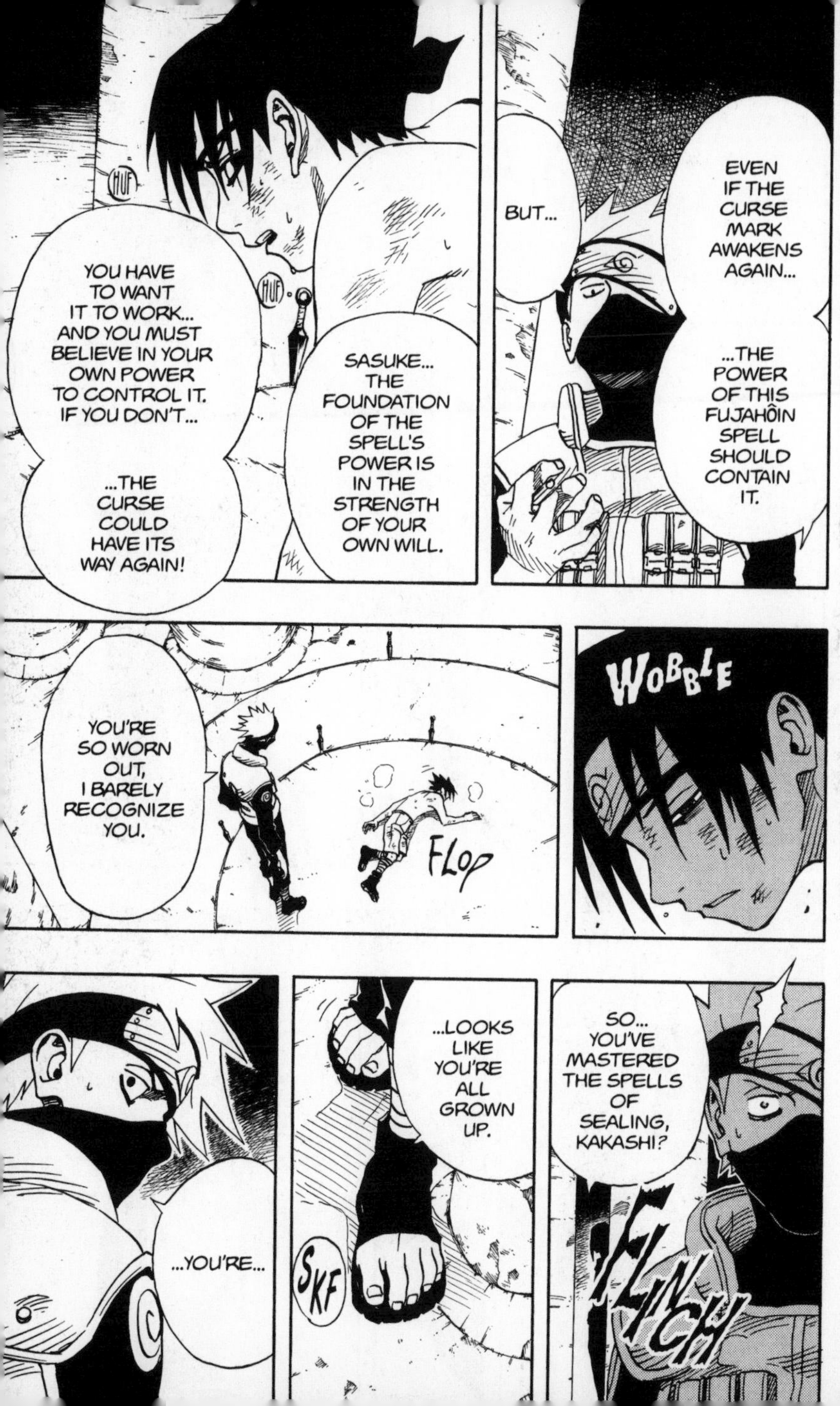
EVEN IF THE CURSE MARK AWAKENS AGAIN...
...THE POWER OF THIS FUJAHÔIN SPELL SHOULD CONTAIN IT.
BUT...
HUF
HUF
SASUKE... THE FOUNDATION OF THE SPELL'S POWER IS IN THE STRENGTH OF YOUR OWN WILL.
YOU HAVE TO WANT IT TO WORK... AND YOU MUST BELIEVE IN YOUR OWN POWER TO CONTROL IT. IF YOU DON'T...
...THE CURSE COULD HAVE ITS WAY AGAIN!
WOBBLE
FLOP
YOU'RE SO WORN OUT, I BARELY RECOGNIZE YOU.
SO... YOU'VE MASTERED THE SPELLS OF SEALING, KAKASHI?
FLINCH
...LOOKS LIKE YOU'RE ALL GROWN UP.
SKF
...YOU'RE...

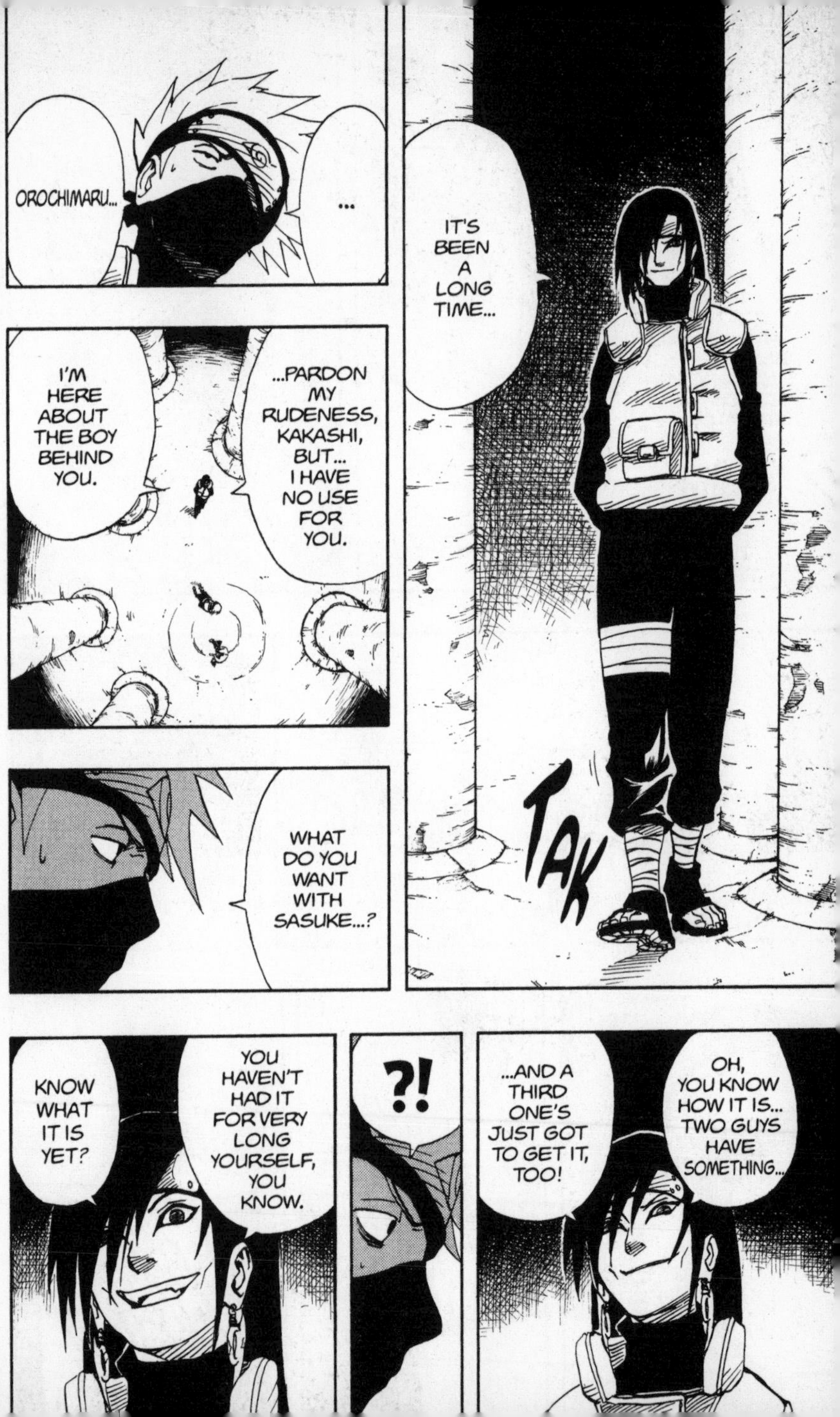

IT'S BEEN A LONG TIME...
TAK
...
OROCHIMARU...
...PARDON MY RUDENESS, KAKASHI, BUT... I HAVE NO USE FOR YOU.
I'M HERE ABOUT THE BOY BEHIND YOU.
WHAT DO YOU WANT WITH SASUKE...?
OH, YOU KNOW HOW IT IS... TWO GUYS HAVE SOMETHING...
...AND A THIRD ONE'S JUST GOT TO GET IT, TOO!
?!
YOU HAVEN'T HAD IT FOR VERY LONG YOURSELF, YOU KNOW.
KNOW WHAT IT IS YET?

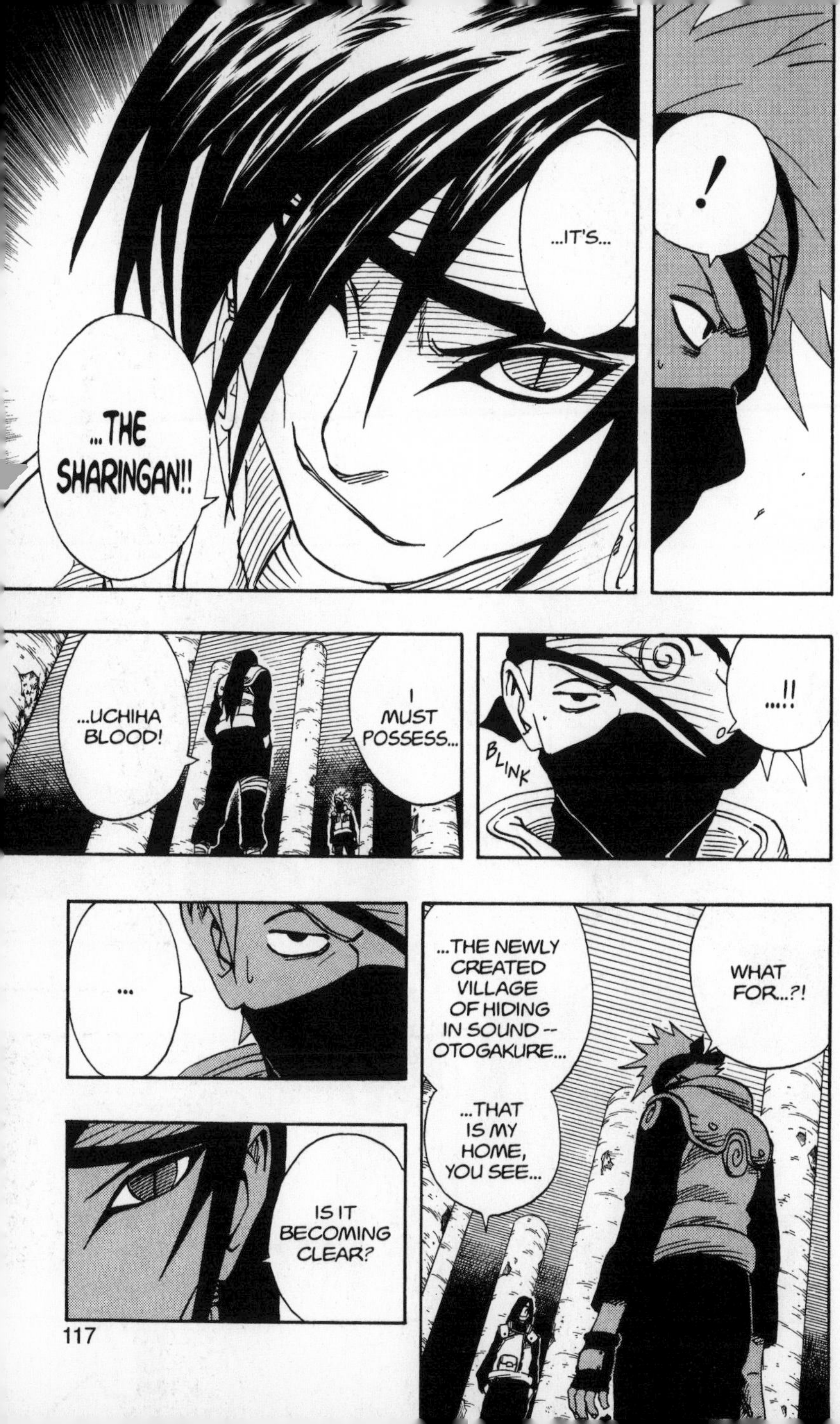
!
...IT'S...
...THE SHARINGAN!!
...!!
BLINK
I MUST POSSESS...
...UCHIHA BLOOD!
WHAT FOR...?!
...THE NEWLY CREATED VILLAGE OF HIDING IN SOUND -- OTOGAKURE...
...THAT IS MY HOME, YOU SEE...
...
IS IT BECOMING CLEAR?

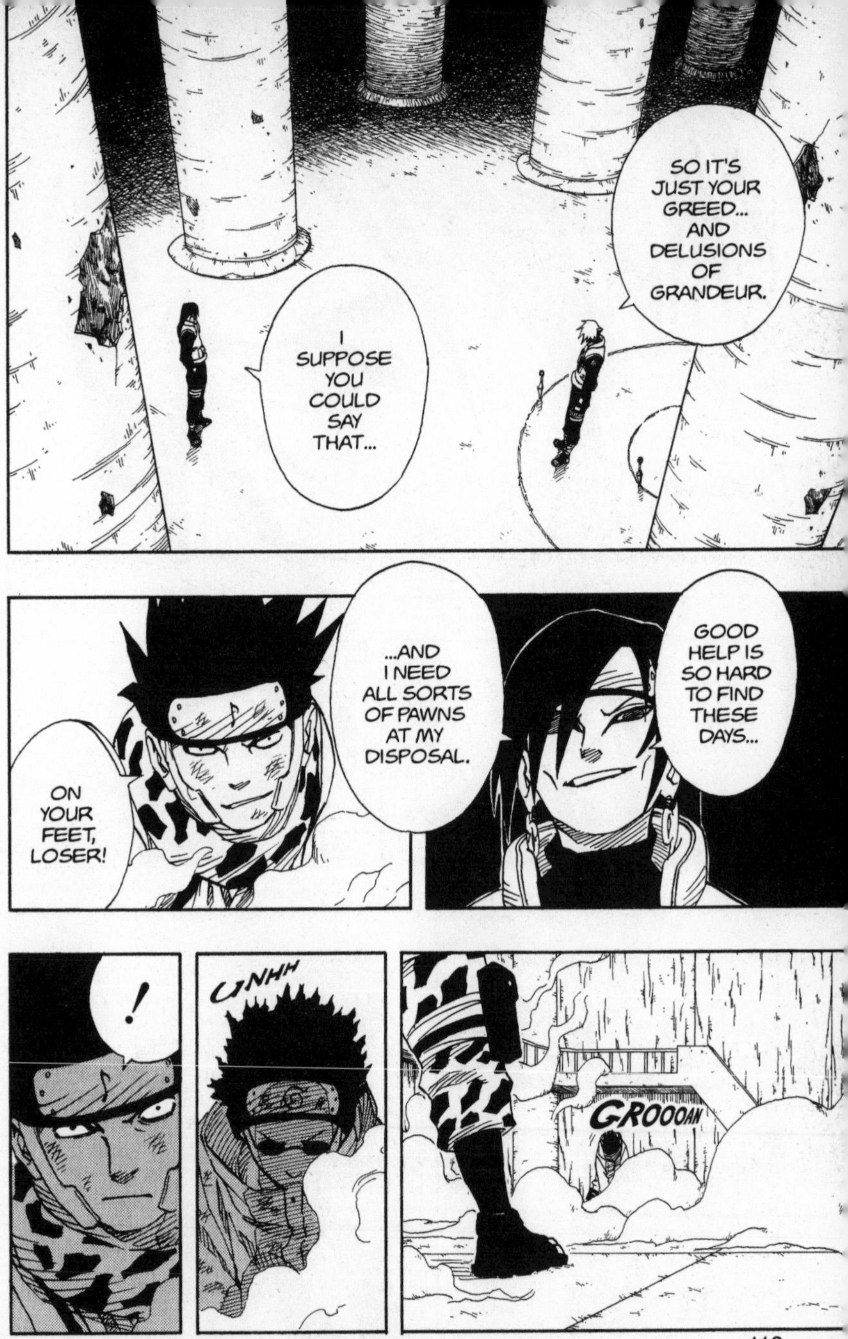
SO IT'S JUST YOUR GREED... AND DELUSIONS OF GRANDEUR.
I SUPPOSE YOU COULD SAY THAT...
GOOD HELP IS SO HARD TO FIND THESE DAYS...
...AND I NEED ALL SORTS OF PAWNS AT MY DISPOSAL.
ON YOUR FEET, LOSER!
GROOOAN
UNHH
!

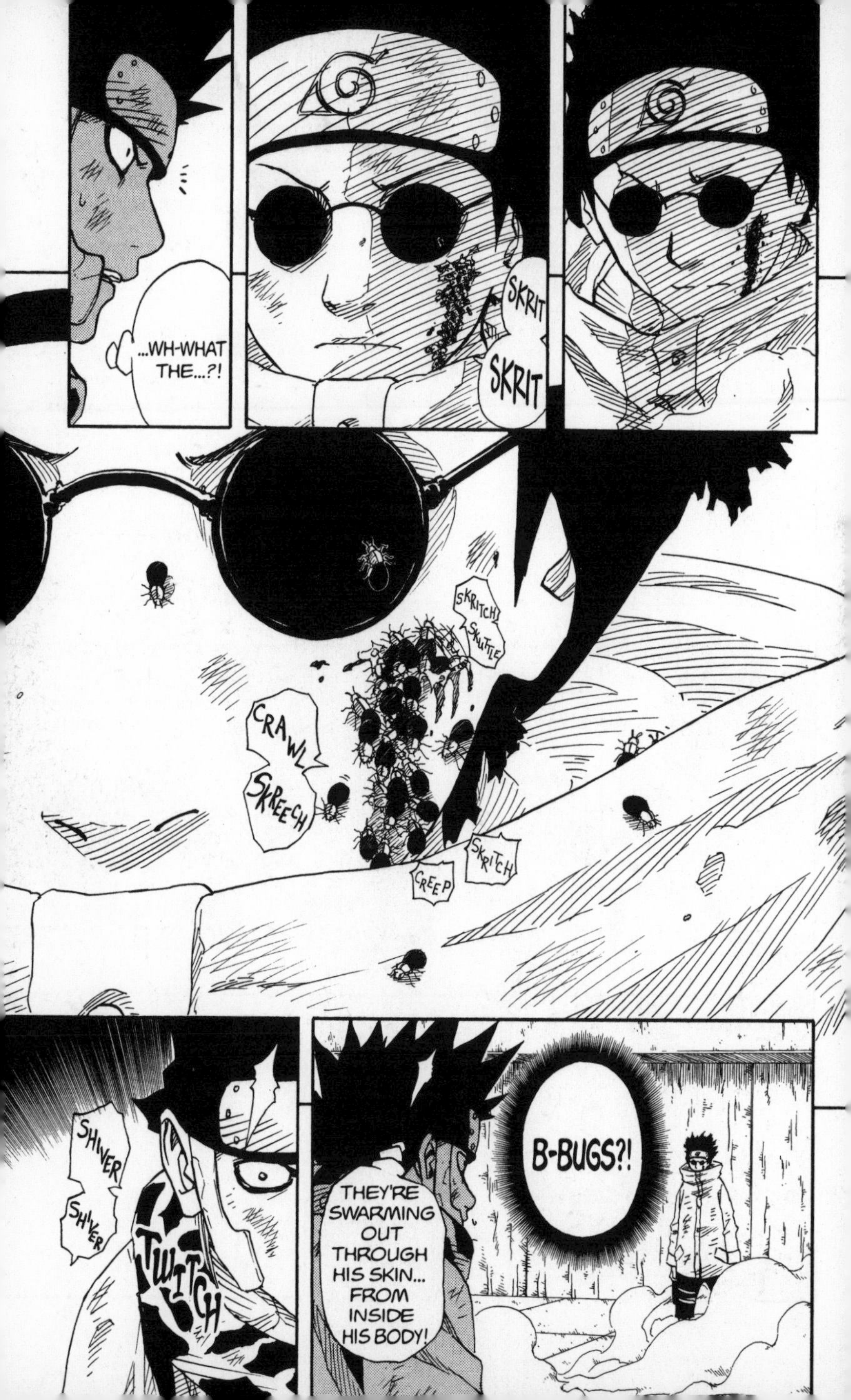
SKRIT
SKRIT
...WH-WHAT THE...?!
SKRITCH
SKUTTLE
CRAWL
SKREECH
SKRITCH
CREEP
B-BUGS?!
THEY'RE SWARMING OUT THROUGH HIS SKIN... FROM INSIDE HIS BODY!
SHIVER
SHIVER
TWITCH

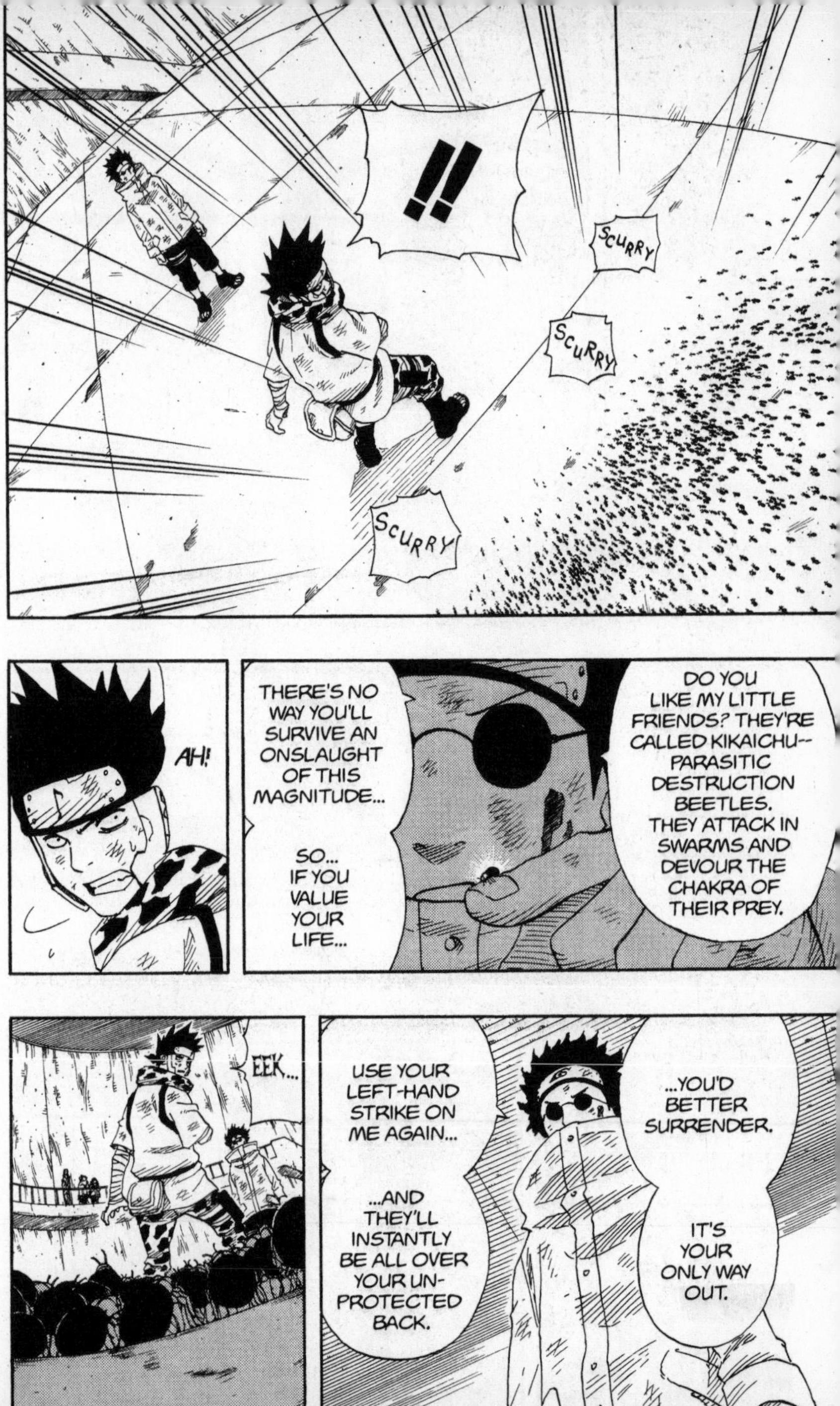
!!
SCURRY
SCURRY
SCURRY
DO YOU LIKE MY LITTLE FRIENDS? THEY'RE CALLED KIKAICHU-- PARASITIC DESTRUCTION BEETLES. THEY ATTACK IN SWARMS AND DEVOUR THE CHAKRA OF THEIR PREY.
THERE'S NO WAY YOU'LL SURVIVE AN ONSLAUGHT OF THIS MAGNITUDE...
SO... IF YOU VALUE YOUR LIFE...
AH!
...YOU'D BETTER SURRENDER.
IT'S YOUR ONLY WAY OUT.
USE YOUR LEFT-HAND STRIKE ON ME AGAIN...
...AND THEY'LL INSTANTLY BE ALL OVER YOUR UN-PROTECTED BACK.
EEK...

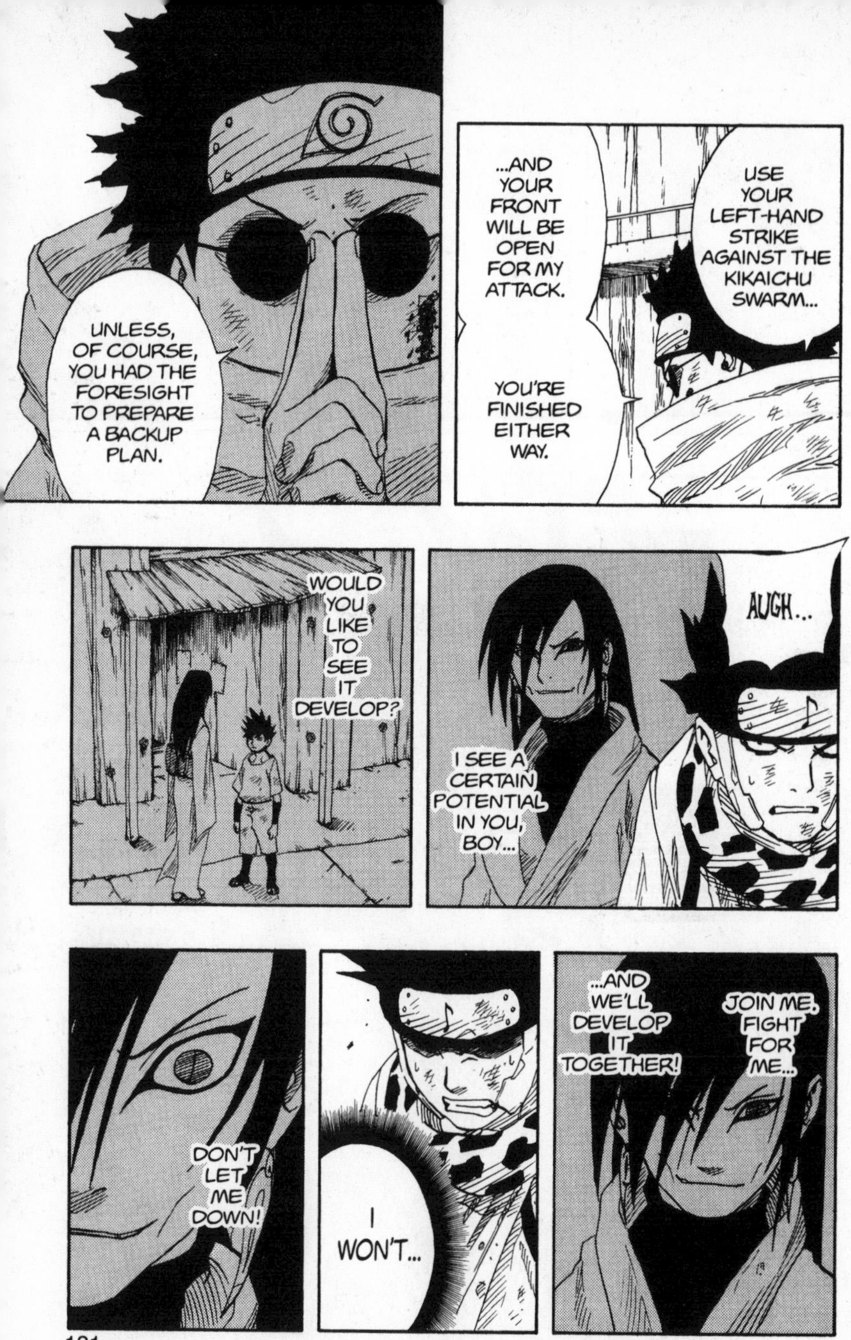
USE YOUR LEFT-HAND STRIKE AGAINST THE KIKAICHU SWARM...
...AND YOUR FRONT WILL BE OPEN FOR MY ATTACK.
YOU'RE FINISHED EITHER WAY.
UNLESS, OF COURSE, YOU HAD THE FORESIGHT TO PREPARE A BACKUP PLAN.
AUGH...
I SEE A CERTAIN POTENTIAL IN YOU, BOY...
WOULD YOU LIKE TO SEE IT DEVELOP?
JOIN ME. FIGHT FOR ME...
...AND WE'LL DEVELOP IT TOGETHER!
I WON'T...
DON'T LET ME DOWN!

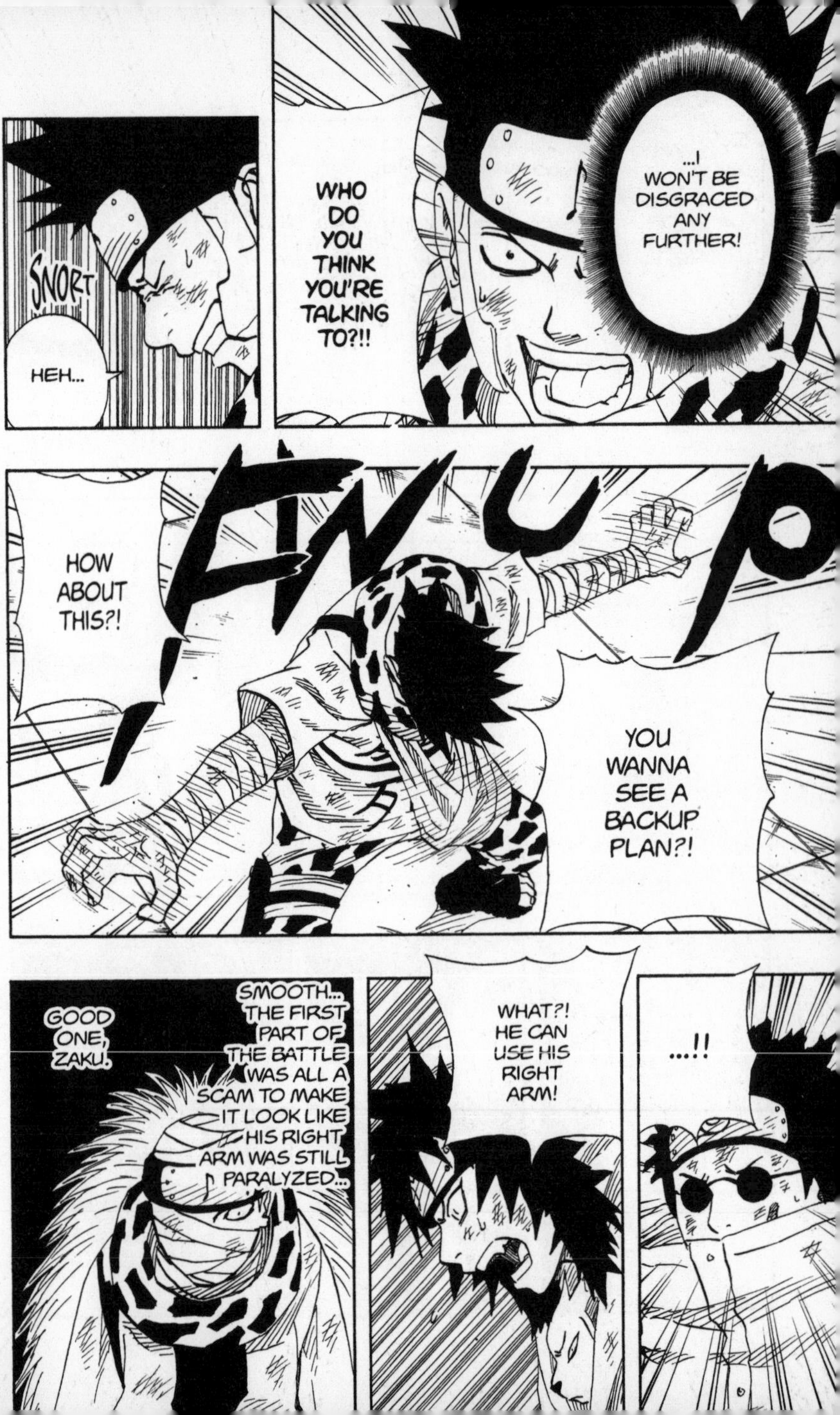
...I WON'T BE DISGRACED ANY FURTHER!
WHO DO YOU THINK YOU'RE TALKING TO?!!
SNORT
HEH...
FWUP
YOU WANNA SEE A BACKUP PLAN?!
HOW ABOUT THIS?!
...!!
WHAT?! HE CAN USE HIS RIGHT ARM!
SMOOTH... THE FIRST PART OF THE BATTLE WAS ALL A SCAM TO MAKE IT LOOK LIKE HIS RIGHT ARM WAS STILL PARALYZED...
GOOD ONE, ZAKU.

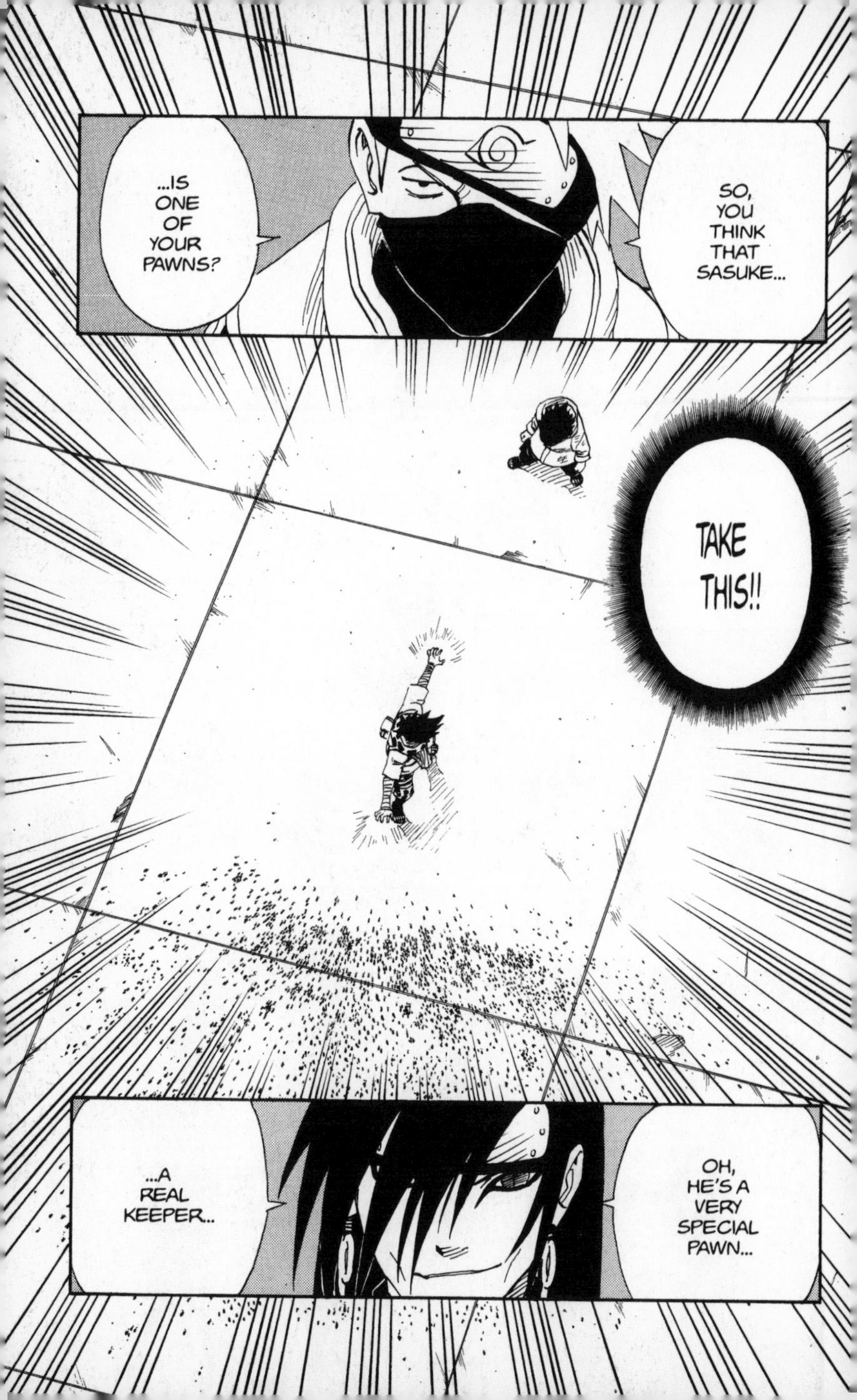
SO, YOU THINK THAT SASUKE...
...IS ONE OF YOUR PAWNS?
TAKE THIS!!
OH, HE'S A VERY SPECIAL PAWN...
...A REAL KEEPER..

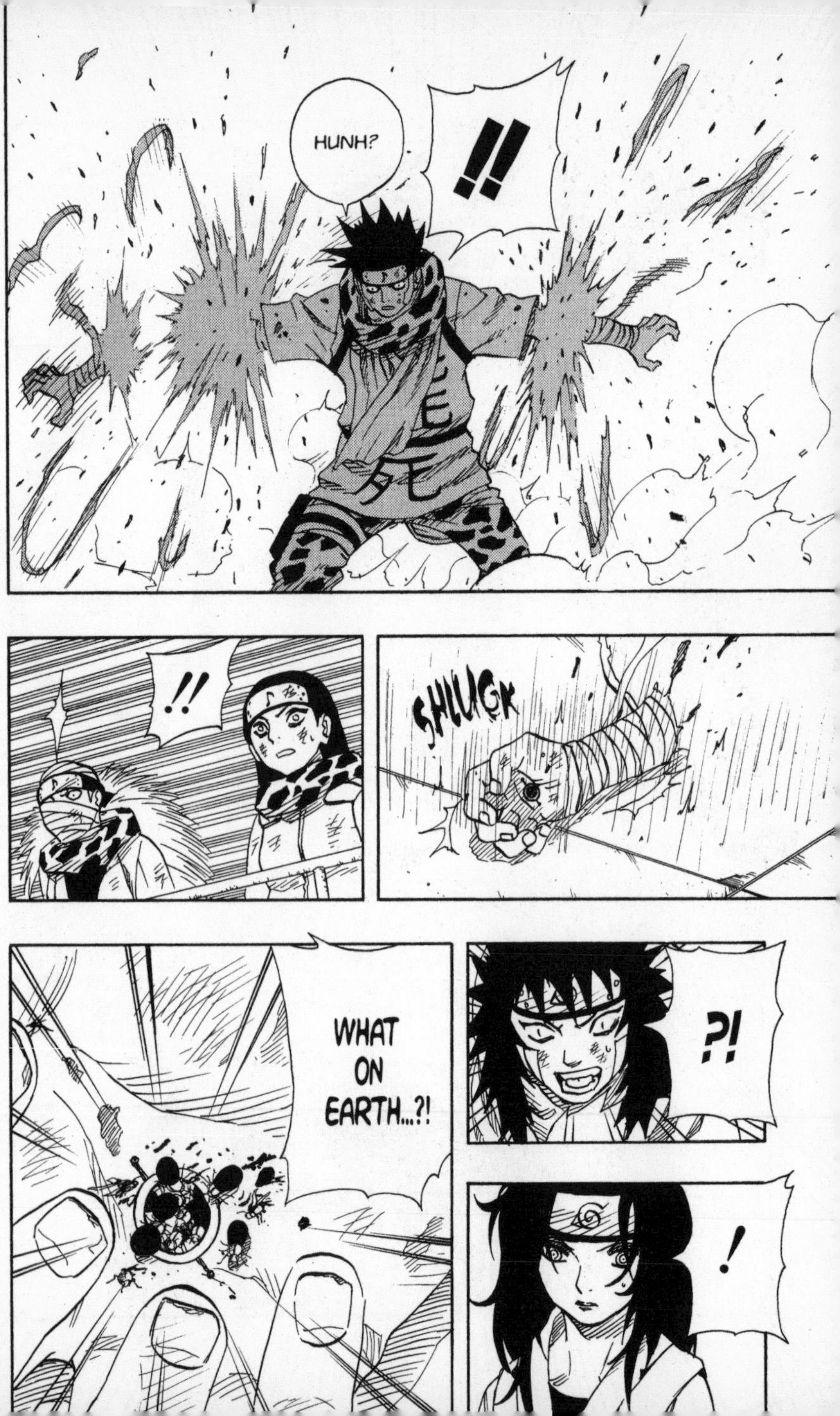
!!
HUNH?
SHLUCK
!!
?!
WHAT ON EARTH...?!
!

READ THIS WAY

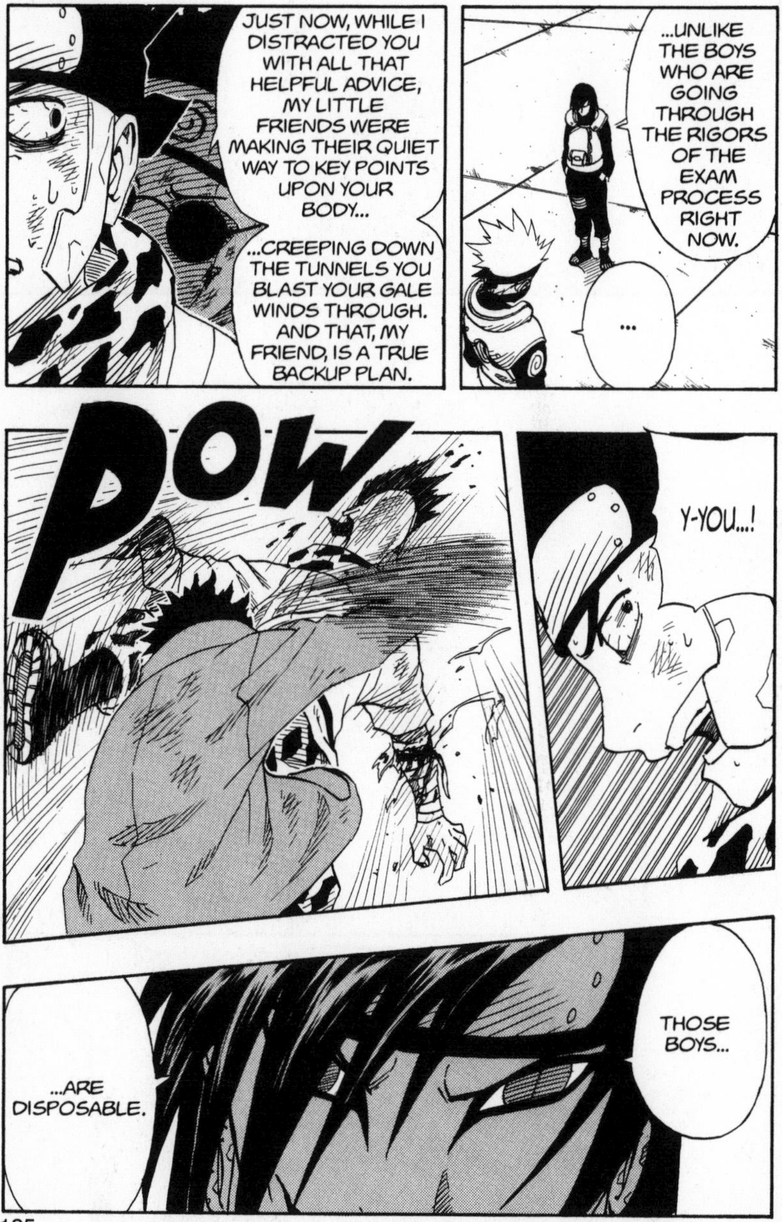

...UNLIKE THE BOYS WHO ARE GOING THROUGH THE RIGORS OF THE EXAM PROCESS RIGHT NOW.
...
JUST NOW, WHILE I DISTRACTED YOU WITH ALL THAT HELPFUL ADVICE, MY LITTLE FRIENDS WERE MAKING THEIR QUIET WAY TO KEY POINTS UPON YOUR BODY...
...CREEPING DOWN THE TUNNELS YOU BLAST YOUR GALE WINDS THROUGH. AND THAT, MY FRIEND, IS A TRUE BACKUP PLAN.
Y-YOU...!
POW
THOSE BOYS...
...ARE DISPOSABLE.

Number 70: The One Who Dies!!

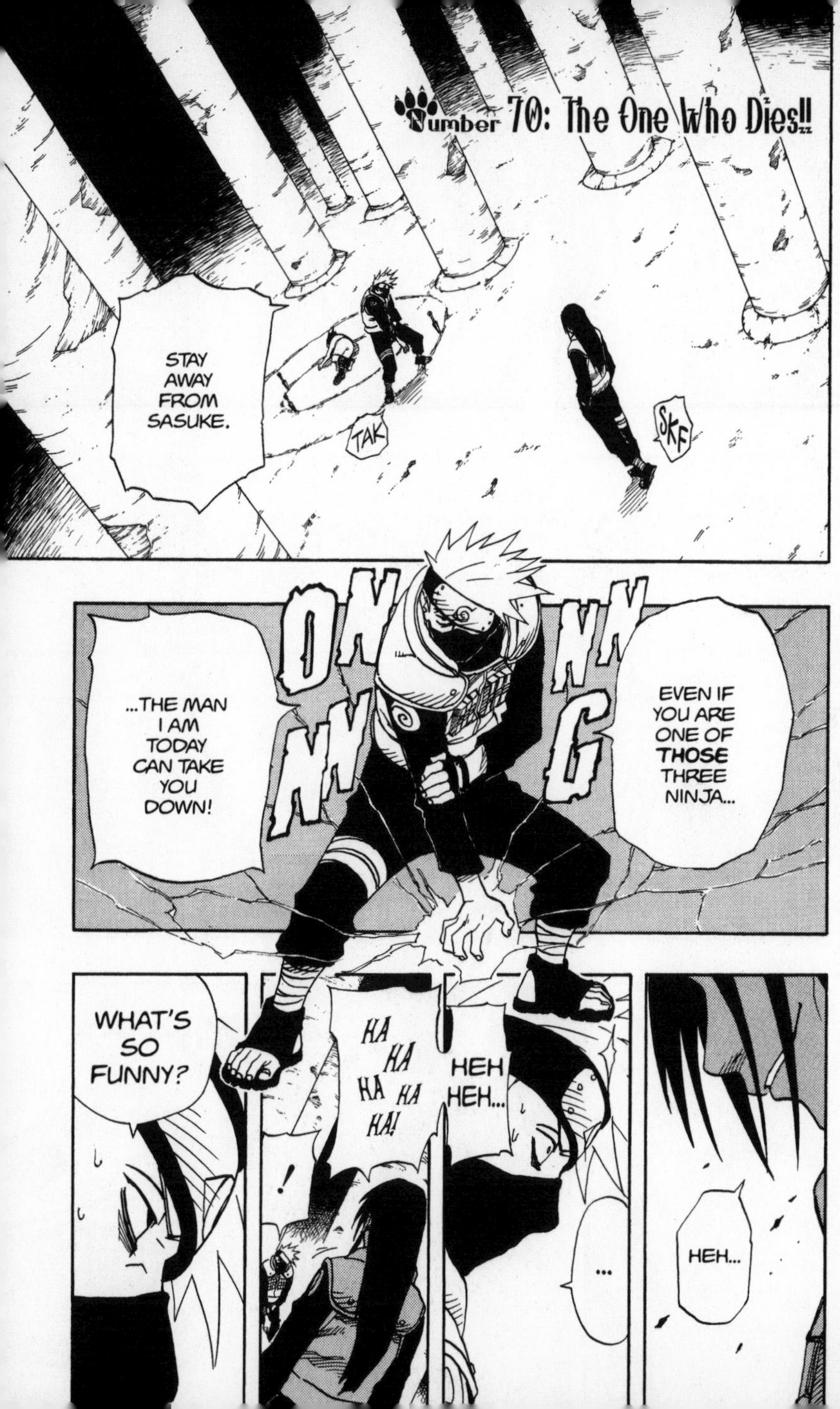
SKF
TAK
STAY AWAY FROM SASUKE.
EVEN IF YOU ARE ONE OF THOSE THREE NINJA...
ONNNNNG
...THE MAN I AM TODAY CAN TAKE YOU DOWN!
HEH...
HEH HEH...
HA HA HA HA HA!
...
!
WHAT'S SO FUNNY?

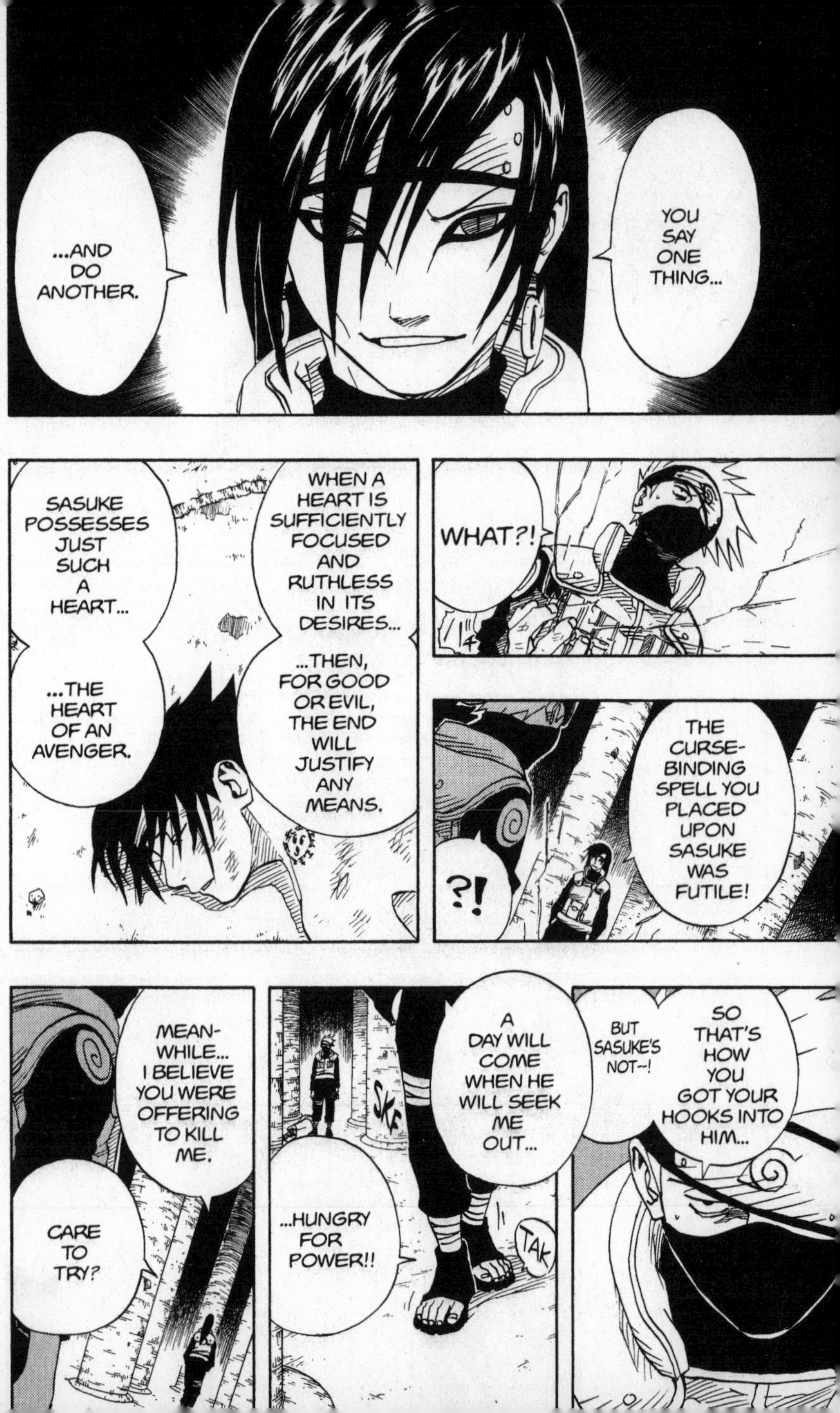
YOU SAY ONE THING...
...AND DO ANOTHER.
WHAT?!
THE CURSE-BINDING SPELL YOU PLACED UPON SASUKE WAS FUTILE!
?!
WHEN A HEART IS SUFFICIENTLY FOCUSED AND RUTHLESS IN ITS DESIRES...
...THEN, FOR GOOD OR EVIL, THE END WILL JUSTIFY ANY MEANS.
SASUKE POSSESSES JUST SUCH A HEART...
...THE HEART OF AN AVENGER.
SO THAT'S HOW YOU GOT YOUR HOOKS INTO HIM...
BUT SASUKE'S NOT--!
A DAY WILL COME WHEN HE WILL SEEK ME OUT...
SKF
...HUNGRY FOR POWER!!
TAK
MEAN-WHILE... I BELIEVE YOU WERE OFFERING TO KILL ME.
CARE TO TRY?

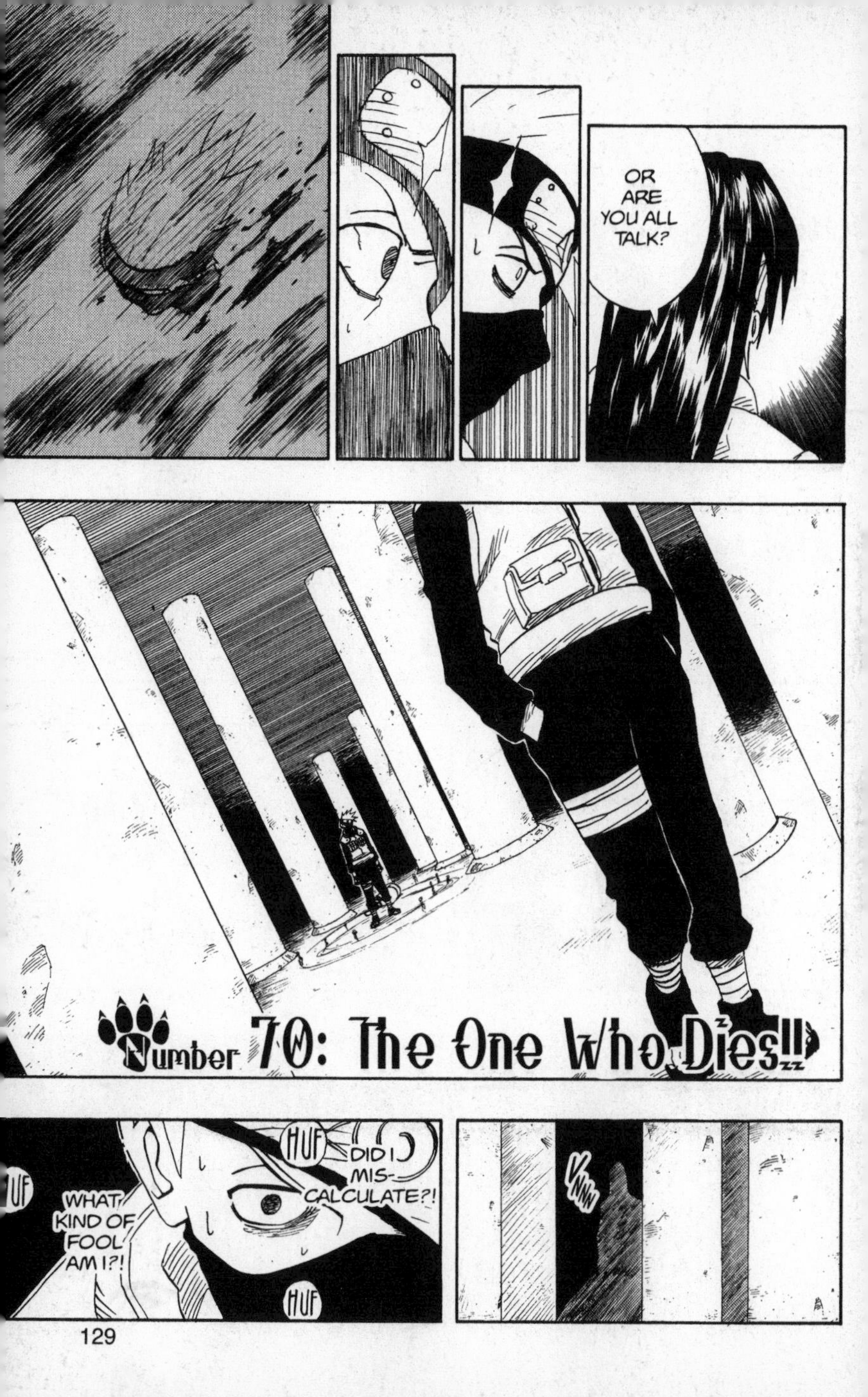
OR ARE YOU ALL TALK?
Number 70: The One Who Dies!!
VNNN
HUF
DID I MIS-CALCULATE?!
HUF
WHAT KIND OF FOOL AM I?!
HUF

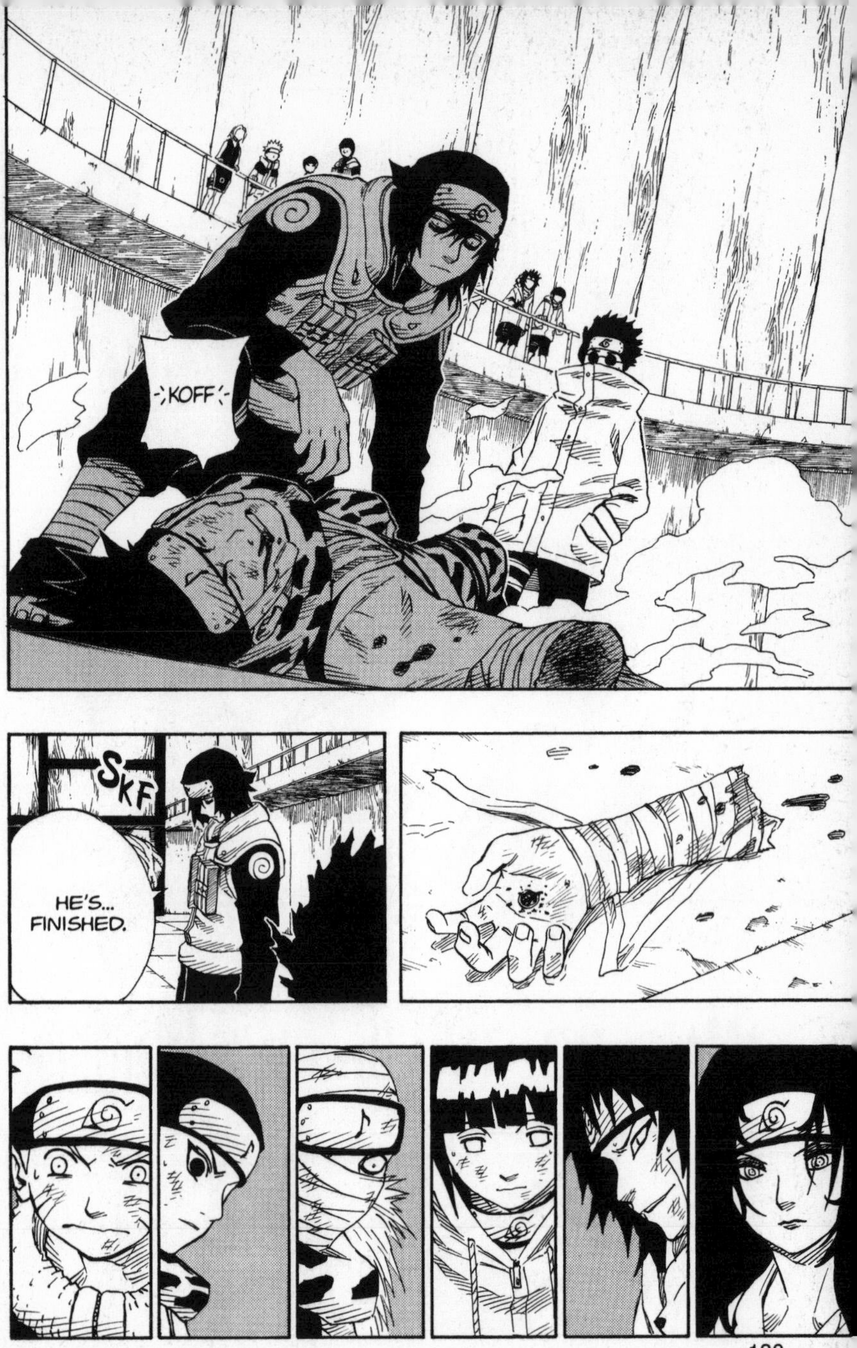
KOFF
SKF
HE'S... FINISHED.

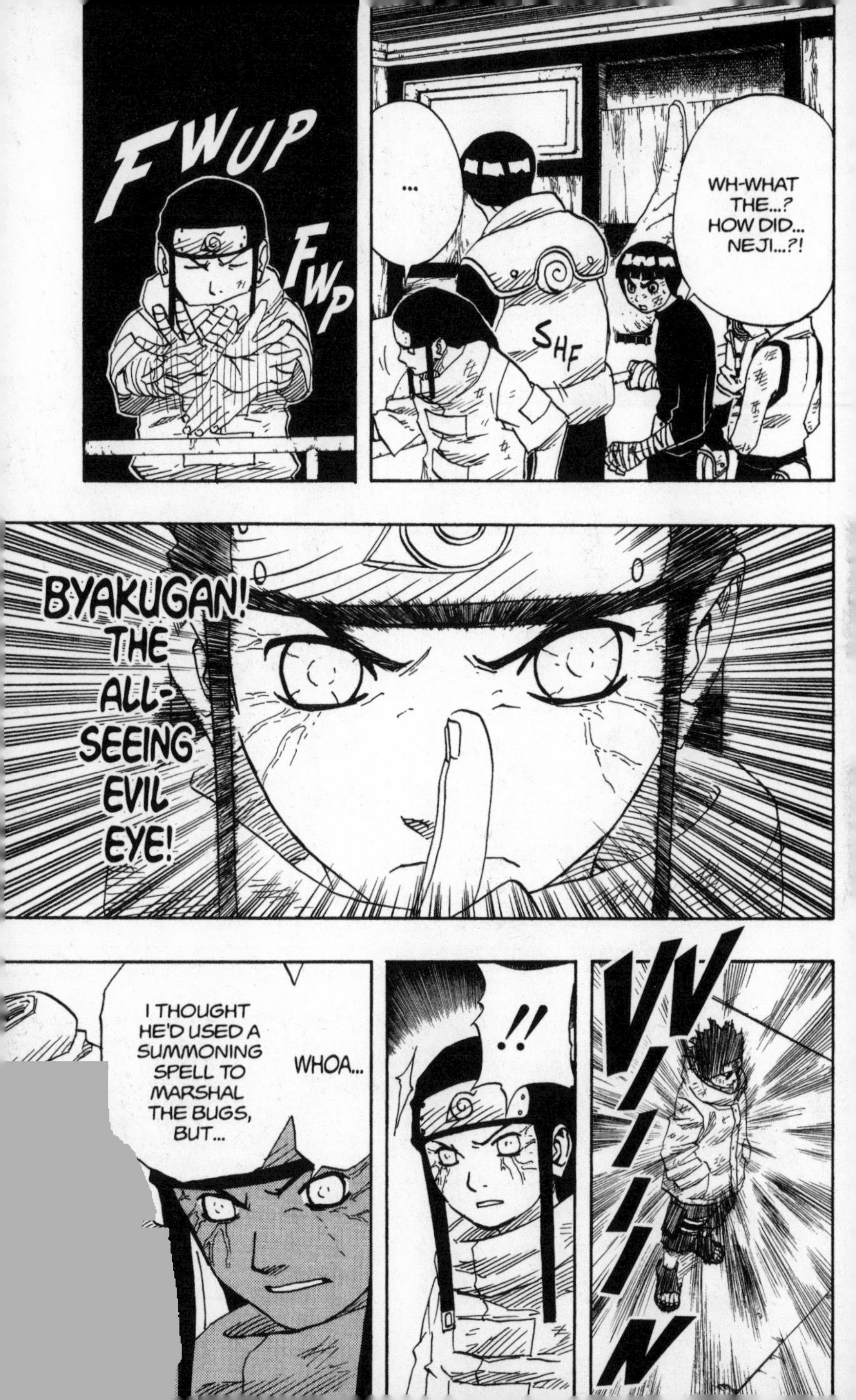
WH-WHAT THE...? HOW DID... NEJI...?!
...
SHF
FWUP
FWP
BYAKUGAN! THE ALL-SEEING EVIL EYE!
!!
WHOA...
I THOUGHT HE'D USED A SUMMONING SPELL TO MARSHAL THE BUGS, BUT...

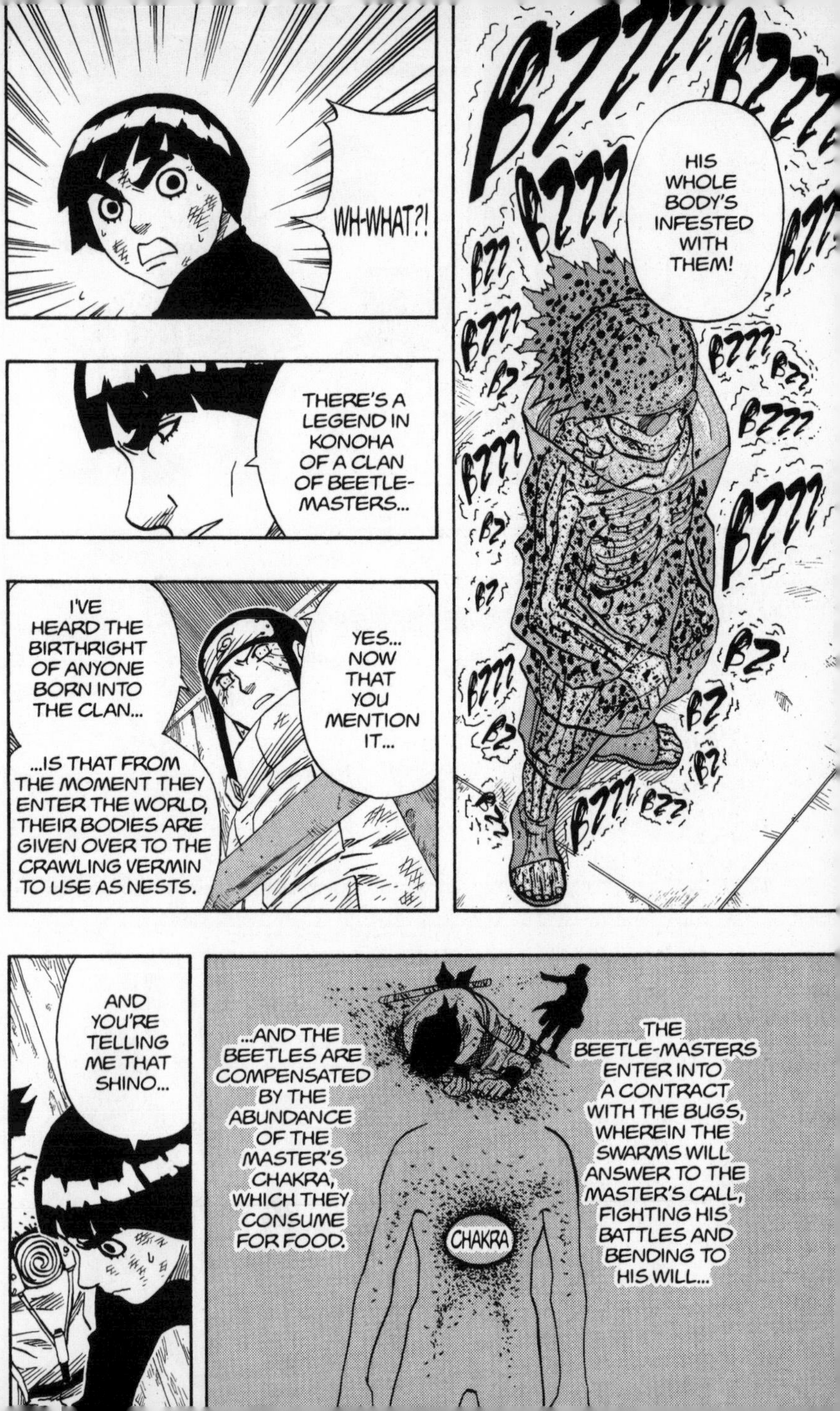

BZZZ BZZZ
BZZZ
HIS WHOLE BODY'S INFESTED WITH THEM!
BZZ BZZZ BZZ BZZZ BZ BZZZ BZZZ BZ BZ BZZZ BZ BZ BZZZ BZ BZ BZZZ BZZ
WH-WHAT?!
THERE'S A LEGEND IN KONOHA OF A CLAN OF BEETLE-MASTERS...
YES... NOW THAT YOU MENTION IT...
I'VE HEARD THE BIRTHRIGHT OF ANYONE BORN INTO THE CLAN...
...IS THAT FROM THE MOMENT THEY ENTER THE WORLD, THEIR BODIES ARE GIVEN OVER TO THE CRAWLING VERMIN TO USE AS NESTS.
THE BEETLE-MASTERS ENTER INTO A CONTRACT WITH THE BUGS, WHEREIN THE SWARMS WILL ANSWER TO THE MASTER'S CALL, FIGHTING HIS BATTLES AND BENDING TO HIS WILL...
...AND THE BEETLES ARE COMPENSATED BY THE ABUNDANCE OF THE MASTER'S CHAKRA, WHICH THEY CONSUME FOR FOOD.
CHAKRA
AND YOU'RE TELLING ME THAT SHINO...

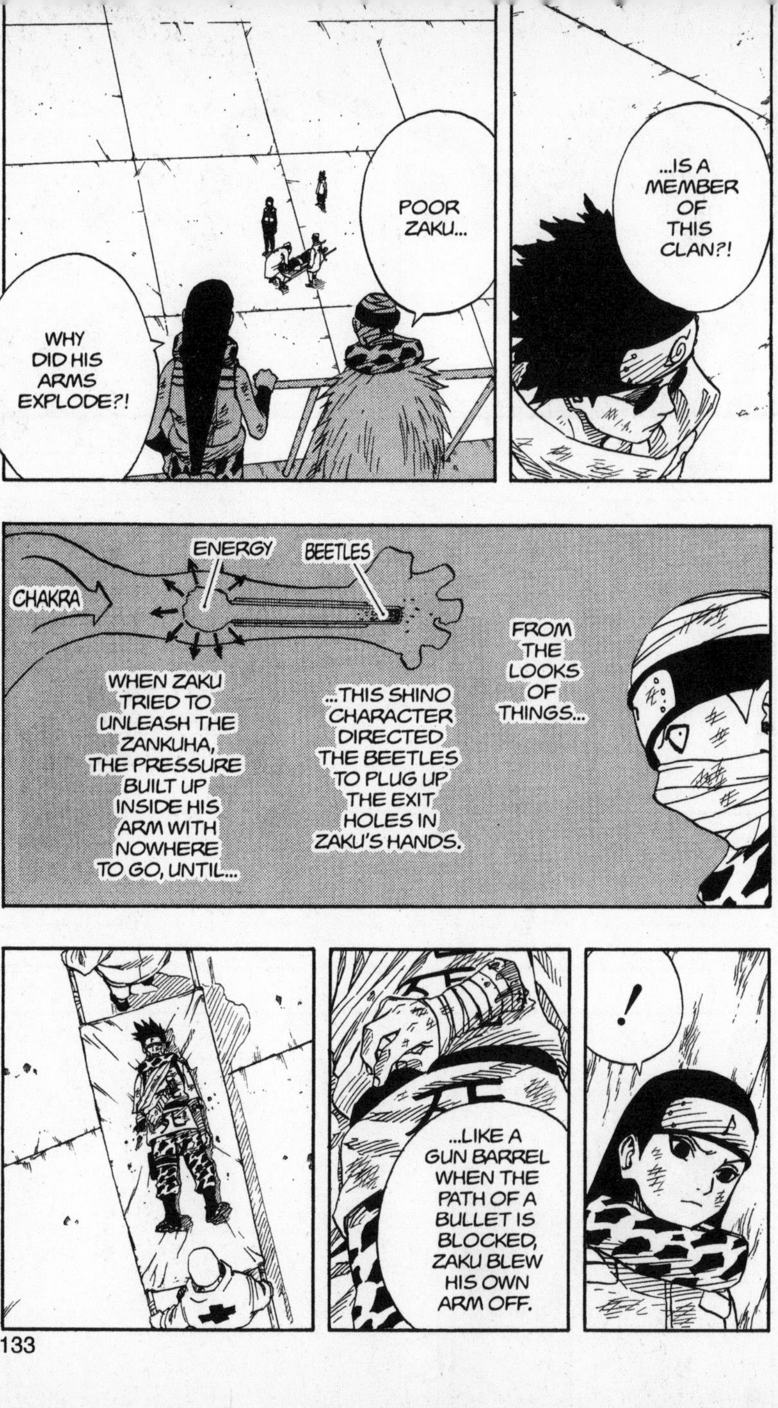
...IS A MEMBER OF THIS CLAN?!
POOR ZAKU...
WHY DID HIS ARMS EXPLODE?!
FROM THE LOOKS OF THINGS...
...THIS SHINO CHARACTER DIRECTED THE BEETLES TO PLUG UP THE EXIT HOLES IN ZAKU'S HANDS.
BEETLES
ENERGY
CHAKRA
WHEN ZAKU TRIED TO UNLEASH THE ZANKUHA, THE PRESSURE BUILT UP INSIDE HIS ARM WITH NOWHERE TO GO, UNTIL...
!
...LIKE A GUN BARREL WHEN THE PATH OF A BULLET IS BLOCKED, ZAKU BLEW HIS OWN ARM OFF.

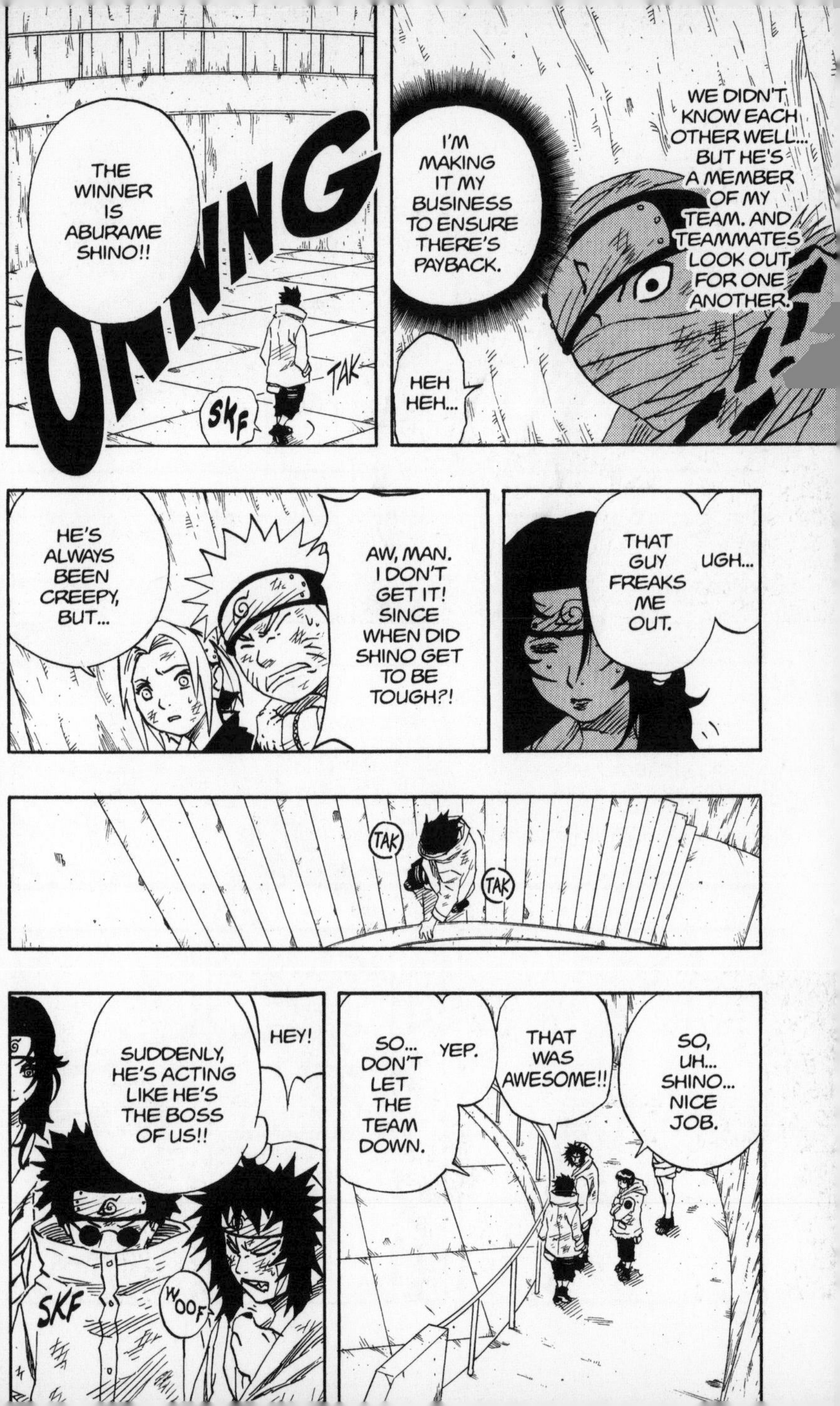
WE DIDN'T KNOW EACH OTHER WELL... BUT HE'S A MEMBER OF MY TEAM. AND TEAMMATES LOOK OUT FOR ONE ANOTHER.
I'M MAKING IT MY BUSINESS TO ENSURE THERE'S PAYBACK.
HEH HEH...
ONNNG
THE WINNER IS ABURAME SHINO!!
TAK
SKF
UGH...
THAT GUY FREAKS ME OUT.
AW, MAN. I DON'T GET IT! SINCE WHEN DID SHINO GET TO BE TOUGH?!
HE'S ALWAYS BEEN CREEPY, BUT...
TAK
TAK
SO, UH... SHINO... NICE JOB.
THAT WAS AWESOME!!
YEP.
SO... DON'T LET THE TEAM DOWN.
HEY!
SUDDENLY, HE'S ACTING LIKE HE'S THE BOSS OF US!!
WOOF
SKF

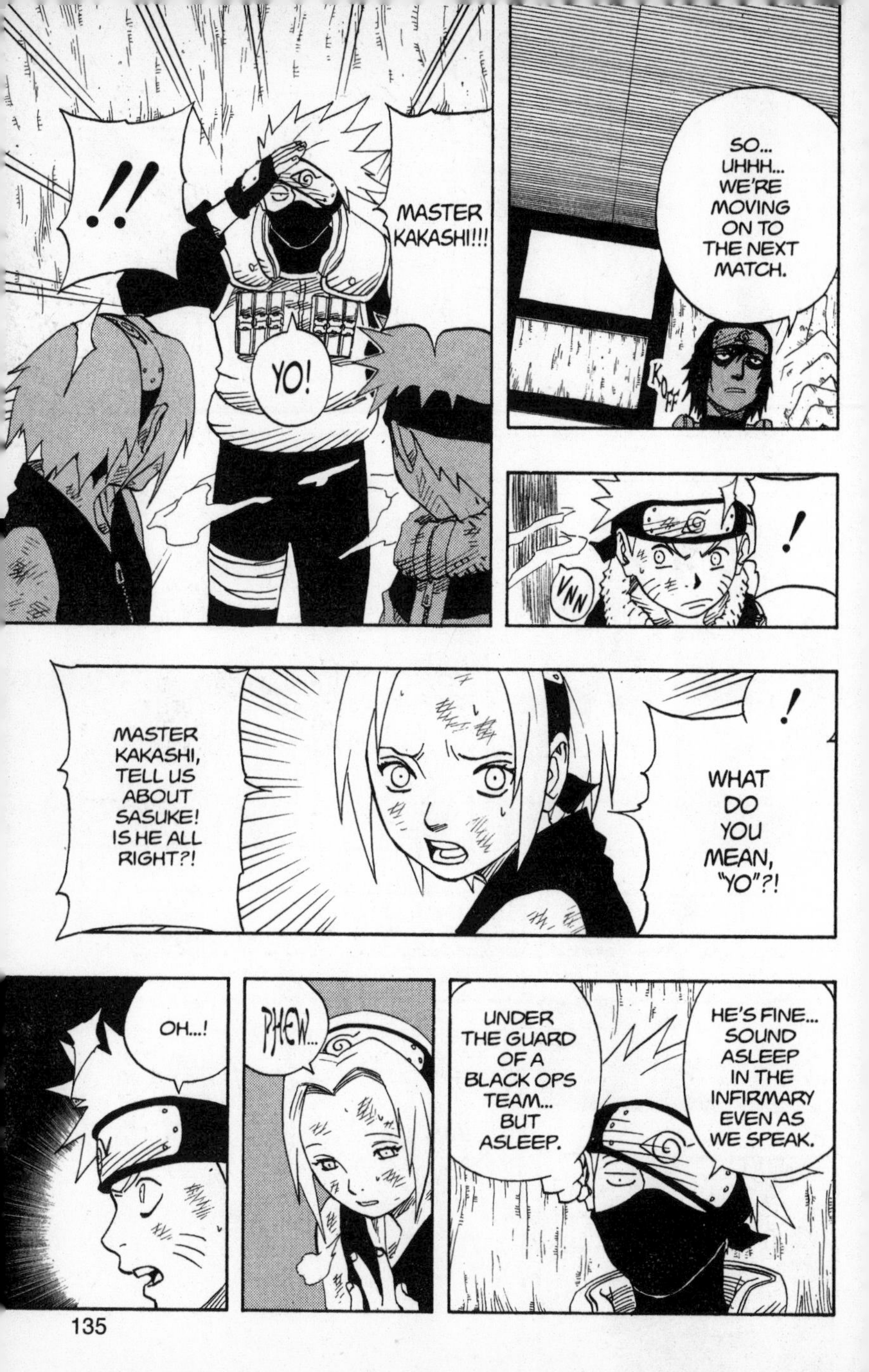
SO... UHHH... WE'RE MOVING ON TO THE NEXT MATCH.
KOFF
!
VNN
MASTER KAKASHI!!!
!!
YO!
!
WHAT DO YOU MEAN, "YO"?!
MASTER KAKASHI, TELL US ABOUT SASUKE! IS HE ALL RIGHT?!
HE'S FINE... SOUND ASLEEP IN THE INFIRMARY EVEN AS WE SPEAK.
UNDER THE GUARD OF A BLACK OPS TEAM... BUT ASLEEP.
PHEW...
OH...!

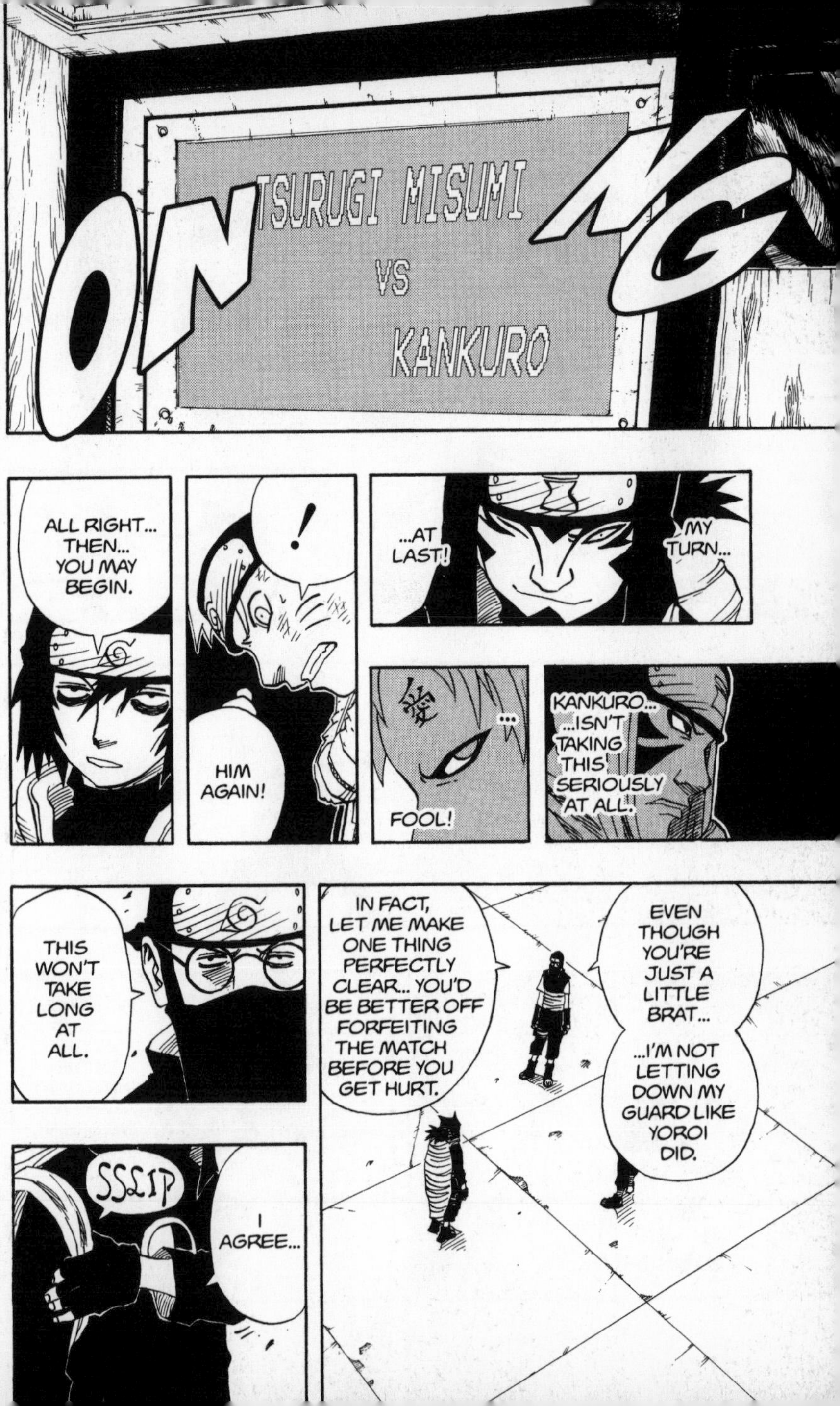
ON
NG
TSURUGI MISUMI VS KANKURO
MY TURN...
...AT LAST!
KANKURO... ...ISN'T TAKING THIS SERIOUSLY AT ALL.
...
FOOL!
!
HIM AGAIN!
ALL RIGHT... THEN... YOU MAY BEGIN.
EVEN THOUGH YOU'RE JUST A LITTLE BRAT...
...I'M NOT LETTING DOWN MY GUARD LIKE YOROI DID.
IN FACT, LET ME MAKE ONE THING PERFECTLY CLEAR... YOU'D BE BETTER OFF FORFEITING THE MATCH BEFORE YOU GET HURT.
THIS WON'T TAKE LONG AT ALL.
SSLIP
I AGREE...

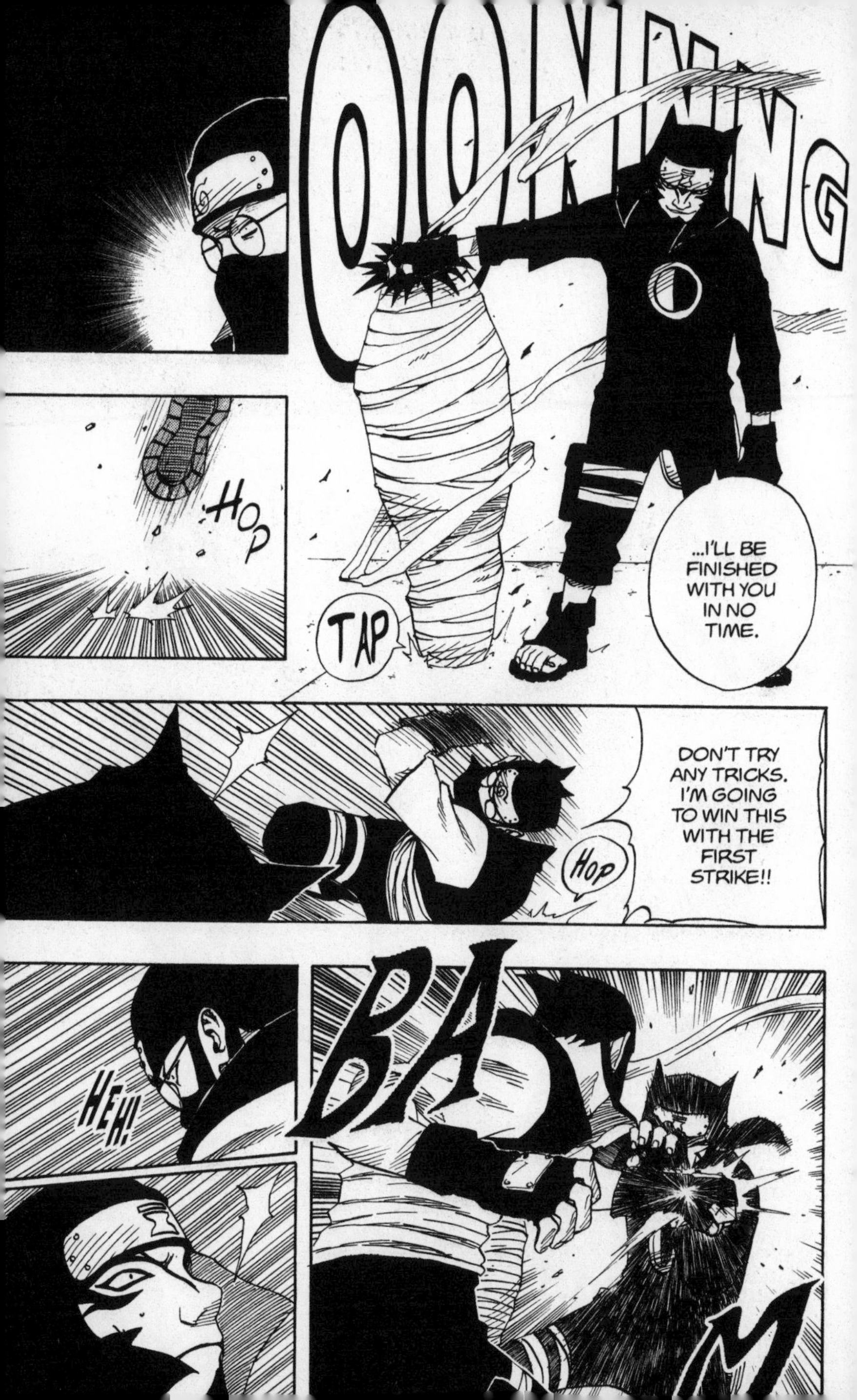
OOINNNG
...I'LL BE FINISHED WITH YOU IN NO TIME.
TAP
HOP
DON'T TRY ANY TRICKS. I'M GOING TO WIN THIS WITH THE FIRST STRIKE!!
HOP
BAM
HEH!

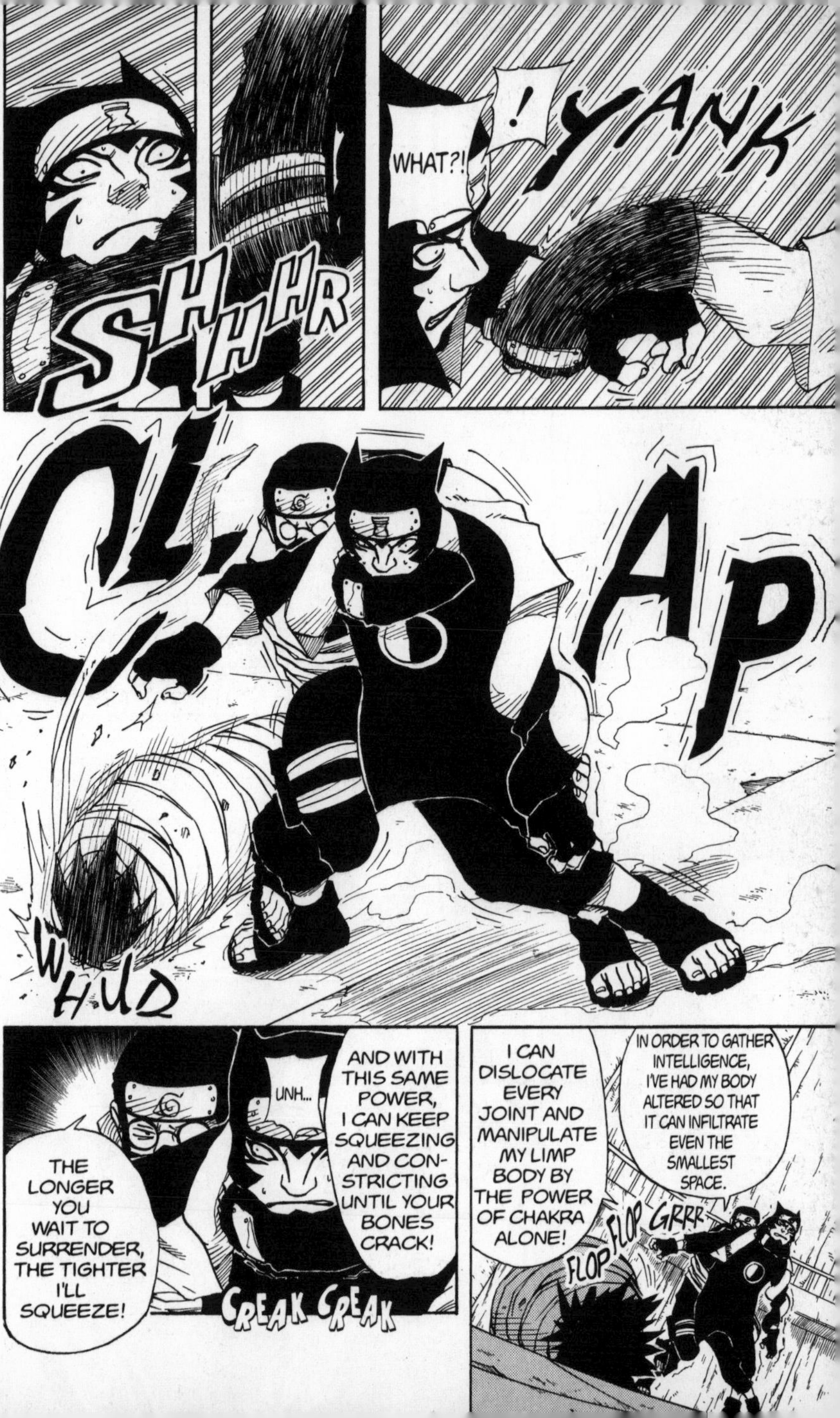
!
WHAT?!
YANK
SHHHR
CLAP
WHUD
IN ORDER TO GATHER INTELLIGENCE, I'VE HAD MY BODY ALTERED SO THAT IT CAN INFILTRATE EVEN THE SMALLEST SPACE.
I CAN DISLOCATE EVERY JOINT AND MANIPULATE MY LIMP BODY BY THE POWER OF CHAKRA ALONE!
GRRR
FLOP FLOP
AND WITH THIS SAME POWER, I CAN KEEP SQUEEZING AND CON-STRICTING UNTIL YOUR BONES CRACK!
UNH...
THE LONGER YOU WAIT TO SURRENDER, THE TIGHTER I'LL SQUEEZE!
CREAK CREAK

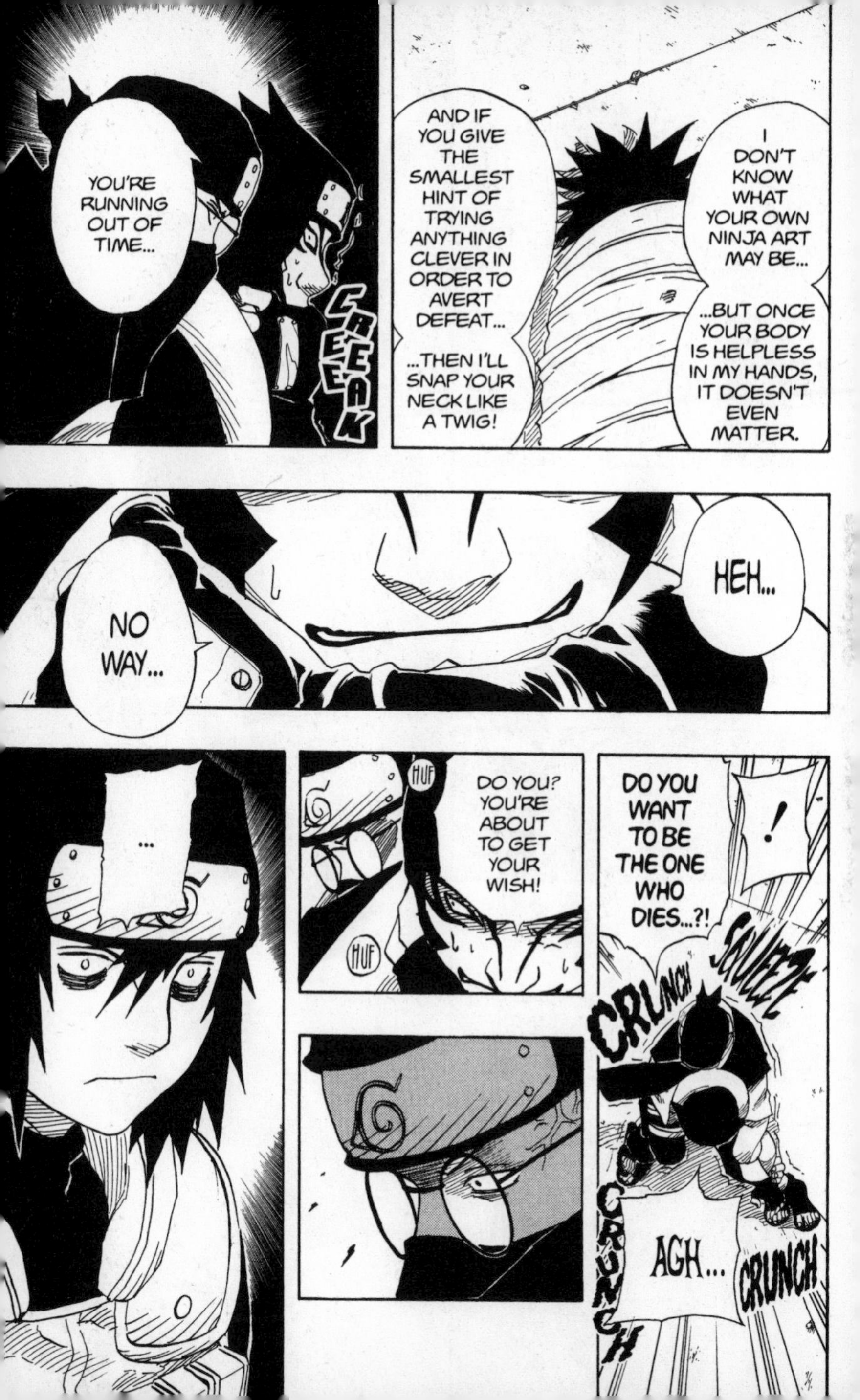

I DON'T KNOW WHAT YOUR OWN NINJA ART MAY BE...
...BUT ONCE YOUR BODY IS HELPLESS IN MY HANDS, IT DOESN'T EVEN MATTER.
AND IF YOU GIVE THE SMALLEST HINT OF TRYING ANYTHING CLEVER IN ORDER TO AVERT DEFEAT...
...THEN I'LL SNAP YOUR NECK LIKE A TWIG!
YOU'RE RUNNING OUT OF TIME...
CREEEAK
HEH...
NO WAY...
!
DO YOU WANT TO BE THE ONE WHO DIES...?!
SQUEEZE
CRUNCH
AGH...
CRUNCH
CRUNCH
HUF
DO YOU? YOU'RE ABOUT TO GET YOUR WISH!
HUF
...

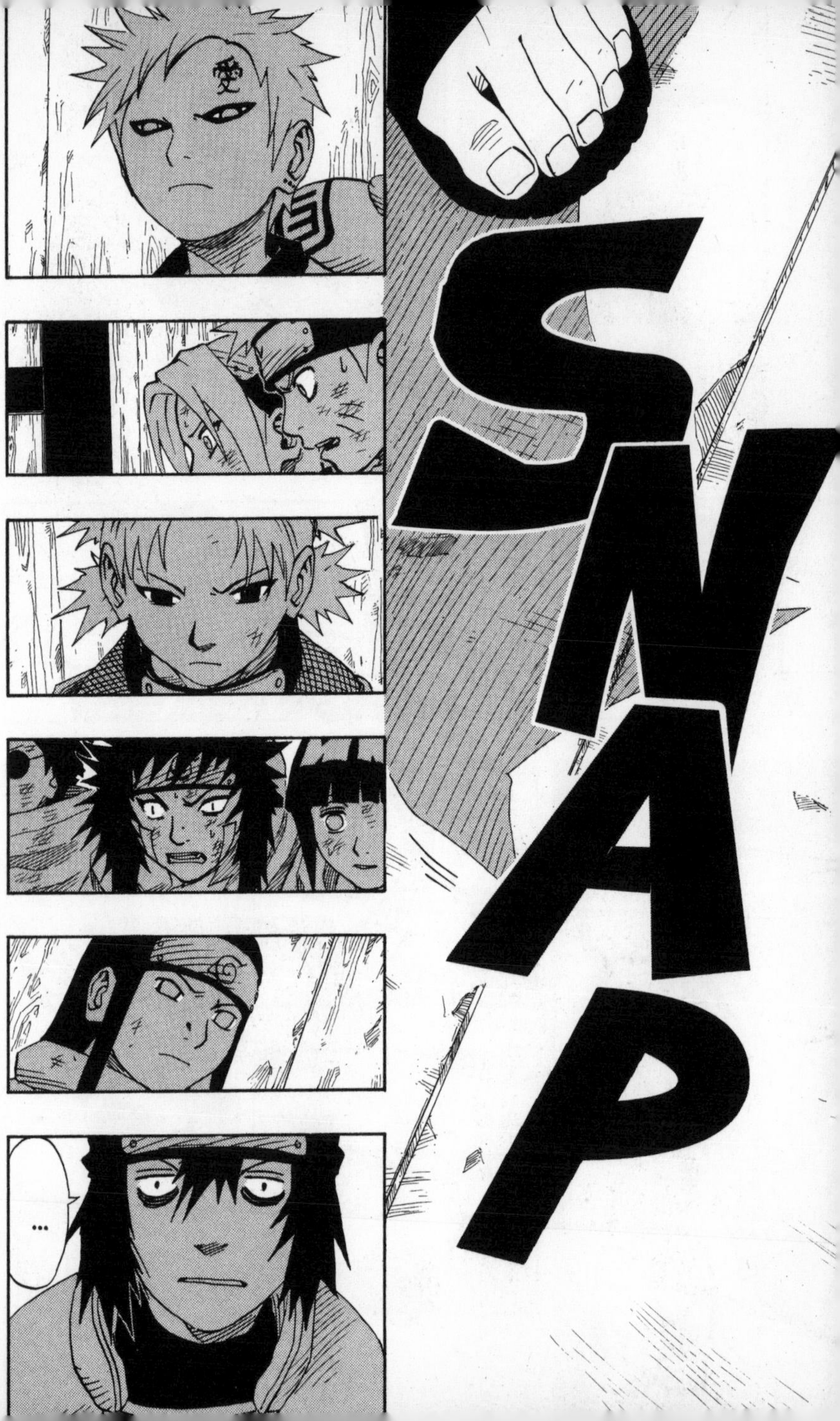
SNAP
...

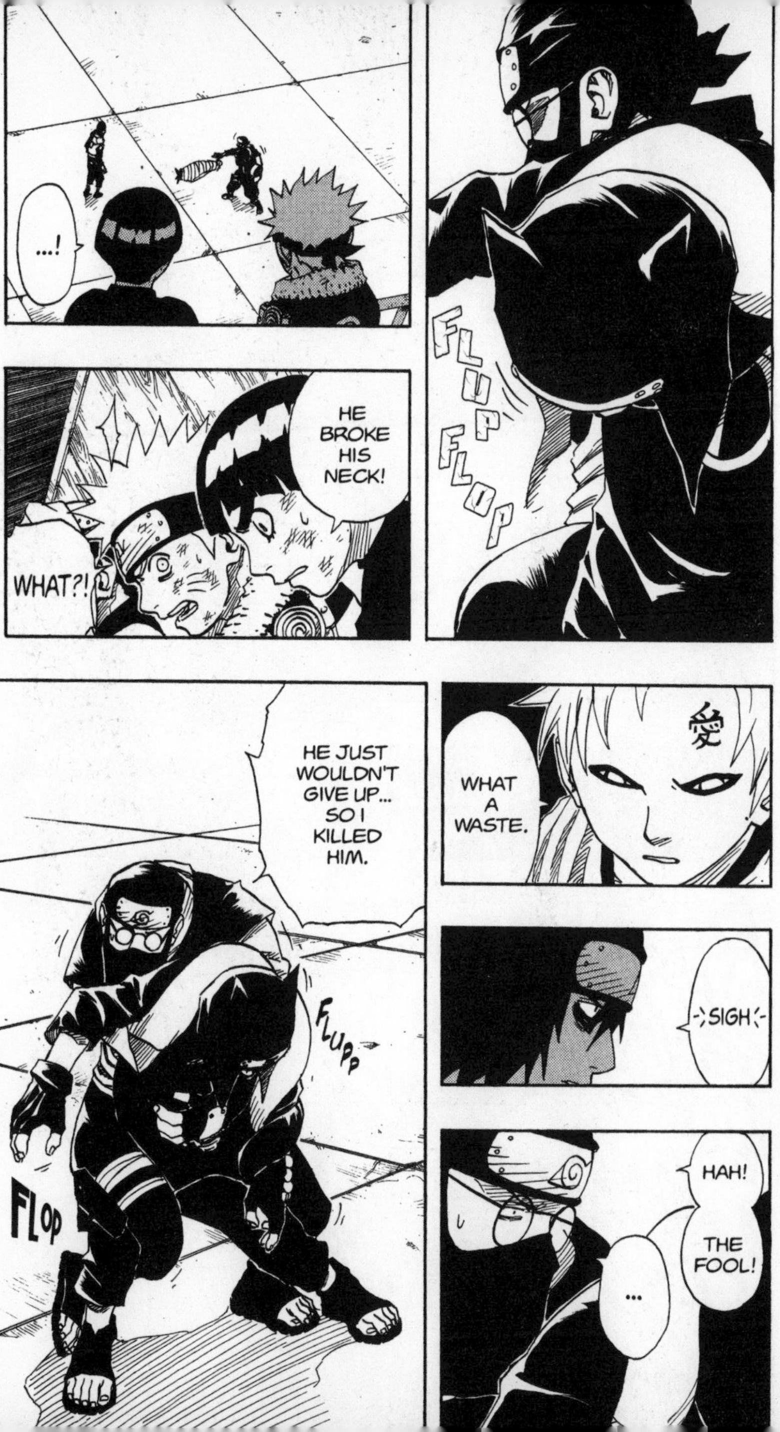
FLUP FLOP
...!
HE BROKE HIS NECK!
WHAT?!
愛
WHAT A WASTE.
SIGH
HAH!
THE FOOL!
...
HE JUST WOULDN'T GIVE UP... SO I KILLED HIM.
FLUPP
FLOP

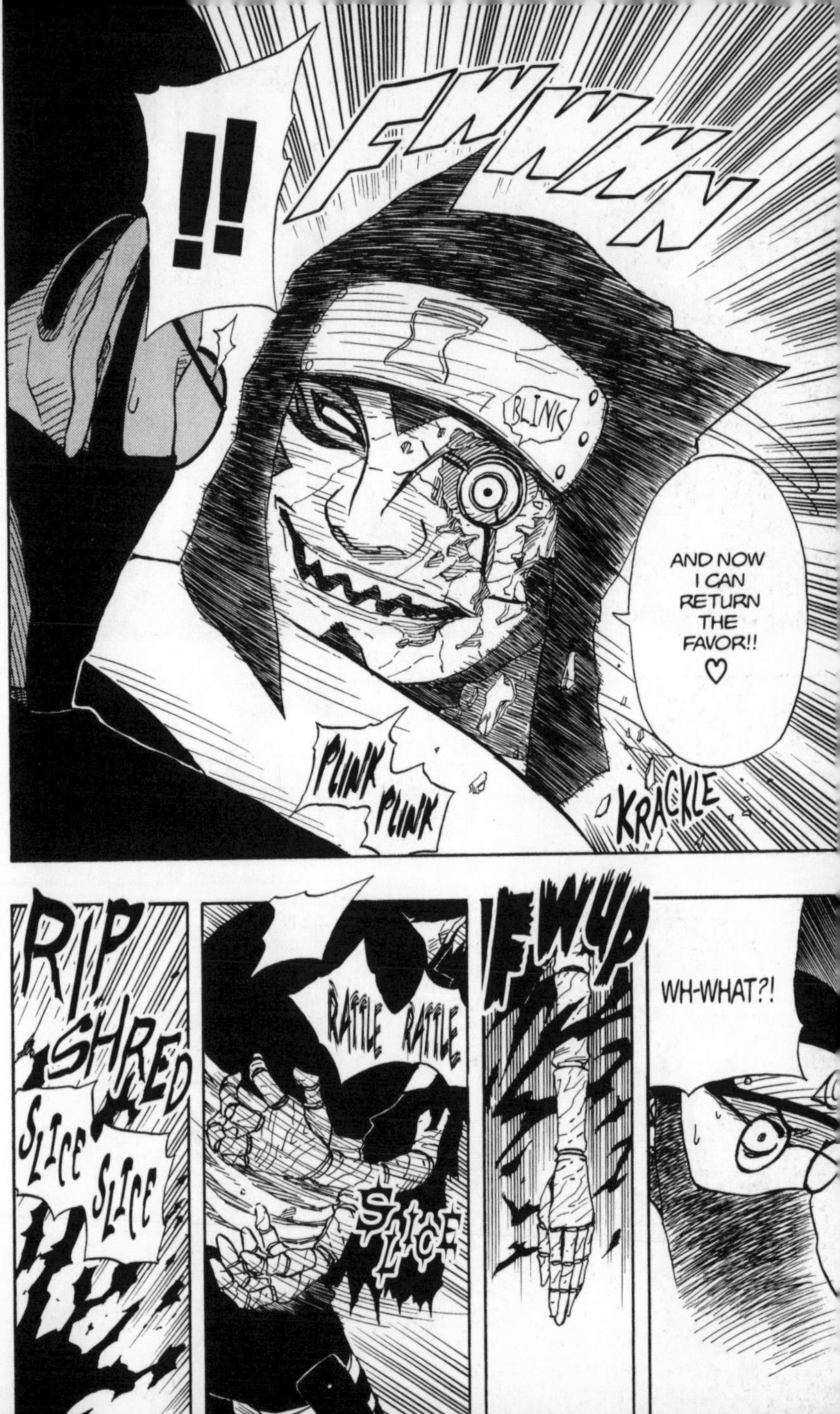
FWHN
!!
BLINK
AND NOW I CAN RETURN THE FAVOR!! ♡
KRACKLE
PLINK PLINK
WH-WHAT?!
FWUP
RATTLE RATTLE
SLICE
RIP
SHRED
SLICE SLICE

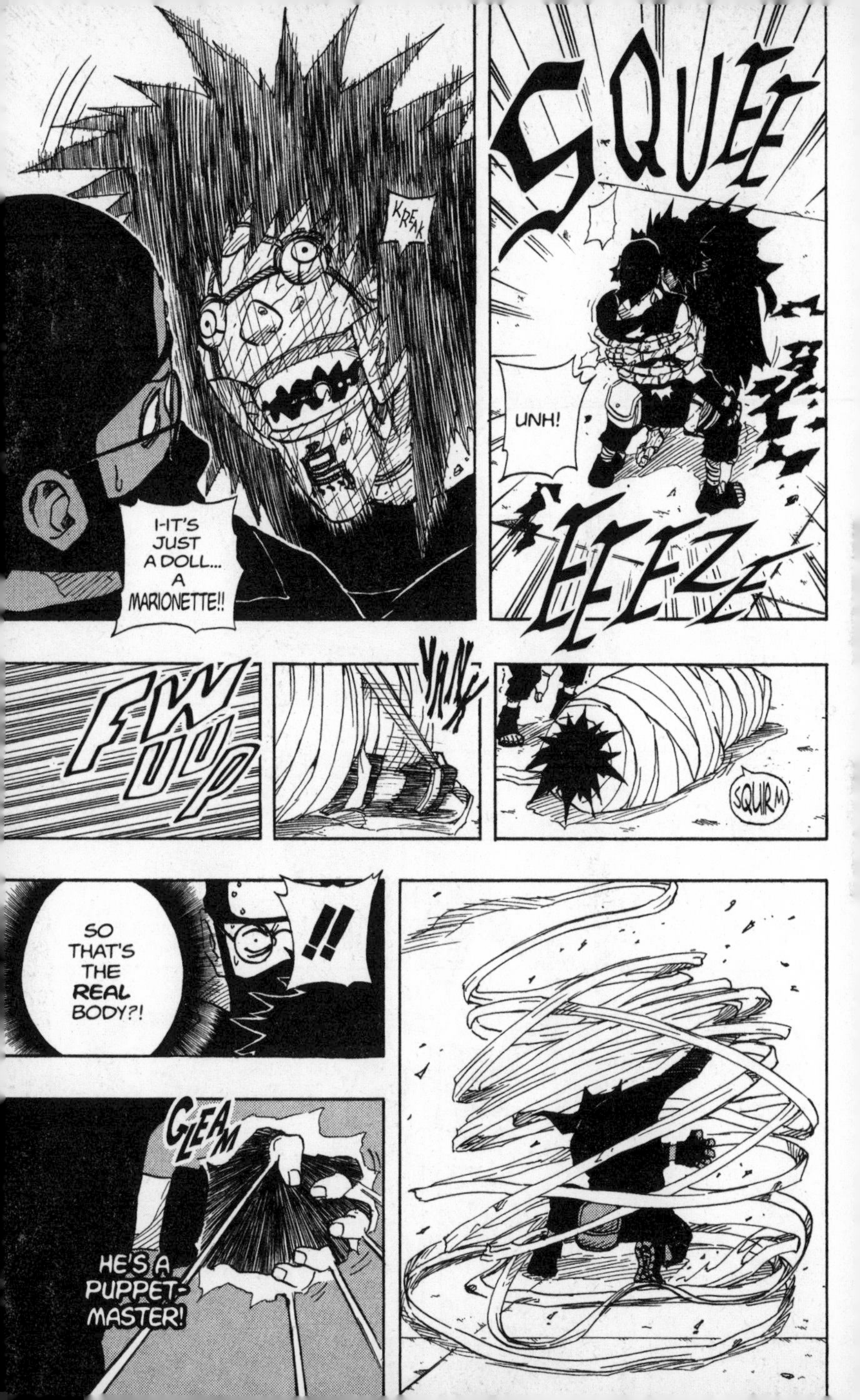
SQUEEEEEZE
UNH!
KREAK
I-IT'S JUST A DOLL... A MARIONETTE!!
SQUIRM
YANK
FWUUP
!!
SO THAT'S THE REAL BODY?!
GLEAM
HE'S A PUPPET-MASTER!

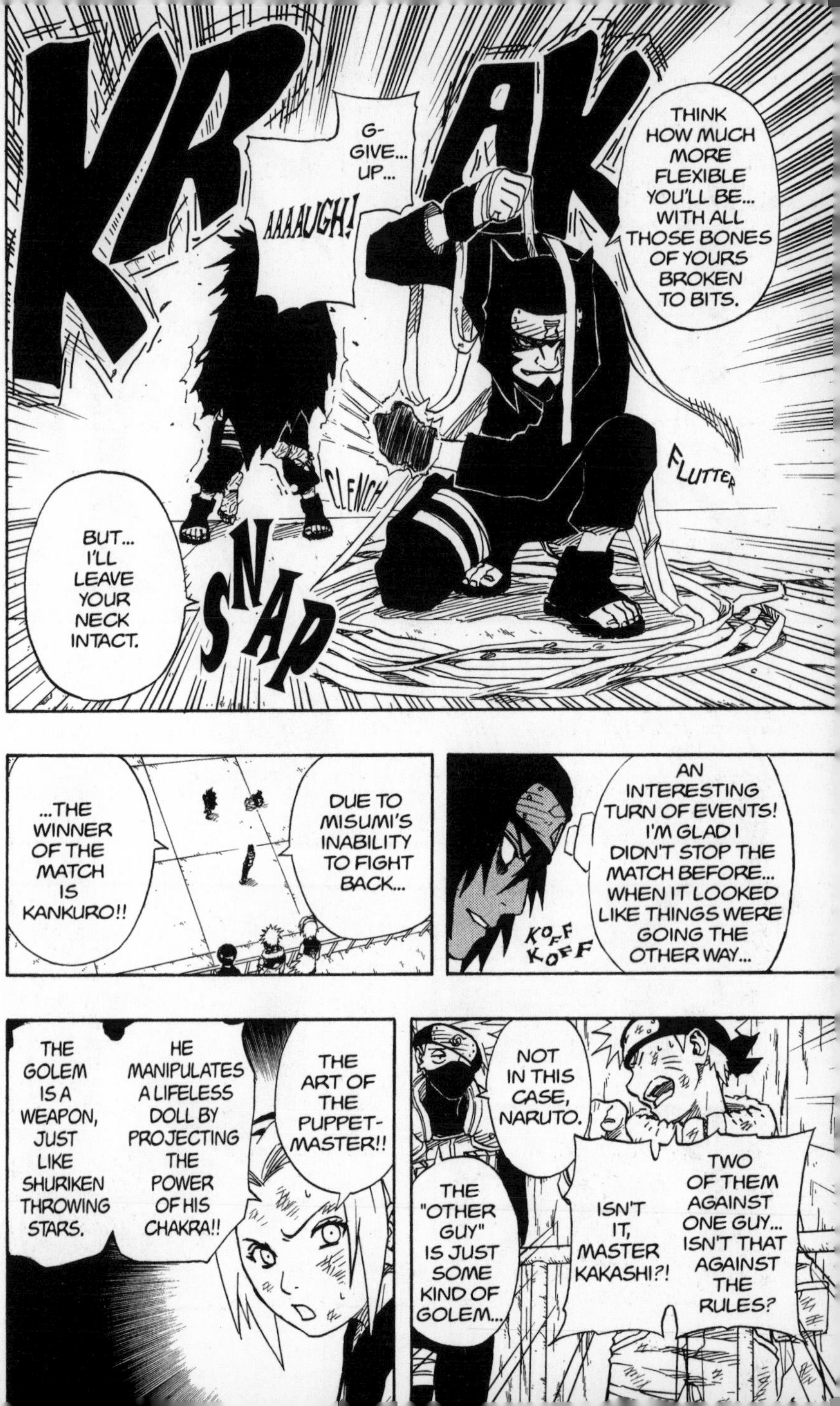
THINK HOW MUCH MORE FLEXIBLE YOU'LL BE... WITH ALL THOSE BONES OF YOURS BROKEN TO BITS.
KRAK
G-GIVE... UP...
AAAAUGH!
FLUTTER
CLENCH
SNAP
BUT... I'LL LEAVE YOUR NECK INTACT.
AN INTERESTING TURN OF EVENTS! I'M GLAD I DIDN'T STOP THE MATCH BEFORE... WHEN IT LOOKED LIKE THINGS WERE GOING THE OTHER WAY...
KOFF KOFF
DUE TO MISUMI'S INABILITY TO FIGHT BACK...
...THE WINNER OF THE MATCH IS KANKURO!!
TWO OF THEM AGAINST ONE GUY... ISN'T THAT AGAINST THE RULES?
ISN'T IT, MASTER KAKASHI?!
NOT IN THIS CASE, NARUTO.
THE "OTHER GUY" IS JUST SOME KIND OF GOLEM...
THE ART OF THE PUPPET-MASTER!!
HE MANIPULATES A LIFELESS DOLL BY PROJECTING THE POWER OF HIS CHAKRA!!
THE GOLEM IS A WEAPON, JUST LIKE SHURIKEN THROWING STARS.

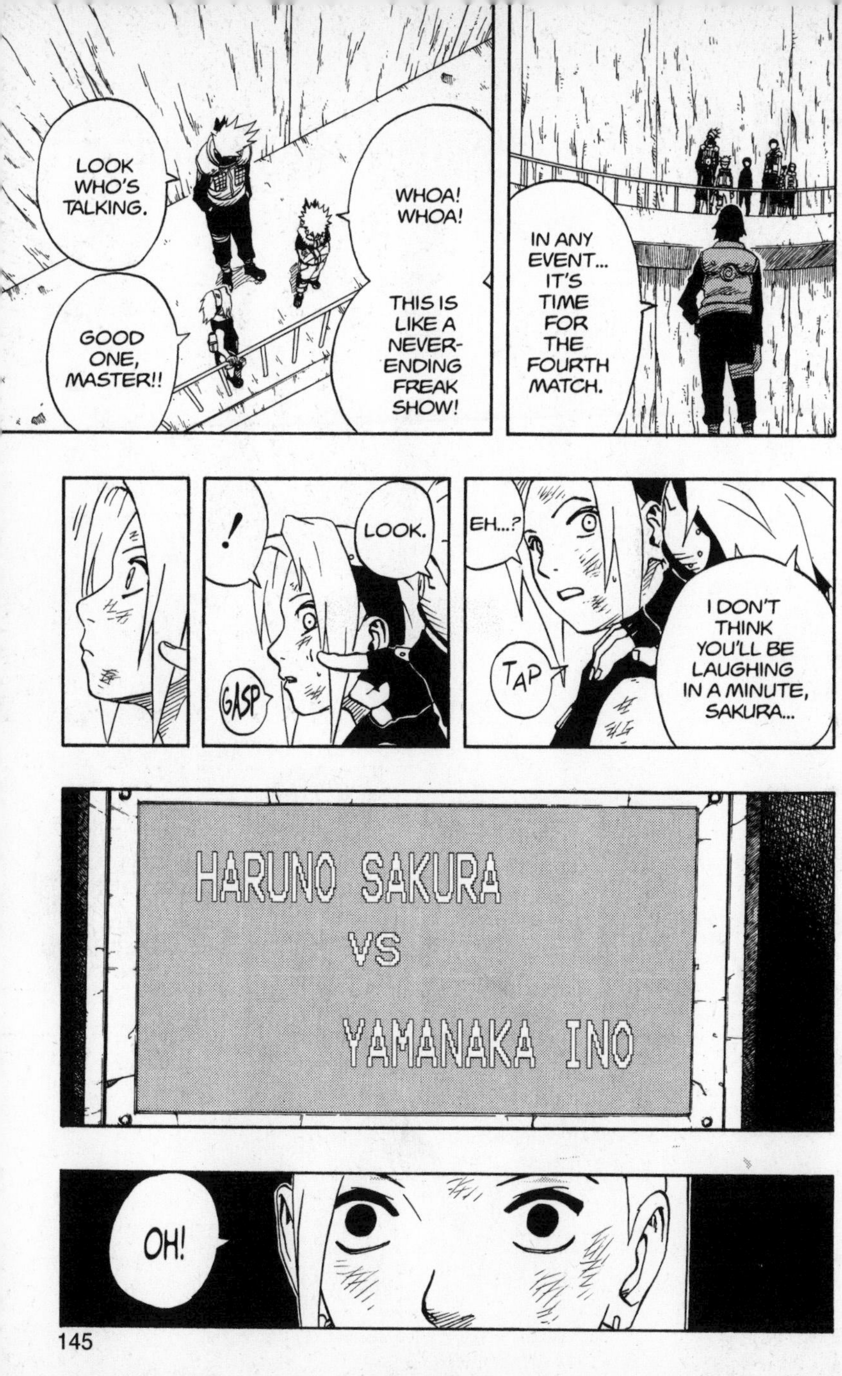
IN ANY EVENT... IT'S TIME FOR THE FOURTH MATCH.
WHOA! WHOA!
THIS IS LIKE A NEVER-ENDING FREAK SHOW!
LOOK WHO'S TALKING.
GOOD ONE, MASTER!!
EH...?
I DON'T THINK YOU'LL BE LAUGHING IN A MINUTE, SAKURA...
TAP
LOOK.
!
GASP
HARUNO SAKURA
VS
YAMANAKA INO
OH!

Number 71: The Insurmountable Wall...!!

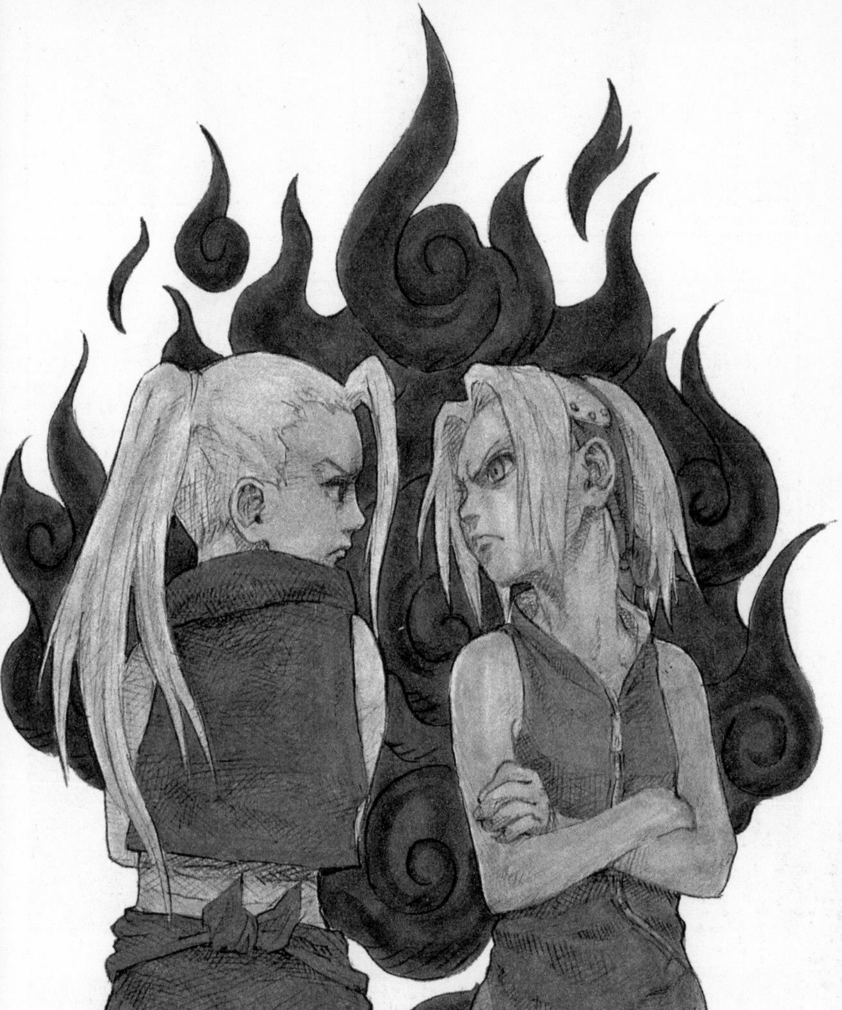

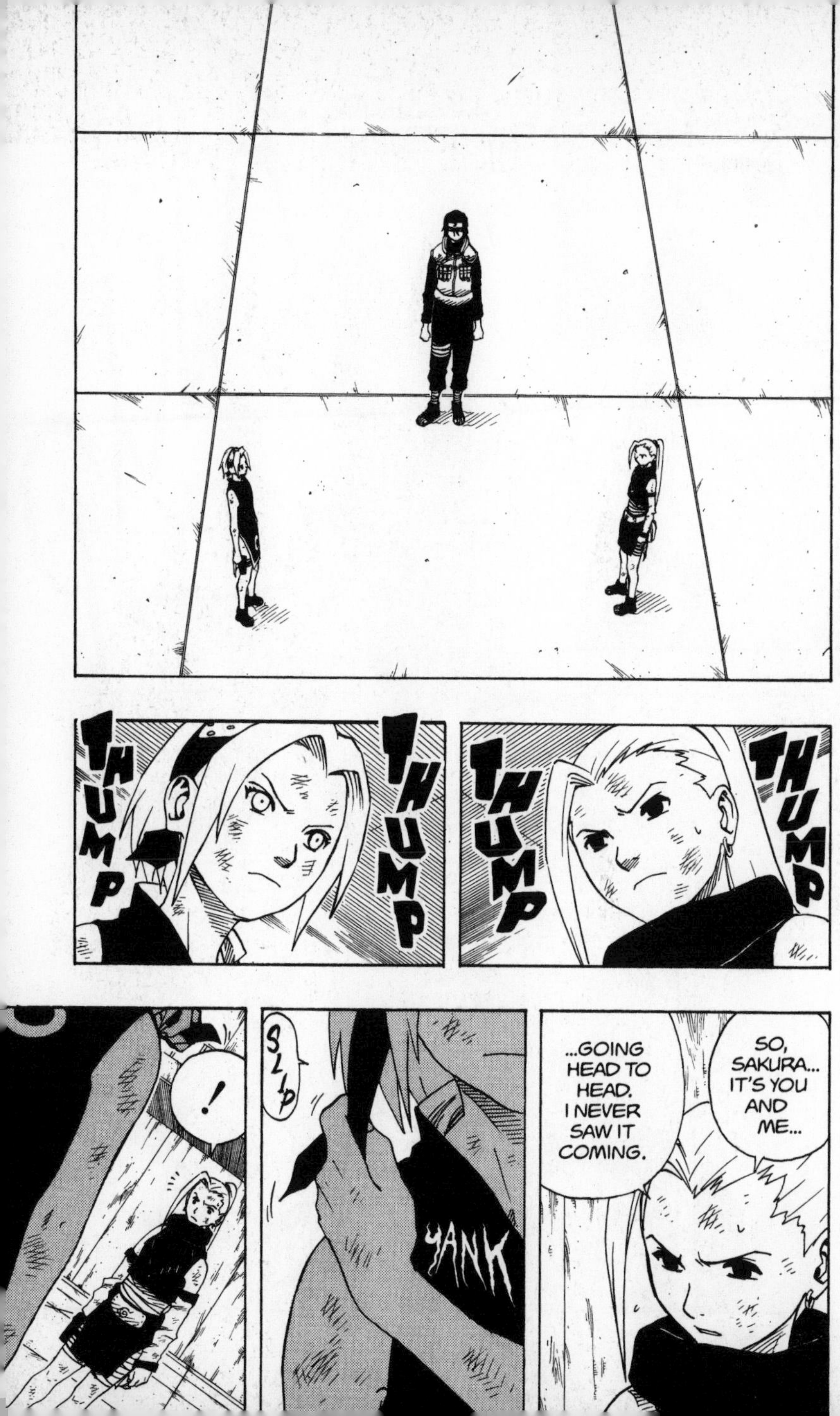
THUMP
THUMP
THUMP
THUMP
SO, SAKURA... IT'S YOU AND ME...
...GOING HEAD TO HEAD. I NEVER SAW IT COMING.
SLIP
YANK
!

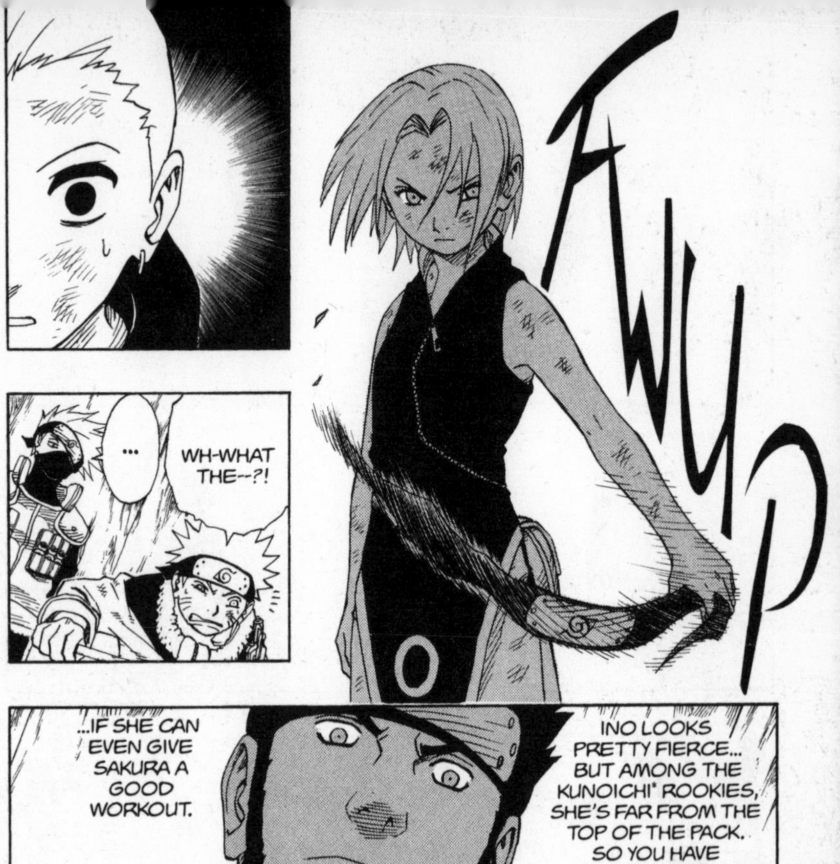
FWUP
...
WH-WHAT THE--?!
INO LOOKS PRETTY FIERCE... BUT AMONG THE KUNOICHI* ROOKIES, SHE'S FAR FROM THE TOP OF THE PACK. SO YOU HAVE TO WONDER...
...IF SHE CAN EVEN GIVE SAKURA A GOOD WORKOUT.

*KUNOICHI = FEMALE SHINOBI

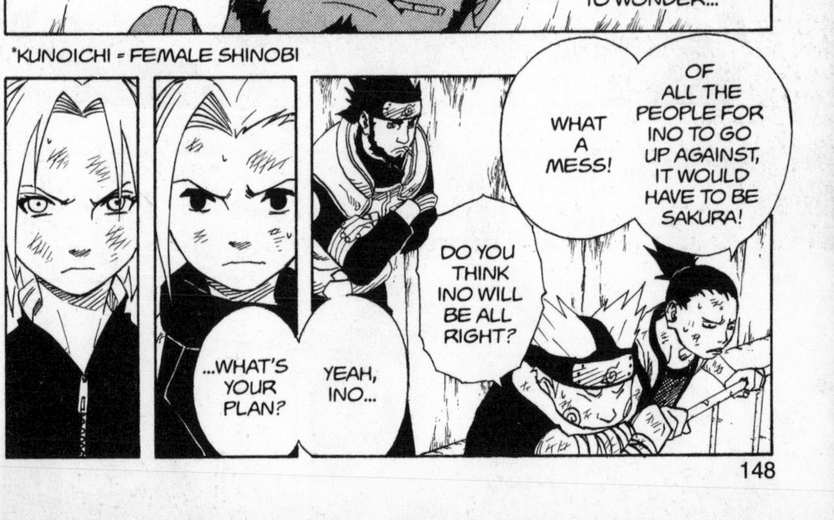
OF ALL THE PEOPLE FOR INO TO GO UP AGAINST, IT WOULD HAVE TO BE SAKURA!
WHAT A MESS!
DO YOU THINK INO WILL BE ALL RIGHT?
YEAH, INO...
...WHAT'S YOUR PLAN?

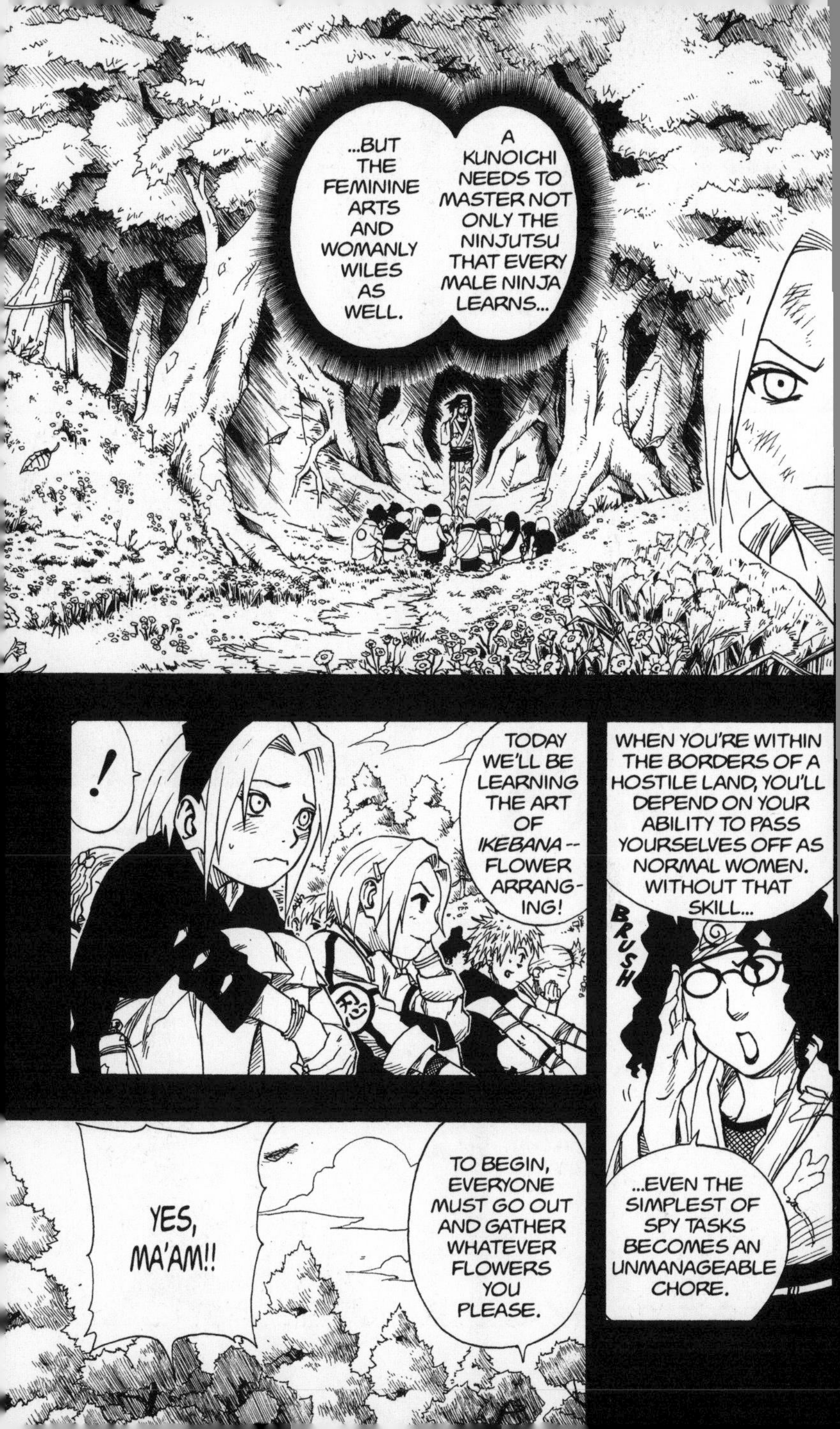
A KUNOICHI NEEDS TO MASTER NOT ONLY THE NINJUTSU THAT EVERY MALE NINJA LEARNS...
...BUT THE FEMININE ARTS AND WOMANLY WILES AS WELL.
WHEN YOU'RE WITHIN THE BORDERS OF A HOSTILE LAND, YOU'LL DEPEND ON YOUR ABILITY TO PASS YOURSELVES OFF AS NORMAL WOMEN. WITHOUT THAT SKILL...
BRUSH
...EVEN THE SIMPLEST OF SPY TASKS BECOMES AN UNMANAGEABLE CHORE.
TODAY WE'LL BE LEARNING THE ART OF *IKEBANA* -- FLOWER ARRANG-ING!
!
TO BEGIN, EVERYONE MUST GO OUT AND GATHER WHATEVER FLOWERS YOU PLEASE.
YES, MA'AM!!

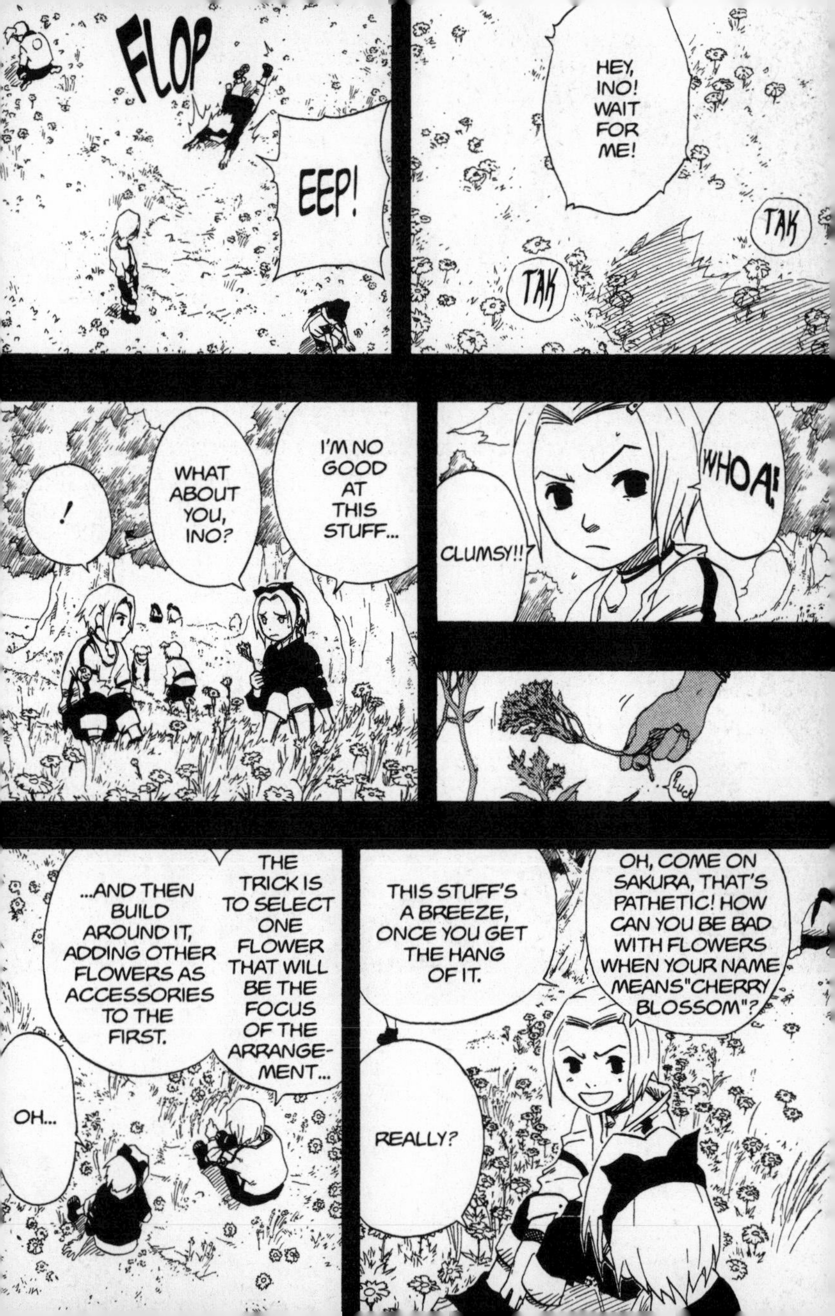
HEY, INO! WAIT FOR ME!
TAK
TAK
FLOP
EEP!
WHOA!
CLUMSY!!
I'M NO GOOD AT THIS STUFF...
WHAT ABOUT YOU, INO?
!
OH, COME ON SAKURA, THAT'S PATHETIC! HOW CAN YOU BE BAD WITH FLOWERS WHEN YOUR NAME MEANS "CHERRY BLOSSOM"?
THIS STUFF'S A BREEZE, ONCE YOU GET THE HANG OF IT.
REALLY?
THE TRICK IS TO SELECT ONE FLOWER THAT WILL BE THE FOCUS OF THE ARRANGE-MENT...
...AND THEN BUILD AROUND IT, ADDING OTHER FLOWERS AS ACCESSORIES TO THE FIRST.
OH...

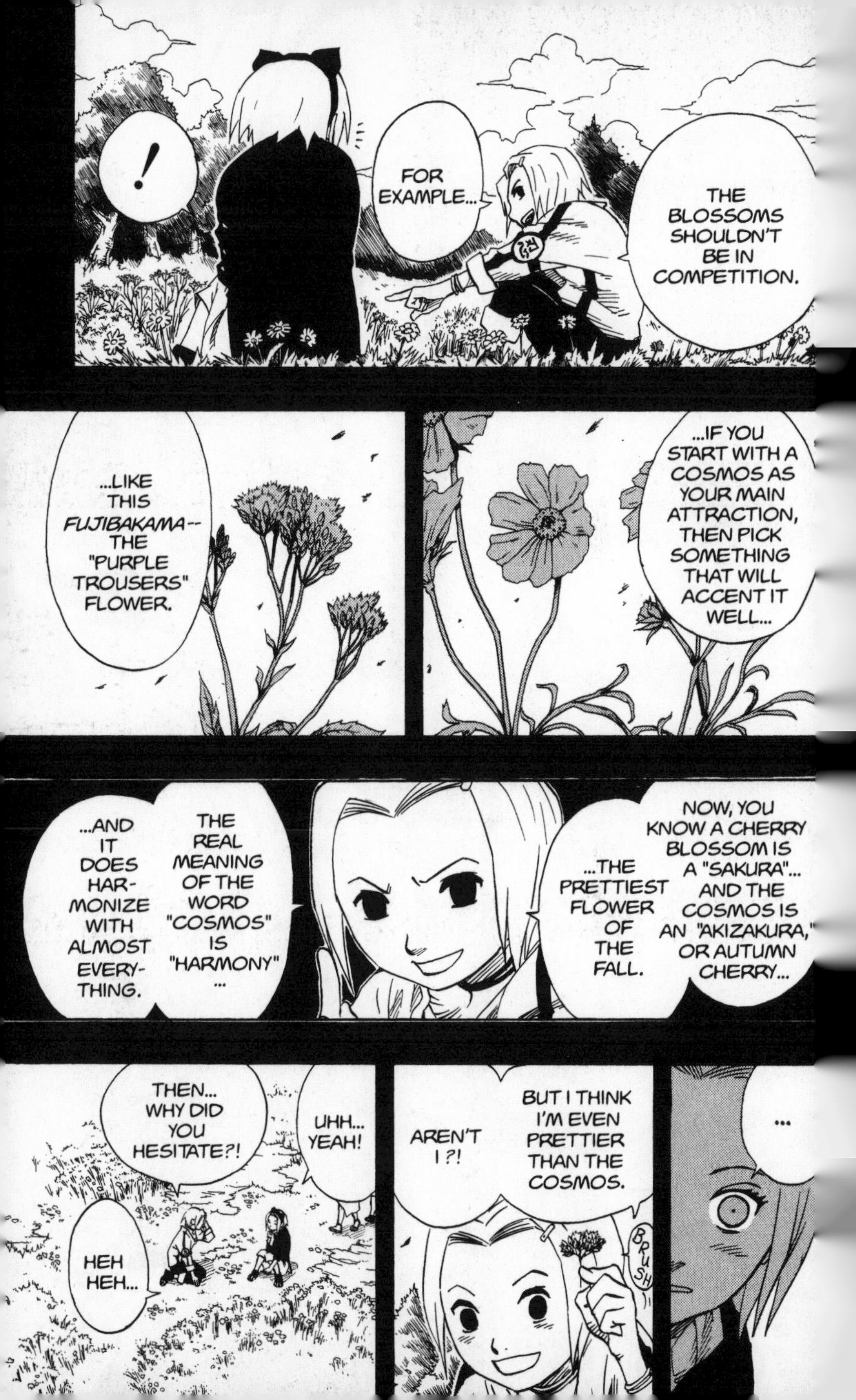
THE BLOSSOMS SHOULDN'T BE IN COMPETITION.
FOR EXAMPLE...
!
...IF YOU START WITH A COSMOS AS YOUR MAIN ATTRACTION, THEN PICK SOMETHING THAT WILL ACCENT IT WELL...
...LIKE THIS *FUJIBAKAMA*-- THE "PURPLE TROUSERS" FLOWER.
NOW, YOU KNOW A CHERRY BLOSSOM IS A "SAKURA"... AND THE COSMOS IS AN "AKIZAKURA," OR AUTUMN CHERRY...
...THE PRETTIEST FLOWER OF THE FALL.
THE REAL MEANING OF THE WORD "COSMOS" IS "HARMONY"...
...AND IT DOES HAR-MONIZE WITH ALMOST EVERY-THING.
...
BUT I THINK I'M EVEN PRETTIER THAN THE COSMOS.
AREN'T I?!
BRUSH
UHH... YEAH!
THEN... WHY DID YOU HESITATE?!
HEH HEH...

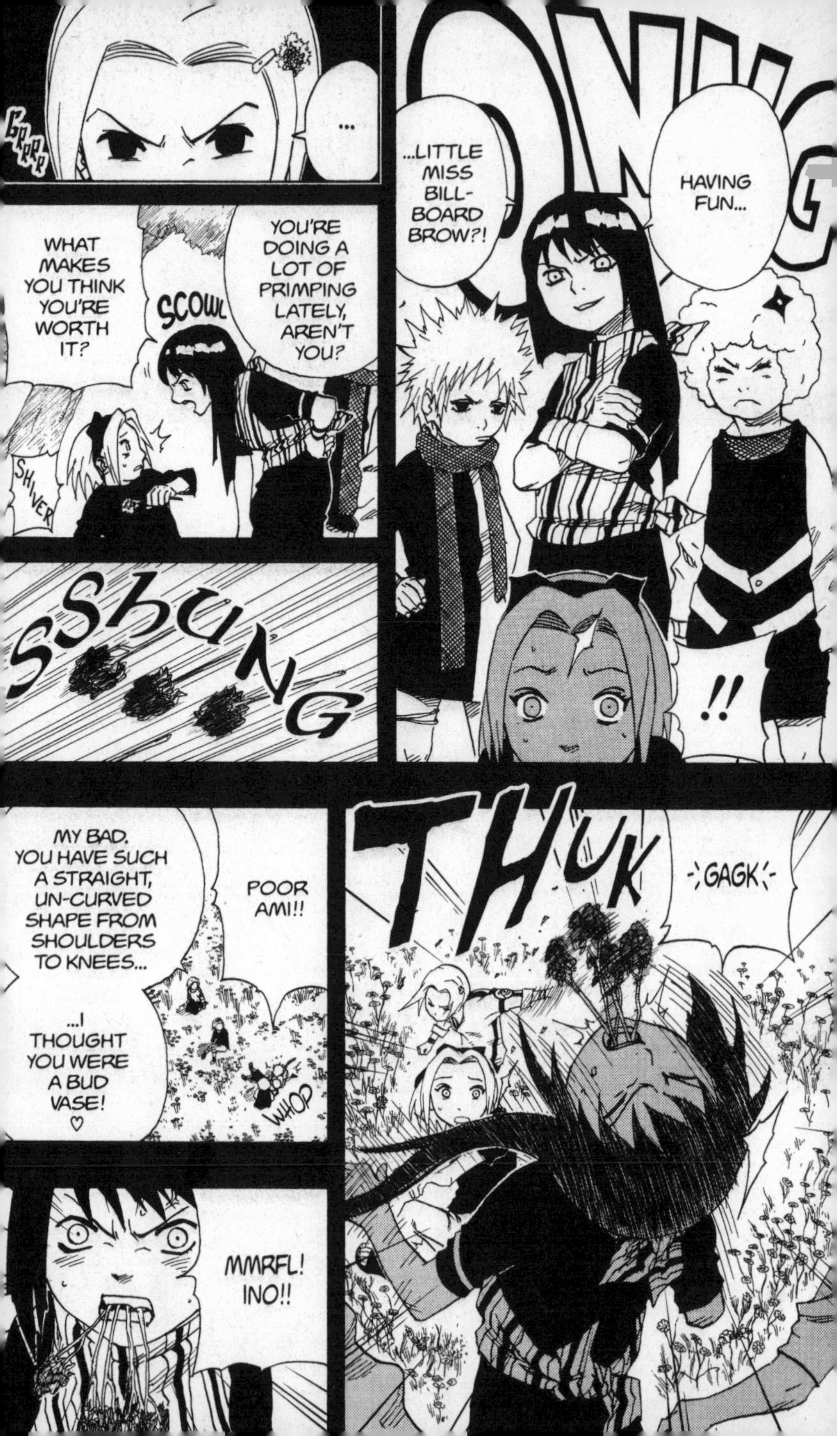
HAVING FUN...
...LITTLE MISS BILL-BOARD BROW?!
!!
...
GRRRR
YOU'RE DOING A LOT OF PRIMPING LATELY, AREN'T YOU?
SCOWL
WHAT MAKES YOU THINK YOU'RE WORTH IT?
SHIVER
SSHUNG
THUK
GAGK
MY BAD. YOU HAVE SUCH A STRAIGHT, UN-CURVED SHAPE FROM SHOULDERS TO KNEES...
POOR AMI!!
...I THOUGHT YOU WERE A BUD VASE! ♡
WHOP
MMRFL! INO!!

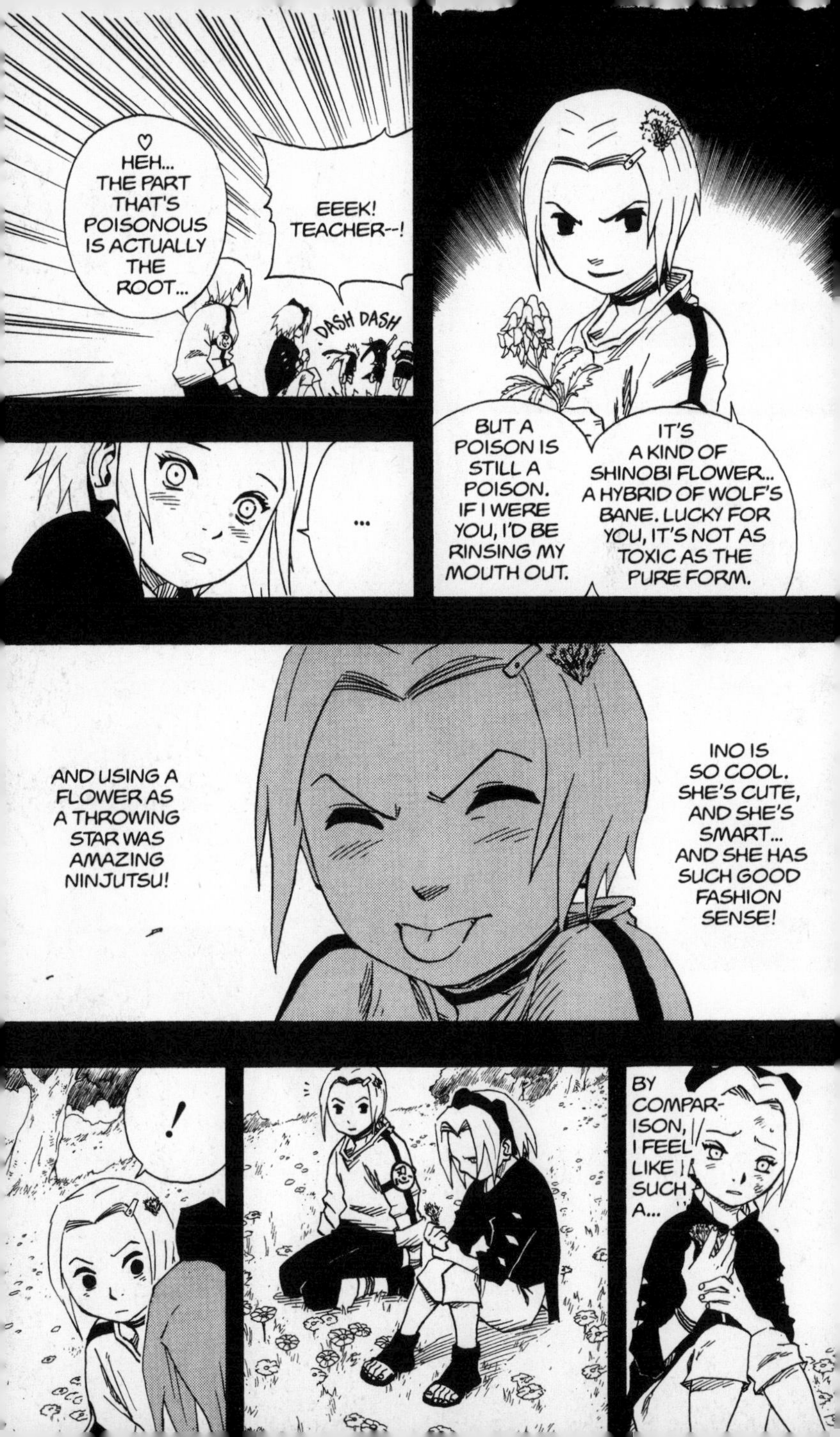
IT'S A KIND OF SHINOBI FLOWER... A HYBRID OF WOLF'S BANE. LUCKY FOR YOU, IT'S NOT AS TOXIC AS THE PURE FORM.
BUT A POISON IS STILL A POISON. IF I WERE YOU, I'D BE RINSING MY MOUTH OUT.
♡ HEH... THE PART THAT'S POISONOUS IS ACTUALLY THE ROOT...
EEEK! TEACHER--!
DASH DASH
...
INO IS SO COOL. SHE'S CUTE, AND SHE'S SMART... AND SHE HAS SUCH GOOD FASHION SENSE!
AND USING A FLOWER AS A THROWING STAR WAS AMAZING NINJUTSU!
BY COMPARISON, I FEEL LIKE I SUCH A...
!

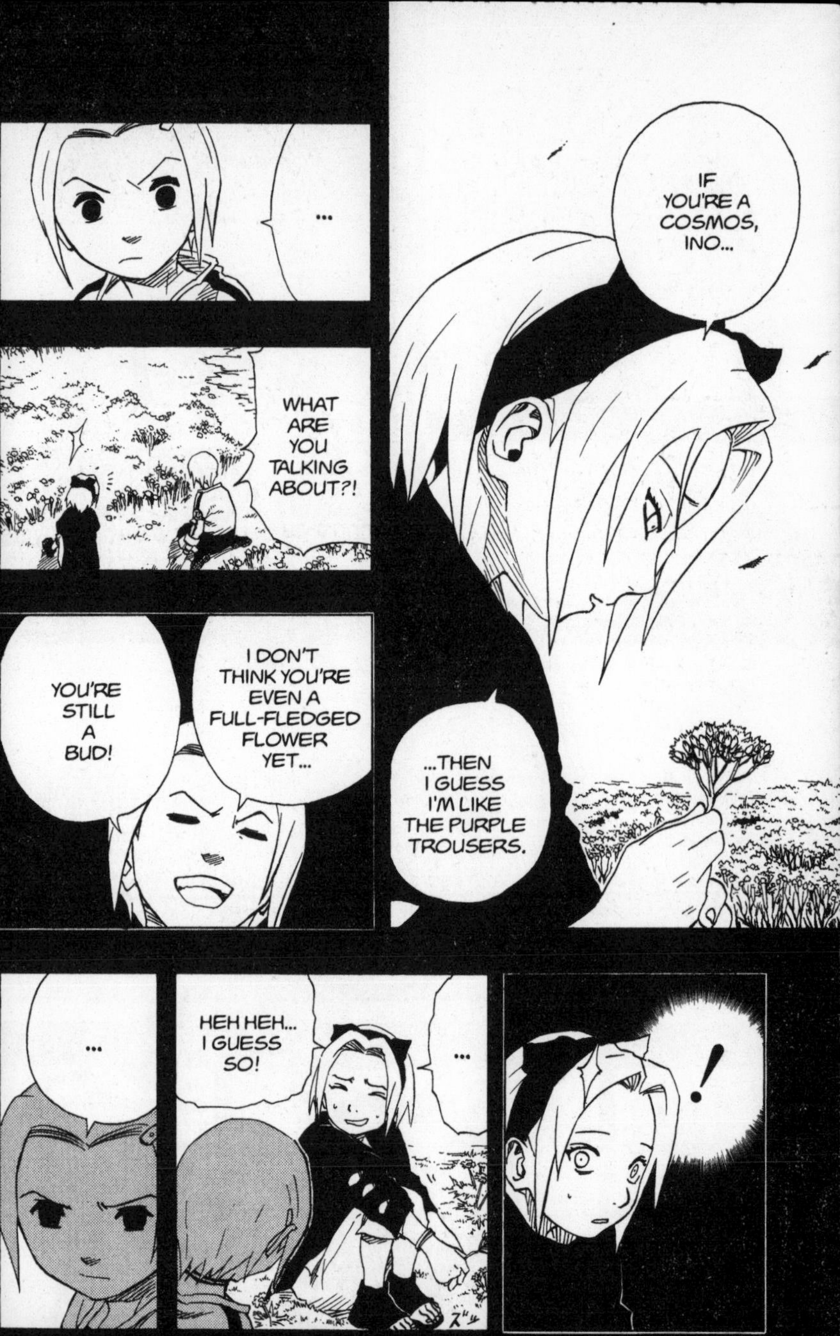
IF YOU'RE A COSMOS, INO...
...THEN I GUESS I'M LIKE THE PURPLE TROUSERS.
...
WHAT ARE YOU TALKING ABOUT?!
I DON'T THINK YOU'RE EVEN A FULL-FLEDGED FLOWER YET...
YOU'RE STILL A BUD!
!
...
HEH HEH... I GUESS SO!
...

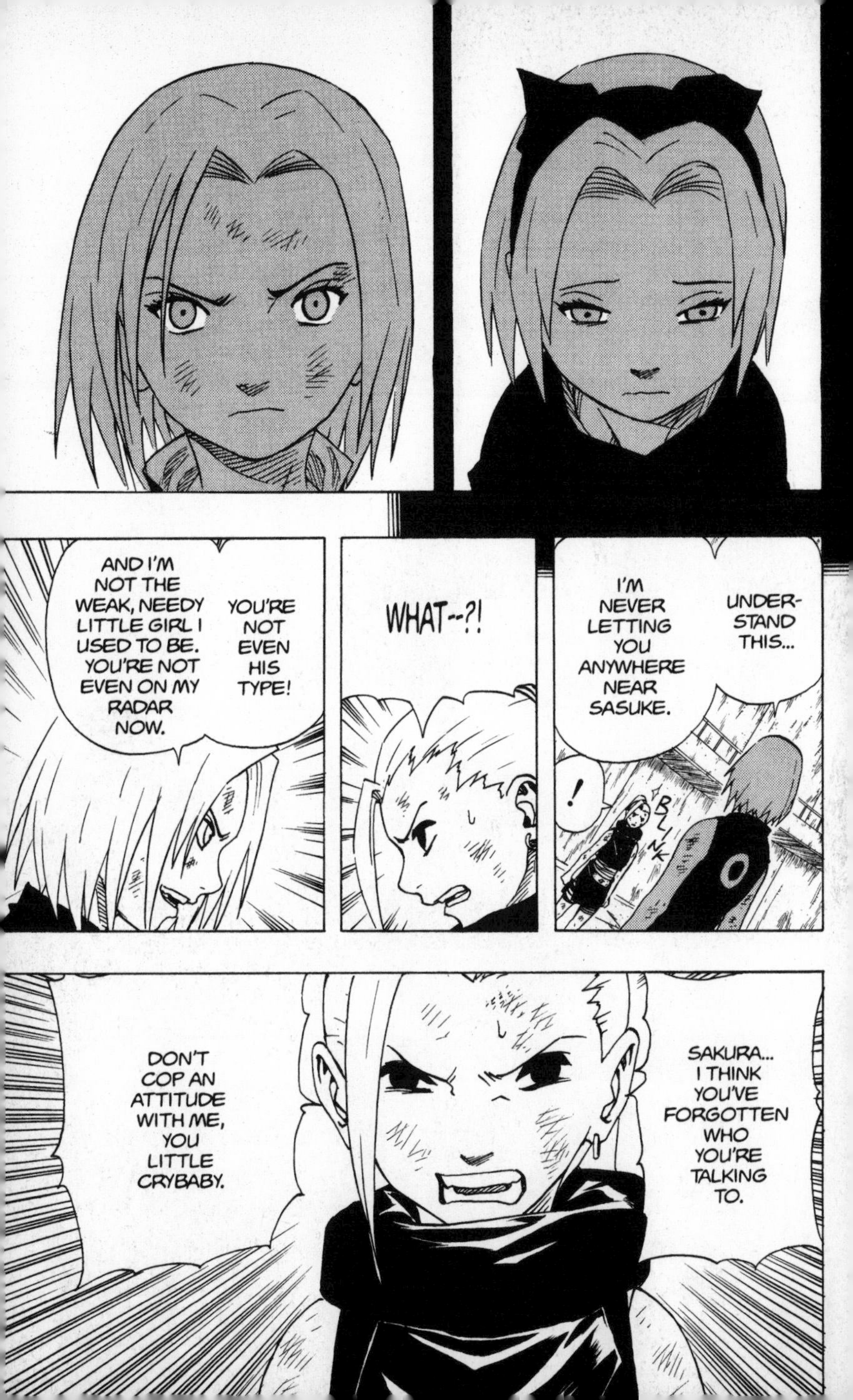
UNDER-STAND THIS...
I'M NEVER LETTING YOU ANYWHERE NEAR SASUKE.
!
BLINK
WHAT--?!
YOU'RE NOT EVEN HIS TYPE!
AND I'M NOT THE WEAK, NEEDY LITTLE GIRL I USED TO BE. YOU'RE NOT EVEN ON MY RADAR NOW.
SAKURA... I THINK YOU'VE FORGOTTEN WHO YOU'RE TALKING TO.
DON'T COP AN ATTITUDE WITH ME, YOU LITTLE CRYBABY.

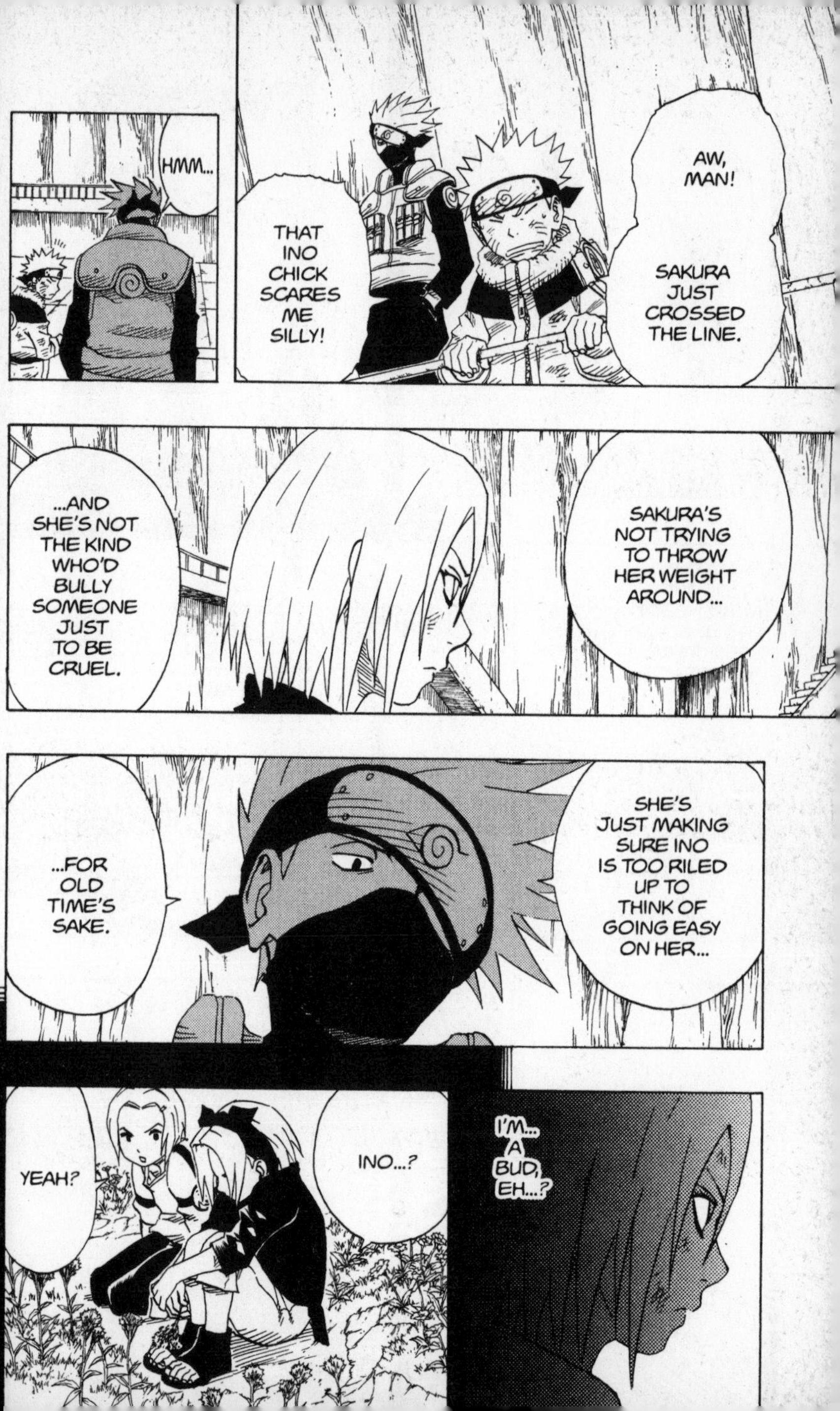
AW, MAN!
SAKURA JUST CROSSED THE LINE.
THAT INO CHICK SCARES ME SILLY!
HMM...
SAKURA'S NOT TRYING TO THROW HER WEIGHT AROUND...
...AND SHE'S NOT THE KIND WHO'D BULLY SOMEONE JUST TO BE CRUEL.
SHE'S JUST MAKING SURE INO IS TOO RILED UP TO THINK OF GOING EASY ON HER...
...FOR OLD TIME'S SAKE.
I'M... A BUD, EH...?
INO...?
YEAH?

READ THIS WAY

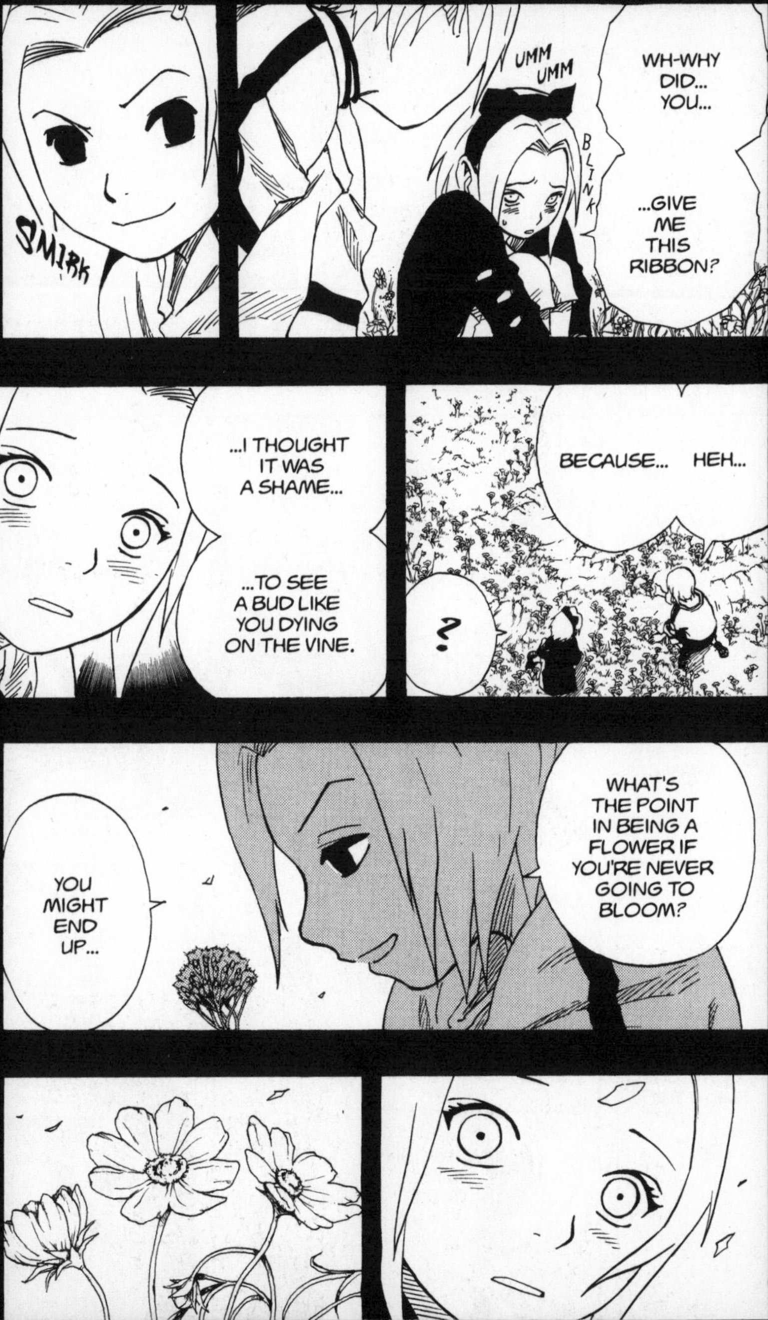

WH-WHY DID... YOU...
...GIVE ME THIS RIBBON?
UMM UMM
BLINK
SMIRK
BECAUSE... HEH...
?
...I THOUGHT IT WAS A SHAME...
...TO SEE A BUD LIKE YOU DYING ON THE VINE.
WHAT'S THE POINT IN BEING A FLOWER IF YOU'RE NEVER GOING TO BLOOM?
YOU MIGHT END UP...

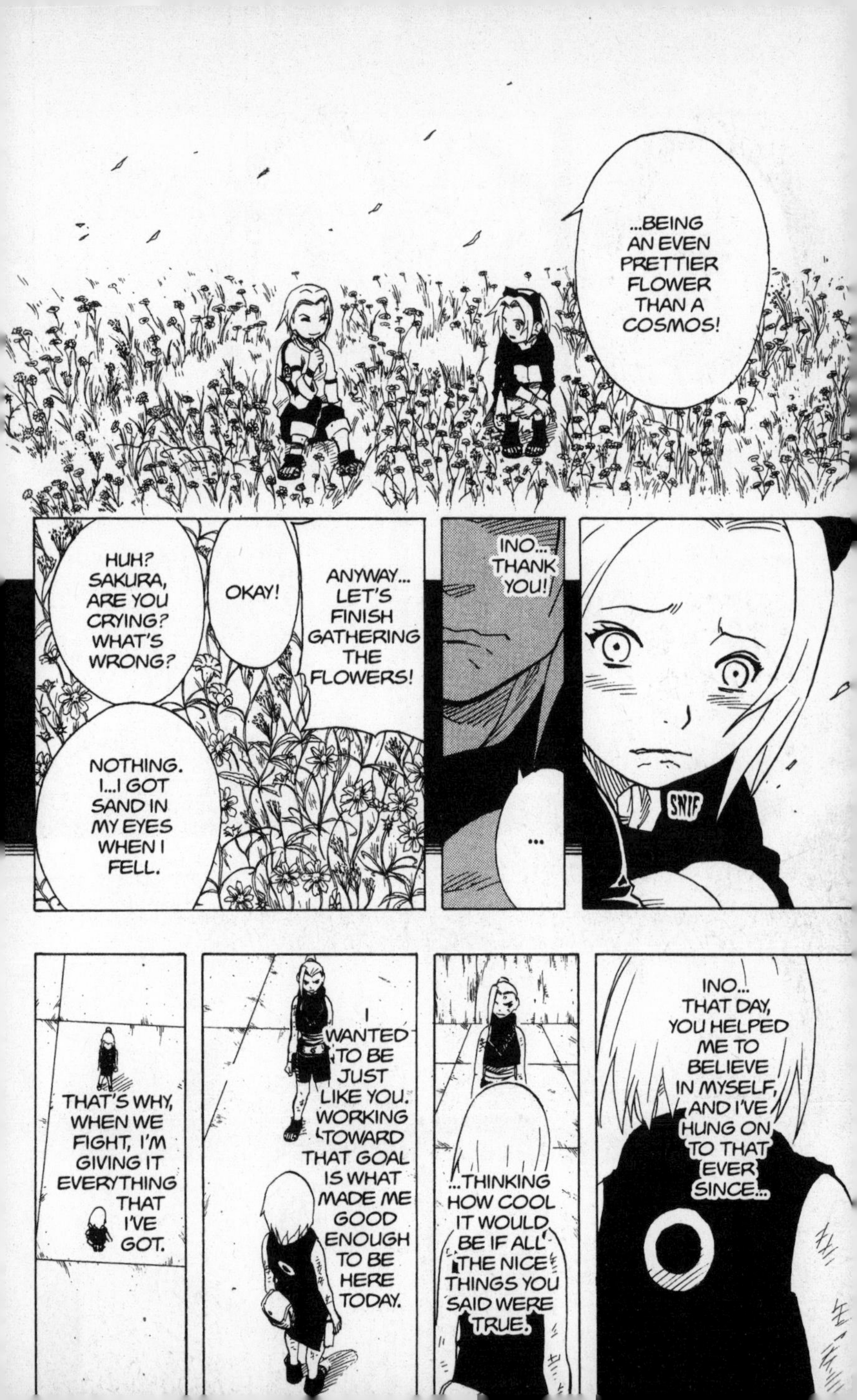
...BEING AN EVEN PRETTIER FLOWER THAN A COSMOS!
SNIF
INO... THANK YOU!
...
ANYWAY... LET'S FINISH GATHERING THE FLOWERS!
OKAY!
HUH? SAKURA, ARE YOU CRYING? WHAT'S WRONG?
NOTHING. I...I GOT SAND IN MY EYES WHEN I FELL.
INO... THAT DAY, YOU HELPED ME TO BELIEVE IN MYSELF, AND I'VE HUNG ON TO THAT EVER SINCE...
...THINKING HOW COOL IT WOULD BE IF ALL THE NICE THINGS YOU SAID WERE TRUE.
I WANTED TO BE JUST LIKE YOU. WORKING TOWARD THAT GOAL IS WHAT MADE ME GOOD ENOUGH TO BE HERE TODAY.
THAT'S WHY, WHEN WE FIGHT, I'M GIVING IT EVERYTHING THAT I'VE GOT.

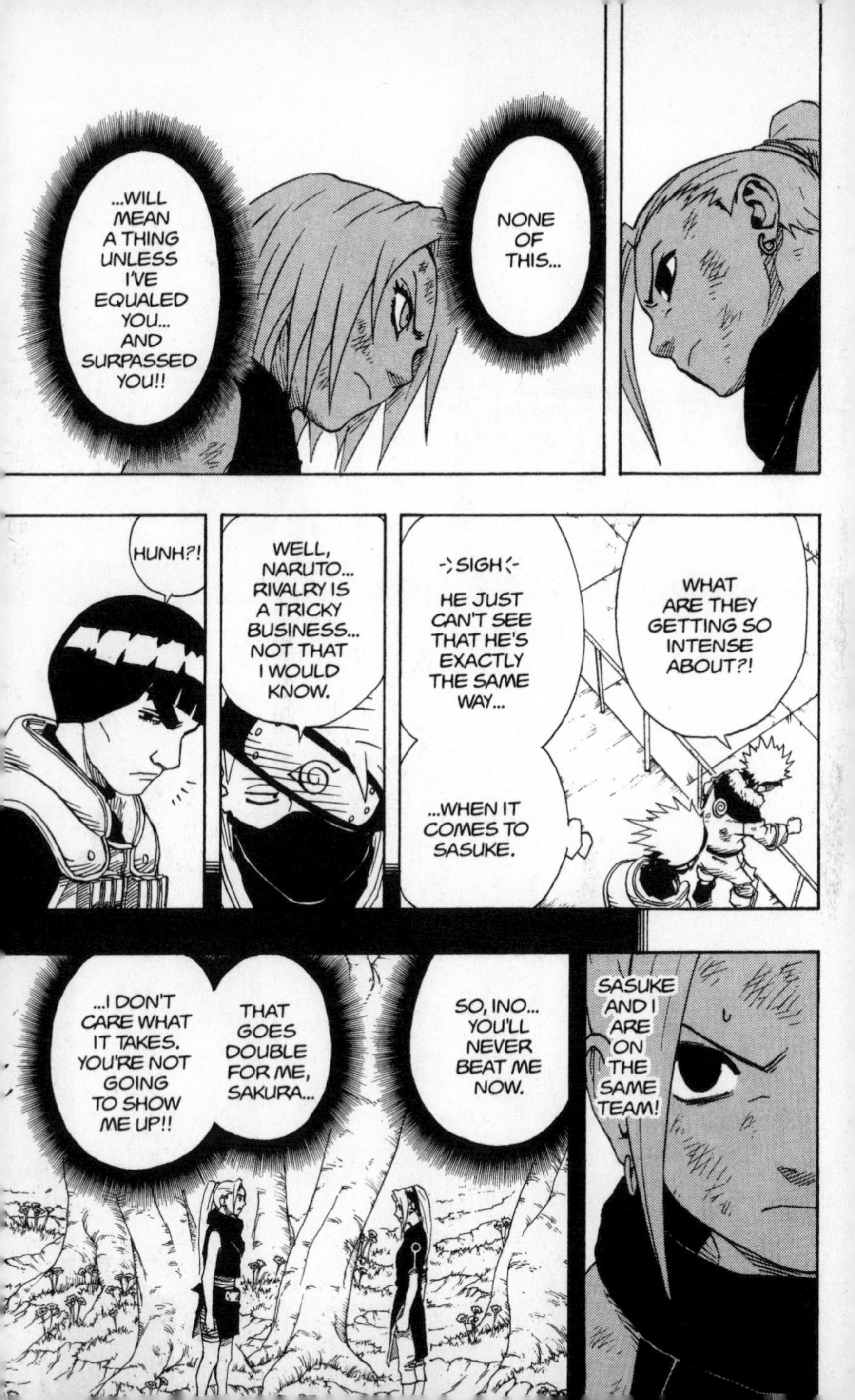
NONE OF THIS...
...WILL MEAN A THING UNLESS I'VE EQUALED YOU... AND SURPASSED YOU!!
WHAT ARE THEY GETTING SO INTENSE ABOUT?!
SIGH
HE JUST CAN'T SEE THAT HE'S EXACTLY THE SAME WAY...
...WHEN IT COMES TO SASUKE.
WELL, NARUTO... RIVALRY IS A TRICKY BUSINESS... NOT THAT I WOULD KNOW.
HUNH?!
SASUKE AND I ARE ON THE SAME TEAM!
SO, INO... YOU'LL NEVER BEAT ME NOW.
THAT GOES DOUBLE FOR ME, SAKURA...
...I DON'T CARE WHAT IT TAKES. YOU'RE NOT GOING TO SHOW ME UP!!

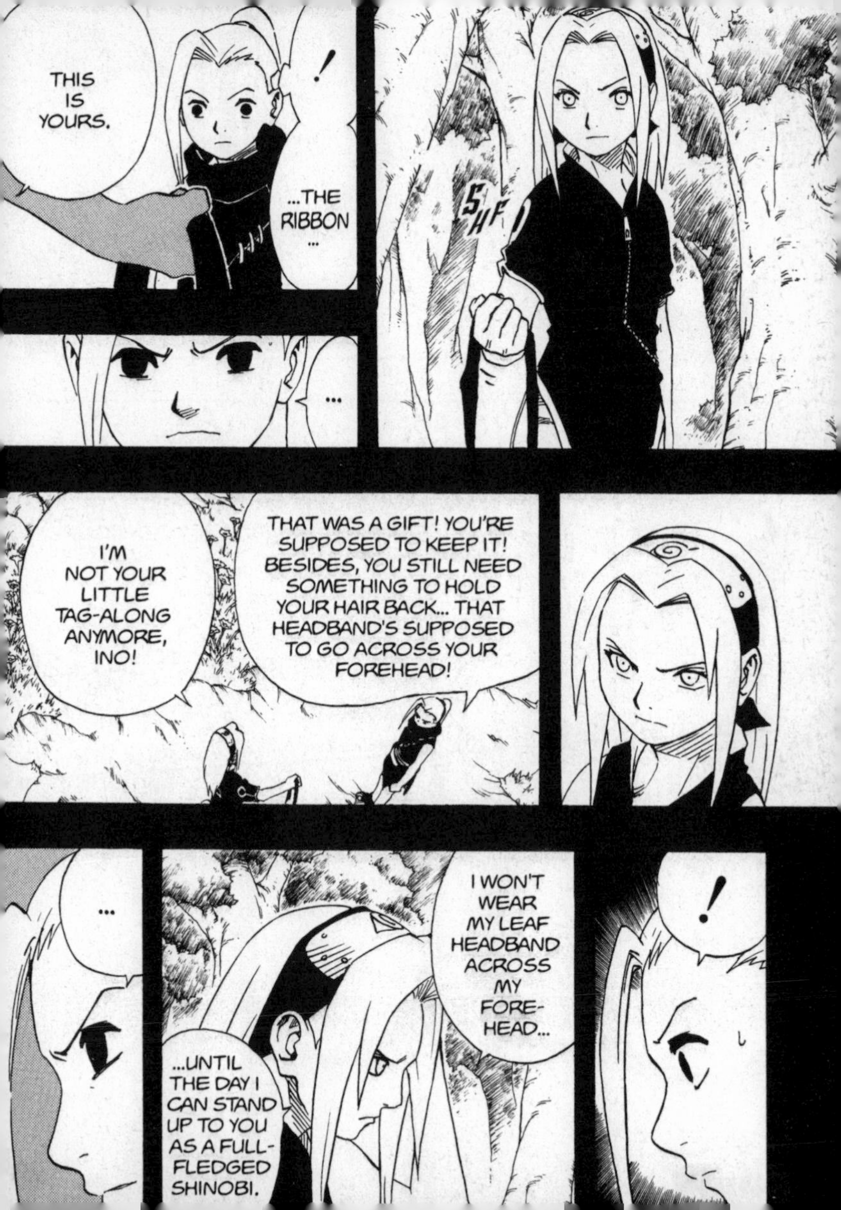
SHF
!
THIS IS YOURS.
...THE RIBBON ...
...
THAT WAS A GIFT! YOU'RE SUPPOSED TO KEEP IT! BESIDES, YOU STILL NEED SOMETHING TO HOLD YOUR HAIR BACK... THAT HEADBAND'S SUPPOSED TO GO ACROSS YOUR FOREHEAD!
I'M NOT YOUR LITTLE TAG-ALONG ANYMORE, INO!
!
I WON'T WEAR MY LEAF HEADBAND ACROSS MY FORE-HEAD...
...UNTIL THE DAY I CAN STAND UP TO YOU AS A FULL-FLEDGED SHINOBI.
...

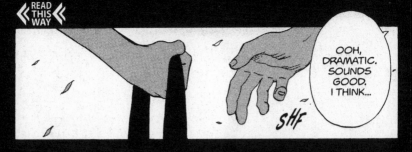

OOH, DRAMATIC. SOUNDS GOOD. I THINK...

SHF

...I'LL DO THE SAME.

...SAKURA.

I GET IT...

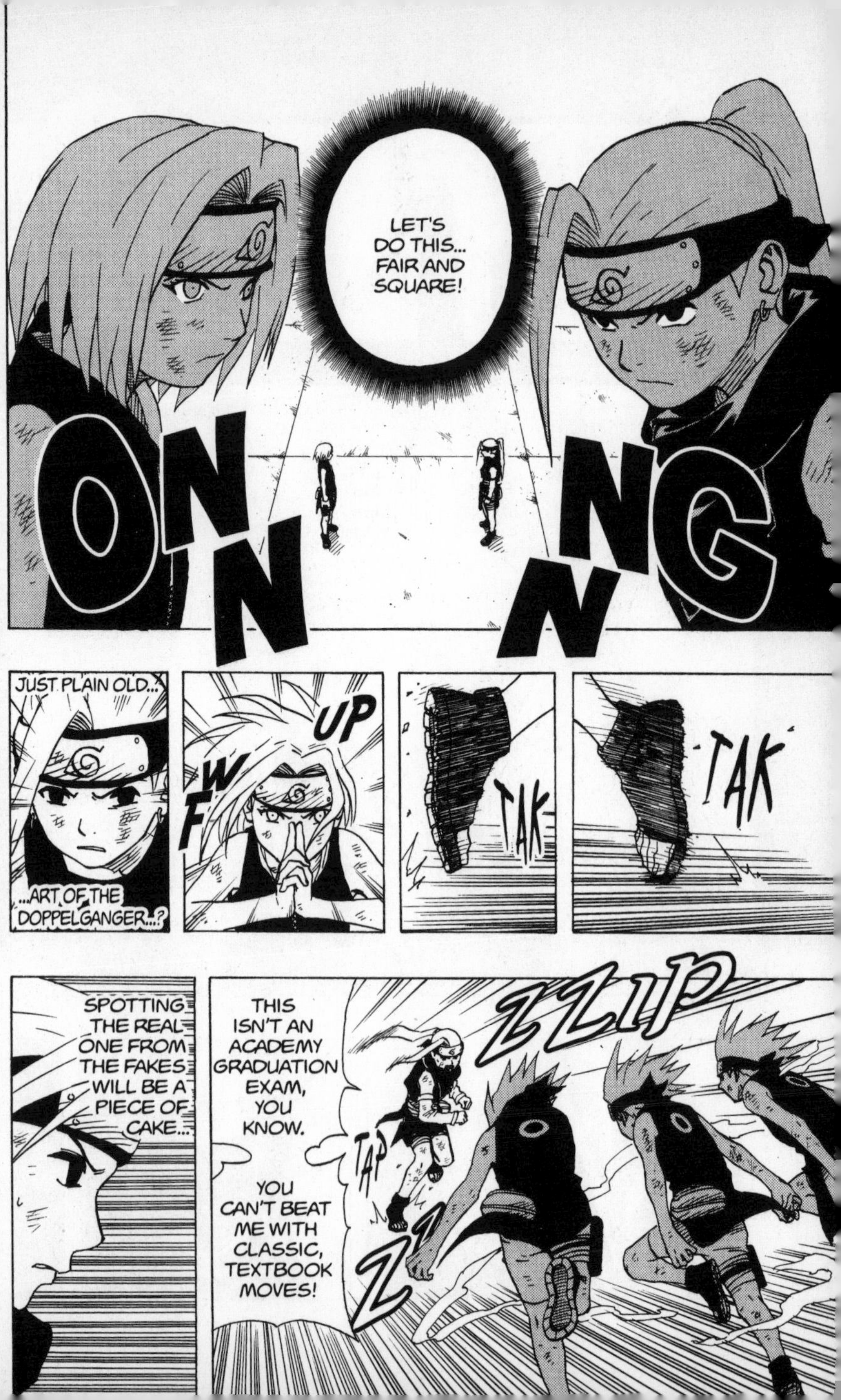
LET'S DO THIS... FAIR AND SQUARE!
ONNNNG
TAK
TAK
FWUP
JUST PLAIN OLD...
...ART OF THE DOPPELGANGER...?
ZZIP
THIS ISN'T AN ACADEMY GRADUATION EXAM, YOU KNOW.
YOU CAN'T BEAT ME WITH CLASSIC, TEXTBOOK MOVES!
TAP
ZZ
SPOTTING THE REAL ONE FROM THE FAKES WILL BE A PIECE OF CAKE...

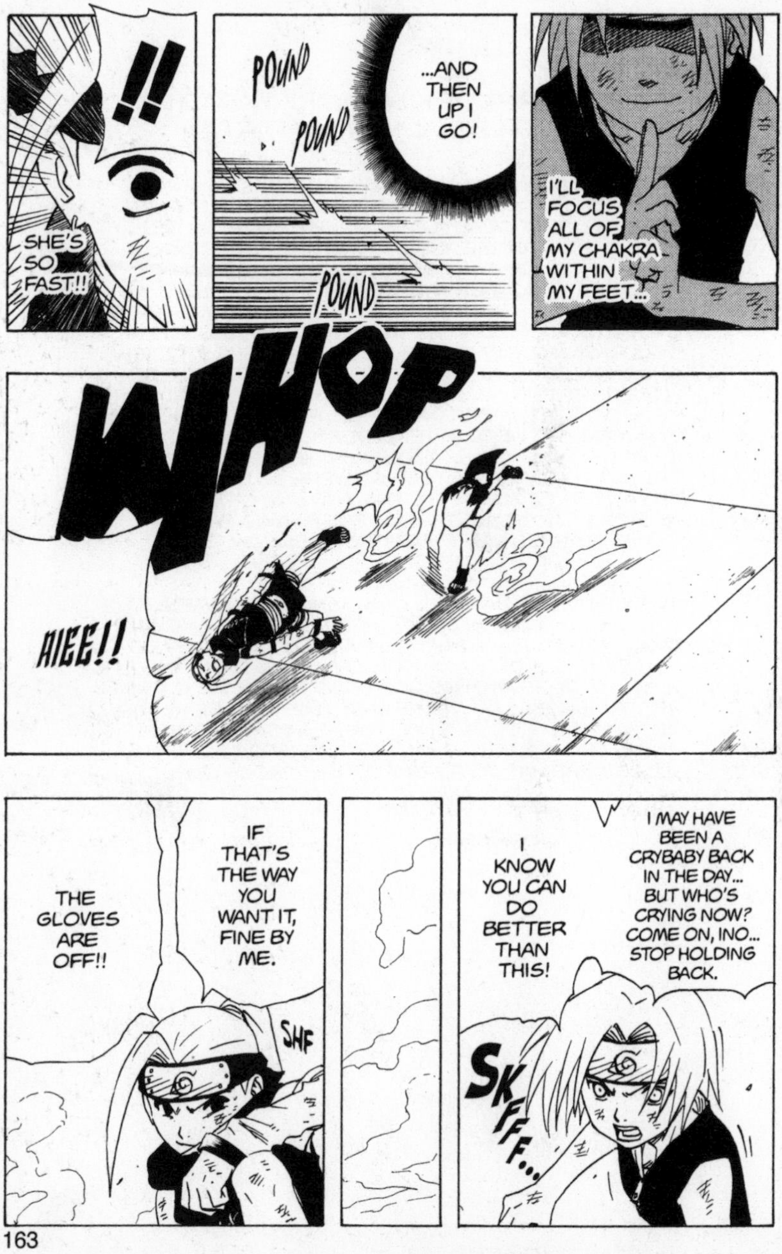
I'LL FOCUS ALL OF MY CHAKRA WITHIN MY FEET...
...AND THEN UP I GO!
POUND
POUND
POUND
!!
SHE'S SO FAST!!
WHOP
AIEE!!
I MAY HAVE BEEN A CRYBABY BACK IN THE DAY... BUT WHO'S CRYING NOW? COME ON, INO... STOP HOLDING BACK.
I KNOW YOU CAN DO BETTER THAN THIS!
SKFFF...
IF THAT'S THE WAY YOU WANT IT, FINE BY ME.
THE GLOVES ARE OFF!!
SHF

THE WORLD OF KISHIMOTO MASASHI
MY PERSONAL HISTORY, PART 7.3

NOWADAYS, EVERY GAMER IS FAMILIAR WITH COMMAND-CONTROLLED ROLE-PLAYING VIDEO GAMES... BUT WHEN *DRAGON QUEST* CAME ALONG, NO ONE HAD EVER SEEN SUCH A THING. IT SEEMED COMPLETELY ALIEN TO ME, AND I HAD TROUBLE UNDERSTANDING IT. EVENTUALLY, THOUGH, MY BROTHER AND I LEARNED (OR THOUGHT WE HAD) THE SKILLS NECESSARY FOR COMPLETE MASTERY OF THE GAME. SO ONE DAY, WE WERE BLISSED OUT PLAYING *DRAGON QUEST* FOR ABOUT A FOUR-HOUR STRETCH... AND THEN, BEING IDIOTS, WE SHUT THE SYSTEM OFF BEFORE REALIZING WE HAD NEVER BOTHERED TO FIND OUT ABOUT THE ALL-IMPORTANT "SPELL FOR RESTORING LIFE" COMMAND. WE WERE UTTERLY DESPONDENT, BUT THEN MY FATHER SHOWED UP AND SURPRISED US BY ASKING TO TRY OUT THE GAME HIMSELF. WE WERE SO EXCITED THAT HE WANTED TO JOIN IN THE FUN, AND ONE OF MY FONDEST MEMORIES IS OF THE THREE OF US PLAYING *DRAGON QUEST* IN AN ALL-NIGHT MARATHON SESSION.

MY FATHER, WHO HAD PREVIOUSLY SHOWN A COMPLETE LACK OF INTEREST IN GAMES, FELL DEEPLY IN LOVE WITH *DRAGON QUEST*, WHICH KIND OF AMAZED ME, BECAUSE FOR ME IT WAS ONLY A PASSING FANCY. THE GAME WAS A HUGE SUCCESS AND HAS CONTINUED TO SPAWN SEQUEL AFTER SEQUEL. IN FACT, THE LAST TIME I CALLED MY PARENTS (A RARE OCCURRENCE THESE DAYS), MY FATHER ANSWERED THE PHONE AND WE TALKED FOR SOME TIME. IT SEEMS HE HAS JUST COMPLETED *DRAGON QUEST 7*.

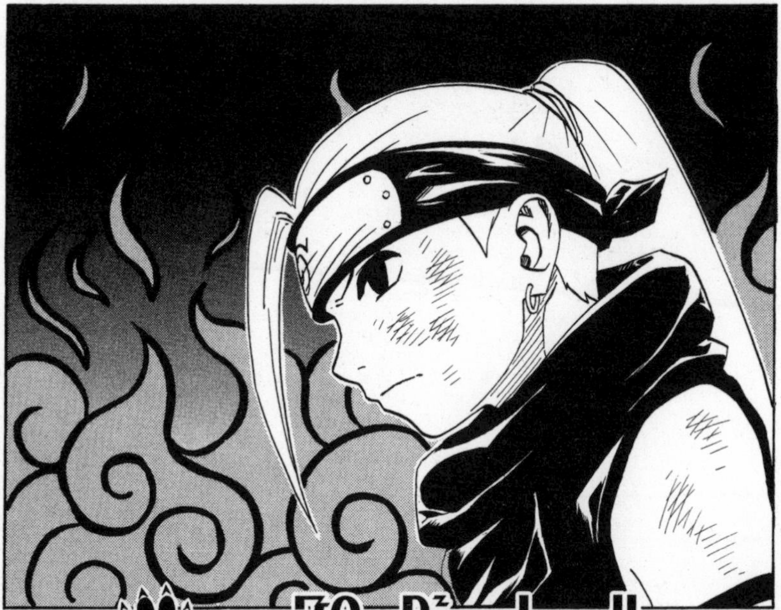

Number 72: Rivals...!!

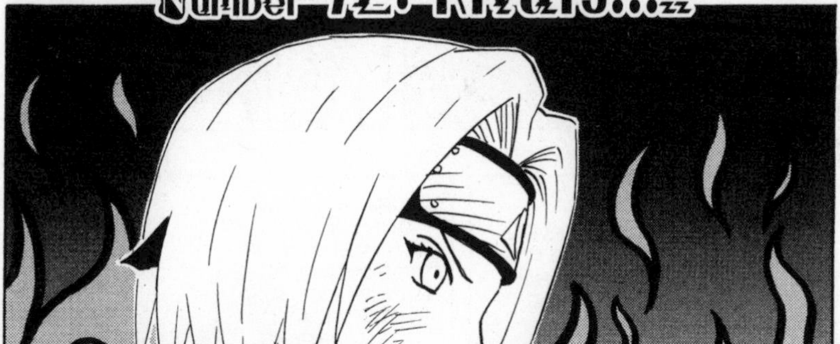

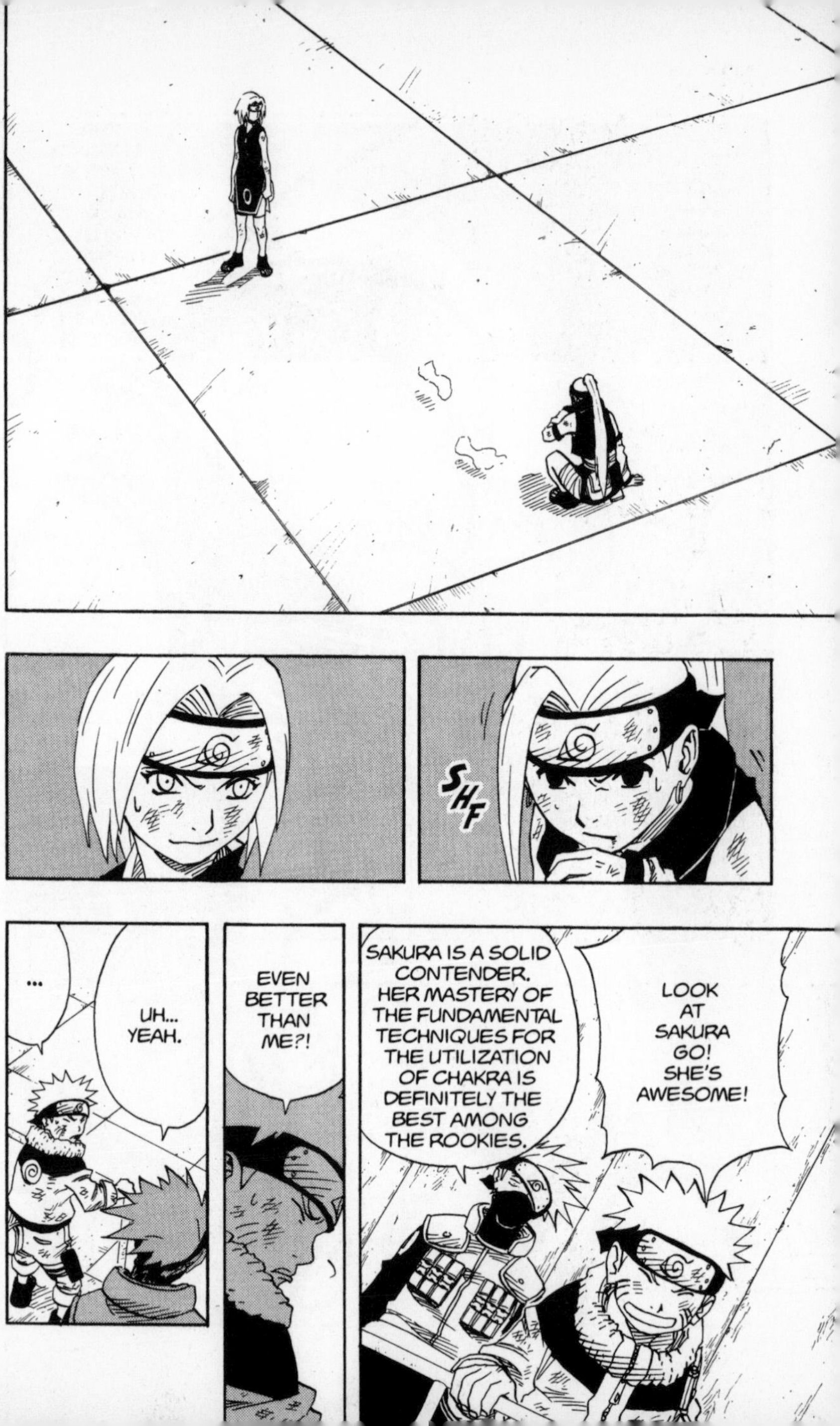
SHF
LOOK AT SAKURA GO! SHE'S AWESOME!
SAKURA IS A SOLID CONTENDER. HER MASTERY OF THE FUNDAMENTAL TECHNIQUES FOR THE UTILIZATION OF CHAKRA IS DEFINITELY THE BEST AMONG THE ROOKIES.
EVEN BETTER THAN ME?!
UH... YEAH.
...

READ THIS WAY

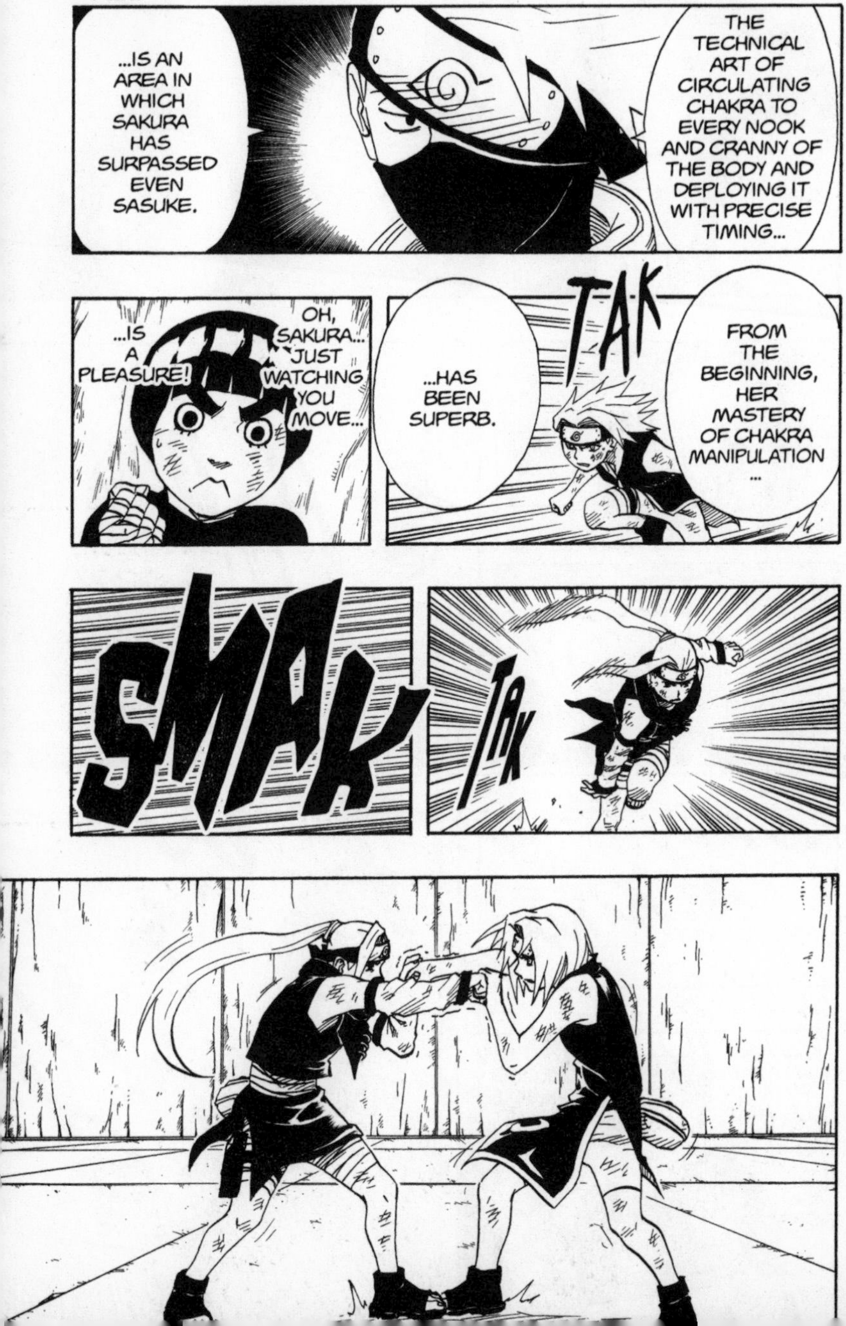
THE TECHNICAL ART OF CIRCULATING CHAKRA TO EVERY NOOK AND CRANNY OF THE BODY AND DEPLOYING IT WITH PRECISE TIMING...
...IS AN AREA IN WHICH SAKURA HAS SURPASSED EVEN SASUKE.
FROM THE BEGINNING, HER MASTERY OF CHAKRA MANIPULATION ...
TAK
...HAS BEEN SUPERB.
OH, SAKURA... JUST WATCHING YOU MOVE...
...IS A PLEASURE!
TAK
SMAK

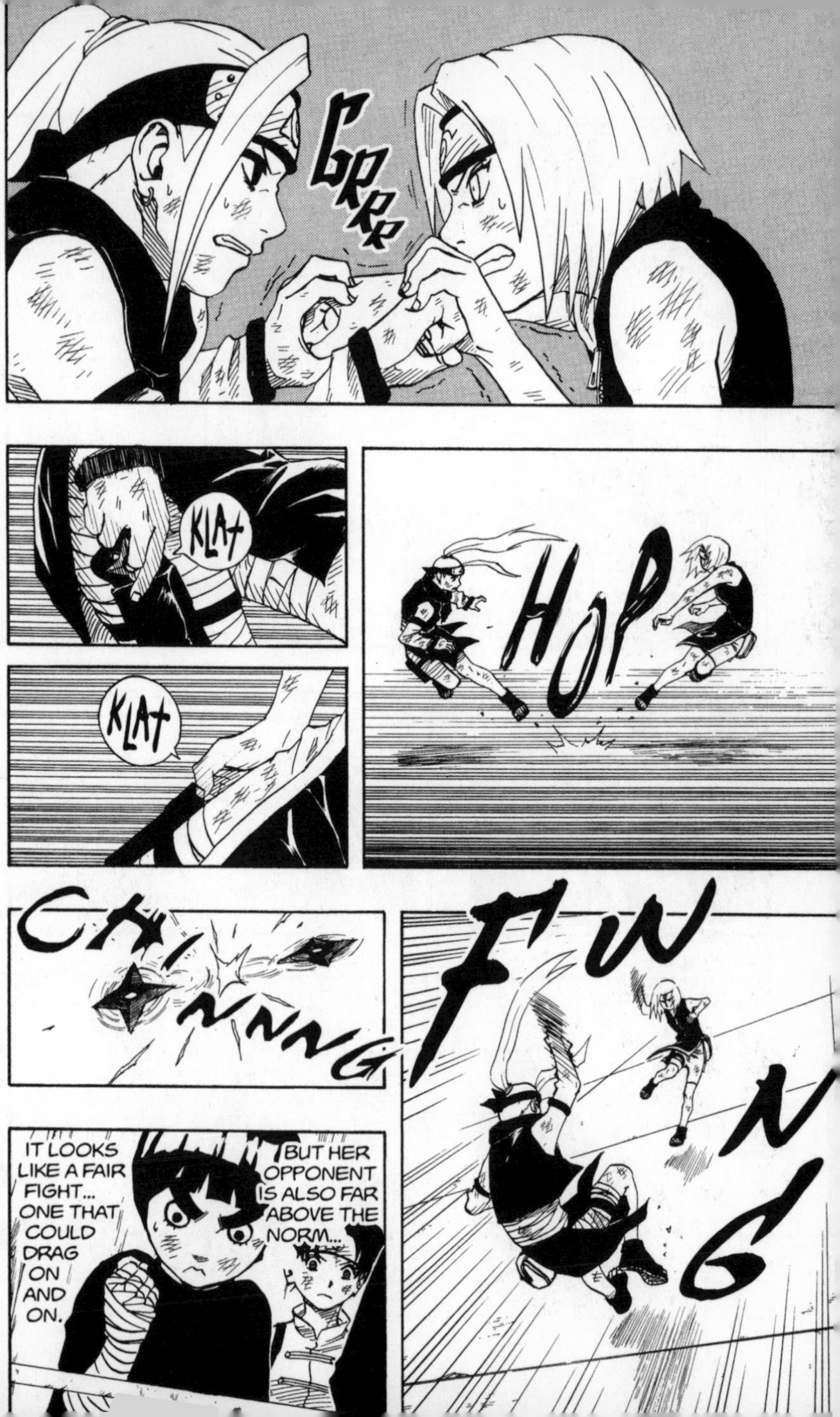
GRRR
HOP
KLAT
KLAT
FWNG
CHINNNG
BUT HER OPPONENT IS ALSO FAR ABOVE THE NORM...
IT LOOKS LIKE A FAIR FIGHT... ONE THAT COULD DRAG ON AND ON.

READ THIS WAY

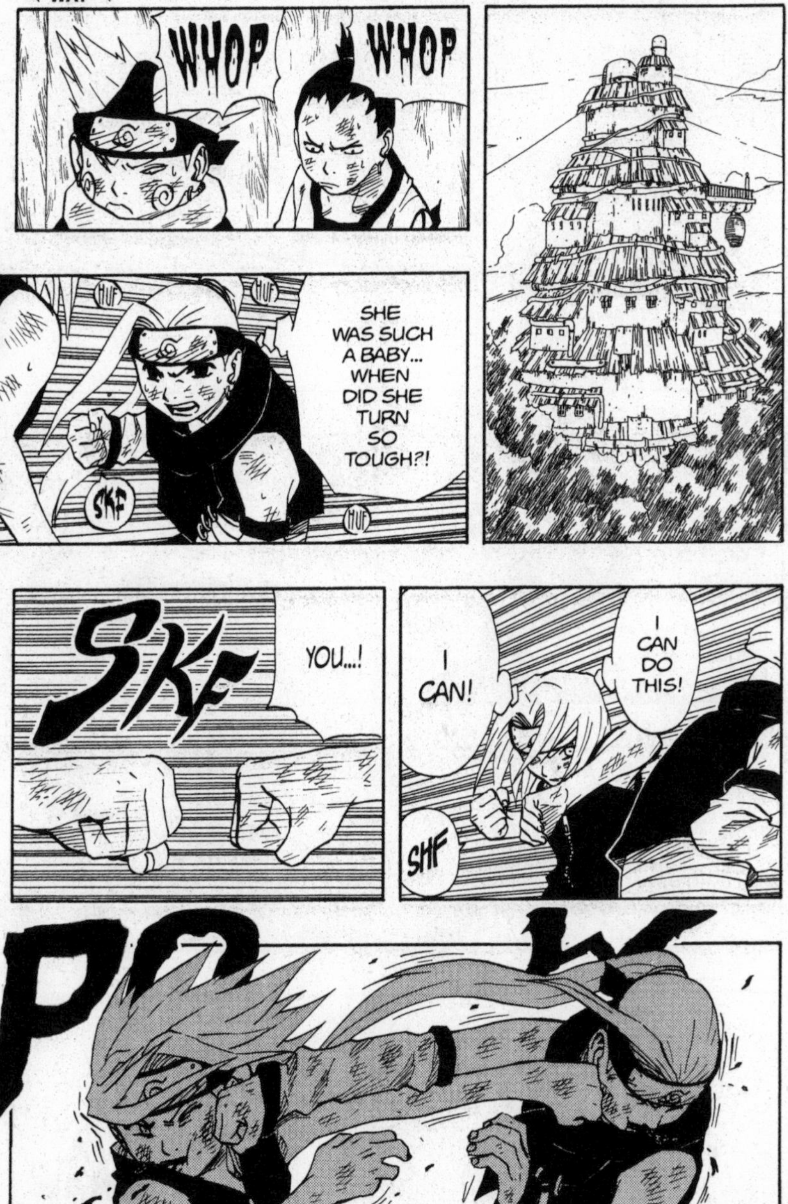

WHOP
WHOP
HUF
HUF
SHE WAS SUCH A BABY... WHEN DID SHE TURN SO TOUGH?!
SKF
HUF
I CAN DO THIS!
I CAN!
SHF
YOU...!
SKF
POW

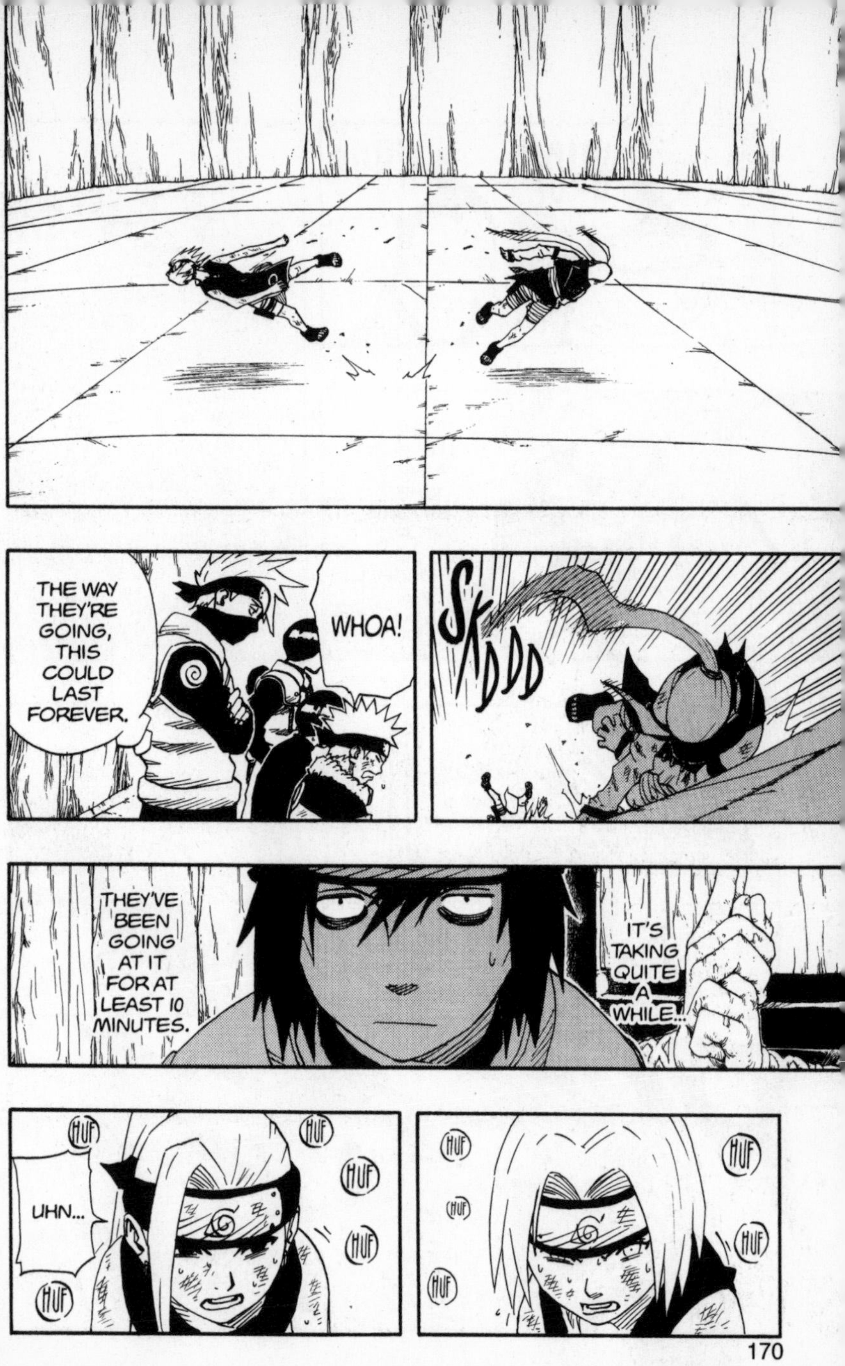
SKDDD
WHOA!
THE WAY THEY'RE GOING, THIS COULD LAST FOREVER.
IT'S TAKING QUITE A WHILE...
THEY'VE BEEN GOING AT IT FOR AT LEAST 10 MINUTES.
HUF HUF HUF HUF HUF HUF
HUF HUF HUF HUF
UHN...

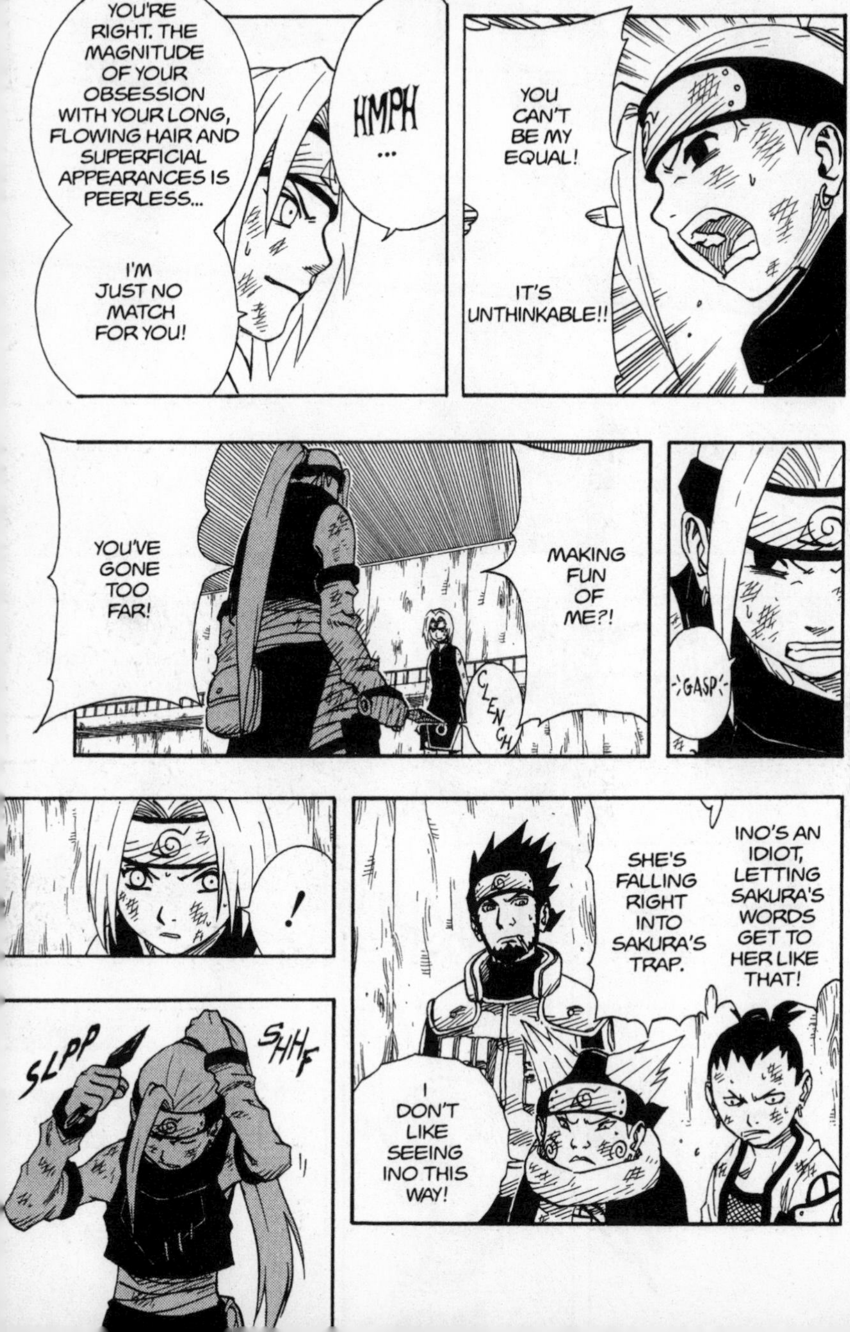

YOU CAN'T BE MY EQUAL!
IT'S UNTHINKABLE!!
HMPH...
YOU'RE RIGHT. THE MAGNITUDE OF YOUR OBSESSION WITH YOUR LONG, FLOWING HAIR AND SUPERFICIAL APPEARANCES IS PEERLESS...
I'M JUST NO MATCH FOR YOU!
GASP
MAKING FUN OF ME?!
CLENCH
YOU'VE GONE TOO FAR!
INO'S AN IDIOT, LETTING SAKURA'S WORDS GET TO HER LIKE THAT!
SHE'S FALLING RIGHT INTO SAKURA'S TRAP.
I DON'T LIKE SEEING INO THIS WAY!
!
SHHF
SLPP

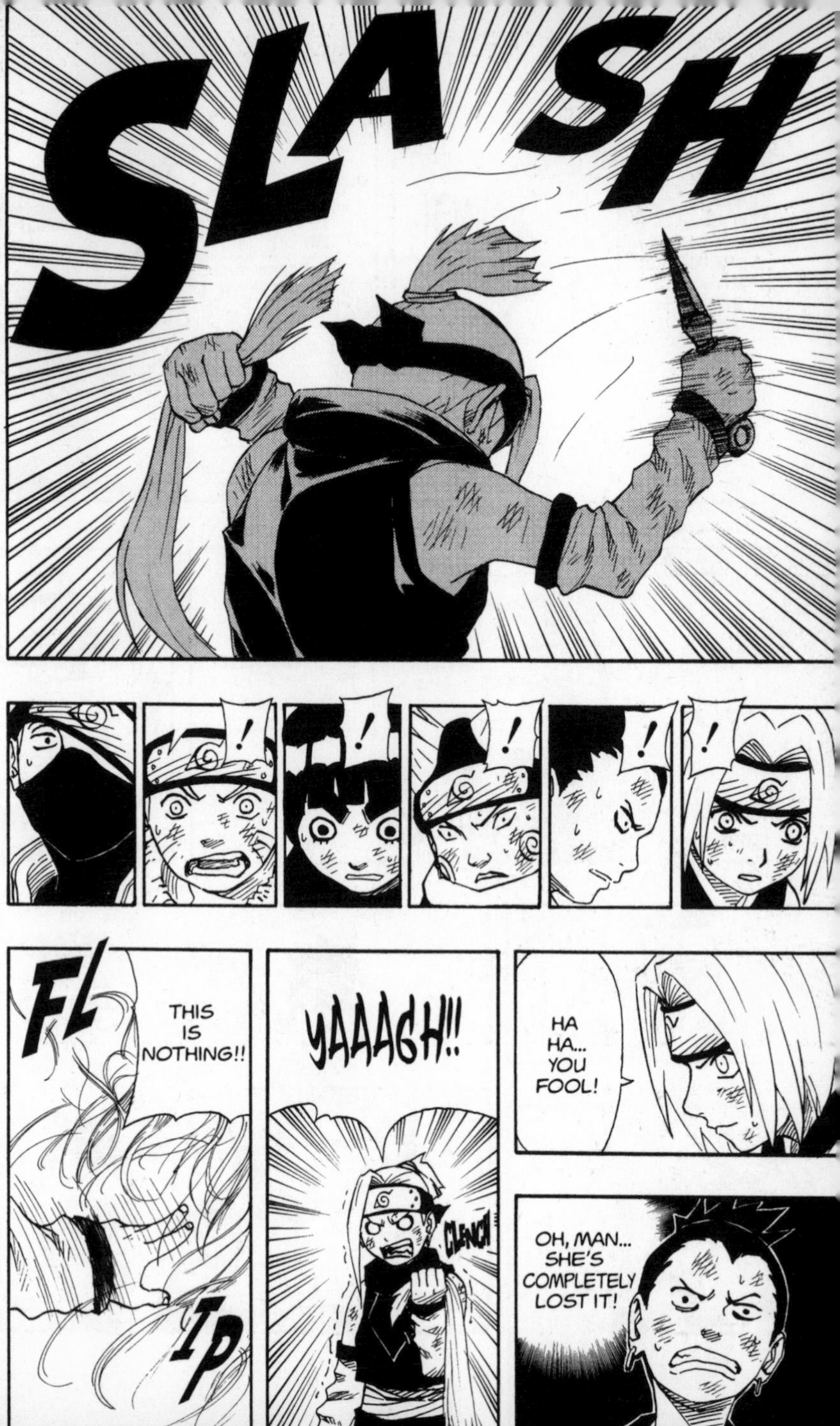

SLASH
!
!
!
!
!
HA HA... YOU FOOL!
OH, MAN... SHE'S COMPLETELY LOST IT!
YAAAGH!!
CLENCH
THIS IS NOTHING!!
FL
IP

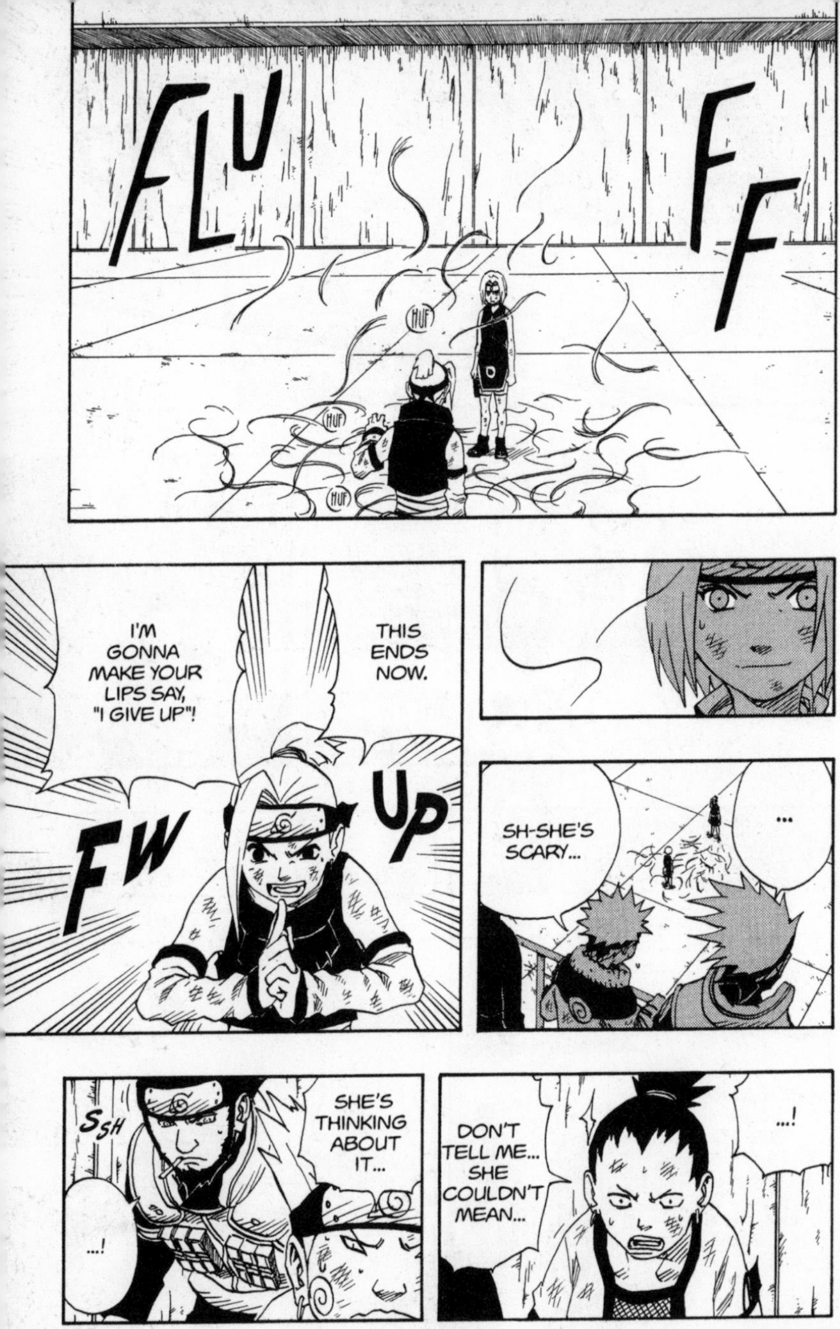
FLUFF
HUF
HUF
HUF
...
SH-SHE'S SCARY...
THIS ENDS NOW.
I'M GONNA MAKE YOUR LIPS SAY, "I GIVE UP"!
FWUP
...!
DON'T TELL ME... SHE COULDN'T MEAN...
SHE'S THINKING ABOUT IT...
SSH
...!

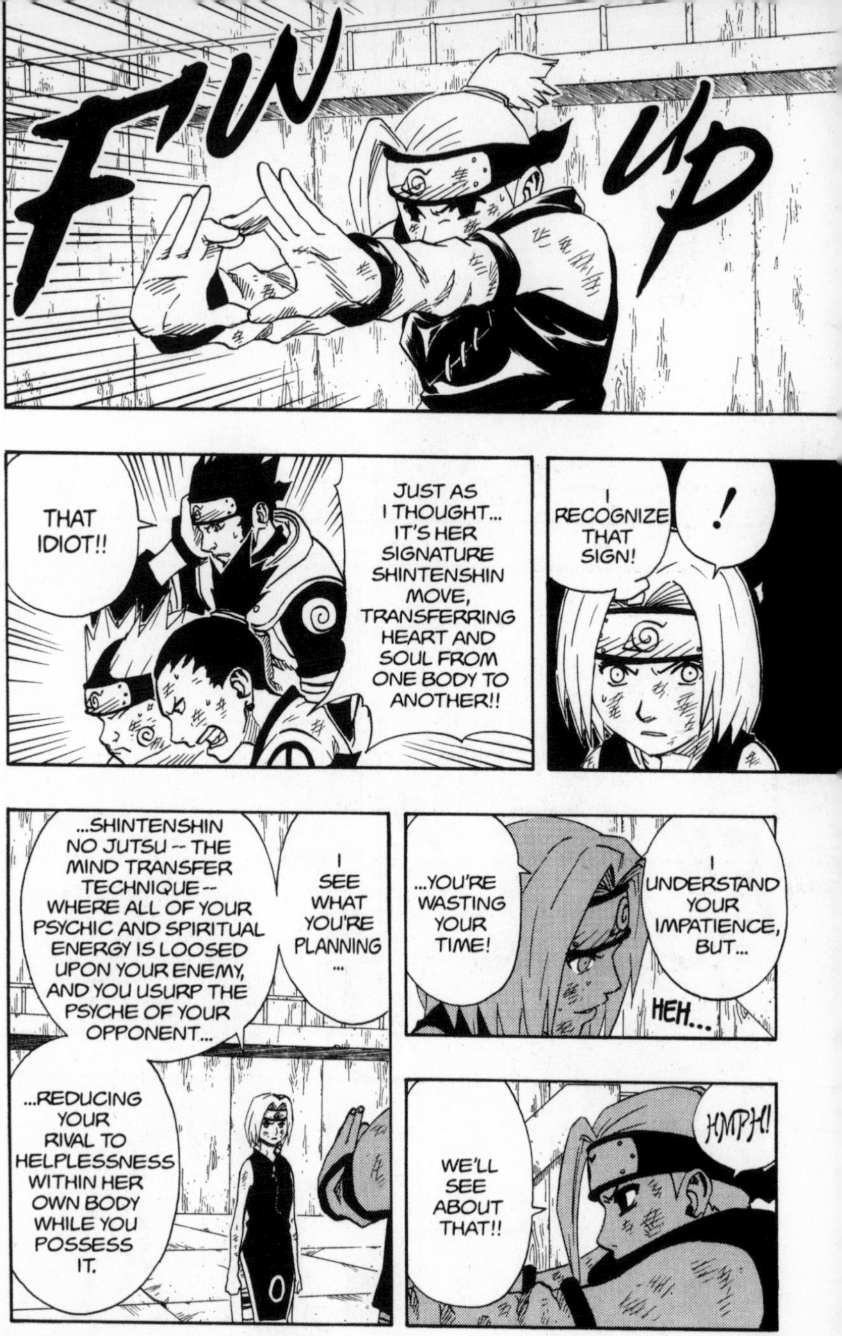
FWUP
!
I RECOGNIZE THAT SIGN!
JUST AS I THOUGHT... IT'S HER SIGNATURE SHINTENSHIN MOVE, TRANSFERRING HEART AND SOUL FROM ONE BODY TO ANOTHER!!
THAT IDIOT!!
I UNDERSTAND YOUR IMPATIENCE, BUT...
HEH...
...YOU'RE WASTING YOUR TIME!
HMPH!
WE'LL SEE ABOUT THAT!!
I SEE WHAT YOU'RE PLANNING...
...SHINTENSHIN NO JUTSU -- THE MIND TRANSFER TECHNIQUE -- WHERE ALL OF YOUR PSYCHIC AND SPIRITUAL ENERGY IS LOOSED UPON YOUR ENEMY, AND YOU USURP THE PSYCHE OF YOUR OPPONENT...
...REDUCING YOUR RIVAL TO HELPLESSNESS WITHIN HER OWN BODY WHILE YOU POSSESS IT.

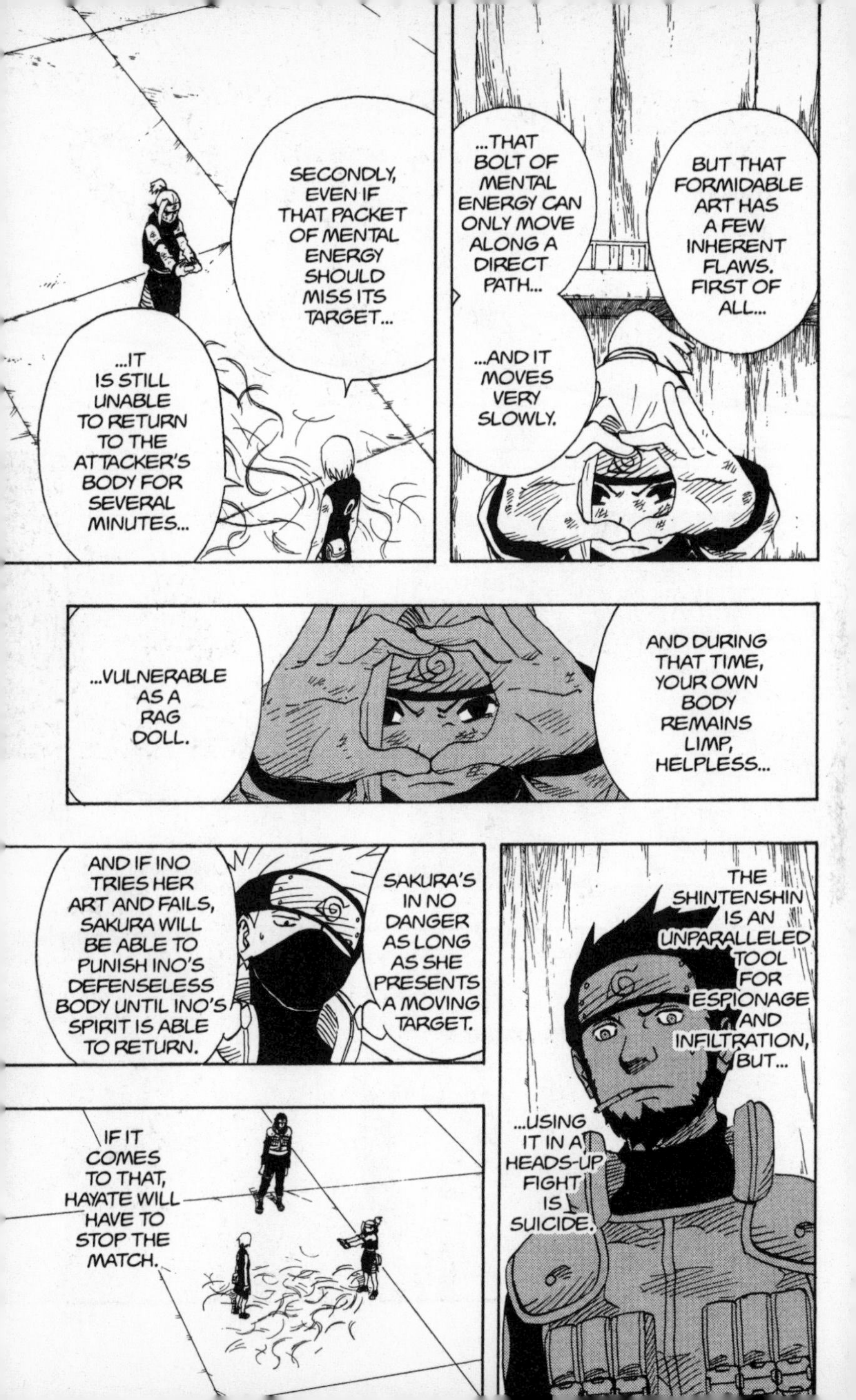
BUT THAT FORMIDABLE ART HAS A FEW INHERENT FLAWS. FIRST OF ALL...
...THAT BOLT OF MENTAL ENERGY CAN ONLY MOVE ALONG A DIRECT PATH...
...AND IT MOVES VERY SLOWLY.
SECONDLY, EVEN IF THAT PACKET OF MENTAL ENERGY SHOULD MISS ITS TARGET...
...IT IS STILL UNABLE TO RETURN TO THE ATTACKER'S BODY FOR SEVERAL MINUTES...
AND DURING THAT TIME, YOUR OWN BODY REMAINS LIMP, HELPLESS...
...VULNERABLE AS A RAG DOLL.
THE SHINTENSHIN IS AN UNPARALLELED TOOL FOR ESPIONAGE AND INFILTRATION, BUT...
...USING IT IN A HEADS-UP FIGHT IS SUICIDE.
SAKURA'S IN NO DANGER AS LONG AS SHE PRESENTS A MOVING TARGET.
AND IF INO TRIES HER ART AND FAILS, SAKURA WILL BE ABLE TO PUNISH INO'S DEFENSELESS BODY UNTIL INO'S SPIRIT IS ABLE TO RETURN.
IF IT COMES TO THAT, HAYATE WILL HAVE TO STOP THE MATCH.

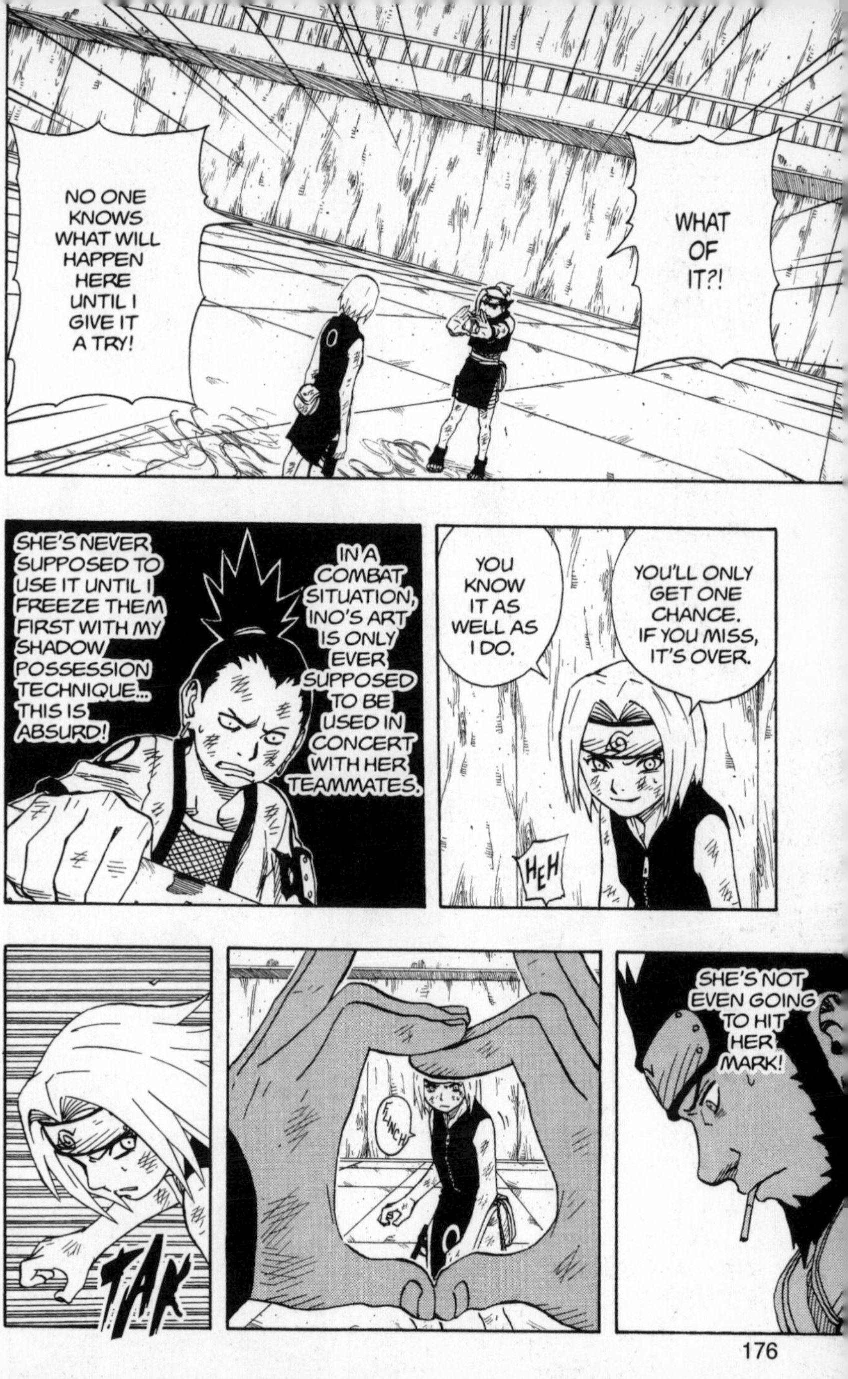
WHAT OF IT?!
NO ONE KNOWS WHAT WILL HAPPEN HERE UNTIL I GIVE IT A TRY!
YOU'LL ONLY GET ONE CHANCE. IF YOU MISS, IT'S OVER.
YOU KNOW IT AS WELL AS I DO.
HEH
IN A COMBAT SITUATION, INO'S ART IS ONLY EVER SUPPOSED TO BE USED IN CONCERT WITH HER TEAMMATES.
SHE'S NEVER SUPPOSED TO USE IT UNTIL I FREEZE THEM FIRST WITH MY SHADOW POSSESSION TECHNIQUE... THIS IS ABSURD!
SHE'S NOT EVEN GOING TO HIT HER MARK!
FLINCH
TAK

READ THIS WAY

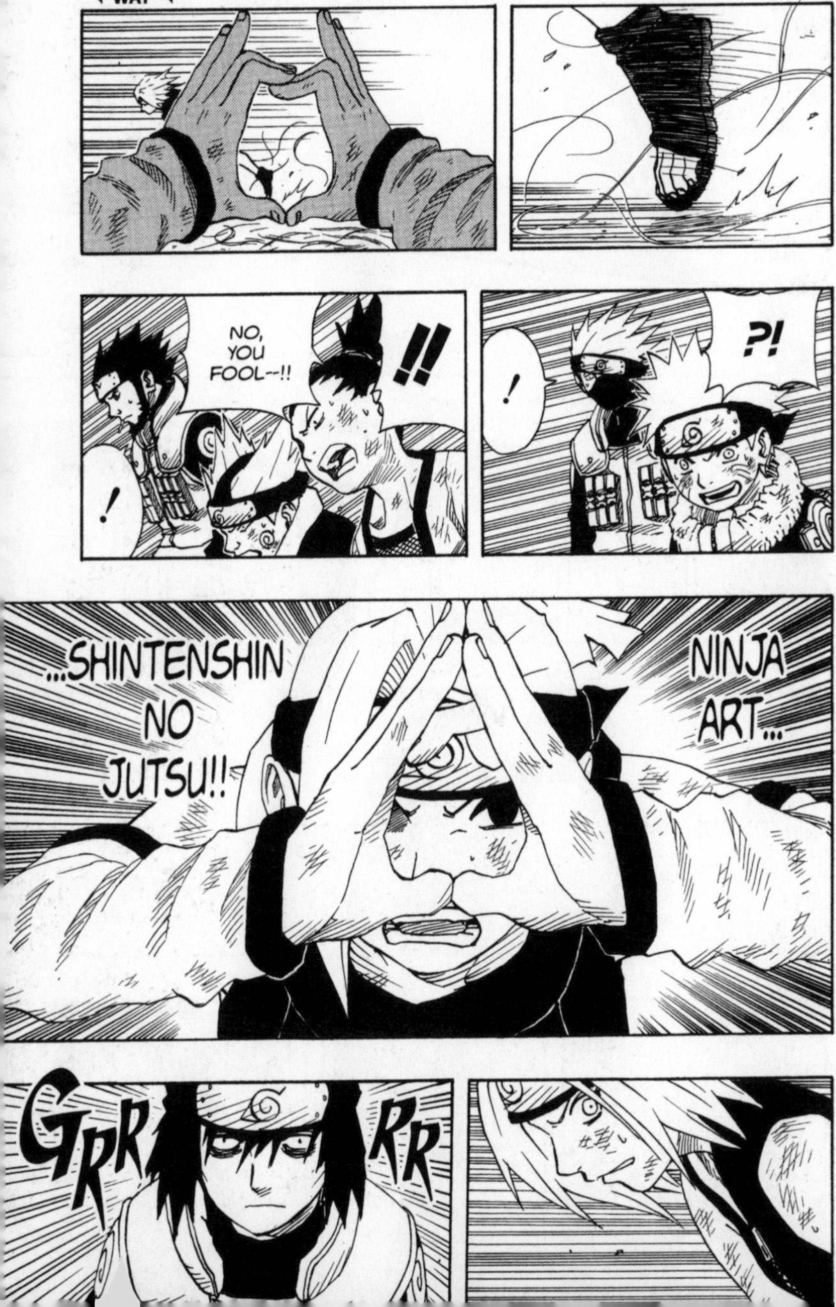

?!
!
!!
NO, YOU FOOL--!!
!
NINJA ART...
...SHINTENSHIN NO JUTSU!!
GRRRR

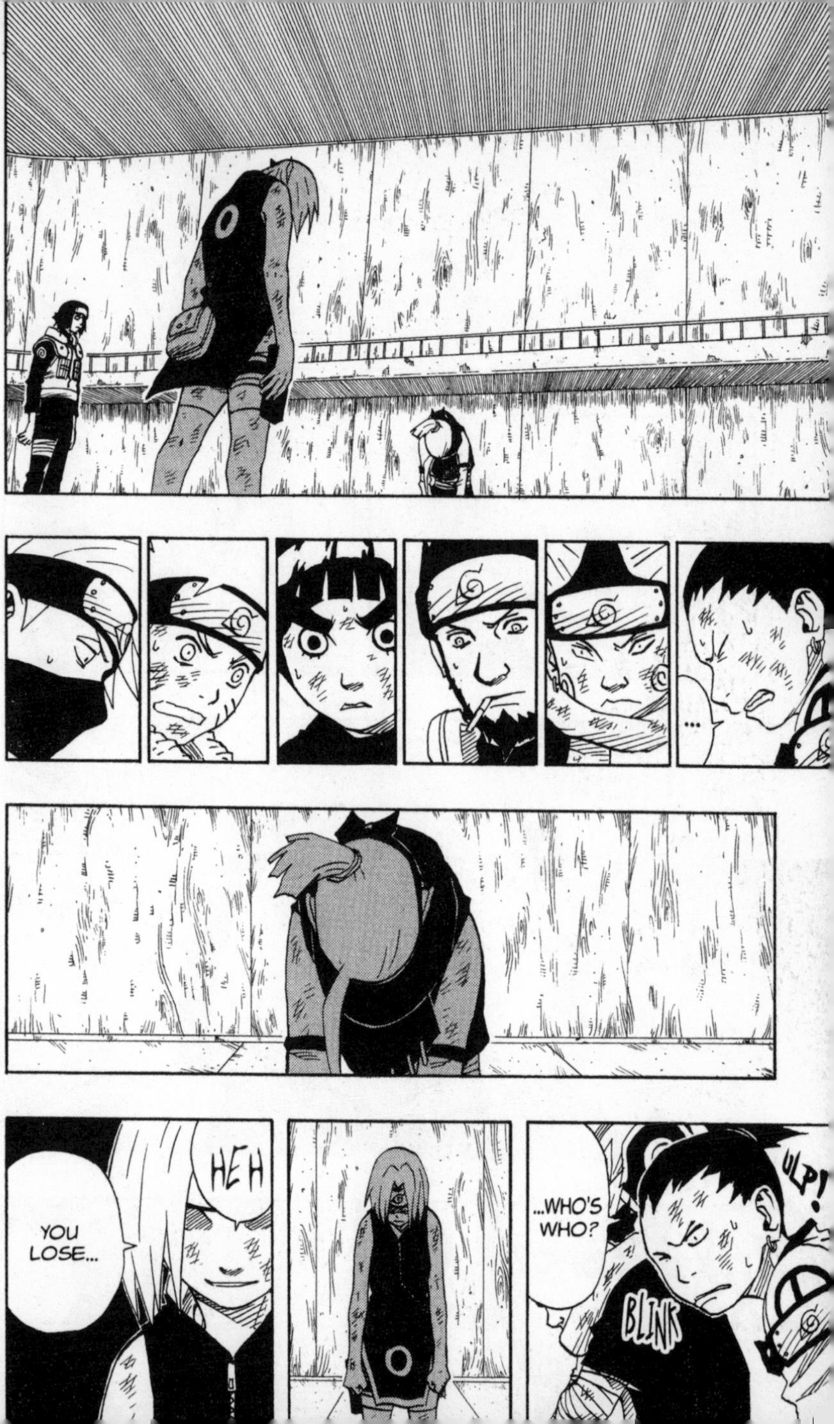
...
ULP!
...WHO'S WHO?
BLINK
HEH
YOU LOSE...

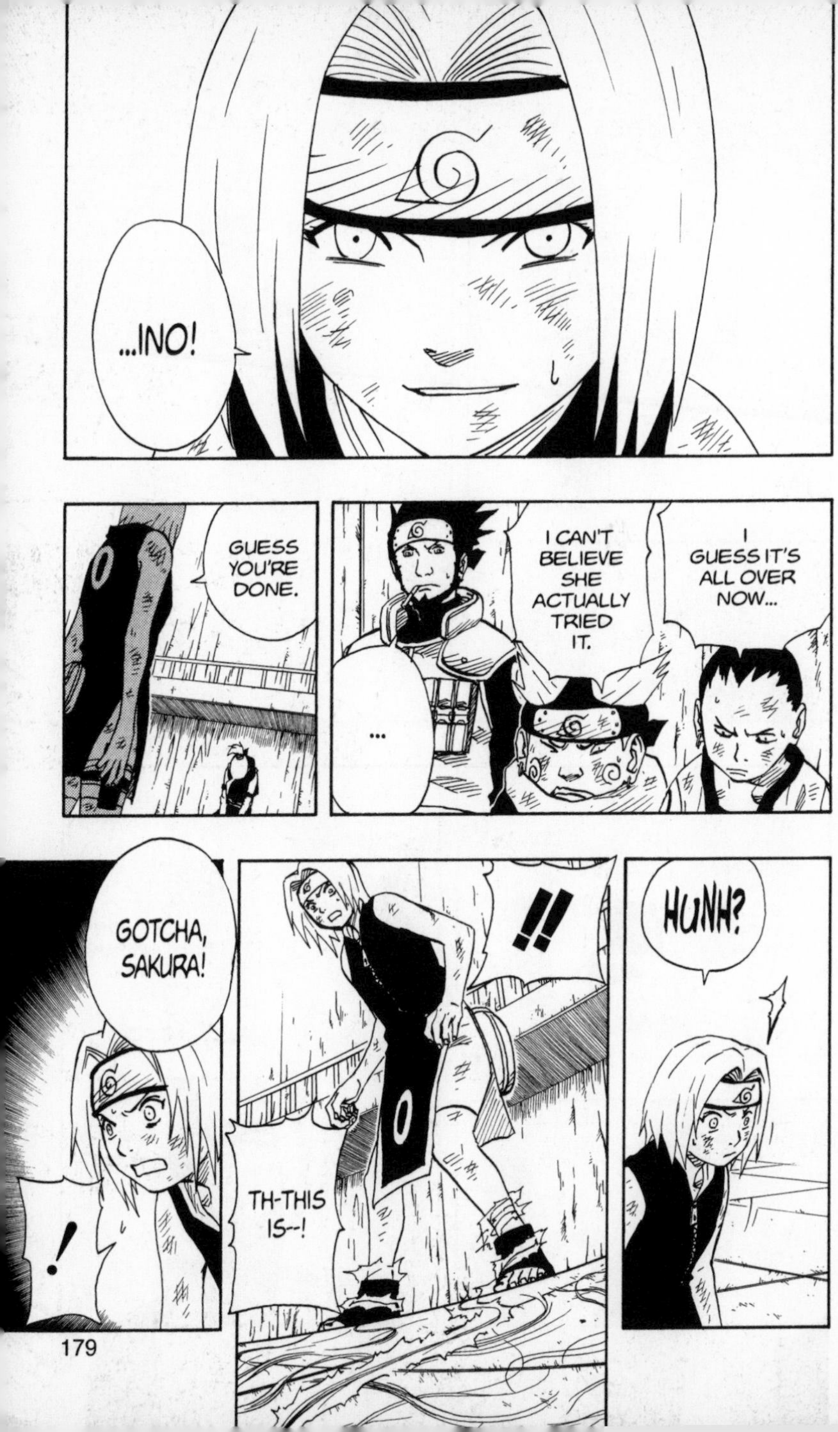
...INO!
I GUESS IT'S ALL OVER NOW...
I CAN'T BELIEVE SHE ACTUALLY TRIED IT.
...
GUESS YOU'RE DONE.
HUNH?
!!
TH-THIS IS--!
GOTCHA, SAKURA!
!

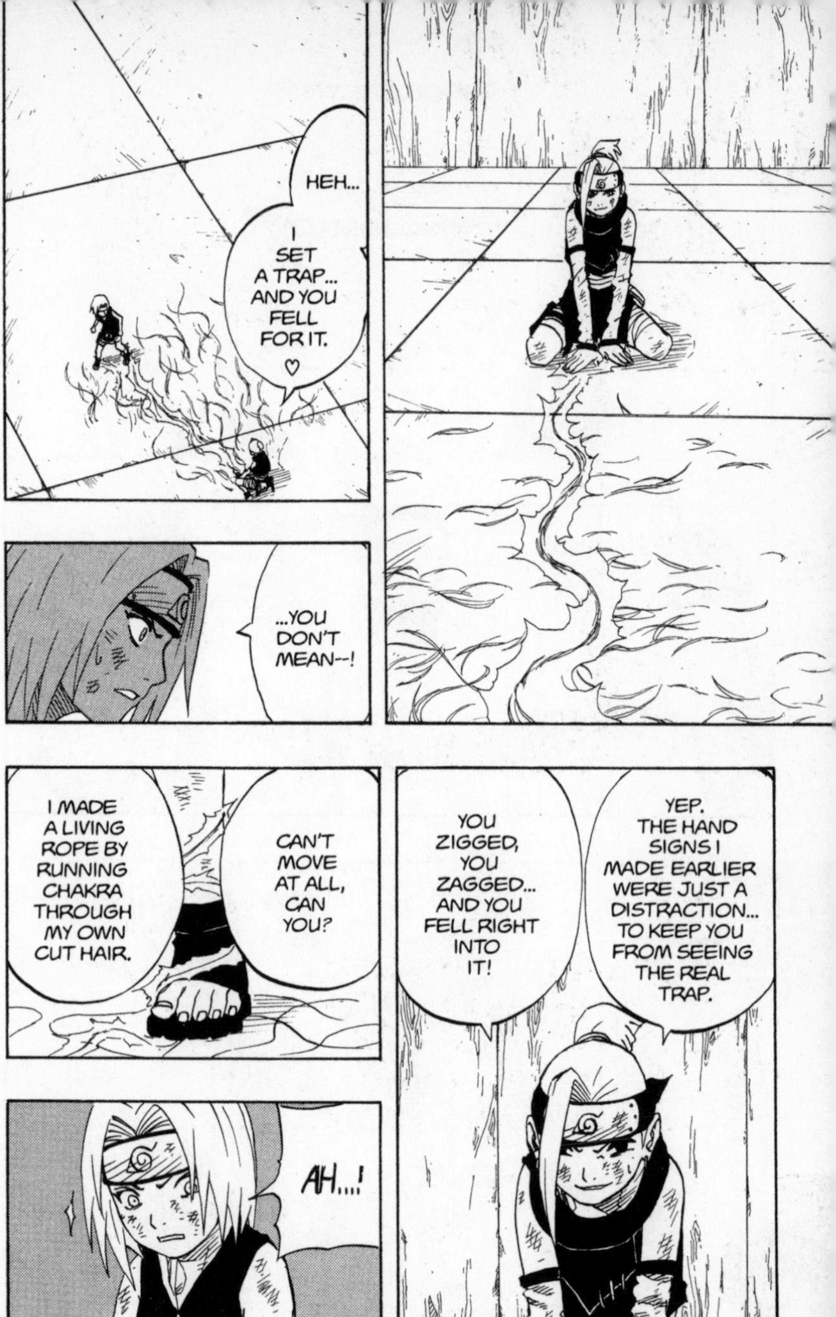
HEH...
I SET A TRAP... AND YOU FELL FOR IT. ♡
...YOU DON'T MEAN--!
YEP. THE HAND SIGNS I MADE EARLIER WERE JUST A DISTRACTION... TO KEEP YOU FROM SEEING THE REAL TRAP.
YOU ZIGGED, YOU ZAGGED... AND YOU FELL RIGHT INTO IT!
CAN'T MOVE AT ALL, CAN YOU?
I MADE A LIVING ROPE BY RUNNING CHAKRA THROUGH MY OWN CUT HAIR.
AH...!

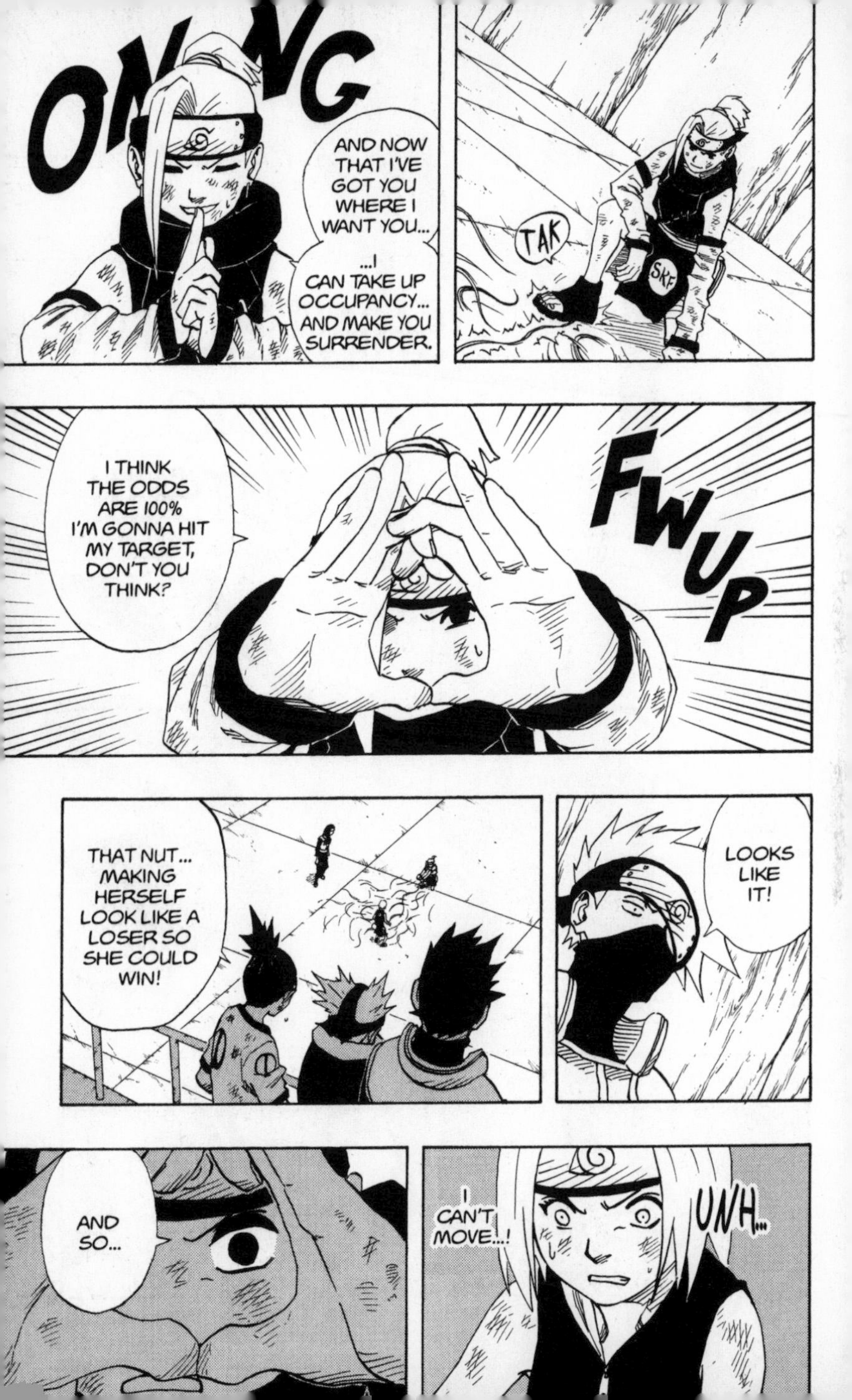
TAK
SKF
ON NG
AND NOW THAT I'VE GOT YOU WHERE I WANT YOU...
...I CAN TAKE UP OCCUPANCY... AND MAKE YOU SURRENDER.
FWUP
I THINK THE ODDS ARE 100% I'M GONNA HIT MY TARGET, DON'T YOU THINK?
LOOKS LIKE IT!
THAT NUT... MAKING HERSELF LOOK LIKE A LOSER SO SHE COULD WIN!
UNH...
I CAN'T MOVE...!
AND SO...

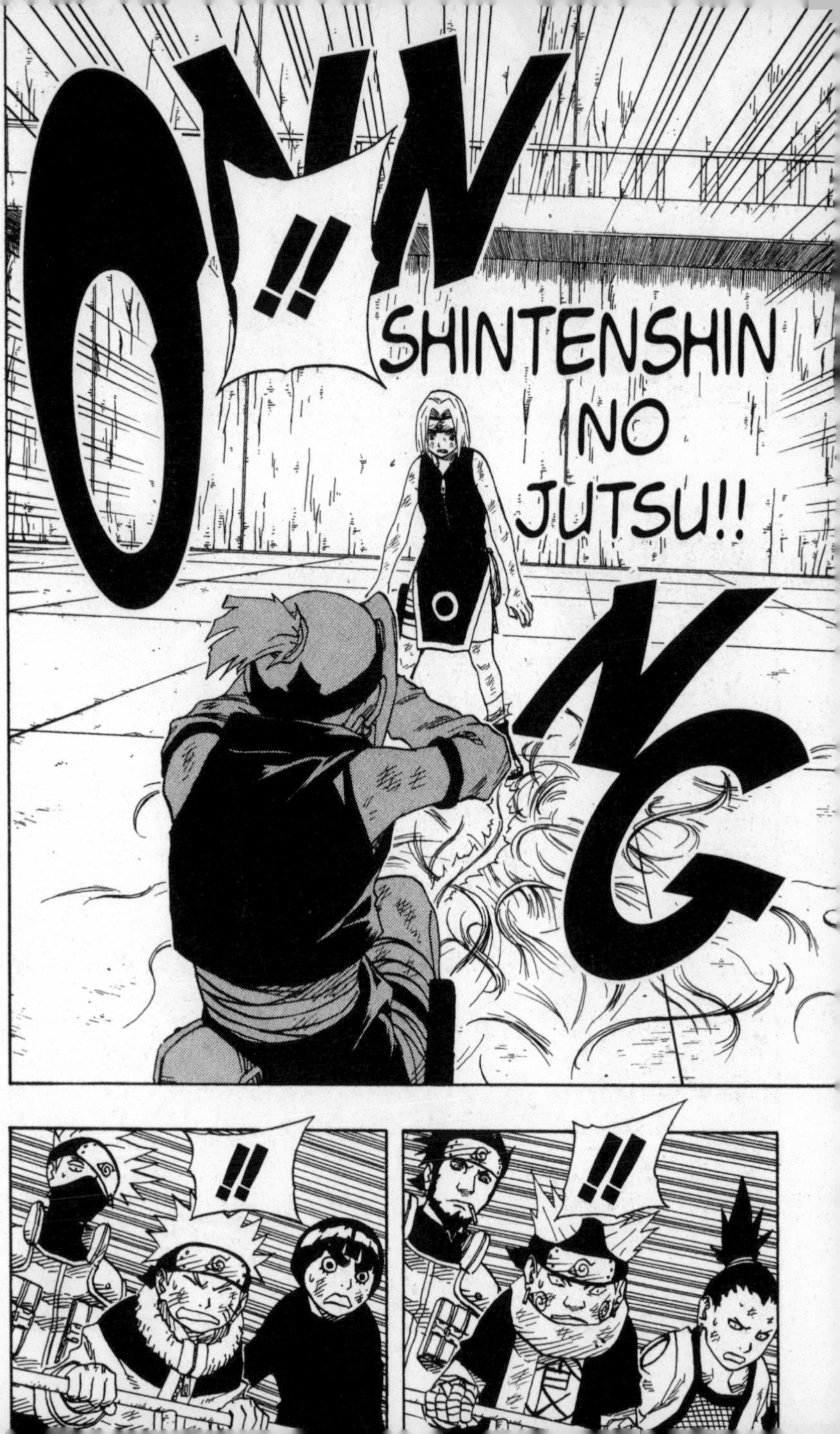

SHINTENSHIN NO JUTSU!!
!!
OWNNG
!!
!!

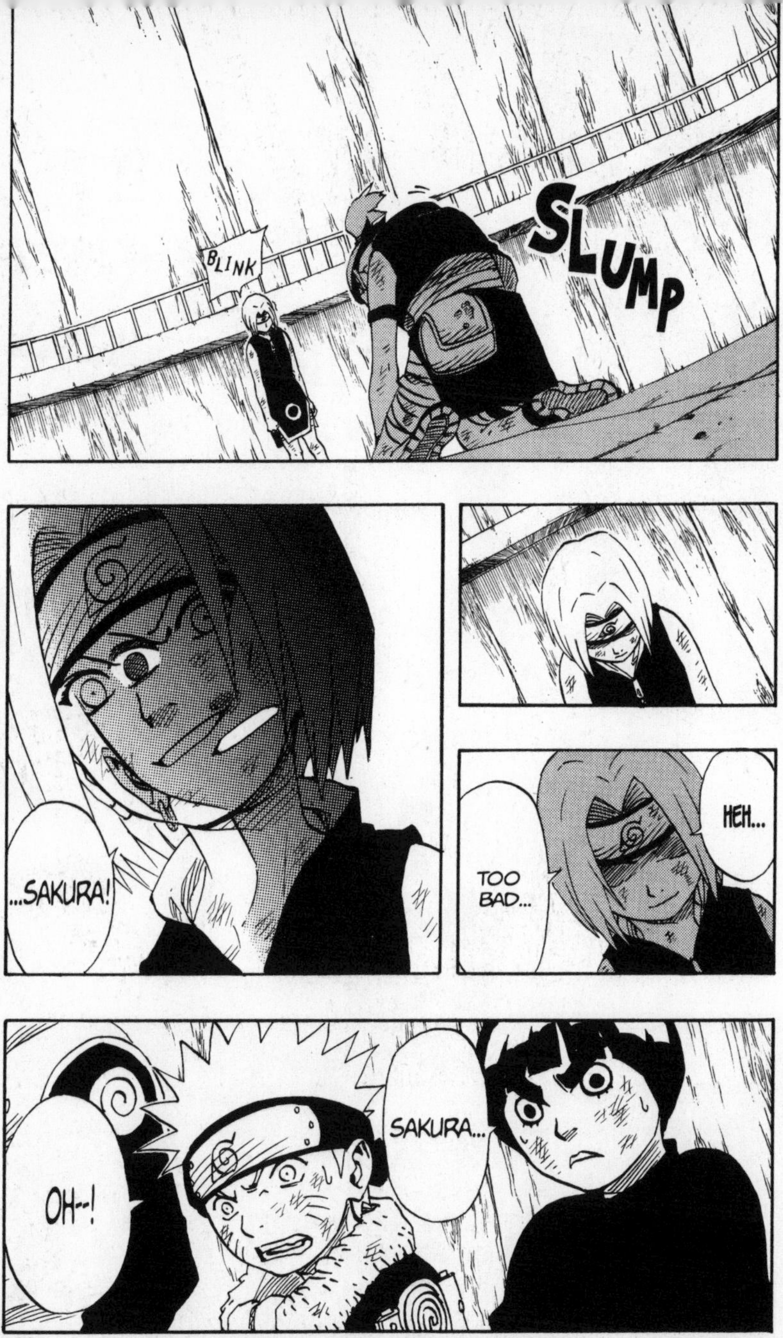
SLUMP
BLINK
HEH...
TOO BAD...
...SAKURA!
SAKURA...
OH--!

TO BE CONTINUED IN NARUTO VOL. 9!

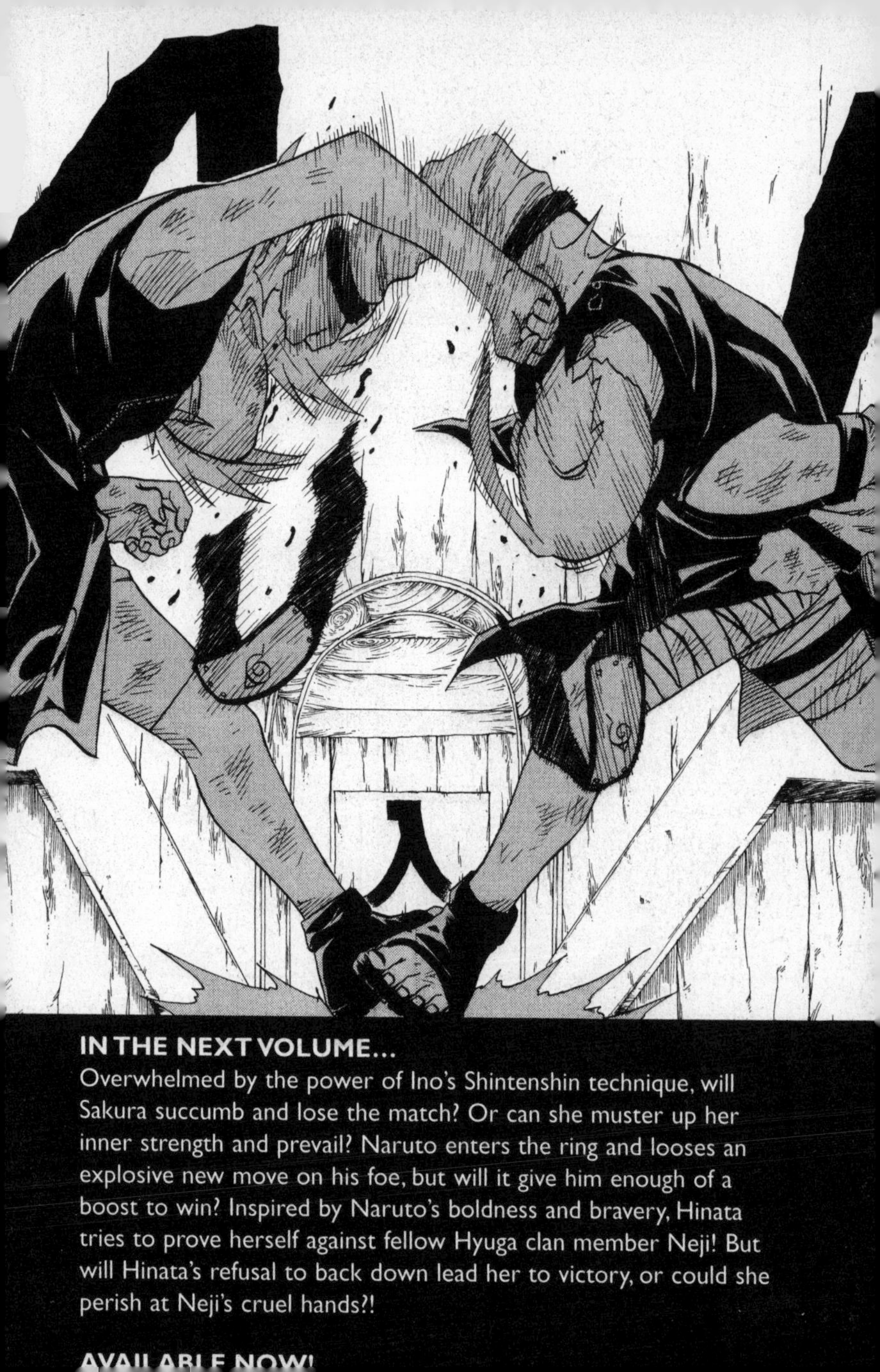

IN THE NEXT VOLUME...

Overwhelmed by the power of Ino's Shintenshin technique, will Sakura succumb and lose the match? Or can she muster up her inner strength and prevail? Naruto enters the ring and looses an explosive new move on his foe, but will it give him enough of a boost to win? Inspired by Naruto's boldness and bravery, Hinata tries to prove herself against fellow Hyuga clan member Neji! But will Hinata's refusal to back down lead her to victory, or could she perish at Neji's cruel hands?!

AVAILABLE NOW!

Secrets of the Village Hidden in the Leaves Revealed!

Get exclusive insider information on your favorite
ninja with these Anime Profile books—complete with:
- Character designs
- Show production information
- Special color illustrations

Episodes 1-37
Plus, creator and voice actor
interviews, and an original pinup!

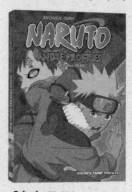

Episodes 38-80
Plus, a fold-out chart connecting
all 55 major characters and an
original poster!

SHONEN JUMP™

NARUTO

ANIME PROFILES™

**Complete your
collection with**
Naruto manga,
fiction, art books,
and anime

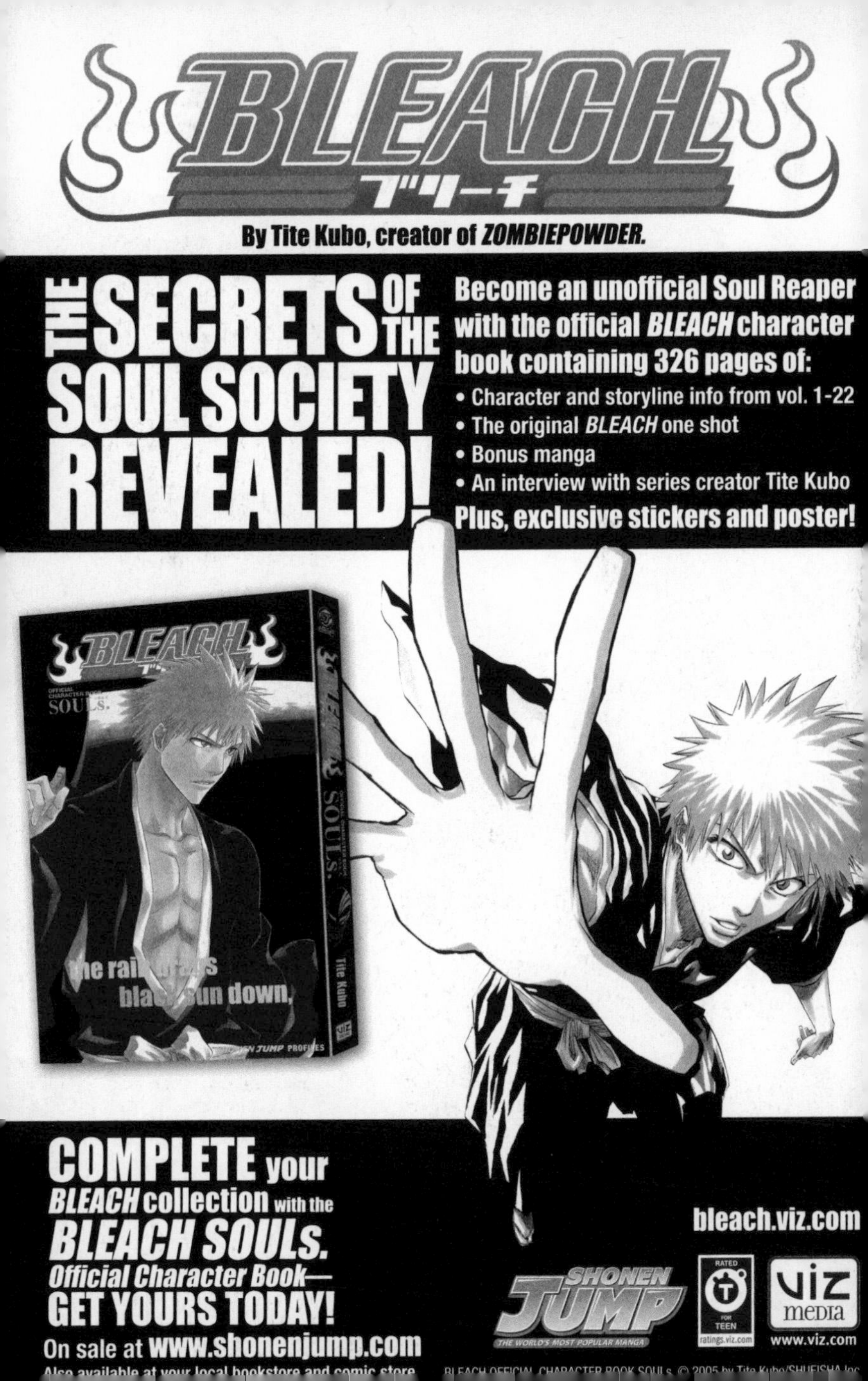

BLEACH
ブリーチ
By Tite Kubo, creator of ZOMBIEPOWDER.
THE SECRETS OF THE SOUL SOCIETY REVEALED!
Become an unofficial Soul Reaper with the official BLEACH character book containing 326 pages of:
• Character and storyline info from vol. 1-22
• The original BLEACH one shot
• Bonus manga
• An interview with series creator Tite Kubo
Plus, exclusive stickers and poster!
BLEACH
OFFICIAL CHARACTER BOOK
SOULs.
Tite Kubo
COMPLETE your BLEACH collection with the BLEACH SOULs. Official Character Book—GET YOURS TODAY!
On sale at www.shonenjump.com
Also available at your local bookstore and comic store
bleach.viz.com
SHONEN JUMP
THE WORLD'S MOST POPULAR MANGA
RATED
T
FOR TEEN
ratings.viz.com
VIZ media
www.viz.com
BLEACH OFFICIAL CHARACTER BOOK SOULs. © 2005 by Tite Kubo/SHUEISHA Inc.

Perspective

3 volumes
in
ONE!!

Get BIG

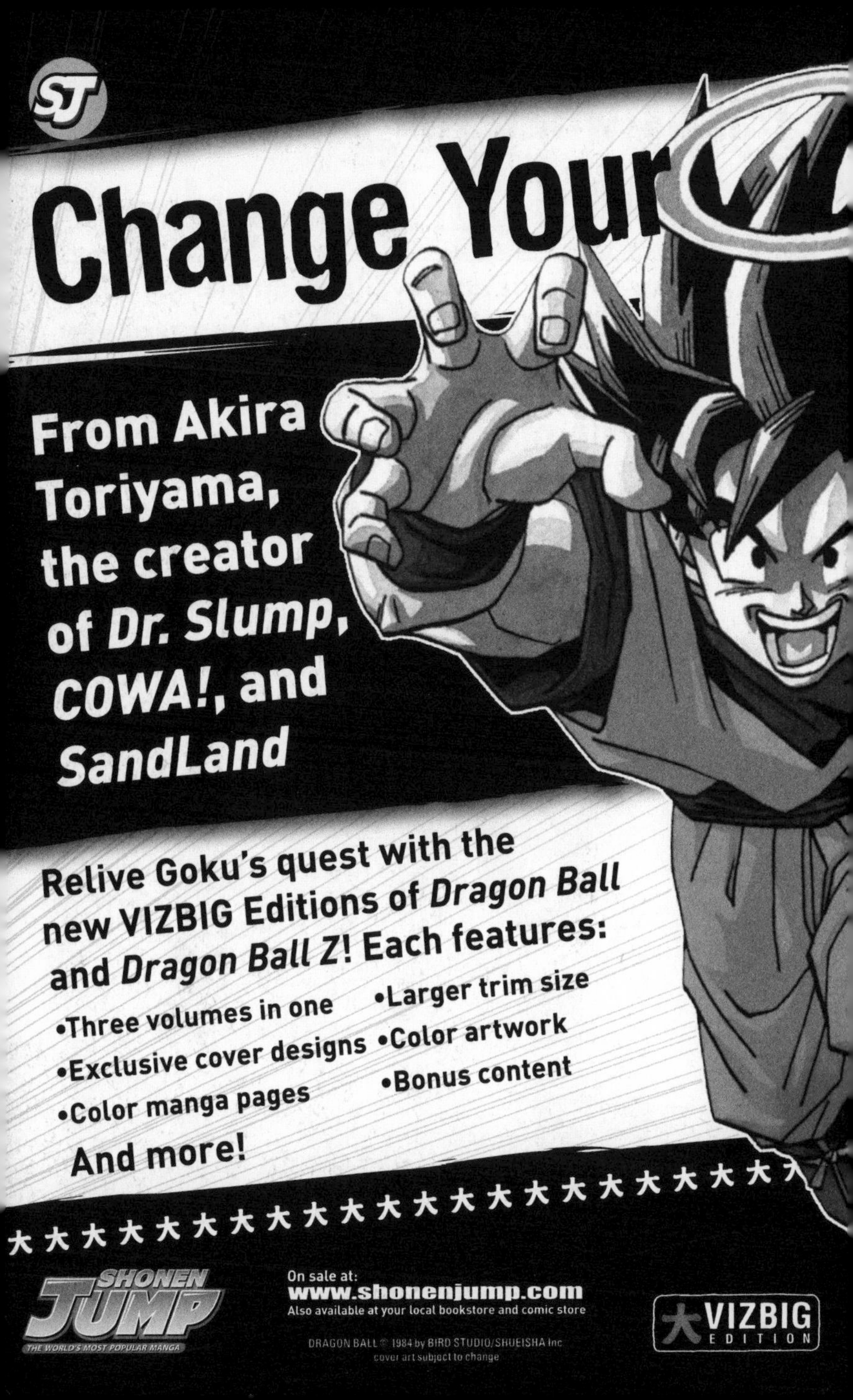
SJ
Change Your
From Akira Toriyama, the creator of Dr. Slump, COWA!, and SandLand
Relive Goku's quest with the new VIZBIG Editions of Dragon Ball and Dragon Ball Z! Each features:
•Three volumes in one
•Exclusive cover designs
•Color manga pages
•Larger trim size
•Color artwork
•Bonus content
And more!
SHONEN JUMP
THE WORLD'S MOST POPULAR MANGA
On sale at:
www.shonenjump.com
Also available at your local bookstore and comic store
DRAGON BALL © 1984 by BIRD STUDIO/SHUEISHA Inc.
cover art subject to change
VIZBIG EDITION

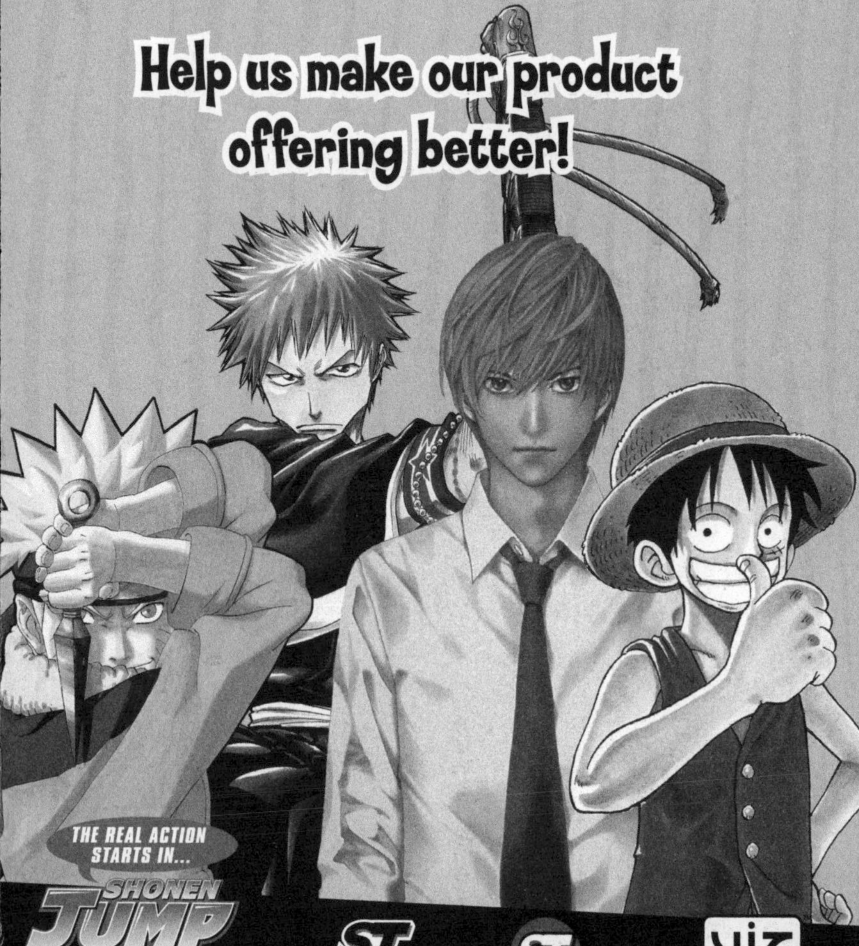
THE REAL ACTION STARTS IN...
SHONEN JUMP
THE WORLD'S MOST POPULAR MANGA
www.shonenjump.com
SJ ADVANCED
SJ
VIZ media